W9-BLS-664

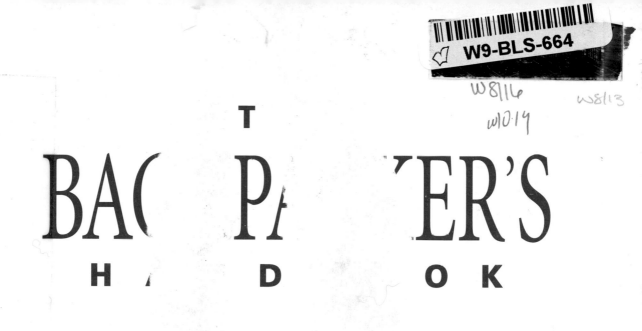

THE BACKPACKER'S HANDBOOK

SECOND EDITION

DISCARD

DISCARD

PROPERTY OF CLPL

THE
BACKPACKER'S
HANDBOOK

SECOND EDITION

Chris Townsend

Ragged Mountain Press

Camden, Maine

International Marine/
Ragged Mountain Press

A Division of The **McGraw·Hill** Companies

10   9   8   7   6   5   4   3   2   1

Copyright © 1997 by Chris Townsend

All rights reserved. The publisher takes no responsibility for the use of any of the materials or methods described in this book, nor for the products thereof. The name "Ragged Mountain Press" and the Ragged Mountain Press logo are trademarks of The McGraw-Hill Companies. Printed in the United States of America.

Library of Congress Cataloging-in-Publication Data

Townsend, Chris.
    The backpacker's handbook / Chris Townsend. — 2nd ed.
        p.   cm.
    Includes bibliographical references (p.   ) and index.
    ISBN 0-07-065315-1 (alk. paper)
        1. Backpacking—Handbooks, manuals, etc.   2. Camping—Handbooks, manuals, etc.   I. Title.
    GV199.6.T69   1997
    796.5'1—dc20   96-38369
                                                                                          CIP

Questions regarding the content of this book should be addressed to:
    Ragged Mountain Press
    P.O. Box 220
    Camden, ME 04843
    207-236-4837

Questions regarding the ordering of this book should be addressed to:
    The McGraw-Hill Companies
    Customer Service Department
    P.O. Box 547
    Blacklick, OH 43004
    Retail customers: 1-800-262-4729
    Bookstores: 1-800-722-4726

A portion of the profits from the sale of each Ragged Mountain Press book
is donated to an environmental cause.

The Backpacker's Handbook is printed on 60-pound Renew Opaque Vellum,
an acid-free paper that contains 50 percent recycled waste paper (preconsumer)
and 10 percent postconsumer waste paper.

Typeset by G&S Typesetters, Austin, Texas
Typeset in Adobe Minion and Adobe Frutiger
Photographs by Chris Townsend
All illustrations by Chris Walsh, except those on pages 39, 71, 114, 141, which are by Mike Clelland
Printed by Quebecor/Fairfield, Fairfield, PA
Design by Joyce C. Weston
Production by Molly Mulhern and Mary Ann Hensel
Edited by Jonathan Eaton, Pamela Benner, and Jerry Novesky

To Denise Thorn for her patience,
love, and companionship.

CONTENTS

PREFACE TO THE
SECOND EDITION

Five years have passed since I wrote the first edition of this book. Since then, I've learned more about backpacking and wilderness living, and many new products for backpackers have appeared on the market. A revised edition seemed necessary to incorporate this new material and to improve and expand on what I said the first time.

As I worked through the original book I found more and more material that I wanted to rewrite or change. Most of the chapters have been substantially rewritten, and I've added new ones on trip planning and adventure travel. There are also new sections on ultralight backpacking, green gear, baking devices, global positioning satellite receivers, and more. With some new material, such as the section on footwear, I've stated my own views more firmly, and have been less cautious about contradicting the advice of others. Throughout I've emphasized gear weight, and I've included kit lists for my own trips so readers can see what I carry.

I make no claim to objectivity. This is a subjective book. In the process of putting my thoughts on paper I've reassessed my views about gear, which in some cases has resulted in a complete reappraisal. New ideas and gear have appeared since the first edition of the book, and these have been incorporated, with notes. Development never stops, but the general principles are fairly constant. Remember: The best reasons for going backpacking are timeless, and in this sense, the gear you use is irrelevant.

So this is very much a new book. At the same time, its subject—wilderness walking—hasn't changed at all. Backpacking is timeless and enduring. I spent two weeks on a solo trip in the Grand Canyon while working on this edition. I traveled from the sub-Alpine forests of the rims down steep, rocky trails to the desert of the inner canyon and back again. I hiked for days along terraces far below the rims and slept under the stars in the heat. At times, autumn rains tumbled from a suddenly dark sky. I watched mule deer and wild turkeys, beautiful white-tailed Kaibab squirrels, and scavenging deer mice. I listened to the roar of rapids, the resoundingly clear sound of a small stone falling from a far cliff, the whisper of wind in the cottonwoods. This is what backpacking is about. It never changes.

ACKNOWLEDGMENTS

Far too many people have added to my store of knowledge and assisted on my walks to thank them all personally here, but some I feel I must single out.

Since the first edition I have learned much about ultralight hiking from Ray and Jenny Jardine, and about winter camping and ski touring from Peter and Pat Lennon.

Although I travel solo more often than not, I have shared trails and campsites with many companions over the years, and I have many valued memories of our walks. I've also spent many hours discussing backpacking with individuals and at organized gatherings. Following the publication of the first edition of this book, many readers wrote to me—a great encouragement. Some readers made useful comments and suggestions about the book.

I can't mention everybody I've hiked with, talked to, or corresponded with, but I would like to thank Chris and Janet Ainsworth, Judy Armstrong, Georgina Collins, Mark Edgington, Ron Ellis, Lou Ann Fellows, Wayne Fuiten, Franjo Goluza, Kris Gravette, Andrew Helliwell, Andy Hicks, Graham Huntington, Alain Kahan, Larry Lake, Alex Lawrence, Duncan MacDonald, Cameron McNeish, Al Micklethwaite, Tony Morfe, Joris Naiman, Dave Rehbehn, Todd Seniff, Pat Silver, Clyde Soles, Wallace Spaulding, Scott Steiner, Douglas K. Stream, Lesya Struz, Denise Thorn, Fran Townsend, John Traynor, Steve Twaites, Stan Walker, and Scott Williamson.

I'd also like to thank all those I've met at the annual gatherings of the American Long Distance Hiker's Association Western Chapter, and all those I've guided on wilderness ski tours.

Many equipment makers, designers, and retailers have been generous with information and equipment. My thanks in particular to Nick Brown of Nikwax and Paramo; Paul Cooper of Bill's Sports Shop, Leadville, Colorado; Morgan J. Connolly of Cascade Designs; Gordon Conyers of Tor Outdoor Products; Richard J. Garcia of Garcia Machine; Hamish Hamilton; Akzo (the makers of Sympatex); Dana Design; Highland Guides Nordic Ski Center, Aviemore, Scotland; Lowe Alpine Systems; and The North Face.

The views expressed in this book are my own. Many who have helped me will not agree with everything I've said.

Many thanks, too, to Jonathan Eaton and Pamela Benner at Ragged Mountain Press, and Jerry Novesky, copyeditor, who've worked hard to make this book what it is.

Into the Wilderness

We celebrate not the trail, but the wild places it passes through.

—*The Pacific Crest Trail Hiker's Handbook,*
Ray Jardine

Do not break into this cabin unless in an emergency. If you do not come to the mountains prepared you do not deserve to be in them.

—Sign on a wilderness outfitter's backcountry cabin in the Canadian Rockies

This is a "how-to" book, an instructional volume on how to move about and live in wild country safely and in comfort. Much of the book concerns the items needed and how to use them—factual stuff leavened with a little bias and opinion, but down-to-earth and functional nevertheless. The scope, theoretically, is worldwide, though you won't find much about tropical travel; my own experience has been mostly in the wild areas of North America and Western Europe, ranging from the hot deserts of the Southwest to the Arctic wastes of Greenland.

I have made several treks lasting many months, the sort that refine your techniques and show you what equipment works. These include through-hikes of the Pacific Crest and the Continental Divide Trails; a 1,600-mile walk along the length of the Canadian Rockies—the first time such a walk has been done; a 1,000-mile south-to-north walk through Canada's Yukon Territory; a 1,300-mile walk through the mountains of Norway and Sweden; and a 1,250-mile walk from Land's End to John O'Groats in Britain. These experiences—more than two decades of backpacking at least 15,000 miles—constitute my credentials for presuming to offer advice to others. I've had many opportunities to make mistakes; these I relate for your amusement, and perhaps for your benefit.

But my highest qualification is my enjoyment of backpacking, and the fact that, for me, it is a way of life, a reason for existing. I want to share that by pointing others in the same direction. This book, an attempt to mesh the reasons for backpacking with the ways to do it, is the result.

Why backpack? Why forgo the comforts of home or hotel for a night under a flimsy nylon sheet? Many people walk in the wilds but seek a return to civilization at night. This is experiencing only part of what the wilderness has to offer; it is akin to dipping your toe in the water instead of taking a refreshing and invigorating swim. Only by living in the wilderness 24 hours a day, day after day, do I gain a feeling of "rightness," of being *with* instead of *against* the earth, the deepest contentment I have found.

The author at a forest camp.

I'm aware that this sounds nearly mystical, but I make no apology. We are too prone to value only what can be defined in logical terms or assigned a cash value. Yet the natural, self-regulating earth cannot be quantified, calculated, and summed up—every attempt to do so uncovers another mystery just beyond our grasp. And this pleases me.

The heart of backpacking lies in the journey, the desire to explore a world beyond our every-day lives, and in so doing explore ourselves. Until comparatively recently, most journeys were like this, because the known world extended little beyond one's hometown. Now, with modern communications and mass transportation, most so-called journeys consist of nothing more than the mechanized moving of bodies from one place to another, a process so sanitized and safe it precludes any sense of adventure or personal involvement. Only when I shoulder my pack and set out into the wilderness do I feel a real journey beginning, even though I may have traveled half-way around the world to take that first step.

A journey requires a beginning and an end, even though what it is really about lies between those two points. Once, I set out into the moun-tains of northwest Scotland with no plan and no idea where I would go. The weather was good, the scenery spectacular, and the campsites pleas-ant, yet after a few days a vague sense of dissatisfaction overtook me, and after a week I abandoned the trip. I had no incentive to keep moving, nothing to give shape to the trip, nothing to define its limits. Thus, I always set a goal, even on dayhikes—a summit, a lake, a distance to cover. Part of me finds this necessary. Once underway, the overall goal is subordinated to the day-by-day, minute-by-minute events and impressions that are my reason for hiking.

By walking through a landscape, you experience it with every one of your senses, you can learn how it works and why it is as it is, and you become, for a time, a part of it. If backpacking has any validity apart from being an enriching personal adventure (good enough in itself, of course), it lies in this. At a time when the balance of nature itself is threatened—when we seem intent on destroying our only life-support system—backpackers in particular should understand that we have to change our ways, to acknowledge that our interests coincide with nature's. If we don't, worrying about preserving wilderness in which we can wander will become irrelevant. Backpackers, therefore, should involve themselves in those environmental and conservation organizations—the Sierra Club, The Nature Conservancy, The Wilderness Society, the John Muir Trust, and others—trying to preserve our still-beautiful world.

Wilderness, defined by the Wilderness Act of 1964, is "an area where the earth and its community of life are untrammeled by man, where man himself is a visitor who does not remain." According to a Sierra Club survey, at least one-third of the earth's land surface—more than 18 million square miles—still is wilderness, untouched by human development. And that only counts areas of more than 1,500 square miles, which excludes many regions. The survey also omits areas showing any human signature,

from the western deserts of the United States (overgrazed by livestock) to most of Iceland (too many four-wheel-drive tracks).

Many areas backpackers visit don't fit the wilderness definition. In Europe in particular, wilderness areas are small, and, if defined in terms of never having been touched by human hand, virtually nonexistent. But, if there is enough land to walk into, enough room to set up a camp and then walk on with that freedom that comes when you escape the constraints of modern living, then it is wilderness, in spirit if not by definition.

All wilderness areas, from the vast expanse of Antarctica (the only continent in the Sierra Club survey considered 100 percent pristine) to the small pockets that still exist even in heavily industrialized countries, need defending. The Sierra Club survey also points out that only 3 percent of the remaining wilderness will be protected by the end of the century, a pitifully small amount. That there are places reachable only on foot, requiring an effort and a commitment to visit, is vitally important. It will be a sad day if the last such spot succumbs to the paved road and the hollow stare of detached tourists.

Ironically, wilderness also needs defending from those who love it. Damaging practices and an increasing number of hikers are turning many popular areas into worn-out remnants of their former selves. Wilderness travelers traditionally lived off the land for shelter as well as for food; they built lean-tos and teepees, cut boughs for mattresses and logs for tables and chairs. Today this would be irresponsible—and often illegal—even in remote corners of the world. There is too little wilderness left, and every scar diminishes what remains.

Even with modern equipment, backpackers have more impact on the land than do daywalkers and, therefore, have more responsibilities.

A timberline lake in the Rocky Mountains—backpacking is the way to enter such wilderness areas.

No-trace, low-impact camping must be the norm if any wild country is to survive. This book emphasizes these techniques, because there are only two solutions to the problems of hikers damaging the wilderness: self-regulation and the practice of minimum-impact techniques by all, or regulation, which already is the norm in many parks worldwide. In some areas, mainly in North America, wilderness camping is allowed only on specified sites; in others, such as several in the Alps, wild camping is forbidden altogether, and people are required to stay in mountain huts. Such restrictions are an anathema to the spirit of freedom inherent in backpacking, but they will become common, and rightly so, unless backpackers learn to leave the wilderness untouched.

CHAPTER ONE

Preparing for the Trail

Take nothing for granted. Not one blessed, cool mountain day or one hellish, desert day or one sweaty, stinky, hiking companion. It is all a gift.

—*Journey on the Crest,* Cindy Ross

Backpacking isn't difficult, but it does require both physical and mental preparation. Every year, first-time hikers set off along the trail unfit, ill-equipped, and with unrealistic expectations. Not surprisingly, many of them never venture into the wilderness again. The better your planning, the more enjoyable your trip will be. You need not know exactly how far you will walk each day, or precisely where you will camp each night (though such detailed planning is useful for beginners), but you should know your capabilities and desires well enough to tailor your trip to them. Setting out to carry 65 pounds 25 miles a day through steep, mountainous terrain just about guarantees exhaustion, frustration, and disappointment unless you are extremely fit and know beforehand you're capable.

FITNESS

Backpacking requires fitness. You need aerobic, or cardiovascular, fitness to walk and climb all day without your heart pounding and your lungs gasping for air. Without muscular fitness, particularly of the legs, you'll be stiff as a board and aching all over on the second day out. Also, if you set out unfit, the likelihood of injury from strains and muscle tears is much higher.

Achieving fitness takes time. I know people who claim they'll get fit over the first few days of an annual backpacking trip. They usually suffer most of the walk, yet with a little preparation, they could enjoy every day.

The best way to train for carrying heavy loads over rough terrain is to carry heavy loads over rough terrain—what sports trainers call "specific training." Although this isn't always practical, it's surprising what you can do if you really want to, even if you live and work in a city. In *Journey Through Britain*, John Hillaby says that he trained for his 1,100-mile, end-to-end walk across Britain by spending the three months prior to the trip walking "from Hampstead to the City [London] each day and farther at the weekends. On these jaunts I carried weight lifters' weights sewn high up in a flat rucksack that didn't look too odd among people making their way to the office in the morning."

At the very least, spend a few weekends getting used to walking with a load before setting off on a longer trip. Walk as much as possible during the week—including up and down stairs. Brisk strolls or runs in the evening help too, especially if there are hills included. In fact, hill running is probably the best way to improve both your aerobic fitness and your leg power in as short a time as possible.

I trained at a fitness center once, before a Canadian Rockies walk. For six months I did hour-long circuit sessions three times a week, hour-long runs on the days between, with one day off a week. It helped, but probably no more than if I'd walked with a pack and exercised at home. If you want to follow a planned exercise program, you might read *The Outdoor Athlete,* by Steve Ilg (Cordillera Press), which includes programs for "mountaineering and advanced backpacking" and "recreational hiking and backpacking," and visit your local fitness center or gym. One thing I did learn from my fitness center training was that you need rest from strenuous exercise. This doesn't just go for exercising at the gym—on walks longer than two weeks, I now aim to take a rest day every week to 10 days.

My current fitness regimen includes hour-long runs over hilly terrain two or three times a week, and at least one full day a week walking or skiing in the mountains. This is apart from the two- to three-day backpacking trips I like to take once a month or so between longer walks.

If you haven't exercised for some time, return to it gradually, especially if you're over 35. Preparing for a walk takes time, anyway. You can't go from being unfit to toting a heavy load 15 mountainous miles a day in a week, or even a month.

THE ART OF WALKING

While the simple act of putting one foot in front of the other seems to require no instruction or comment, there are, in fact, good and bad ways to walk, and good and bad walkers. Good walkers can walk effortlessly all day, while bad ones may be exhausted after a few hours.

The way to make walking seem effortless is to walk slowly and steadily, to find a *rhythm* that lets you glide along, and a *pace* you can keep up

The best way to train for carrying heavy loads is to carry heavy loads! Hiking in the Yosemite wilderness.

for hours. Without a comfortable rhythm, every step seems tiring, which is why crossing boulder fields, brush-choked forest, and other broken terrain is so exhausting. Inexperienced walkers often start off at a rapid pace, leaving the experienced plodding slowly behind. As in the fable of the tortoise and the hare, slower walkers often catch up and pass exhausted novices long before a day's walk is complete.

The ability to maintain a steady pace hour after hour has to be developed. If you need a rest, take one; otherwise, you'll exhaust yourself.

The difference between novices and experts was demonstrated graphically to me when I was leading backpacking treks for an Outward Bound school in the Scottish Highlands. I let the students set their own pace, often following them or traversing above the group at a higher level. But one day, the course supervisor, an experienced mountaineer, turned up and said he'd lead the day's walk—and he meant *lead*. Off he went, the group following in his footsteps, while I brought up the rear. Initially, we followed a flat river valley, and soon the students were muttering about the supervisor's slow pace. The faint trail began to climb after a while, and on we went at the same slow pace, with some of the students close to rebellion. Eventually, we came to the base of a steep, grassy slope with no trail. The supervisor didn't pause—he just headed up as if the terrain hadn't altered. After a few hundred yards, the tenor of the students changed. "Isn't he ever going to stop?" they complained. One or two fell behind. Intercepting a trail, we turned up it, switchbacking steadily to a high pass. By now some of the students seemed in danger of collapse, so I hurried ahead to the supervisor and said they needed a rest. He seemed surprised. "I'll see you later then," he said, and started down, his pace unaltered, leaving the students slumped with relief.

This story reveals one of the problems of walking in a group: each person has his or her own pace. The best way to deal with this is not to walk as a large group, but to establish pairs or smaller groups of walkers with similar abilities, which will allow people to proceed at their own pace, meeting up at rest stops and in camp. If a large group must stay together, perhaps because of bad weather or difficult route finding, let the slowest member set the pace, perhaps leading at least some of the time. It is neither fair nor safe to let the slowest member fall far behind the group, and if this happens to you, you should object.

The ability to walk economically, using the least energy, comes only with experience. It may help to try to create a rhythm in your head if one doesn't develop naturally. I sometimes do this on long climbs if the right pace is hard to find and I'm constantly stopping to catch my breath. I often repeat rhythmic chants consisting of any words that come to mind (I find the poems of Robert Service or Longfellow are good—I need to repeat only a few lines). If I begin to speed up, I chant out loud, which slows me down. It is impossible to walk at a faster-than-normal pace for a long time, but walking at a slower one is surprisingly tiring, since it is hard to establish a rhythm.

Once in a great while all the aspects of walking come together, and then I have an hour or a day when I simply glide along, seemingly expending no energy. When this happens, distance melts under my feet, and I feel I could stride on forever. I can't force such moments and I don't know where they come from, but the more I walk, the more often they happen. Not surprisingly, they occur most often on really long treks. On such days, I'll walk for five hours and 12 miles and more without a break, yet with such little effort that I don't realize how long and far I've traveled until I finally stop. I never feel any effects afterward, except perhaps greater contentment.

Distance

"How far can I walk in a day?" is a perennial question asked by walkers and non-walkers alike. The answer depends on your fitness, the length of your stride, how many hours you walk, the weight you're carrying, and the terrain. There are formulas for making calculations, including a good one proposed last century by W. Naismith, a luminary of the Scottish Mountaineering Club. Naismith's formula allows one hour for every 3 miles, plus an extra half hour for every 1,000 feet of ascent. I've used this as a guide for years and it seems to work; a 15-mile day with 4,000 feet of ascent takes me, on average, eight hours, including stops. Of course, 15 miles on a map will be longer on the ground, since map miles are flat miles, unlike most terrain. As slopes steepen, the distance increases.

Additional Distance Hiked for Slopes of Different Angles Over 1 Mile on the Map

Slope angle	Height gained	Additional distance traveled
10°	930 feet	1.5%/80 feet
20°	1,920 feet	6.5%/340 feet
30°	3,050 feet	15.5%/815 feet
40°	4,435 feet	31.0%/1,615 feet
45°	5,280 feet/1mile	41.0%/2,186 feet
50°	6,295 feet	56.0%/2,936 feet
60°	9,146 feet	100%/5,289 feet/1 mile

The time I spend between leaving one camp and setting up the next is usually eight to 10 hours, not all of it spent walking. I once measured my pace against distance posts on a flat, paved road

in the Great Divide Basin during a Continental Divide walk. While carrying a 55-pound pack, I went about 3¾ miles per hour. At that rate I would cover 37 miles in 10 hours if I did nothing but walk. In practice, however, I probably spend no more than seven hours of a 10-hour day walking, averaging about 2½ miles per hour if the terrain isn't too rugged. That speed, for me, is fast enough. Backpacking is about living in the wilderness, not running through it. I cover distance most quickly on roads—tarmac, gravel, or dirt—because I always want to leave them behind as soon as possible.

How far you can push yourself to walk in a day is less important than how far you are happy walking in a day. This distance can be worked out if you keep records of your trips. I plan walks on the basis of 15 miles per day on trails and over easy terrain. For difficult cross-country travel, I estimate 12 miles a day.

When planning treks, it also helps to know how far you can walk over a complete trip. You can get an idea by analyzing your previous walks. For example, I averaged 16 miles per day on the 2,600-mile Pacific Crest Trail (PCT), a 1,600-mile Canadian Rockies walk, and a 1,300-mile Scandinavian mountains walk, and 16¾ miles per day on the 3,000-mile Continental Divide, which seems amazingly consistent. A closer look, however, reveals that daily distances varied from 6 to 30 miles, and the time spent between camps varied from three to 15 hours. All these walks were mainly on trails. My 1,000-mile Yukon walk was mostly cross-country, and on that my average dropped to 12½ miles per day.

One problem with a two-week summer backpacking trip is that many people spend the first week struggling to get fit, and the second week turning the efforts of the first week into hard muscle and greater lung power. By the time they're ready to go home, they're at peak fitness.

The solution is to temper your desires. It's easy in winter to make ambitious plans for spring hikes that fall apart the first day out as you struggle to carry your pack half the distance you intended. On all walks, I take it easy until I feel comfortable being on the move again. This breaking-in period may last only a few hours on a weekend trip, or as long as a couple of weeks on a long summer trek. On two-week trips, it's a good idea to take it easy the first two or three days by walking less distance than you hope to cover later in the trip, especially if you're not as fit as you intended to be.

Pedometers

In theory, pedometers measure how far you travel during a specific time. The trouble is that all pedometers work by converting the number of steps taken into distance, and this works only if your strides are regular. In the wilderness, with its ups and downs, bogs, scree, boulders, and logs, maintaining a regular stride hour after hour is difficult. I've tried pedometers, but they've never produced any reliable figures for me.

GOING ALONE

It is customary to advise hikers never to go alone, but I can hardly do so since I travel solo more often than not—I feel it is the best way to experience the wilderness. The heightened awareness that comes with solo walking is always absent when I'm with others. Solitude is immeasurably rewarding. Going alone also gives me the freedom of self-determination. I can choose to walk 12 hours one day but only three the next, or to spend half a day watching otters or lying in the tent wondering if the rain will ever stop without having to consult anyone else.

Of course, solo walking has its dangers, and it is up to the individual to calculate what risks he

or she is prepared to take. I'm always aware when crossing steep boulder fields or fording streams that if I slip there is no one to go for help. The solo walker must weigh every action very carefully and assess every risk. In the Canadian Rockies I once spent eight days struggling cross-country through rugged terrain in the foothills. I was constantly aware that even a minor accident could have serious consequences, especially since I was also way off route. Such situations demand greater care than trail travel, where a twisted ankle may mean no more than a painful limp out to the road, and potential rescuers may not be too far away.

Leaving Word

You always should leave word with somebody about where you are going and when you will be back, especially if you are going out alone. The route details you leave may be precise or vague—but some indication of your plans must be left with a responsible person. If you're leaving a car anywhere, you should tell someone when you'll be back for it. This isn't a problem in places where you must register a trail permit, but elsewhere an abandoned car could cause concern, or even lead to an unnecessary rescue attempt. (Indeed, a few days after writing this, I saw a television interview of a walker who'd been surprised to find a rescue helicopter landing outside the remote mountain hut he was using. He had been reported missing after his car was noticed at a forest trailhead, despite the fact that he had left detailed plans of his 10-day trek with his wife and family.) Unfortunately, leaving a note in your car is inadvisable because it is an open invitation to thieves.

Whenever you've said you'll let someone know you're safe, you *must* do so. Too many hours have been spent by rescue teams searching for a walker, who was back home or relaxing in a café, because someone expecting word didn't receive it.

SLACKPACKING AND POWERHIKING

Different hiking styles produce different outlooks—philosophies even, if that's not too grand a word for a simple pleasure. Some hikers stride along the trail, aiming for the maximum mileage per hour, day, or week. Others dash up and down the peaks, bagging as many summits as possible. The more contemplative meander forests and meadows, studying flowers, watching clouds, or simply staring into the distance when the spirit moves them.

The name *slackpacker* was first coined to describe Appalachian Trail (AT) hikers who, while intent on walking the entire 2,150 miles, nevertheless also plan on doing so as casually as possible. One of the walkers to whom the description was first applied holds the record for the slowest continuous Appalachian Trail walk. O.d.Coyote (his "trail" name—an AT tradition—that has become his real name) took 263 days for his hike, an average of 8 miles a day.

In the September/October 1994 issue of *Appalachian Trailway News,* the journal of the Appalachian Trail Conference, O.d.Coyote describes slackpacking as an "attempt to backpack in a manner that is never trying, difficult, or tense, but in a slowly free-flowing way that drifts with whatever currents of interest, attraction, or stimulation are blowing at that moment."

The converse of slackpacking is *powerhiking,* which emphasizes maximum mileage by walking fast for long hours. I'm not sure where this term comes from—I first discovered it in the writings of Ray Jardine, whose fast hikes of the Appalachian and Pacific Crest Trails with his wife, Jenny, prove they are experts in the discipline. Ultimately, powerhiking merges into *trail running,* and I was interested to hear from one powerhiker that he'd run sections of the Appalachian Trail while through-hiking.

Is one extreme better than the other? O.d.Coyote clearly believes slackpacking is superior, that powerhiking can be "trying, difficult, or tense," and, in any case, prevents a walker from experiencing all that a trail has to offer. But in *Running Wild,* long-distance runner John Annerino, who has run the length of the Grand Canyon on both the north and south sides of the Colorado River, says, "And so I run, run like the wind, the wind pushing me across a rainbow of joy that now extends from one end of the Grand Canyon to the other. . . . The running is a fantasy come alive; there is no effort, nor is there the faintest hint of pain. It is pure flight."

O.d.Coyote says that slackpacking means escaping from "our culture's slavish devotion to efficiency," and banishing "the gnawing rat of goal-orientation" by relearning how to play. Some powerhikers, he suspects, have internalized these values and become temperamentally incapable of slackpacking. But British long-distance wilderness runner Mike Cudahy, who has run the 270-mile Pennine Way in England in under three days, offers this explanation for the "indescribable joy" that can occur on a long, hard run: "Perhaps the artificiality of a conventional and sophisticated society is stripped away and the simple, ingenuous nature of a creature of the earth is laid bare."

The obvious conclusion is that different approaches are right for different people. There's nothing wrong with walking the Appalachian Trail at 8 miles a day, or running the length of the Grand Canyon in a week—as long as it satisfies and rejuvenates the participant. In recent years there has been a growing and unfortunate tendency among walkers to criticize each other for being too fast or too slow, for bagging peaks or collecting miles, for going alone, for going out in large groups, for taking part in organized walks, for sticking to trails, for not sticking to trails — for being, in fact, different from the critic.

I've tried most forms of wilderness walking and running, including attempting 100 miles in 48 hours, and more than one two-day mountain marathon race. I've also wandered mountains slowly, averaging maybe 10 miles a day. Overall, I prefer the latter approach, but I would not call it superior. At times during long runs I have felt flashes of what Annerino describes, but these moments have never made up for my exhaustion and aching limbs. I gain the greatest fulfillment on backpacking trips lasting weeks at a time. How far I walk on such trips doesn't seem to matter. It's living in the wilds 24 hours a day, day after day, that is important to me. I still enjoy walking fast and am quite happy doing 25 to 30 miles a day in easy terrain with a light load. I don't like having to do so, though; I like to know I can stop whenever I want, for as long as I want. So I'm both a slackpacker and a powerhiker.

There are practical reasons for occasionally powerhiking. For one thing, being able to travel fast if necessary can be important for safety. In *The Pacific Crest Trail Hiker's Handbook* (AdventureLore Press), Ray Jardine points out that on long walks, the faster you travel between supply points the fewer supplies you need carry, the lighter your pack, and the more enjoyable the walking. With a lighter pack you can walk faster and longer. I am no more tired after 30 miles with a 20-pound pack than I am after 15 with 50 pounds. But when I'm not trying to cover a certain distance in a set time, I will carry extra weight and walk more slowly in order to be more comfortable in camp.

To experience all that walking has to offer, it's worth trying different approaches. If you generally amble along, stopping frequently, try pushing yourself occasionally to see what it feels like. If you always zoom over the hills, eating up miles, then slow down once in a while, take long rest stops, look around.

PLANNING

In its simplest form, planning means packing your gear and setting off with no prescribed route or goal in mind. This is what I sometimes do in areas I know well, especially when the weather may affect my plans. I have even done it in areas I've never visited before to see what's there. Quite recently, due to an eleventh-hour assignment to attend and write about a mountain race, I found myself in the Colorado Rockies with 10 days to spare and no plans. Having no route, no clear destination, worried me at first. Where would I go, and why? But there was freedom in not knowing. I didn't have to walk a certain distance each day. There were no deadlines, no food drops, no campsites to book in advance. I could wander at will. Or not wander, for that matter. The Colorado Rockies are ideal for such an apparently aimless venture, because their small pockets of wilderness can be escaped easily when you need to resupply or want a day or two in town.

Usually, though, a little more planning is required. Guidebooks, maps, and magazine articles all can provide information on where to go, and there is an increasing amount of information available on the Internet. Videos and interactive CD-ROMs can also provide information (and inspiration). Once you've selected an area, up-to-date information can be obtained from the land managers—the National Park Service, the Forest Service, the Bureau of Land Management, or state forest or park services. They will also tell you about permits. Most areas don't require these, but many national parks and some wilderness areas with easy access do. The number of permits issued may be severely restricted in the most popular places, making it essential to apply for permits long before your trip. If you want to backpack popular trails in national parks like Grand Canyon or Yosemite, you need to apply for a permit many months in advance and must be flexible about your route. Whatever you think about limiting numbers by permit (personally I would rather see access made more difficult by long walk-ins in place of

entry roads and backcountry parking lots), it means that even in popular areas you won't meet too many people. There remain vast areas of less-frequented wilderness where permits aren't needed, and even the most crowded summer trails are usually quiet out of season. On a two-week ski-backpacking trip through the High Sierra in May, my group encountered only two other parties, both on the same day.

Not so long ago in many national parks and wilderness areas, you could camp legally only in specific sites that were nearly always crowded and were well known as food sources to local wildlife. Many areas now allow you to camp where you like, which gives far greater freedom. The last time I was in Yosemite, I deliberately avoided popular sites, which meant I mostly camped far from others and had no problems

The author in the Grand Canyon.

with the infamous Yosemite bears. Where good campsites are few, such as the Grand Canyon, there still are restrictions on campsites in the most visited areas, though wild camping is allowed elsewhere in the park.

Long-Distance Trails

Detailed planning is advisable for a long-distance hike, especially one that will take several months or more. And there seems to be an increasing number of these. The big three are the 2,100-mile Appalachian Trail, the 2,600-mile Pacific Crest Trail, and the 3,000-mile Continental Divide Trail (CDT). People have set off on these with no more than a hazy idea of the route or what to expect, yet they've completed the hike. Far more, however, give up within the first few days or weeks—and this includes those who do some planning. Only 15 to 20 percent of PCT hikers complete the first hundred miles.

There are various reasons for failure. Heavy packs, sore feet, exhaustion, overly ambitious mileage goals, unexpected weather, terrain, and trail conditions are the most common. Read the accounts of other hikers, check guidebooks for information on weather and terrain, and study the planning guides that are available for popular trails. The best of these is Ray Jardine's *The Pacific Crest Trail Hiker's Handbook.* The book is so good, in fact, that I'd recommend it even if you're planning a Continental Divide, Appalachian Trail, or other long-distance hike.

A surprising number of hikers set off each spring for Mount Katahdin, Maine (the northernmost point of the AT), or the Canadian or Mexican borders on the PCT or CDT, with little or no previous backpacking experience. This in itself ensures a high failure rate. A gradual progression—an apprenticeship, in fact—should precede a multi-month trip. Before attempting

one of the big three, try hiking a shorter but challenging trail, such as the John Muir, Colorado, or Long Trail. My first solo distance hike, a 17-day, 270-mile trip along Britain's Pennine Way, followed several years of two- to five-day trips. Two years later, I made a 1,250-mile Britain end-to-end hike. Then, after another three years of shorter trips, I set out on the Pacific Crest Trail. I still made lots of mistakes, but I had enough knowledge and determination to finish the walk. If it had been my first distance hike, I doubt I would have managed more than a few hundred miles.

Preparation for a long trek doesn't mean just dealing with logistics—knowing where to send food supplies, where stores and post offices are, how far you can realistically walk per day—it also means accepting that at times you will be wet, cold, or hungry, and the trail will be hard to follow. Adventures are unpredictable by definition. Every long walk I've done included moments when I felt like quitting—but I've always continued, knowing the moment would pass. If the time ever comes when the moment *doesn't* pass, I'll stop. If backpacking isn't enjoyable, it is pointless. Completing the trail doesn't matter—it's what happens along the way that's significant.

Mapping Long Routes

For me, the ultimate backpacking experience is to spend weeks or months in wilderness areas without benefit of long-distance trails, or sometimes without any trails at all. Walking a route of my own is more exciting and satisfying than following a route someone else has planned.

Planning such a walk can be difficult, however. Compiling information takes time and there are always gaps. The easiest approach is to link shorter trails, which is what I did for the southern half of a walk over the length of the Canadian Rockies. Even there, though, I was forced to travel cross-country on one trail-less section.

First, of course, you have to decide where you want to start and finish. This inspiration can come from the nature of the land, from the writings of others, and occasionally from photographs. My first long-distance walk from Land's End to John O'Groats was inspired by John Hillaby's *Journey Through Britain.* Soon after that walk I read Hamish Brown's *Hamish's Mountain Walk,* about the first continuous round of the Munros, Scottish mountains over 3,000 feet high. Brown's walk inspired a couple of 500-mile walks in the Scottish Highlands, but the idea of a *really* long walk there was put aside in favor of other ventures. A PCT walk was inspired by a slide show of the Yosemite backcountry and by Colin Fletcher's *The Thousand-Mile Summer.* On that walk, I learned of the CDT, so it was that trail I hiked next. On a ski-backpacking trip in the Canadian Rockies I came upon Ben Gadd's *The Handbook of the Canadian Rockies,* and read that no one had hiked the length of the range. Another dream was born. A later Yukon trip was, in a sense, a continuation of this walk into an area I'd read about in the writings of Jack London and Robert Service.

I always thought that one day I would tramp all the Munros in one go. The spur that turned a vague thought into a concrete plan came from another book, Andrew Dempster's fascinating *The Munro Phenomenon,* a sentence of which flew off the page: "It is interesting and almost strange that no one has yet attempted all the Munros and Tops in a single expedition." I knew instantly that I wanted to try this—a round of all 517 3,000-foot summits in Scotland.

The thought of being the first to do something lends excitement and adventure to an expedi-

tion. Yes, the heart of any backpacking trip is spending weeks at a time living in wild country, and it is the great pleasure and satisfaction of doing this that sends me back again and again. But a goal gives a walk focus, a shape, a beginning and an end.

The initial buzz of excitement eventually gives way to a sober assessment of what is involved. This is the point at which ventures come closest to being abandoned. The planning often seems more daunting than the walk itself, but once begun, it's usually enjoyable.

My planning for a Scottish summits walk involves working through a pile of maps and plotting a cat's cradle of a route linking 517 summits by the easiest and quickest path, though "easiest" and "quickest" are often not the same. At the time of this writing (the winter before I hope to do the walk), I've planned a detailed 800-mile route over the first 200 summits. From this I estimate the total route will be something over 2,000 miles. (A reasonably accurate way to estimate the length of a route, by the way, is to measure the straight-line distance between the start and finish and then add half as much.)

There is no such thing as too much information, but it's easy to have too little. When planning a long hike, I write to national parks, forest services, and other land management bodies; tourist information offices; and any other contact addresses I can find. In really remote areas like the Yukon, local knowledge is invaluable. On my walk through that area I changed my route several times based on information received from locals.

For the initial route planning I use small-scale (1:250,000) maps covering large areas before purchasing the appropriate topographic maps and working out a more detailed line. I'm always aware, however, that cross-country routes may be impassable on the ground or that a far more obvious way may show itself, so I don't stick rigidly to my pre-hike plans.

One of the big problems with planning a hike is resupply. On trails like the AT and PCT, regularly updated lists of facilities like post offices and grocery stores are available. There are even companies that will ship food parcels to you. Hikers may be rare or even unheard of in other places, so it's always best to write and ask about amenities. For more details, see Chapter 7 (pages 192–193).

Planning a long walk takes time and energy, and the adventure itself can vanish in a welter of lists, logistics, maps, and food. This is only temporary, of course. When you take that first step, all the organization fades into the background. Then it is just you and the wilderness.

CHAPTER TWO

The Load on Your Back: Choosing and Using Equipment

*S*oon, my apartment furniture disappeared
under an avalanche of maps; and I found myself
eat-and-sleep deep in routes and loads, clothing
and cameras, sleeping bags and pemmican.

—*The Thousand-Mile Summer,* Colin Fletcher

One aspect of backpacking that puts off many
people is the prospect of carrying everything you
need for days, maybe even weeks, on your back.
To the uninitiated, the resulting load looks back-
breakingly heavy, a burden that will take all the
joy out of walking, all the pleasure from a day in
the mountains. For the uninformed novice, this
may be the case. It certainly was for me when I
began. I am not a masochist; however, I don't like
aching shoulders, sore hips, and trail-pounded,
blistered feet. Nor do I like being wet or cold.
After suffering all those in my first few backpacking attempts, I developed an interest in
equipment and techniques.

While experience and technique play a large
part, no amount of hiking skill will allow an
inadequately designed pack to carry 50 pounds
comfortably, or make a leaking rain jacket waterproof. The right equipment can make the difference between a trip you want to repeat and a
nightmare that will make you shudder every time
you see a pack. I've met walkers who recoil at

mere mention of the word backpacking, muttering about their one attempt of the Appalachian
Trail and how their backs ached, their knees gave
way, their tents leaked, and they suffered for
weeks afterward. It doesn't have to be like that.

My interest in equipment was born from a
couple of hillside soakings that ended in night
descents and near hypothermia, and from lug-
ging around a heavy cotton tent that leaked at
the merest hint of rain in a pack that resembled a
medieval torture rack. Not that I ever carried the
tent up any hills—reaching a valley campground
from a bus stop was exhausting enough. I used
this equipment through ignorance; I didn't know
anything better existed.

Two experiences showed me what was possible. Once, another hiker expressed horror at
the sight of my huge pack frame. "No hipbelt?"
he exclaimed. "What's a hipbelt?" I replied. He
handed me his pack, an even bigger one than
mine. I put it on and tightened the hipbelt. The

Peace in the Wilderness

It is good to be alone. I don't go far the first
day, camping in a spruce grove above a cool,
rushing stream after only a couple of hours.
Miles traveled are irrelevant; I am content just
to be here.

weight of the pack seemed to melt away. Ever since, I've viewed a hipbelt as the key feature of any pack designed for heavy loads.

The other occasion was on a roadside campground when I was using a wooden-poled, cotton ridge tent that weighed a ton. Sitting outside this monstrosity, which was neither wind- nor waterproof, I watched a walker with a moderate-size pack come down from the mountains and pitch a tiny green nylon tent. The next morning he packed everything up, shouldered his modest load, and headed, effortlessly it seemed, back into the wilderness. The realization that it was possible to backpack in comfort led me to visit outdoor shops, write away for equipment catalogs, and read everything I could find about backpacking.

Later, I worked in an equipment shop and started writing reviews of gear for outdoor magazines. I've been doing this since the late 1970s, and have acquired a fairly detailed knowledge of what equipment is available, and more important, what to look for in equipment. My interest in gear may seem to give it greater importance than it deserves—after all, it's only a tool. Backpacking is not about having the latest tent or trying out the new, guaranteed-to-keep-you-comfortable-in-all-weather-conditions clothing system. If you know enough about equipment to select what really works, however, when you're in the wilderness you won't need to think about your gear. You can get on with what you are really there for—experiencing the natural world. Worrying about rain because you don't trust your rain gear to keep you dry, or about the temperature at night because of your threadbare sleeping bag, will come between you and the environment, and may even come to dominate your thoughts on your walk. In extreme circumstances, inadequate gear could even be life threatening. So it's worth taking your time choosing equipment. It will be with you for many miles and many nights.

WEIGHT

Three major factors govern choice of gear: *performance, durability,* and *weight.* The first is simple—an item must do what is required of it. Rain gear must keep out the rain; a stove must bring water to a boil. How long it goes on doing so efficiently is a measure of its durability. It may be easy to make items that perform well and last for ages, but the backpacker's (and equipment designer's) problem is the weight of such gear. Backpackers probably spend more time trying to reduce the weight of their packs than they do on all other aspects of trip planning. Such time is usually well spent. A 2-pound weight saving means another day's food can be carried; the difference between a 35-pound pack and a 45-pound one is considerable, especially near the end of a long, hard day.

Equipment can be divided into two categories: *standard* and *lightweight.* In the first, compromises have been made between weight and durability to produce gear that is reasonably light but strong enough to withstand years of average use or the rigors of a multi-month expedition. With this equipment, a load for a week-long summer solo trip—without food or non-essentials such as chair kits, lanterns, cameras, or books, but including fuel, maps, boots, and clothing—weighs 25 to 30 pounds. Extra items for a longer trip that may run into autumn or winter push this up to 35 to 40 pounds. If you're traveling with a group, shared camping and cooking equipment will reduce this a little, while the need for specialized gear for winter conditions will add to it.

Gear for a Two-Week, Solo, Late-Summer, High-Mountain Trip

On this walk I wasn't intent on hiking a great distance (100 miles was the total), so weight wasn't a major consideration—hence the roomy tent, self-inflating mat, candle lantern, and changes of clothes.

The expectation of warm days with little rain but sub-freezing temperatures at night were the reasons for the fleece and the ultralight rain gear. In fact, the coldest overnight temperature was only 39°F (4°C), and heavy thunderstorms meant I wore my rain jacket every day. The fleece was welcome in camp, though, and the ultralight rain gear completely adequate. I took a polyester/cotton shirt rather than a windshirt—a nice luxury in camp, though it wasn't worth the extra weight. I did the whole walk in sandals, usually without socks, sometimes with them.

(A note on weights and measures: gear that I've used I've also weighed, so the weights quoted throughout this chapter may differ from those provided by manufacturers. Elsewhere catalog weights are given when available.)

Gear	Weight in Ounces
Pack	
5,000 cu. in. internal frame	90.0
Shelter	
Two-person two-pole tunnel tent	77.0
18 oz. goose-down sleeping bag	33.5
Self-inflating mat	19.0
Kitchen	
White-gas stove with 34 oz. fuel bottle	21.5
1 qt. stainless steel/aluminum pot with lid	7.5
1 pt. stainless steel cup	4.0
Pot grab	2.0
2 spoons	2.0
Pot scrub	1.0
Matches	2.0
1 qt. water bottle	5.0
4 qt. waterbag	2.5
Footwear	
Running shoes	22.5
Sports sandals	19.0

Clothing	
1 pair medium-weight Ragg wool socks	4.5
2 pair lightweight synthetic socks	2.5
Polyester/cotton shorts	5.0
Nylon microfiber trail pants	11.0
Nylon underpants	2.0
Polypro long-sleeved crew-neck top	4.5
Cotton T-shirt	5.5
Polyester/cotton long-sleeved shirt	12.0
Mid-weight pile sweater	15.0
Bandanna	2.0
Waterproof/breathable jacket	11.5
Waterproof/breathable rain pants	4.5
Fleece hat	2.0
Sun hat	4.0

Essential accessories	
Headlamp and spare batteries	6.5
Compass and whistle	1.5
Maps	8.0
First aid kit	4.5
Repair kit	4.0
Hiking poles	21.0
Wrist altimeter/watch	1.5
Sunscreen	2.0
Knife	1.0
Wash kit	2.0
Toilet paper	2.0
Toilet trowel	2.0
Iodine crystals	4.0
Dark glasses	2.0

Optional accessories	
Notebook, pens, travel documents	18.5
Paperbacks	12.0
Mini binoculars	4.5
Candle lantern	9.5

Total:	**31.5 pounds**

To this must be added food and fuel, which totaled around 20 pounds when the trip started. My camera gear weighed another 10 pounds. Allowing for trekking poles and clothing worn (around 3 pounds), my pack weighed about 58 pounds at the start, and 38 pounds at the finish.

Gear for a Solo, Wet Summer Weekend Trip in the Mountains

On this short trip I wanted to climb several peaks, so a light pack was essential. I walked in and camped high the first evening; on the main day of the trip I walked 20 miles, with a 9,600-foot ascent. The lowest overnight temperature was 42°F (6°C); I never had to wear the fleece top. On the long day, I wore the long pants and the windshirt because there was a cool breeze, but no rain.

Gear	Weight in Ounces
Pack	
4,000 cu. in. internal frame	74.0
Shelter	
One-person single-hoop tent	70.0
10 oz. goose-down sleeping bag	24.0
Three-quarter-length closed-cell foam pad	8.0
Kitchen	
Mini cartridge stove	5.5
9 oz. butane/propane cartridge	12.0
Foil wind screen	2.0
1 qt. stainless steel/aluminum pot with foil lid	6.0
1 pt. stainless steel cup	4.0
Mini pot grab	1.0
2 spoons	2.0
Dishcloth	0.5
Matches/lighter	1.0
1 qt. water bottle	5.0
4 qt. waterbag	2.5
Footwear	
Running shoes	25.0

Clothing	
Polypro long-sleeved crew-neck top	4.0
Nylon underpants	2.0
Polyester/cotton shorts	5.0
Nylon microfiber trail pants	11.0
Microfleece sweater	11.0
Nylon microfiber windshirt	7.5
Waterproof/breathable jacket	19.0
Waterproof/breathable rain pants	4.5
Sun hat	4.0
Lightweight nylon socks	1.0
Medium-weight nylon socks	3.0
Essential accessories	
Headlamp and spare batteries	6.5
Compass and whistle	1.5
Maps	4.0
First aid kit	4.5
Repair kit	4.0
Wrist altimeter/watch	1.5
Sunscreen	2.0
Knife	1.0
Wash kit	2.0
Toilet paper	2.0
Toilet trowel	2.0
Dark glasses	2.0
Optional accessories	
Notebook and pen	8.0
Paperback book	6.0
Total:	**22.5 pounds**

To this must be added 4 pounds of food and 3 pounds of camera gear, to give a starting total of 29.5 pounds, of which about 2 pounds was worn.

Weight is subjective. When you set out deep into the wilderness carrying two weeks' supplies in a 70-pound pack, the 40-pound load you emerge with feels amazingly light. But set off cold with 40 pounds for a weekend, and the burden will seem unbearable. There are limits, of course. I once carried more than 110 pounds (including snowshoes, ice ax, crampons, and 23 days' food) through the snowbound High Sierra. I couldn't lift my pack; instead I had to sit down, slide my arms through the shoulder straps, then roll forward to all fours before

Gear for a Two-Week Desert Canyon Trip in Autumn

This was a trip to the Grand Canyon during which I planned to camp both at the bottom of the canyon and on the north rim at 8,000 feet. Although I expected hot weather in the canyon (with overnight lows in the mid-50s), because it was a late-October hike I knew that snow and cold weather were likely on the north rim. I carried the long johns, down vest, and wool socks for campwear and to sleep in on the coldest nights. (The lowest overnight temperature in the tent was 32°F (0°C); I slept in the warm clothing once and wore it in camp on several evenings and mornings. It was worth carrying.) It was also in case of cold or wet weather that I carried the trail shoes and the waterproof jacket—I needed them for the last two days, when I crossed from the north to south rim in rain, hail, and wind. For the rest of the 155-mile walk I wore sandals, shorts, a shirt, and a sun hat. The only mistake I made with my gear selection was the fuel cartridges. At the Grand Canyon I was unable to buy the 9-ounce butane/propane cartridges I usually use, and I had to purchase 6-ounce isobutane ones instead. I knew three 9-ounce cartridges would have been enough for the whole trip, but because I was unfamiliar with the smaller isobutane cartridges, I took six 6-ounce ones—I only used 3½ however. The facilities on the north rim had closed for the winter at the time of the trip; I had left a cache of six days' food and three fuel cartridges in the canyon, so I didn't have to carry 12 days' worth of food or return to the south rim to resupply.

Gear	Weight in Ounces
Pack	
5,000 cu. in. internal frame	90.0
Shelter	
Solo single-hoop tent	60.0
10 oz. goose-down sleeping bag	24.0
Three-quarter-length closed-cell foam pad	8.0
Kitchen	
Mini cartridge stove	5.5
(3) 6 oz. isobutane cartridges	24.0
Foil wind screen	2.0
1 qt. titanium pot with lid	5.0
1 pt. stainless steel cup	4.0
2 plastic spoons	1.0
Dishcloth	0.5

slowly standing up. Carrying this much weight was not fun, and I was exhausted by the end of every 12-mile day. I wouldn't do it again. Since then, I have started sections of long treks in remote wilderness with 80 pounds in my pack and found even that too much. Only after the first week do such loads slim down to bearable weight. My current aim is never to carry more than 70 pounds on any trip; I find 50 pounds manageable, as long as my pack can support the load and I'm not planning on covering more than 12 to 15 miles a day or ascending thousands of feet. If I want to cover more distance or climb, then 30 pounds is my target pack weight.

If the total weight seems excessive, I look for items to eliminate. (It's a bit late to decide you could do with a lighter tent or sleeping bag when you're packing for a trip, which is why your original gear choices are so important.) When the only difference between two items is weight, I go for the lighter one every time. The big items—tent, sleeping bag, pack, stove—add weight to the pack most rapidly, but it all has to be carried.

I like to know the weight of *everything* I consider carrying, down to the smallest item. I use an angler's spring balance that measures to the nearest half ounce. If you can't decide between two items and the store where you're shopping doesn't have a scale, it might be worth taking yours along. Catalog weights are often inaccurate. I also find it helps to have maximum target weights and to disregard all heavier items.

Matches/lighter	1.0	Compass and whistle	1.5
(4) 1 qt. water bottles	14.5	Maps	8.0
4 qt. waterbag	2.5	First aid kit	4.5
		Repair kit	4.0
Footwear		Wrist altimeter/watch	1.5
Trail shoes	32.5	Sunscreen	4.0
Sports sandals	21.5	Knife	1.0
		Wash kit	2.0
Clothing		Toilet paper	2.0
Synthetic sun shirt	8.5	Toilet trowel	2.0
Nylon underpants	2.0	Iodine pills	2.0
Polyester long johns	4.5	Dark glasses	2.0
Polyester/cotton shorts	5.0		
Nylon microfiber trail pants	11.0	**Optional accessories**	
Microfleece sweater	11.0	Notebook and pens	12.0
Down vest	13.5	Mini binoculars	4.5
Waterproof/breathable jacket	11.5	Paperback book	6.0
Sun hat	4.0		
Fleece hat	2.0	**Total:**	**29.5 pounds**
Lightweight nylon socks	1.0		
Medium-weight nylon socks	2.5		
Medium-weight wool socks	3.5		

Essential accessories

Trekking poles	23.0
Headlamp and spare batteries	6.5
Candle lantern and 3 candles	10.5

To this must be added about 12 pounds of food and 10 pounds of camera gear, to give a starting total of about 52 pounds, of which about 4.5 pounds was worn or in use most days. I also always carried at least a quart of water— twice I carried 8 quarts. On the last day, my pack weighed about 40 pounds.

Equipment for a 12-day autumn hike in the Grand Canyon.

Gear for a Spring Ski Trip in High Mountains

Ten of us skied through the High Sierra from North Lake to June Lake in May, a 12-day trip split into eight and four days by a resupply/rest day at Mammoth Lakes. To keep the weight down, I took a lightweight sleeping bag and foam pad, sleeping in clothes on the coldest nights—12°F (−11°C) was the lowest overnight temperature. Most nights were in the 20s. My gear was only just adequate for these conditions. I would now save weight with lightweight crampons; at the time I only had an old, heavy pair. These were used once.

Personal Gear	Weight in Ounces
Pack	
7,000 cu. in. internal frame	115.0
Sleeping	
18 oz. goose-down sleeping bag	33.5
Three-quarter-length closed-cell foam pad	8.0
Clothing	
Polyester long-sleeved crew-neck top	5.5
Polyester/cotton shorts	5.0
Nylon microfiber trail pants	11.0
Stretch pile pants	7.0
Waterproof/breathable jacket	19.0
Waterproof/breathable pants	4.5
Lightweight pile jacket	12.0
Nylon windshirt	9.5
Down vest	13.5
Fleece hat	2.0
Sun hat	4.0
Polypro liner gloves	1.5
Pile gloves	3.0
Nylon-shelled pile mitts	3.0
Heavyweight wool/polypro socks	5.0
Medium-weight wool/polypro socks	4.0
Lightweight synthetic socks	1.0
2 pair nylon underpants	3.5
Bandanna	1.0
Supergaiters	17.0
Sports sandals	19.0
Accessories	
2 pair dark glasses	3.5
Compass and whistle	1.5
Notebook, pens, permit	11.5
Paperback book	6.0
Maps	4.0
1 pt. stainless steel cup	4.0
Plastic bowl	3.0
Spoon	1.0
1 qt. water bottle	5.0
Knife	3.5
Headlamp and spare batteries	6.5
Matches and lighters	1.0
Wrist altimeter/watch	1.5
Wash kit	2.0
Sunscreen/lip salve	8.0
Mini binoculars	6.5
Ski gear	
Nordic ski boots	92.0
Nordic mountain skis, cable bindings	109.0
Adjustable ski poles	22.0
Spare pole	11.0
Wax kit	10.0
Climbing skins	14.0
Snow shovel	21.0
Ice ax	11.0
Crampons	35.0
Total:	**45 pounds**

Communal Gear	
Tents (3 tunnels, 1 semi-geodesic)	495.0
3 white-gas stoves and fuel bottles	58.5
Pans and utensils	48.0
100 ft. 8 mm rope	32.0
First aid kit	24.0
Repair kit	39.0
Total:	**43.5 pounds**

My share of the communal total was about 4½ pounds, which brought total weight to about 50 pounds. Of this, about 17½ pounds is ski gear and clothing worn, leaving a pack weight of 32 pounds. We set off with eight days' food (18 pounds each); I had an additional 10 pounds of camera gear. Because we carried the ski gear up to the snow, my initial pack weight was about 70 pounds. The average weight for the trip was about 50 pounds.

The author and his gear plus food for 10 days during a three-month walk through Canada's Yukon Territory.

As an exercise, I once compiled two lists of gear from a mail-order catalog. The first consisted of standard items, chosen regardless of weight; the second contained the lightest gear in each category. The difference between items was small, often no more than a few ounces, yet the overall weights were 25 pounds for the lightweight gear, 35 for the standard. (See table, page 24.)

The Ultralight Approach

The ultralight approach involves using the lightest gear possible and carrying the absolute minimum. If you leave an item at home you reduce its weight by 100 percent. The leading exponents of this approach are Ray and Jenny Jardine, who have hiked the Appalachian and Pacific Crest Trails with packs averaging an astonishing 8½ pounds without food. Their techniques and equipment are described in the excellent book, *The Pacific Crest Trail Hiker's Handbook.*

This approach works best in summer conditions on good trails, and it's suited to those who like to keep moving and spend as little time in camp as possible. It also requires expertise and fitness—there's no back-up gear to get you out of trouble. I've tried the ultralight approach on long weekends when I wanted to cover high mileage. On these trips, my companion and I managed to get our pack weights down to around 13 pounds each, including food. Personally, I wouldn't want to travel with such minimal gear for long, but if you're interested in high daily mileage and stoic enough to endure minimal comfort in camp in bad weather, this could be the way to go.

Previously, I wrote that "much ultralight equipment wouldn't last if used day in and day out." This was based on having used some of the few commercially available ultralight gear items. I didn't consider the possibility of making my own gear, which is what the Jardines do. Their gear, carefully made from quality materials, has proved durable for long-distance hiking. After their 1994 Pacific Coast Trail hike, I was privileged to spend a few days hiking in the Cascades with Ray. I borrowed Jenny's 13-ounce pack for

Target Weights

Gear	Ounces	Gear	Ounces
Footwear		**Clothing, summer**	
Sports sandals	25	Synthetic T-shirt	4
Running shoes	25	Fleece top	16
Trail shoes	32	Shorts	6
Three-season boots	40	Synthetic long johns	4
Winter boots (suitable for crampons)	64	Summer-weight trousers	12
Note: these weights are for a pair, size 9½; scale up or down for different sizes.		Windproof top	12
		Waterproof jacket	16
		Rain pants	8
Shelter		Warm hat	2
Groundsheet	10	Sun hat	4
Bivy bag	20		
Tarp, solo	20	**Clothing, winter**	
Tarp, duo	32	Synthetic zip-neck shirt	8
Bivy tent	40	Fleece top	20
Solo tent, three-season	64	Windproof fleece top (for wet/cold)	25
Duo tent, three-season	6 lbs. 96	Down top (for dry/cold)	20
Duo tent, winter mountain	128	Synthetic long johns/pile pants	8
Sleeping bag (summer)	25	Long pants	24
Sleeping bag (three-season)	3 lbs. 48	Waterproof/breathable jacket	28
Sleeping bag (winter)	64	Waterproof/breathable pants	20
Closed-cell foam mat	9	Warm hat	2
Self-inflating mat	less than 1 lb. 14	Windproof pile-lined cap	4
		Liner gloves	2
Cooking gear		Warm gloves/mitts	4
Stove (cartridge)	less than 1 lb. 14	Shell gloves/mitts	5
Stove (multi-fuel/white-gas)	16		
Stove (alcohol with solo cookset)	30	**Packs**	
Stove (alcohol with duo cookset)	44	Ultra-lightweight trip (3,000 cu. in.)	40
1 qt. pot with lid	8	Summer weekend (3,500 to 4,000 cu. in.)	4 lbs. 64
Cookset with 1½ and 2 qt. pans, lid	26	Extended summer/short winter trip (4,500 to 5,500 cu. in.)	5.5 lbs. 90
		Wilderness expedition (6,000+ cu. in.)	120

this. It was hard to tell it just had seen three months of hard usage.

Green Gear

A welcome development is the growing use by outdoor companies of recycled materials in both finished items and packaging. Whatever the companies' motivation, using recycled materials does less damage to the environment than using virgin materials.

But when pile clothing made from recycled materials first appeared, there was some doubt as to whether it would perform as well as clothing made from virgin material. After extensive use of gear made from recycled materials, I'm glad to say I can't tell the difference. It's now possible to buy clothing, boots, and even packs made from 100 percent recycled materials, as well as products containing varying amounts of recycled material. If there's a choice between identical recycled and non-recycled products, I now always choose the first. I hope it won't be long before it's possible to head into the wilderness with all gear made from recycled materials. One company, Ecotrek, already makes products mainly from recycled material, including packs and fleece jackets.

Using gear made from recycled material is only the first step, of course. What happens when you've finished with it? Donating it to a worthy cause, selling it, or passing it along to friends are preferable to sending it to a landfill. And here's a good idea: vauDe has established the Ecolog Recycling Network, which accepts worn-out equipment for recycling.

The key to long equipment life is maintenance. Annie Getchell's *The Essential Outdoor Gear Manual* (Ragged Mountain Press) covers repair and care of everything from packs to kayaks. It should be on every backpacker's bookshelf. Repair centers exist, but unless you live near one or near an outdoor store that will forward gear, you have to mail your gear to them—they're only worth using for major problems you can't fix yourself.

CHECKLISTS

When, where, and for how long you go will determine what you carry for any walk. You need to know about the weather, the terrain, and the environment, and you should prepare for the most extreme conditions you may encounter. I work from a complete list of all my gear, then distill a shorter list for the walk at hand. Because I know what each item weighs, I can work out how much gear I'll be carrying. Adding about 2 pounds of food per day, plus the weight of my camera gear, tells me what the total load will be. At that point I review the list again to see if anything can be left out or replaced with a lighter alternative. For a major trip that will last many months, I repeat this process obsessively. With experience, you'll probably find that your first list needs only a little tinkering.

CHOOSING AND BUYING

The highly competitive nature of the outdoor equipment market means that styles and names change rapidly—companies come and go, brand names are taken over, new materials emerge. While some changes are cosmetic, some involve new designs. There are basically four sources for the latest information on equipment: specialty stores, mail-order companies, manufacturers and importers, and outdoor magazines (see Appendix 3).

If you can find a good store with staff who use the equipment they sell regularly and know what they're talking about, support it. The employees in such a store can keep you well informed and advised. But even the best retailer only stocks a fraction of what is available.

One alternative to the retail store is mail order. A number of companies, including Campmor, L.L. Bean, and REI, produce informative catalogs, which often feature equipment comparison charts and "house brand" items not available elsewhere. Manufacturers' catalogs and brochures are worth writing for and often give a lot of information on materials, though some don't include essential details such as weight.

For an objective viewpoint, consult the outdoor magazines. Most test and review gear, often in great detail. They also carry news of the latest gear and advertisements from most of the big companies, plus many smaller specialty manufacturers whose products you may never find in a store or mail-order catalog.

The leading specialty magazine for many years has been *Backpacker,* which regularly carries detailed comparative test reports on gear, and also publishes an annual gear guide issue that lists the specifications of thousands of items. (The information can be accessed electronically through the magazine's Electronic Trailhead on America Online.) *Outside* covers a wider field, and often has features of interest to backpackers. In Canada, the same applies to *Explore.*

Quality

Today, outdoor companies are international and you can buy the best gear worldwide. Much high-quality equipment from reputable companies is made in the Far East, once known only for budget items, and several American companies have factories in Europe. You may want to buy gear made in your home country for patriotic reasons, but you don't need to do so to ensure you're getting good quality.

What you *should* do is check carefully and thoroughly every bit of gear you buy. However reputable the company, and however good the quality control, a faulty item occasionally slips through. It is better to discover that your tent door zipper jams or that the snaps fall off your jacket when you're home rather than when you're out in a raging blizzard. Make sure everything works. Check that stitching is neat and unbroken, and that seam ends are finished properly. (With filled garments and sleeping bags, you usually can't see the work inside, but if the outside is put together well, chances are the interior is too.) All waterproof/breathable garments should have taped seams; check that the tapes are flat and run in straight lines. The same applies to tents with pre-taped seams (on some, you'll have to seal the seams yourself). You should be able to spot any gross manufacturing defects before they cause problems in the field.

Cost

Your life might depend on the performance of your equipment. Buy the best you can afford. During a mountaintop blizzard, a few dollars saved on a cheap jacket is meaningless. This doesn't mean you need to buy the most expensive items, or that you shouldn't go hiking if you can't afford top-of-the-line gear. There are huge price ranges—especially in clothing, where high prices often just mean the latest style, color, or fabric rather than better performance. (Indeed, the most expensive garments are often too complex and heavy for backpacking.) The simplest, lightest designs—not the most costly—are best.

Depending on where you plan to go, there are critical gear items for which money should be no object, but other items need not be expensive or may not even be needed. Remember: Good gear isn't a substitute for skill. Equipment is of no use if you don't know what to do with it. An experienced backpacker can function more efficiently and safely with minimum basic gear than can a novice with the latest high-tech designs.

Color

When I began backpacking, most items were green, brown, or blue. In the 1980s, however, there came an explosion of brilliant colors and multi-hued equipment that shows no sign of abating, to the point where some green-clad hikers are crying "visual pollution."

For many years I was in favor of being inconspicuous when outdoors. Indeed, a group of backpacking friends and I once acquired the nickname "the green cagoule brigade," because that was what we all wore. I've moderated my views for two reasons, though. The first was the upsurge of interest in "survivalism" (not to be confused with general survival techniques, though the two unfortunately overlap a little), and the use of the hills and forests for pseudo-military activities. I don't go into the wilds in order to pretend I'm in the S.A.S. or the Marines, and I don't want to be associated with those who do. Green and brown (and especially camouflage) clothing seems to imply such an allegiance (four of us were once mistaken for soldiers skiing in the Alps because of our olive-green windproof clothing). I now prefer to wear at least one item that doesn't look like military surplus.

The main reason I've changed, however, has been because of photography. On the Pacific Crest Trail in 1982, I wore dark blue and green clothing and used a sludge-brown tent. In the photographs, I look like a black smudge, and the tent blends neatly into the trees. A bright garment, especially a red one, can give the splash of color that makes a striking (or salable) photograph.

I still prefer fairly dull, pale colors for my tent, but I always like to carry at least one item of reasonably bright clothing or a colorful pack. As for safety, I always carry at least one or two bright orange or red stuff sacks in my pack that could be used to signal if necessary.

Testing

Many manufacturers spend a great deal of time and money conducting tests on equipment and fabrics, the results of which often are touted in catalogs and advertisements. There are tests for everything from waterproofness to wind resistance. But test methods vary, so comparing results can be difficult. Moreover, although tests can *suggest* how a garment will work in the outdoors, they don't guarantee performance—and "performance" is often a subjective judgment, anyway. This applies especially to clothing and sleeping bags—what keeps one person cozy may not be enough to stop someone else from shivering. Read and note laboratory test results by all means, but don't assume an item that *tests* perfectly will *perform* perfectly in the real world.

FINAL THOUGHTS

The chapters that follow cover the intricacies of equipment and how to use it. Technical details on gear and techniques are interwoven because no equipment, however good, is of any use if you don't know what to do with it.

The views here are my own, and experienced backpackers will undoubtedly find much to disagree with. Those who don't have experience and thus no strong views (prejudices?) of their own should note that much of the equipment I describe is what has worked well for me, but no one can try out even a fraction of what is available. I've named names only to make it easier to illustrate details; other gear is as good as what I've selected. So, take what I've said as a guide, not as a rule.

CHAPTER THREE

Footwear and Wilderness Travel

Grandma Gatewood, the fabulous woman who hiked the entire 2,000-mile Appalachian Trail three times—the first time at age 67—wore sneakers. If Grandma Gatewood could hike 2,000 miles in sneakers, does Joe Athlete really need heavy boots with lug soles?

—*Backwoods Ethics,* Laura and Guy Waterman

More backpacking trips are ruined by sore feet than by all other causes combined. Pounded by the ground below and the weight of you and your pack above, your feet receive harsher treatment than any other part of your body. Feet are marvelously complex—flexible and tough at the same time—but they need care and protection if they are to carry you and your load mile after mile through the wilderness in comfort. This protection is provided by your footwear.

A variety of accessories can make walking easier and safer—from staffs to socks, and, for snow travel, ice axes, crampons, snowshoes, and skis. The last two items don't constitute walking accessories per se, but they greatly aid travel in deep snow, especially with a heavy pack.

BOOTS AND SHOES: PURPOSE AND FIT

The main purposes of backpacking footwear are to *protect* your feet and ankles against bruising

and abrasion from rough wilderness terrain, to *cushion* the soles of your feet from the constant hammering of miles of walking, and to provide *good grip* on slippery, steep, and wet terrain.

Protection for the sole of the foot comes from layers of cushioning; these must be thick enough to prevent stones from bruising the feet, but soft enough to allow a natural toe-to-heel flex. Thick soles also insulate against snow and cold ground, and the heat of desert sand and rock. The *tread* cut out of the outer sole offers grip; the best grips not only give security on rough terrain but also minimize damage to the ground.

Footwear should also provide *support* for your foot and ankle, though this is less important than some people think. Support comes from a fit that is snug enough to stop the foot from slipping around inside the shoe, but not so tight that it prevents the foot from expanding as it swells. The ankle is supported by a stiff lower heel counter, or heel cup (see "Heel Counters and Toe Boxes" and the illustration on page 39), and not simply by a high-cut boot; some running shoes give more ankle support than some boots do.

Keeping your feet dry isn't a major purpose of footwear—no boot or shoe that allows adequate respiration can be waterproof. Top-quality leather is fairly water resistant, but only boots with "breathable" membrane inserts can be considered waterproof; how long they stay so is open

Wildlife

Moving softly, I begin to meet local residents: fat black-and-gold marmots scuttling among rocks on the high passes, brown flickers swooping through trees, red-tailed hawks soaring overhead, and elk crashing through the undergrowth, antlers held high. I hear the elk, too—their weird bugling call heralding autumn. On one steep trail I glance down to see a tiny mouse emerge from a hole in a log and prospect its way across a rill. Then it scurries back to take an even tinier offspring gently in its jaws for the journey across the water.

to question. Plastic and rubber boots are waterproof, of course, but lead to hot, sweaty feet.

Fit

Take your time when choosing footwear—if the fit isn't right, you'll suffer badly. Nothing is worse than footwear that hurts your feet. The types of boots and shoes available, construction methods, and materials are all points to consider, but the most modern, high-tech, waterproof, breathable, expensive boots are worse than useless if they don't fit. Given the bewildering variety of foot

shapes, good fit is more than a question of finding the right size. For that reason, it is unwise to set your heart on a particular model of boot or shoe before you go shopping, however seductive the advertising message.

All footwear is built around a *last*, a rough approximation of a human foot, which varies in shape according to the bootmaker's view of what a foot looks like. Lasts sometimes are designated "American," "European," or "British." Ignore such descriptions.

In the 1980s, manufacturers introduced the *sprung* or *anatomic last*, which has a curved sole that mimics the forward flex of the foot when walking. Boots produced on a sprung last have what is often called a *rocker sole* that, instead of resisting the forward roll of the foot, helps it with what boot manufacturer Scarpa calls "increased toe spring." The first time I used boots made on a sprung last I was amazed at the extra comfort of the curved sole; it seemed to make walking easier than the old-style straight last. A curved sole is a feature I now look for.

Women's feet are generally narrower and smaller than men's feet, and there are boots manufactured on lasts specifically designed for women. Of course, men with small, narrow feet may find women's boots fit them best, just as women with larger, wider feet may prefer men's boots.

Allow yourself several hours for purchasing footwear, and try to visit a store at a quiet time, not on a busy Saturday afternoon. Feet swell during the day, so it is best to try on new footwear later in the day rather than earlier. Take your hiking socks with you. If you forget them, most stores provide suitable socks to wear while trying on footwear. Use your normal shoe size only as a starting point; sizes vary from maker to maker and, just to make matters more confusing, there are two sizing systems. A store may stock footwear made in the United States, Italy,

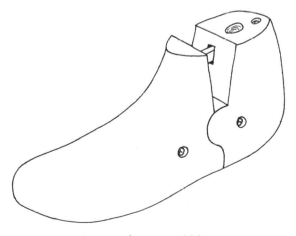

A sprung (or anatomic) last.

Boot size comparison table.

Austria, South Korea, and other countries, so you can't expect consistency.

Make sure you try on both shoes. One of your feet is almost certainly larger than the other, perhaps by as much as half a size. *Make sure the larger foot has the best fit.* An extra sock or insole can pad a slightly large boot, but nothing can be done for one that is too small.

Light- and medium-weight boots and shoes are fairly easy to fit because they conform quickly to your feet and generally hold their shape, especially if they're a combination of nylon and suede. Heavier boots are stiffer, and tend to be uncomfortable when first worn, which makes finding a good fit in the store more difficult; on the other hand, because they are so unforgiving, a good fit is essential, even though they eventually stretch (in width, not length) and mold to your feet. Even more care is needed when fitting traditional and heavy leather boots.

With any shoe or boot, you want a snug but not a tight fit. Check the length first: If your toes touch the end, leaving no space at the heel, the shoe is too small. When you slide your foot forward in an unlaced shoe, you should just be able to insert a finger between the shoe and your heel. If you can't do this, the shoe is too short and will bruise your toes, especially on long downhills. If there is room for more than one finger, the shoe is too big. When the shoe is laced up, your heel

Fitting My Foot

A good store should be able to measure your feet with a *Brannock device,* which not only measures the length and width of your feet but also the ball-to-heel (arch) length. It's well worth doing. I had my feet measured in this way by Paul Cooper of Bill's Sport Shop in Leadville, Colorado, and the result was quite a shock. For 20 years I'd believed I measured size 9EE. I'd had problems finding footwear that was wide enough in the forefoot; EE width always seemed best. I initially asked Paul Cooper if he had any running shoes in a EE. He suggested I have my feet measured first, because they probably weren't as wide as I thought. "Of course they are," I said confidently. They weren't. The figures on the Brannock device were clear: I have size 9 feet in a D width. Why, then, did I have such trouble finding footwear to fit? Because my *arch length* is size 11, and if the size difference between the whole foot and the arch is more than one size, fit will be a problem. In my case, it means that the widest part of my foot is more forward than usual, beyond the point at which most footwear starts to narrow. Paul Cooper made me a pair of custom insoles, assuring me that these could be the solution. They match my feet exactly. I'm still looking for footwear that fits well, but at least now I know what to look for—shoes with broad, rather than narrow, toes.

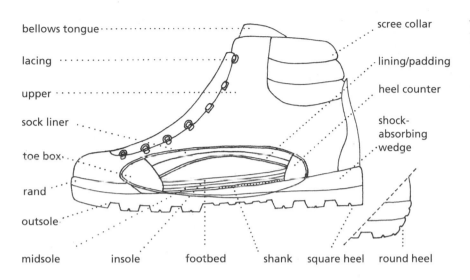

bellows tongue
lacing
upper
sock liner
toe box
rand
outsole
midsole
insole
footbed
shank
square heel
round heel
scree collar
lining/padding
heel counter
shock-absorbing wedge

The basic components of a lightweight hiking boot.

shouldn't move up and down or side to side more than a quarter of an inch when you walk. If it does, chances are you'll get blisters, and the shoe will not support you adequately on rough terrain.

Footwear should be wide enough to let your toes wiggle easily, but not so wide that your feet slide about. Many boots are available in a variety of widths, which increases the chances of finding a good fit. Insoles make a difference in width and volume—take them out to make a larger boot, put in thicker ones for a closer fit. Vasque and Merrell produce lightweight boots that feature a choice of three footbeds in different widths; Vasque calls it the "Variable Fit System," and Merrell the "Custom Fit System." I've tried the Merrell system and it works.

Once you find footwear that seems roughly the right length and width, walk around the store; find inclines if possible to see if your foot slips. Note any pressure points or discomfort— on a long walk these will be magnified. The uppers should be spacious enough not to press too hard on your feet, but snug enough with the laces tightened to keep your feet from moving around. In particular, check the base of the tongue, where shoes commonly rub.

Part with your money only when you're confident you have the best fit possible, then take the shoes home and wear them around the house to check the fit further. If you decide they don't fit after all, a good store should exchange footwear that hasn't been waxed or worn outside.

Breaking In

Gone, thankfully, are the days when boots had to be worn for many short, gentle strolls before you dared subject your feet to them on a real walk. Today, you can set off on a 15-mile walk the day you buy a pair of lightweight boots and suffer not a blister; a short break-in period is advisable, though not essential, for medium-weight models. Only if you have particularly tender feet or heavyweight boots (which I don't recommend) will you need to wear your boots for a long time before setting off on a major trek.

Custom-Made Footwear

A made-to-measure service for those who can't find a suitable off-the-shelf pair of boots is offered by several companies. I once had boots made for me by the Swedish bootmakers Lundhags. Working off a sketched outline of my feet, they produced a well-fitting pair of their 3-pound Mountaineer boots, which I immediately took on a two-week walk in the Pyrenees. They proved very comfortable. I had no problems with sore spots or blisters, though unfortunately the lack of a heel counter made them unsuitable for off-trail travel. Peter Limmer of New Hampshire is the best-known name for custom-made boots, but the wait for a pair of his boots can be a year or longer. Other makers include Mekan Boots in Salt Lake City, Utah, and Morin Custom Boots in Evergreen, Colorado. Your local outdoor store may know of other bootmakers.

If you have to mail-order boots, most companies have clear instructions for obtaining the right size. But nothing beats trying on boots in a store.

Lightweight vs. Heavyweight

Before the early 1980s, virtually all boots were what we now call heavyweight—with leather inners and outers, leather midsoles, steel shanks, and heavily lugged rubber soles. A typical pair of size 9s weighed around 4 pounds and required dozens, if not hundreds, of miles of walking to break in. Lighter boots were available, but they were neither very supportive nor very durable.

The introduction of lightweight leathers, synthetic fabrics, and running-shoe features in the early 1980s revolutionized what we wear in the wilderness. Most backpackers were won over, though some stayed—and still stay—loyal to the old heavyweights. My conversion came nearly 1,500 miles into a Pacific Crest Trail walk in 1982. My heavy, traditional boots had been

giving me hot, sore feet on flat sections of trail, and I'd ended up carrying them and wearing my running shoes (brought along for campwear) much of the time. Only in the snow of the High Sierra did I need the boots. When the time came to resole them, I replaced them with a pair of the new fabric/suede walking shoes, the Asolo Approach (so called because they were designed for the approach marches of Himalayan climbing expeditions whose members had likewise taken to wearing running shoes rather than boots). They weighed less than half the weight of my boots. The staff in the store where I bought the shoes were horrified on hearing I intended to wear them to backpack more than 1,000 miles. My feet, however, released from their stiff leather prisons, rejoiced, and my daily mileage went up. Although full of holes by the end, the shoes gave all the support and grip of my old boots, with vastly increased comfort. I have not worn heavy, traditional footwear since.

That lighter footwear is less tiring seems indisputable. The general estimate is that every pound on your feet equals 5 pounds on your back. Therefore, wearing 2-pound rather than 4-pound boots is like removing 10 pounds from your pack. A heavier boot may also mean thicker materials and, often, more padding. In all but winter conditions this can lead to hot, sweaty feet. Hot feet swell and are more prone to blistering; sweat-soaked feet blister, too.

Boots weighing more than 3 pounds make my feet ache after about 12 miles, and after 15 miles all I want to do is stop. Yet in running shoes I can cover twice that distance before my feet complain.

The ultimate in weight saving is to wear no shoes at all, of course. This idea might seem crazy and a good way to hurt your feet (it certainly is when it's cold), but in summer, walking barefoot is perfectly feasible. I occasionally walk

Walking Style

Heavy boots are bulldozers on the trail. They enable a walker to stumble along, kicking rocks and gouging chunks out of the path. In part, the rigidity of the boots forces such a gait on the walker.

Lightweight, flexible footwear engenders a better walking style. You can move faster and more gently, with less effort; you can step around and over rocks instead of banging into them; gliding, instead of trudging, you can cover more miles with the same effort. How much more? Ray Jardine in *The Pacific Crest Trail Hiker's Handbook* estimates that "each additional 1¾ ounces removed from a boot (3 ounces for the pair) will add about a mile to the day's hiking progress." This means, he says, that changing from boots weighing a little over 3 pounds to running shoes weighing 1 pound means you could walk 7 miles more a day with no extra effort.

short distances barefoot when my feet feel hot and sweaty in my shoes, and I often wander around camp barefoot. Wearing sandals (as I do for most summer hiking) is close to going barefoot. If you're interested in this idea, Richard Frazine's *The Barefoot Hiker* (Ten Speed Press) is worth reading. It has inspired me to go barefoot more often.

The Ankle-Support Myth

The argument that heavy footwear is necessary for ankle support is false.

To begin with, most walking boots offer little ankle support—they have soft ankle cuffs that give easily under any pressure. (Try standing on the outer edge of a standard walking boot and you'll feel the strain on your ankle.) Only boots with high, stiffened ankles give real ankle support. My high-top telemark ski boots with plastic reinforcements in the ankles give good ankle

support; I can balance on the edges without strain and traverse steep, icy slopes on my skis without my ankles aching. Because the stiff ankle support restricts foot movement so much, however, I loosen the laces when walking in these boots so that my ankles can flex fairly normally. Stiff-ankled boots and natural foot movement do not go together.

What actually holds your ankle in place over the sole of a shoe is a rigid heel counter (see "Heel Counters and Toe Boxes" later in this chapter), something found in good-quality running shoes, as well as most boots. I once tested a pair of high-top leather boots without heel cups. On rough terrain they were worse than useless—my foot slid off the insole constantly. I ended up using them for walking on good paths between campsites. For mountain ascents, I wore the running shoes I'd brought along as campwear—they had heel cups and were more stable than the boots.

Some of the greatest strain on your ankles occurs when you run over steep, rough ground. Yet mountain runners, who do this regularly (sometimes for days on end), never wear boots. Try running in boots and you'll see why. The disadvantages of heavy, stiff boots are all magnified, and your feet will quickly feel tired and restricted. What you need for traversing steep, rugged terrain are strong, flexible ankles and lightweight, flexible footwear. Exercises to strengthen your ankles are a good idea, certainly better than splinting them in heavy, rigid boots.

The Stiffness Myth

The other argument in favor of heavy boots is that stiff soles protect your feet from rough terrain and heavy loads. In my experience, restricting normal foot movement does the opposite.

Stiff soles can't flex enough to accommodate to the terrain, and they prevent you from placing your feet naturally. Your gait will be slow and clumsy, and this can lead to injury as your feet are repeatedly forced into the same unnatural position. Also, straining against the stiffness requires energy, and is therefore tiring.

What you need is footwear that *cushions* your feet. The way to do this is with thick, shock-absorbing, but flexible soles, and footwear that is as light as possible. Flexibility enables you to place the whole sole in contact with the ground, even when it's steep, rather than digging in your heels or boot edges, which jars your legs and often digs holes into the hillside.

Sole stiffness is required only on steep, hard-packed snow. Then, a bit of lateral stiffness makes it easier to kick the boot edges into the snow. Crampons can also be used with such boots.

FOOTWEAR TYPES, MATERIALS, AND CONSTRUCTION

Boots and shoes are complex constructions, and there are many ways of making them, using many different materials. It's possible to buy and use footwear happily without knowing whether it has a "graded flex nylon midsole" or "EVA wedges" or is "Blake sewn." What may be more important to you is whether the boots contain any recycled materials (many now do). The selection is enormous, and choosing footwear can be daunting. However, if you go to a store that has a good selection and a knowledgeable, helpful staff, you won't go far wrong. For those who want to know more, here are some technical details and a few subjective views. If you prefer to skip the technical talk, just browse through the boxed discussions of footwear categories in the pages that follow. I haven't listed makes of shoes and boots in any categories other than sandals. There are simply too many—44 in *Backpacker*

magazine's 1995 Gear Guide, not including running shoes.

Uppers: Leather

Leather is still the main outer material for quality boots, although synthetics now dominate midsoles and linings, and a fabric/leather combination is the standard for the uppers of running and trail shoes, and is common in the lightest boots. When I began backpacking, finding out what kind of leather a boot was made from was easy: it was either *top-grain* or *split-grain.* The former, made from the outer layer of the cow's hide, is tougher and more water resistant. Split-grain leather is often coated with polyurethane or polyvinyl chloride (PVC) to make it more water resistant and attractive, though this shiny layer soon cracks and allows the leather to soak up water like a sponge, while the remaining coating impedes drying. (For this reason, I avoid coated leathers.)

It is still useful to know whether leather is top- or split-grain, but many manufacturers no longer divulge this information. Instead they offer a vast variety of fancy names for leather, few of which mean much. If the boot looks good, you usually have to take it on trust that the leather is good, a leap of faith that can be assisted by the reputation of the manufacturer. Anfibio (Italian for "waterproof"), Crochetta, and Gallusser are three names of quality leathers worth looking for. Nubuck (sometimes spelled Nubuc or Nubuk) leather is full-grain leather whose top surface has been sanded down to give a soft finish similar to suede; it's much tougher and more water resistant than suede, however. More and more bootmakers use Nubuck leather because it doesn't show scuffs and scratches as smooth leathers do. It also has a sensuously soft feel. But Nubuck may be made from different sorts of leather, so the name alone isn't an indi-

Running/Approach Shoes

Shoes designed for off-road or hill running make ideal lightweight backpacking footwear, as do the trail shoes made by many boot companies. Construction usually features suede/synthetic fabric uppers, shock-absorbing midsoles, shaped removable footbeds, and strong heel counters. Because these shoes are not very warm, I wouldn't recommend them for snow or very cold weather, but for summer trails, dry or wet, they're my first choice of footwear. Most running-shoe companies make at least one model suitable for off-road use. Avoid road-running shoes with soles that do not have enough tread for good grip on rough, wet ground.

If you want more solidity or stiffness than most running shoes provide, some trail shoes incorporate toe boxes, graded nylon midsoles, and even half-length metal shanks.

A typical running shoe weighs around 25 ounces. Trail shoes weigh in at a couple of pounds.

Running shoes are ideal for summer hiking (also known as trail or approach).

cation of quality. Some top-grain leather boots have the rough, inner surface facing out, though this is less common now that Nubuck is available. Rough-out and Nubuck leathers are easily distinguishable from suede by their thickness and solidity.

One type of leather is different from the others—a water-repellent substance is chemically bonded to the leather fibers during tanning. This leather goes by various names, such as Watershed, Prime WeatherTuff, and Pittards WR100. I've found this leather performs as advertised, especially when new. In time, though, the waterproofing breaks down and waxing is required.

Suede is the inside half of a split leather and has a rough surface; it's often used to strengthen the wear points of fabric footwear. Although it is not as durable, supportive, or water resistant as top-grain leather or the best splits, good-quality suede is still worth considering for lightweight footwear.

There was a trend against leather in the early 1980s because of its association with heavyweight traditional boots. With changes in outsoles, midsoles, and linings, and the introduction of high-quality lightweight leathers, however, some leather boots are as light as most synthetic ones, and leather has regained its popularity. Leather lasts longer than other upper materials, it keeps your feet dry longer, and it absorbs and then passes moisture (sweat) quickly and efficiently. It is also flexible and comfortable.

Uppers: Fabric/Leather

The first lightweight boots and trail shoes aped the nylon/suede design of the running shoes on which they were based. Many such boots and shoes are still around, and they work well for

Lightweight fabric boots are comfortable and suited to all but winter hiking.

trail hiking in all but the coldest, snowiest conditions. Their problems stem more from design than materials. Uppers are mostly fabric, often nylon mesh in shoes but usually texturized nylon (though sometimes polyester) in boots, reinforced with leather or suede. This design requires many stitched seams, which are vulnerable to abrasion and thus not durable in rough, rocky terrain, where boot uppers take a hammering. (I found this out the hard way while scrambling and walking on the incredibly rough and sharp gabbro rock of the Cuillin Hills on Scotland's Isle of Skye. After two weeks, my nylon/suede boots were in shreds, virtually every seam having ripped open.)

Waterproofness is not a strong point of fabric/leather footwear either, unless it has a "breathable" membrane insert. This is due to the seams. Also, grit and dirt can penetrate nylon much more easily than it can leather; membranes therefore do not last as long as in leather boots. This is the case whether the synthetic part of the boot is lightweight nylon or the much-tougher Cordura.

So why consider fabric/leather footwear at all? Because it's cooler than most leather footwear for warm-weather use, it needs little or no breaking in, it's comfortable, and it dries more quickly. It's also used on the lightest, most flexible footwear.

Wet Feet/Dry Feet: One reason many people wear leather boots is to keep their feet dry. On weekend hikes, many boots will indeed do this, at least when fairly new. On longer trips, however, it becomes more difficult; on walks lasting several months it's impossible. This is because leather boots need to be fully dried and then waxed after a day or so in wet conditions if they are to continue to keep your feet dry. Fabric boots with waterproof sock liners need less care, but, in my experience, the liners don't stay waterproof for long.

Drying boots on a long walk in wet weather just can't be done. For example, I walked 1,300 miles up the length of Norway and Sweden during a very wet summer. Because much of the route was over rough terrain, I wore lightweight leather boots. For most of the walk these were sodden—which doubled the weight, reduced the breathability, and softened the leather so it gave less support. I would have been far better off with fabric/leather shoes, which wouldn't have gained as much weight when wet, would have been much more breathable, and would have dried more quickly when it wasn't raining. My feet still would have been wet, of course, but they'd have been much more comfortable. I'd rather have cool, wet feet than hot, sweaty feet.

In warm weather, wet feet aren't a problem—as long as you can keep them dry overnight. When it's cold, the answer is thick socks, preferably ones with a high wool content, changed regularly. During a 40-day walk through wet,

Lightweight Boots

This is the most popular footwear category. Lightweight boots weigh from 2 to 3 pounds. This category includes most synthetic/suede boots and a few leather ones. The advantages of lightweights are comfort and weight. However, they are not very waterproof (except, for a while, those with sock liners), and the seams are vulnerable. They have many of the design features of running shoes, along with a higher ankle, rands (either full or just at the toe and heel), cushioned linings, sewn-in tongues, and, on some models, graded flexible midsoles and half-length shanks.

A pair of lightweight leather boots after a 1,000-mile walk.

thawing snow in the High Sierra in 1982, my heavy leather boots were soaked most of the time. (I couldn't have done this trek in running shoes because I often wore crampons or needed to kick steps, though now I would wear lighter boots.) By the end of each day my wool socks were soaked. To keep my feet as warm and dry as possible, I alternated two pairs of thick wool socks, hanging the previous day's wet socks on the back of my pack to dry each morning, while wearing the pair I'd dried the day before. A third dry pair was kept for wearing in the tent. It worked—I had no blisters or other foot problems during the walk.

Uppers: Plastic

Plastic is now the dominant material for mountaineering and downhill ski boots, and it's becoming popular for telemark boots—it is better than leather at providing the rigidity, waterproofness, and warmth such pursuits require. Walking-boot uppers need to be flexible, however, and permeable to moisture so that sweat can escape. I've tried walking in both plastic ski mountaineering and plastic climbing boots—an experience to avoid. I have never had such sore and blistered heels, nor such aching feet. With their rigid soles and outer shells, such boots work against, rather than with, your feet. After a 25-mile day walk in freezing conditions in a pair of these boots, my feet were soaked in sweat and far too hot. Plastic walking boots are better but still have problems. Climbing boots are always supportive. Although that walk covered reasonably gentle terrain, the boots didn't support my feet as leather ones do. It seems that plastic either can be supportive or flexible but, unlike leather, not both.

My experience with plastic boots also left me

wondering how they would perform in warmer conditions, and how they could be dried out on a backpacking trip. Plastic boots may appear again in the future if the technical problems are solved, but for now the best alternative to leather is nylon.

Heel Counters and Toe Boxes

Heels need to be held in place and prevented from twisting, and toes need to be protected from rocks and anything else you may stub them against. A *heel counter* is a stiff piece of material—usually synthetic though sometimes leather—built into the rear of a boot or shoe that cups the heel and holds it in place. You can't

usually see them, though at least one company (One Sport) puts them on the outside of some boots, but they can be felt under the leather of the heel. Heel counters are essential. A soft, sloppy heel without a counter won't support your ankle, no matter how high the upper.

Toe boxes are made from similar material inserted in the front of a boot, although some boots dispense with this construction in favor of a thick rubber rand around the boot toe.

Linings and Padding

Traditionally, linings were made from soft leather—as they still are in some boots— but lighter, less-absorbent, harder-wearing,

---

Medium-Weight Boots

Weighing from 3 to 4 pounds, medium-weight boots are good for mountain and winter back-packing where cold, wet weather is expected and crampons may be needed. The best models combine the durability and support of traditional boots with the long-term comfort of the new designs. Although many have one-piece leather constructions, some models are fabric/ leather combinations. Most medium-weight boots incorporate a sole stiffener—either graded nylon midsoles or half-length shanks, or both—and can be fitted with crampons for hard snow and ice. Generally, these boots are designed to cope with rugged, off-trail terrain in any weather. The best ones are made on curved lasts and feature one-piece top-grain leather, synthetic linings, padded sewn-in tongues, heel counters, toe boxes, footbeds, and shock-absorbing midsoles or dual-density outsoles. Many also include waterproof/breathable sock liners.

The proper fitting of medium-weight boots is critical, and a short break-in period is advisable.

Medium-weight leather boots suitable for hiking in snow and cold, wet weather.

Key Features: Three-Season Boots and Shoes

- A good fit. This is more important than anything else. Badly fitting footwear means blisters and sore feet, regardless of the quality.
- Light weight. One pound on your feet equals 5 pounds on your back.
- Deep lugs for good grip on rough ground.
- Thick, shock-absorbing midsoles for cushioning and comfort.

- A solid heel counter to center your foot over the sole.
- A removable footbed for extra cushioning and fit adjustment.
- A soft ankle cuff to minimize rubbing (in boots).
- Speed hooks or pulleys for quick, easy lacing.
- A sewn-in tongue to prevent water leaks.

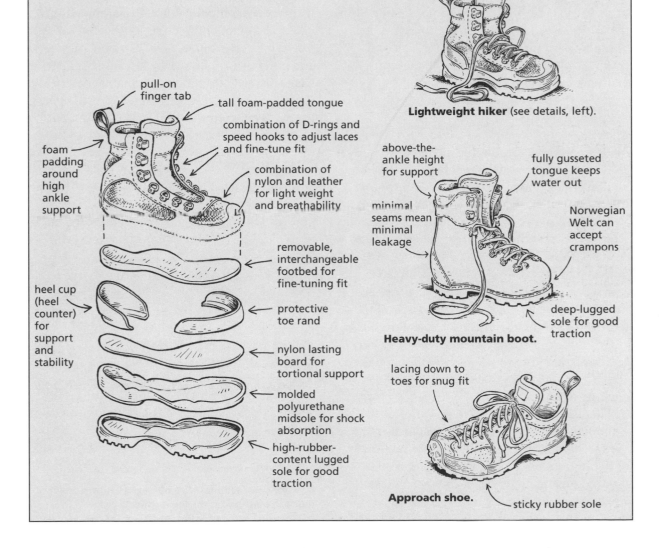

Lightweight hiker (see details, left).

pull-on finger tab

tall foam-padded tongue

combination of D-rings and speed hooks to adjust laces and fine-tune fit

foam padding around high ankle support

combination of nylon and leather for light weight and breathability

removable, interchangeable footbed for fine-tuning fit

heel cup (heel counter) for support and stability

protective toe rand

nylon lasting board for tortional support

molded polyurethane midsole for shock absorption

high-rubber-content lugged sole for good traction

above-the-ankle height for support

fully gusseted tongue keeps water out

minimal seams mean minimal leakage

Norwegian Welt can accept crampons

deep-lugged sole for good traction

Heavy-duty mountain boot.

lacing down to toes for snug fit

Approach shoe.

sticky rubber sole

quicker-drying, moisture-wicking, non-rotting synthetics are taking over. The main one is Cambrelle, though there are others such as Sportee (found in Vasque boots). I find these new linings vastly superior to their leather counterparts. Some wearers have found an odor problem with synthetic linings, though I haven't.

Many boots have thin layers of foam padding between the lining and the outer, usually around the ankle and upper tongue areas, but occasionally throughout the boot. Such padding does provide more cushioning for the foot, but it also makes boots warmer, something to be avoided in hot weather. Foam also absorbs water and is slow-drying. I prefer boots with minimum padding; I rely on socks for warmth.

Sock Liners

Many boots now feature *sock liners,* or *booties,* made from vapor-permeable membranes such as Gore-Tex and Sympatex hung between the lining and the outer. These certainly make the boots waterproof when they are new—but how long they last is a matter of great debate. Some people swear by them; others swear at them. My experience with such liners suggests that they last longest and perform best in boots with few seams and with water-repellent leather rather than nylon/suede outers. I've found Sympatex to be the most durable. Even so, such boots leak after no more than a few weeks in wet weather, so I'm not convinced the feature adds enough to a boot's performance to be worth seeking out or paying extra for.

There are disadvantages to these liners, too. Although they allow some water vapor through, they are far less breathable than running shoes or lightweight boots without sock liners. This reduced breathability means they are a bit hot and sweaty in summer weather, especially if the uppers get saturated—which is why water-repellent leathers are best for the outers of boots with sock liners. And if you do get them wet inside (by stepping in a deep pool or creek), they are slow-drying because, although vapor can pass through the membrane, liquid cannot.

A few boots have non-breathable waterproof liners. These are only suitable for cold, wet conditions. Overall, I'd avoid them.

Running shoes and boots have recently appeared with liners that can be pumped up to vary the support they provide. I've tried a boot with such a liner and, although pumping it up does increase side-to-side support (useful when traversing very steep terrain), the boots are hot, and potentially quite sweaty, because the liner has to be made from non-breathable materials; they are only suitable for use in wet, cold conditions. It's an interesting gimmick, but not one I've found necessary.

The Tongue

Sewn-in, gusseted tongues with light padding inside are the most comfortable and water resistant, and they're found on most boots; the only

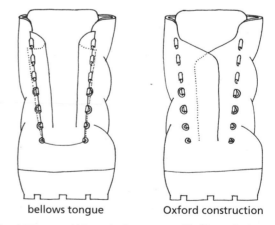

bellows tongue   Oxford construction

Boot tongues. Although the gusseted bellows design is found in most boots, the less-common Oxford construction is superior in snow.

disadvantage to gusseted tongues is that snow can collect in the gussets and soak into the boot if gaiters aren't worn. *Oxford construction,* in which two flaps of leather (basically extensions of the upper) fold over the inner tongue, which may or may not be sewn in, is a better design for snow. These flaps are often held in place by small hook-and-loop tabs. Some heavier boots have a gusseted tongue with another tongue sewn in only at the base behind it to achieve the same purpose. On high-ankle and stiff leather boots, the tongue may be hinged so that it flexes easily.

Lacing

The several methods for lacing up boots use D-rings, hooks, and eyelets. *D-rings* may be plastic and sewn to the upper (the norm on shoes and ultralight boots), or metal and attached to a swivel clip riveted to the upper. The easiest to use is a combination of several rows of D-rings above the base of the tongue, followed by several rows of *hooks* (or *speed laces*) at the top. With this system you can fully open the boot by unhooking the laces at the top, yet quickly tighten them. This may seem trivial, but it's not when you're trying to don a stiff, half-frozen boot while wearing thick mitts in a small tent with a blizzard outside. Boots laced with D-rings alone involve far more fiddling with the laces and are harder to tighten precisely. A new approach from Asolo is to use tiny *pulleys* instead of D-rings. This makes it very easy to adjust the fit evenly across the foot. I've only had a brief try with pulley lacing, but it seems superior to D-ring lacing.

Old-style *eyelets* are rare on boots now, though they are found more often on shoes. Although the most awkward system to use, eyelets are the least susceptible to breakage.

Laces are usually made from braided nylon, which rarely breaks, though they may wear through from abrasion after much use. Round laces seem to last longer than flat ones, though not by much. I used to carry spare laces but gave it up long ago; it's been years since I had a lace snap, even on long walks. If or when one does, I'll replace it with a length of the nylon cord I always carry.

Scree Collars

Many boots have one or more rolls of foam-padded soft leather or synthetic material at the cuff to keep out stones, grass seeds, mud, and other debris, but for this to work well the boots have to be laced up so tightly that they restrict ankle movement. The collars themselves don't seem to cause any problems, so their presence or absence can be ignored when choosing a boot.

Seams

Traditional wisdom says the fewer seams the better, because seams may admit water and can abrade, allowing the boot to disintegrate; thus, one-piece leather boots with seams only at the heel and around the tongue should prove the most durable and water resistant.

I agree. Having used quite a few pairs of shoes and boots made from several pieces of stitched fabric and leather, I've found their life expectancy limited by how long the seams remain intact. Side seams usually split first (which can be postponed, but not prevented, by coating them heavily with a seam sealer or quick-setting flexible epoxy. This also decreases the likelihood of leaks).

I don't rely solely on one-piece leather construction for footwear, however, since many excellent boots, especially lightweights, are made from several pieces of material, and I prefer the comfort of a lighter-weight boot to a heavier one-piece pair. But for long treks, especially in winter conditions, I still prefer one-piece leather boots, so it's a difficult trade-off. I learned this the hard way: During a walk along the length of the Canadian Rockies I used two pairs of sectional leather boots from different makers; each split at the side seams after around 750 miles. I believe that only a one-piece leather boot would have lasted the whole walk.

Whether you should wear just one pair of boots or shoes for an entire long-distance hike is debatable. I increasingly agree that footwear should be changed after a while because the internal structure can begin to break down, and the cushioning in the sole can compact and lead to foot problems. This is especially so with running shoes and lightweight boots with Evazote (EVA) or similar midsoles. Traditional boots with leather midsoles maintain their structure longer.

Insoles and Midsoles

The boot sole must support the foot and protect it from shock. It should be flexible enough to allow a natural gait. The standard rule is that it should be stiff enough to deal with rugged terrain. I used to agree with the stiffness rule, but extensive hiking in rugged terrain in sports sandals and very flexible shoes has convinced me that this is a fallacy, and that maximum flexibility is more important.

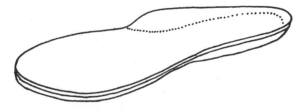

Removable, shaped footbeds provide better support than flat insoles and provide a bit of cushioning, particularly shock-absorbing padded footbeds of neoprene rubber or Sorbothane.

Most boots and shoes now have either an *insole* or a *footbed* immediately under the foot; the latter has a curved foot shape and should be removable for drying and for replacement when worn out. Footbeds give better support than flat insoles because they support the entire length of the foot. Some are made from dual-density foam or have pads of shock-absorbing material built into the footbed under the heel and forefoot. Many, however, are thin and thus provide little cushioning; this can be increased by adding thicker footbeds of neoprene or other shock-absorbing material. Some footbeds, such as those made from Sorbothane, are relatively heavy, adding up to 5 ounces to the weight of a pair of boots, and may also be hot in warm weather. My preference is for Eagle Rock insoles, which are made from a soft, flexible rubber-like material called Poron 4000. This cushions well but doesn't overheat in hot weather because it's quite breathable. For extra cushioning, Poron insoles with Sorbothane inserts are available.

If your feet tend to swell a lot (as is likely on long-distance walks and in hot weather), removing the footbeds will make your footwear more roomy. I've often done this toward the end of a long day out.

The best insole of all, though quite expensive, is a custom-made one that fits your foot exactly, cupping each toe and the ball of your foot. Originally conceived for Alpine ski boots, custom-made insoles are now offered for walking and running footwear, and many stores have the facilities for making them. The process takes time; the material has to be heat-molded to the shape of each foot. I obtained a pair partway through a Canadian Rockies walk when the insoles in one pair of boots gave me blisters; the custom-made inserts prevented any movement of my feet inside the boots, and minimized further blistering. They just lasted the rest of the

Shock-absorbing footbeds—shaped on the left, flat on the right.

walk—about 1,250 miles, which is longer than most footbeds last.

Under the footbed lies the *midsole* or *lasting board,* a flat, foot-shaped piece of material. The stiffness of a shoe or boot is in part due to the material from which the midsole is made. A fiberboard midsole is common in running and trail shoes and the lightest boots. In inexpensive footwear, the midsoles may be cardboard. (There are reports of cardboard midsoles breaking up when wet, though this hasn't happened to any I've used.) Many boots now feature stiff plastic or nylon midsoles graded for flex according to the size of the boot. This means that small boots have the same relative stiffness as larger boots (other stiffening materials can render small boots too stiff, and large ones too bendy). Many manufacturers vary the stiffness of the different midsoles—the stiffest is reserved for mountaineering boots, and the most flexible for what is usually described as "easy trail use" with a light load. You can judge flex by bending the boot: A

stiff, hard-to-bend shoe is fine for kicking steps in snow but it's tiring for most walking. I regard flexible footwear as best for backpacking.

The lightest, most flexible shoes and boots may not have a midsole at all. Instead, when the insole is removed, a line of stitching will be seen running round the edge of the sole. This is known as *sliplasting* and is the construction I prefer for all walking where much snow isn't expected. Some running shoes have *combination lasting*—the front is sliplasted but there is a half-midsole in the heel. This gives a flexible forefoot but a more rigid heel.

The traditional midsole stiffener is a half- or three-quarter-length steel shank, only a half-inch or so wide, placed forward from the heel to give solidity to the rear of the foot as well as lateral stability and support to the arch, while allowing the front of the foot to flex when walking. Full-length shanks are for rigid mountaineering boots, not for walking; even half-length midsoles are needed only for kicking steps on snow. Some

Heavyweight and Traditional Boots

Having almost disappeared in the early 1980s with the success of the new lightweights for walking and plastic footwear for mountaineering, heavyweight boots (4 pounds and up) have enjoyed something of a comeback for general mountaineering—trips that combine hiking with scrambling or easy rock climbing, and the need to wear crampons for long periods—the type carried out on easy Alpine snow ascents in summer. In these situations or when traversing narrow rock ledges, light- and medium-weight footwear is too soft and flexible, while plastic boots are too rigid on easier terrain. Traditional heavyweight designs with leather midsoles, full- or three-quarter-length steel shanks, thick one-piece uppers, Vibram Montagna soles, and Norwegian welts are still available. These designs have been improved, however, by including lighter-weight features such as graded nylon midsoles, footbeds, synthetic linings, curved soles, and shock-absorbing heel inserts.

Heavyweights require a considerable breaking-in period. I find them uncomfortable and tiring to walk in and haven't worn a pair for many years. They are only appropriate if your trips include serious mountaineering, in which case your activities are outside the scope of this book. The little snow and ice climbing I do when backpacking I accomplish using medium-weight boots that accept flexible crampons and are far more comfortable on easier terrain; on steep, rocky terrain where scrambling and easy climbing may be required, I find lightweight footwear perfectly adequate.

boots combine a steel shank with a flexible synthetic midsole.

Many boots incorporate a midsole of a shock-absorbing material. This is usually EVA in lightweight boots and shoes, and the much longer-wearing polyurethane in mid- and heavyweight boots, though polyurethane is used in some trail shoes. These midsoles are often shaped like a tapered wedge, thickest under the heel. They absorb shock well, and I wouldn't consider footwear without them—the difference they make to how your feet feel at the end of a long day is startling. They are designed to protect against the shock of heel strike—the impact when your heel hits the ground—which jars the knees and lower back as well as the feet. Cushioning also is needed at the ball of the foot, and the best shock-absorbing wedges are quite thick under the forefoot as well as the heel.

As an alternative to a wedge midsole, a few boots feature a layer of Sorbothane in the heel between the midsole and outsole. I have not tried these but have heard that they work well.

The most recent development is the *footframe*, a cupped polyurethane unit that combines the shock-absorbing midsole with the rand. This cradles the foot and is said to provide better cushioning as well as good side-to-side support and stability. One Sport and Merrell utilize them; Asolo has developed one that incorporates a heel cup into the same unit.

Outsole

This is the part of the shoe that contacts the ground. The traditional Vibram carbon-rubber lugsole has been joined by a wide variety of other outsole patterns and materials, including many made by individual bootmakers. Any pattern of studs, bars, or other shapes seems to grip well on most terrain.

The type of rubber used makes a difference, however, and some footwear utilizes the "sticky rubber" that has revolutionized rock-climbing footwear. Companies using this include Five.Ten, La Sportiva, and Merrell. I've used Five.Ten shoes and Five.Ten Stealth Sandals and found the sole

Nordic Ski-Touring Boots

Most ski-touring (cross-country) ski boots use one-piece leather uppers, Norwegian welt construction, half- to three-quarter-length steel shanks, and leather midsoles. Outsoles have an extended, squared-off toe containing a metal plate with three holes for locating the binding pins, plus a tread for walking. I've skied many miles on the Vibram Ferret 75MM, a good-quality sole. A more recent development is a boot with a bar embedded at the toe that clips into a lightweight binding. These were first introduced for racing and track skiing, but the latest versions—the Rottefella New Nordic Norm Backcountry and the Salomon Nordic System Country—are designed for wilderness use and are worth considering by backpackers who aren't intent on tackling steep mountain slopes.

Ski-touring boots need lateral rigidity to prevent them from twisting off the ski during turns, plus moderate flex that allows for

Telemark touring boot with Vibram sole.

Artex ATC 30 boot with New Nordic Norm Backcountry sole.

a good kick and easy gliding. Nordic skiing has seen a recent renaissance, and with it has come a wealth of footwear—but only some of it is suitable for backcountry touring. The stiffest, tallest boots with plastic cuffs and a forward cant are designed for telemarking on downhill pistes, while lightweight, general or in-track touring boots just aren't robust enough for ski-backpacking. (Nor are they suitable if you have to carry your skis for long periods—which, believe me, happens all too often—since they have smooth, flexible soles that don't grip well and can't be fitted with crampons.) The best designs are a compromise between flexibility (for ease of touring the flats) and rigidity (for downhill turning control). If you're mainly interested in forest touring and have no desire to telemark, then leather boots weighing 4 to 4½ pounds will be fine. Mountain skiers should look for heavier boots with reinforced ankles (perhaps even with plastic clips) for greater support on steep downhills.

A selection of soles—all of these are adequate for rugged terrain.

has good grip, ideal for scrambling and difficult terrain. An alternative I've not tried but which has had good reviews is Salomon's Contragrip sole, designed in conjunction with a tire company; One Sport uses Goodyear Indy 500 Rubber in several models of boots and shoes.

There has been some concern about the damage that heavily lugged soles do to soft ground, and some manufacturers claim their soles minimize this damage by not collecting debris in the tread. Studded soles seem to work best in this respect, but unless all your walking will be done on gentle trails, grip is the most important quality of outsoles. This should not be compromised, especially if you're walking on steep, rugged terrain.

Many new soles, including some from Vibram, are made from a dual-density rubber—a soft upper layer for shock absorption and a hard outer layer for durability. I've used boots with this type of sole and find it a good alternative to the EVA-style wedge.

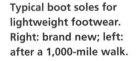

Typical boot soles for lightweight footwear. Right: brand new; left: after a 1,000-mile walk.

Descending steep and rough slopes.
1. Walking down on your heels.

2. Flexing the ankles.

3. Descending sideways.

4. Don't lean back! If you don't keep your
weight forward over your feet you'll slip,
whatever method you use for descending.

Sports Sandals

Sports sandals are a major new development and very different from other types of footwear; specifications and construction for shoes and boots don't pertain to them.

My first reaction to the appearance of sports sandals was that they might be fine for leaping out of rafts in the Colorado River, but their only use to the backpacker was as campwear and for river crossings.

Nonetheless, I decided to find out what these new sandals could do. The results were surprising. I'd assumed all the talk surrounding the sandals was just hype—no way could a sandal compare with a boot, or even a running shoe. I was wrong. In the right circumstances, good sports sandals are much better than any other footwear. Sports sandals, I'm now convinced, are the best innovation in footwear for walking in many years.

Sports sandals aren't just traditional sandals with a trendy name. To be suitable for walking any distance they have to support the feet; cushion against hard, rough, and hot surfaces; and grip well. The best of them do all this very well.

Essential features are thick, shock-absorbing soles; a patterned outsole for grip; and a strapping system that holds the heel and forefoot

Sports sandals are excellent for warm-weather hiking.

firmly. Straps may be leather, synthetic leather, or nylon webbing. The last two materials absorb little moisture and dry quickly, and would be my choice. Closure is usually by hook-and-loop fabric, though some models use snap buckles. A broad and fairly rigid heel strap, preferably reinforced, helps keep the heel centered over the sole. I also look for raised or rimmed edges that can protect the feet—especially the toes—from bumping against rocks and stones.

Like other footwear, sports sandals need to fit

Heavier soles with deeper treads should outlast lighter ones, though it's hard to predict tread life. Wear depends on the ground surface—tarmac wears out soles fastest, followed by rocks and scree. On soft forest duff, soles last forever. I have found that on long walks, lightweight studded soles last 800 to 1,000 miles, while the traditional Vibram Montagna lasts at least 1,250 miles.

There is little controversy over sole patterns, but *heel design* has generated heated discussions. Indeed, some designs have been blamed for fatal accidents. The debate is over the lack of a *forward heel bar* under the instep, together with the *rounded heel* (derived from running shoe

outsoles), and how these features perform when descending steep slopes, especially wet, grassy ones. Traditional soles have a deep bar at the front of the heel and a square-cut rear edge, making descents safe, say proponents. Newer sole designs, they say, don't allow you to dig in the back of the heel for grip or use the front bar to halt slips; instead, the sloped heel makes slipping more likely. This criticism has prompted some makers to add deep serrations to their sloping heels and to replace the forward edge.

After experimenting with different soles and observing other walkers, I've concluded that it all depends on how you walk downhill. If you properly. Your foot shouldn't hang over the sole at the sides or at the toe or heel, and the straps should hold the foot snugly in place without rubbing. Try sandals on and walk around the store to see if they rub anywhere, just as you would with boots. If you're going to wear them without socks, you'll probably need a size smaller than your boot size.

Although I haven't had any problems with sandals, they obviously do have limitations. They are best suited to warm or dry conditions, though they can be worn with socks when it's cool and dry. Just how superior to other footwear sports sandals are in hot weather I first learned on a trek in the Himalayas, when I walked more than 75 miles on rugged, steep, stony trails in a pair. My feet stayed dry and cool, and never felt sore or swollen. Nor did I suffer any blisters. Sweaty socks weren't a problem—I wore socks only in cold temperatures and in camp. When streams crossed the trail I just sloshed straight through, unlike the others in the party who had to stop to remove boots and socks. Wearing sandals toughens up your feet, too, as I found at the end of the Nepal trek, when I did a 2,000-foot scree run in them. The stones that slid between my feet and the sandals were irritating, but they didn't bruise or cut my feet.

Since then, I've worn sandals for two-week trips with a 50-pound pack in the Colorado Rockies and in the Grand Canyon, and on many weekend walks. They're now my standard backup footwear because they're comfortable around camp.

I haven't worn sandals for trips longer than two weeks, though other hikers have done so with great success. In 1995, Scott Williamson walked the Florida Trail and the Appalachian Trail, plus the country in between, while Hamish Brown hiked the 900-mile crest of the Atlas Mountains in Morocco. Both wore sandals. The previous year, Ray and Jenny Jardine wore sandals over a significant portion of the Pacific Crest Trail, Ray reporting that the soles of his feet dried out on this trip and developed painful, deep cracks that took a long time to heal. Checking for this would be advisable on a long trip. Perhaps a moisturizer or sunscreen could be used to minimize this. (Another hint: Your feet don't usually see much sunlight. In sandals they are exposed, and just like any other part of your body they can sunburn. Sunscreen is essential for protection.)

Sports sandals weigh from 20 to 30 ounces, comparable to running shoes. I've used models from Reebok, Merrell, Five.Ten, Rockport, Teva, and Reef Brazil, and found them all excellent.

descend using the back or sides of the heel for support, you're more likely to slip in a boot with a smooth, sloping heel than one with a serrated or square-cut edge. If you descend as I do, however—with your boots flat on the ground, pointing downhill, and your weight over your feet—heel design is irrelevant. I've descended long, steep slopes covered with slippery vegetation in smooth, sloped-heel footwear without slipping or feeling insecure. I've noticed that too many people who fall descending slippery hills kept their boots angled *across* the slope and descended using the edges of the sole. If you use the sole edges and heel for support, a stiffer boot works better and some form of serration or a

square-cut heel is needed for safe descents. Of course, if you descend hills the way I recommend, you must have flexible footwear.

Rounded heels are advertised as minimizing heel strike, because they allow a gradual "roll" from the heel to sole instead of the jarring impact from the edge of a square-cut heel hitting the ground, but I haven't noticed any difference in practice. A shock-absorbing insole seems far more important for reducing heel-strike injury.

Rands

The most likely place for water to penetrate a boot is where the sole and the upper meet. Some boots have a rubber *rand* running around this joint, while others have just toe or toe and heel rands, or bumpers. Rands work as they're supposed to, especially on lightweight boots, which have thinner uppers that are more vulnerable to damage. Rands aren't necessary on heavier boots.

Stitching vs. Bonding

Joining the sole to the uppers is the critical part of footwear manufacture. If that connection fails, the shoe or boot will fall apart. Stitching used to be the only way of holding footwear together, but is now used mainly in boots made for mountaineering or Nordic ski touring rather than for walking. The most common stitched construction is the *Norwegian welt,* sometimes called *stitchdown construction,* in which the upper is

turned out from the boot, then sewn to a leather midsole with two or three rows of stitching. These stitches are visible and exposed, but they can be protected by daubing with sealant.

Currently, on most footwear the uppers are *heat-bonded* to the sole. (Some are also *Blake-* or *Littleway-stitched,* which means the uppers are turned in and stitched to a midsole, to which the outsole is bonded.) Unlike the Norwegian welt, the quality of these construction methods usually cannot be checked. A bonded sole failed on me only once, many years ago. On that occasion, the sole started to peel away from the boot at the toe after only 250 miles. I was on a long trek and far from a repair shop, so I patched the boots with glue from my repair kit almost every night, and nursed them through another 500 miles. I wouldn't like to repeat the experience.

FOOTWEAR CARE AND REPAIR

Although most footwear is fairly tough, proper care is needed to ensure a long life. Washing off all mud and dirt after each use is a good idea; if it dries on the uppers, they can harden and crack, especially if they're leather. A stiff brush (I use an old toothbrush) helps to remove mud from seams, stitching, and tongue gussets. Excessive heat is even more likely to cause the leather to harden and split, and it's also hard on nylon. Wet footwear should never be dried in a hot place such as next to a car heater, a house radiator, or a campfire. Even mid-day sunshine can be too warm, and if you stay in a mountain hut or hostel with a drying room, you should keep your footwear out of there as well. Any leather should never become too hot to touch. Footwear should be left in a cool, dry place to dry slowly, with the insoles removed and the tongues fully open. If they are really sodden, stuffing them with newspaper will help the drying process. Fabric/leather

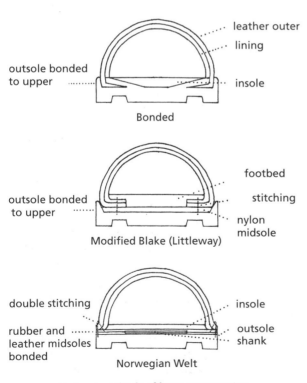

Various methods of boot construction.

Footwear needs regular treatment if it is to last.

shoes without any internal padding dry quickly, but foam-lined leather boots can take a long time—at least several days for medium-weight leather boots.

Drying footwear can be a problem on long treks, when it is tempting to dry sodden boots by a fire. I'm occasionally guilty of this. The second half of the Canadian Rockies walk was mostly cross-country in wet terrain, and my lightweight leather boots were soaked by the end of most days. I often helped them dry out by standing them a little too close to my campfire. As a result, I was forced to wear boots with cracked uppers and peeling soles for the last few snowy weeks of the trek.

When wet footwear has dried, it needs to be treated to restore suppleness and water repellency. Proofing compounds such as Nikwax Fabric and Leather Footwear Proofing, Aquaseal, Zepel, Scotchguard, and similar products can be sprayed or painted on synthetic and suede foot-

wear. Don't expect miracles though—this type of footwear is inherently lacking in waterproofness. Treatment will limit the amount of water it absorbs, and thus the time it takes to dry, but it won't make it waterproof. On long walks I don't treat such footwear and have found it dries fairly quickly in warm weather, even when it hasn't been treated for weeks.

Leather footwear is different. Proper treatment increases the water repellency and prolongs life by keeping the leather supple. What constitutes proper treatment depends in part on the type of leather. Virtually all leathers are now chemically treated rather than oil-tanned, and therefore require dressing with wax rather than oil. Liquids such as Neat's Foot Oil can over-soften leather; I'd only use them for leather that has been allowed to dry out and harden.

For regular leather treatment, use wax. Of the many types available my preference is Nikwax, a tough, durable proofing. Biwell, Sno-Seal, Aquaseal, and others all have their adherents, and many companies tout their own products. Manufacturers also suggest that you don't wax some of the specially tanned leathers until they are scuffed, as they won't absorb wax before then. And at least one leather, Pittards WR100, is said to need no treatment at all because the water repellency is permanently tanned in. I'm skeptical about such claims. Boots get such a battering that any leather eventually gets scratched, abraded, and dried out. At the very least, applying wax will keep it supple. No one wax is vastly superior to any other. If you can't find any wax at all, try ordinary shoe polish—at least one boot company believes it works just as well as specialty products.

Boots should be waxed the evening before use (and before long-term storage) to allow the wax to penetrate. Nick Brown, the man behind Nikwax, says that over-treatment is bad for boots, whatever type of wax is used. He says several thin coats are more effective than one thick one. Although you can apply wax with a rag, Brown says fingers do the best job, since their warmth helps to melt the wax, improving penetration.

Wax *does not* provide long-term waterproofing. There is a ratio between the amount of wax you apply, the degree of waterproofness obtained, and the breathability of your boots. Several layers of wax will mean better and longer-lasting water resistance, but also less breathability. If you wear leather boots in warm weather (which I don't recommend), I'd go easy on the wax or your feet will get wetter from sweat than from the occasional summer shower. In cold, wet conditions, especially in snow, heavily waxed boots are necessary. Freshly waxed boots can still get wet after just a few hours in dew-wet grass or melting snow, but they will dry out more quickly and absorb less moisture than ones that haven't been treated. I also apply a welt-seal, such as Sno-Seal, to seams and exposed stitching; it protects seams and prevents them from leaking for a while.

Boots used to have to be dry before they could be waxed, and this still applies with most waxes. However, Aqueous Wax for Leather, from Nikwax, is a concentrated, water-based emulsion that can be painted onto wet leather. I've found it works well. It's especially useful on long walks in wet conditions when your boots may never be totally dry. For that reason I now carry it on walks lasting more than a few weeks.

Uppers on lightweight boots often wear out at the same time as the soles. Resoling is then hardly worthwhile, but top-quality lightweights in good condition can be worth repairing; I have had running shoes successfully resoled. Medium-weight boots should last the life of at least two soles; heavyweights even more (I had a pair that was on their fourth sole when I retired them).

The key is to have boots resoled before the mid-sole becomes worn and needs replacing, which can be very expensive. EVA wedges usually need replacing along with the soles. For your own safety, don't let soles wear down too much.

Many outdoor stores accept boots for repair and send them to either a local cobbler or a national repair store. If you can't find a repair service, contact the manufacturer for advice.

SOCKS

Too many people spend a great deal of time choosing boots and then buy whatever socks the store has on hand. I used to be like that. Socks are important, however, and deserve more careful consideration. They cushion feet, prevent abrasion, wick away moisture, and keep feet at the right temperature. For a decade and more I used 80/20 wool/nylon socks with terry-loop inners, because that was what my local outdoor stores sold. Only when I began to write about socks did I ask myself why I wore this type. The answer was based solely on availability—I realized they didn't give me what I wanted from socks.

I can see why socks with fluffy, terry-loop inners are popular: They look very comfortable and warm, far nicer than the old, knitted, Ragg wool socks. On the first day out they feel wonderful, and, if you wash them properly after every use, they last fairly long. But on a backpacking trip you can't wash your socks every day; indeed, you may end up wearing one pair of socks for several days, even weeks, at a time, with just an occasional quick rinse in a cold pan of water to freshen them up. After a few days' constant wear, many terry-loop socks mat down into a hard, sweaty mass, and rinsing them out in cold stream water does not restore their initial fluffiness. Even repeated machine washings won't revive some types. Such socks provide little insulation or comfort underfoot—I relegate them to the spares shelf, which is crammed with dozens of pairs of terry-loop socks that may have had only two weeks' use.

I went back to wearing standard Ragg wool socks, which I found vastly superior. I've taken both types on two-week treks and worn them for the same number of days. The more open structure of the Ragg socks reduces matting; when rinsed in cold water, they're almost as good as new. The old problems of raised toe seams that rubbed, and slack ankles that slipped down, have been solved by new stitching methods that create flat seams, and the addition of elasticized material to the cuff. There are many brands of Ragg socks available—I've found Norwegian ones such as Devold and Janus best.

Wool is the accepted material for socks because socks need to cushion the foot, keep it warm in winter yet cool in summer, absorb and wick away sweat, and keep it warm when wet—all of which wool does. Nylon or other synthetic material often is added as a reinforcement at the heel and toe. I wouldn't buy a Ragg sock that was less than 50 percent wool, however, and 80 percent or more is better. I tried stretchy, 88 percent acrylic/10 percent stretch nylon/2 percent Lycra loopstitch Thorlo-Padd Hiking Socks (calf-length, 3 ounces) which are supposed to make your feet feel more comfortable than any other sock because of their complex construction, which involves thicker sections under the heel and around the front of the foot. They are adequate, though a bit hot in hot weather. They don't mat down as much as wool loop-pile socks, and they wash out better in cold water. However, they do become saturated with sweat quicker than wool socks, and when wet they feel cooler than wool. But anyone allergic to wool would find the Thorlo-Padd socks or one of the many

When socks develop holes like this, they should be retired. This was after several hundred miles' use.

similar models made from wicking synthetic materials, available from companies like Wigwam, a good alternative. Pile or fleece socks aren't a good idea, however, as they don't wick moisture very well.

Thorlo-Padd also makes wool socks similar to its Hiking Socks. These Thorlo-Padd Trekking Socks consist of 45 percent acrylic, 38 percent wool, 9 percent stretch nylon, 6 percent Hollofil, and 2 percent spandex. They are calf-length and weigh 4 ounces. I bought a pair for my Yukon Wilderness walk, and found them very comfortable, hard-wearing, and softer underfoot when walking on hard surfaces than my Ragg socks. This was due to a particular terry-loop construction that didn't mat down until after several days' wear, and which fluffed up again when washed. The Trekking Socks were cool when wet, however, and slow-drying despite the low wool content. I liked the stretch uppers, which didn't sag after several days' wear as my old Ragg ones do (they're 100 percent wool and don't have Lycra in the cuffs).

I still use both Ragg socks and Thorlo-Padd Trekking Socks. I wore the latter on a 1,300-mile Scandinavian mountain walk—four pairs just lasted the distance, averaging about 300 miles a pair. However, I have since discovered a sock that is far better than anything else for cold-weather use (in summer I now wear thin synthetic socks when I wear socks at all). These socks come from Wild Country, better known for tents, and are called Mountain Toesters. I came across them when a pair that had been worn for a week were thrown at me with the comment "smell those!" I did, and they didn't, at least not much. I've worn them for over a week with hardly any matting and not much odor, and they've fluffed up perfectly when washed. They're made from 49 percent merino wool, 49 percent texturized polypropylene, and 2 percent Lycra. Like other modern socks, they have a thick loop-pile underfoot but are thinner up the legs. A medium-size, calf-length pair weighs 5 ounces. Mountain Toesters are very warm, ideal for winter but a bit hot in summer. For three-season use there is a lighter version called Winter Toesters, made from the same materials, which I've also found very good.

I think the main reason for the performance of these socks is the high-quality merino wool. Another maker who uses this is SmartWool.

Thick wool socks go with boots and cool, wet weather. When wearing shoes rather than boots in warm weather I prefer lighter, thinner, cooler socks made from wicking synthetic fabrics such as Tactel nylon, polypropylene, or polyesters such as CoolMax, Thermax, and Capilene. These weigh only 1 to 2 ounces a pair and are usually sold as liner socks for wearing under thicker ones. Ordinary nylon socks also work well in the heat. Many thin socks have cotton in them, however. These should be avoided because cotton soaks up sweat, takes ages to dry, and rucks up under the foot, leading to rubbing and blisters.

I've also been impressed by the various double-layer socks available. These usually are made from synthetics, though some have a wool content. They're actually two thin socks attached at the toe and ankle and can be awkward to put on if the layers become twisted, but once on they are very comfortable, quite warm, and quick-drying. I wear them in shoes and lightweight boots when it's too cool for thin socks. They weigh about 2½ ounces a pair. Alternatively, you could wear one of the thicker liner socks with a terry-loop bottom made by Wigwam and Thorlo.

Whatever type of socks you wear, make sure that they fit well. This is difficult to determine in the store because most socks come pre-packed and can't be tried on. Sock sizes bear no relation to shoe sizes, so you'll need to check the label to find the size that should fit. Nor are sizes standardized between makes—a good reason for sticking to the same brand of socks once you've found some that fit well. Before you use the socks it's also worthwhile checking for loose threads, knots, or harsh stitching that might cause blisters and sore spots. Flat seams at the toe are essential; bulky seams rub and can cause blisters. The leg length of socks is optional. Calf-length socks can be turned down over boot tops to keep out stones and grit. Knee-length stockings could be useful in winter for extra warmth;

they're essential with knickers, though few people wear these anymore.

How many pairs of socks to wear is a matter of debate and personal taste. I was taught to wear two thick pairs, but abandoned this years ago because of my foot structure—I simply can't find boots to fit my feet plus two pairs of thick socks. I now wear different socks with different footwear in different weather; thick socks with medium-weight boots in cold weather, medium-weight socks with lightweight boots or shoes in cool weather, and thin socks with shoes when it's warm.

A popular approach is to wear a thick outer pair with a pair of thin synthetic liner socks. The theory is that the liners help reduce friction and remove sweat quickly. I've tried this but haven't found any increase in comfort over a single pair of socks. This, I think, is because modern socks are soft next to the skin and are efficient at wicking moisture. When socks were made from rough, scratchy wool, liners were probably more comfortable. If you use liner socks, they need rinsing out regularly; they dry quickly, of course.

Oversocks

To keep your feet dry, you could try *oversocks* made from a waterproof/breathable fabric. There are several available, including Gore-Tex ones from Manzella, Rocky, and REI; Triad (a chemically treated polyester membrane) ones from Fox River, Ov'r'Sox, and Tecnica; and SealSkinz, made from a DuPont membrane. In all of them, a waterproof membrane is sandwiched between thin synthetic layers.

I've tried two Gore-Tex versions, weighing 3 and 4 ounces, respectively, and the SealSkinz, which weigh 3¾ ounces. Both Gore-Tex models were calf-length and had taped seams, but one was open at the top and made from non-stretch material; the others had an elasticized cuff and

were made from stretchy fabric. When the first type appeared in Britain, pairs were given to all the gear reviewers for the outdoor press, myself included. We all found the socks worked well and kept feet dry when new, but they started to leak and then split at the seams after about two weeks' use. The second design is better—the close-fitting cuff, which keeps moisture and debris out, is a big advantage. I've tried them over silk liners and they kept my feet dry and warm, but they didn't last much longer than the first pair. Neither pair was very comfortable—they were so thick that I could only wear a thin sock under them, and I missed the cushioning effect of thick wool. The seams could be felt, too. The lack of durability means they're not suited to constant wearing, though they could be carried for use on boggy ground or in heavy rain. Overall, I don't think they're useful for backpacking, especially since they are expensive—six times the cost of a pair of Ragg socks. The less-expensive SealSkinz oversocks have a different lining and can be worn next to the skin. I haven't worn them enough to assess the durability, but I have found them waterproof and much more comfortable than Gore-Tex socks, partly because they're foot-shaped and have no seams, though they're not quite as breathable. Wearing thin synthetic liner socks helps minimize this. For really wet terrain and weather, I think Seal-Skinz and similarly priced oversocks are worth considering, especially if you wear shoes or sandals rather than boots.

Caring for Socks

On long trips, I carry three pairs of socks and try to change them every couple of days, though I have worn a pair for as many as 10 days. I like to keep one pair dry for campwear unless I'm carrying booties or pile socks for that purpose.

Clean socks are warmer, more comfortable, and wick moisture better than dirty ones. Whenever possible, I rinse socks in water taken from a stream or lake, using a cooking pot as a makeshift washbowl. Turning them inside out helps ensure sweat is removed from the inside and the socks can fluff up again. Rinsed socks can be hung on a line in camp or just draped over a rock or branch to dry. Wool socks take time to dry, so it's often necessary to hang them on the back of the pack to finish the process the next day.

At home, socks should be either hand-washed or put through the wool cycle on a washing machine (inside-out), then line-dried. Non-detergent powders remove less of the wool's natural lanolin. I use Ecover, available from Seventh Generation, or Nikwax Loft, and also add TX.10 in place of fabric conditioner. Fabric softeners are good for socks—you want them as soft as possible. However, the performance of some wicking synthetics can be affected by fabric softeners, so check the washing instructions for your socks before you throw the packaging away. Heat is bad for wool socks because it too removes lanolin from the wool and can cause synthetics to shrink, especially those containing polypropylene. Socks shouldn't be tumble-dried on a hot setting or draped over a hot radiator or near a fire.

GAITERS

Neither breathable-membrane sock liners nor Gore-Tex socks will keep your boots, socks, and feet dry and warm for long in deep snow. Only *gaiters* can do this. The lightest and simplest of these waterproof coverings for the lower leg are short (8 inches high), and sometimes are called *stop tous* or *anklets,* which are worn to keep stones and bits of grass out of the boot. I tried a coated nylon pair once, but they were too hot, probably because they prevented moisture vapor from escaping out of the boot tops. Ones made from uncoated nylon or waterproof/breathable fabrics are available and would probably perform better. The most interesting I've seen are Outdoor Research's Flex-Tex Low Gaiters, which are made from uncoated Spandura (stretch Cordura), and Patagonia's Instigaiters, made from waterproof stretch nylon/Lycra and weighing 5.5 ounces.

Knee-length gaiters are the standard design and come in two types: those that cover only the upper part of the boot, and *supergaiters* that cover the entire boot. Both styles usually have full-length zippers on the back, side, or front. Ones with front zippers are easier to put on, but they must have a hook-and-loop (Velcro) flap over the zipper to keep out moisture. Some dispense with the zipper and just use Velcro. The lower edge of a gaiter is elasticized or randed so that it grips the boot. There may also be an elasticized section around the ankle. A drawcord tightens the gaiter in below the knee.

In spite of their benefits, I don't like gaiters and only wear them when the alternative is wet, cold feet, which I like even less. Generally I only carry gaiters when I'm likely to encounter deep snow. On ski tours or winter walks in snow-covered terrain, I wear supergaiters all day. These grip the lower edge of the boot with a tight-fitting rubber rand that also runs under the instep in a thick band. They keep boots dry and unscuffed for days on end unless you ski through a lot of melting snow or wade rivers. No other gaiters come close in terms of performance. The front zipper means you can put on and lace up boots without removing the gaiters, so I fit supergaiters to my touring boots at the start of the ski season and don't remove them until the end, though I do flip them off the boot toes between tours to prevent the tension from curling my boots. Supergaiter rands, which are replaceable, wear quickly on rocky, rooty terrain, so I only use these gaiters for skiing or walking in snow. But in these circumstances, there is nothing better. Most supergaiters are made from Gore-Tex or other waterproof/breathable material. There aren't many brands. Wild Country Glacier Supergaiters, Berghaus Yetis, Black Diamond Superfit Supergaiters, and Outdoor Research X-Gaiters are all well regarded. I've used the first two and found them excellent. Supergaiters come in several sizes, and it's important to get the right fit. They won't fit very flexible boots properly but, despite what some makers say, they don't only fit fully stiffened boots. Supergaiters aren't light—they weigh 16 to 20 ounces a pair—but under the conditions you'll need them the weight isn't that important. For serious Arctic trips, insulated supergaiters are available.

Ordinary gaiters come in coated and uncoated nylon, waterproof/breathable fabrics, and nylon/cotton blends. They have an adjustable cord, strap, or wire that fits under the instep. These straps fray and eventually break, so look for gaiters with reinforced eyelets on the edge so you can replace broken straps. I'd avoid gaiters with fancy buckles, which only work with the original strap. Weights of gaiters range from 5 to 12 ounces a pair. The heaviest ones, made from fabrics such as Cordura, are the most durable, and therefore best for regular wear.

CAMPWEAR

On trips of one week or less, I often don't bother with spare footwear, especially if the weather is likely to keep me in my tent. On long treks, however, I find it essential to be able to change my footwear in the evening, so I carry sports sandals or running shoes as spare footwear for trail and camp use. My morale gets a boost when I don clean socks and light, cool footwear on my hot,

Insulated booties are nice for cold weather.

sore feet after a hard day, and my feet feel such relief that the change must be good for them. For campwear, I carry a pair of clean, dry socks that I try not to wear for walking (though somehow I often end up doing so). In cold weather I use thick wool socks, in summer often just thin liners.

If the weather during a trip is apt to be very cold and snowy, and I'm with a group and don't want to spend all evening in the tent, or if I plan to use huts or shelters, I carry *insulated booties.* These are very warm, and the mere thought of them is comforting when one's feet are cold and wet, but many are useless on anything except flat ground due to the smooth soles—climbing down a bank to fetch water from a stream or pond in booties can seem like a major expedition. Booties are available with both down and synthetic fill. Although the synthetic ones are slightly heavier, I prefer them—I don't have to worry about getting them wet when wandering around in the snow. There isn't a wide selection, but features vary. If you're going to wander around camp, your booties need a closed-cell foam insole, preferably sewn in, to insulate your feet from the ground. For many years I've used REI Polarguard Booties, which weigh 11¼ ounces in the large size and have packcloth soles, closed-cell insoles, nylon outers, a warm polyester/cotton/nylon lining, and a front drawcord. Later versions use Polarguard/Thinsulate insulation and Cordura soles, and weigh 11 ounces. There are similar models available, including down-filled ones such as Sierra Designs' Hot Shooties, with a 2-ounce down fill, closed-cell foam insoles, leather outsoles, and Velcro closures (total weight: 9 ounces).

On solo winter trips, when I spend most if not all my camp time in the tent (probably in a sleeping bag), I often carry pile socks for tent wear, since they are much warmer weight-for-weight than wool ones. For years I've used Helly-Hansen fiber-pile boot liners, which just reach my ankle and weigh 3½ ounces. The current catalog shows calf-length ones, which must weigh a little more. The name suggests they could be worn in boots, but I wouldn't do this except around camp because pile and fleece don't wick moisture quickly and are non-absorbent. They are, however, wonderful to pull on cold, wet feet at the end of the day; great for sleeping in; and nice for wearing in the tent when you aren't in the sleeping bag. There are plenty of similar socks, usually made from Polartec 200 fleece and often promoted for wearing with sports sandals. But since they don't have proper soles, they cannot be worn outside the tent, which is a nuisance.

A solution would be a pair of *mukluks* (soft, weatherproof overboots that can be worn over pile socks, wool socks, or even insulated booties). Outdoor Research's Modular Mukluks are a good example; they're made from Gore-Tex and Cordura, have removable closed-cell insoles, reach up to the knee, and weigh just 7½ ounces, making them an alternative to insulated booties. Of course, for short excursions outside the tent you could just pull stuff sacks or plastic bags over your pile socks or even don your boots again if the snow's not too deep.

TREKKING POLES AND STAFFS

For years I never considered using trekking poles or staffs. But when I started using Nordic skis in winter and spring I discovered that when I had to carry the skis on my pack, using the poles when walking improved my balance. After a while, I realized that I didn't need skis on my pack for a staff to be useful, and I began picking up stout sticks to help me climb steep inclines and ford streams. Staff in hand, I can negotiate steep scree slopes, boulder fields, and tussocky tundra with confidence, not fearing that my unwieldy burden will tip me over.

But a staff has even more uses. On level ground and good trails it helps maintain a walking rhythm. When crossing boggy ground or snow, it can probe for hidden rocks and deep

Hiking poles provide stability on rough ground and take some of the stress off knees and ankles.

spots as well as provide support. It can hold back bushes, barbed wire, stinging plants, and other trail obstructions, and even fend off aggressive dogs. Perhaps most useful of all, it saves energy: I am convinced it takes some weight off my feet, particularly when I lean heavily on it as I climb steep slopes. The German mountaineering equipment company Edelrid quotes "mountain doctor" Gottfried Neureuther as saying that "each placement of the ski pole takes between 5 and 8 kilograms (10 to 18 pounds) weight off the lower part of the body, which is equivalent to a total of 13 tons during a one-hour walk on flat ground and an amazing 34 tons total load reduction when walking downhill."

Edelrid recommends using two poles rather than one, and this is what I now do. All the advantages of one staff are more than doubled when you use two. Walking with two sticks uses the upper body muscles and takes much of the strain off legs and hips. On steep terrain, especially direct descents, you can always have three points of contact with the ground, which gives much greater stability. I can walk faster and farther when using two hiking sticks before I begin to feel tired, and I no longer have aching knees at the end of days with lots of steep descents.

My hiking sticks have other uses. During rest stops, they turn my pack into a backrest. In camp they can be used as poles to turn a fly-sheet door into an awning, or support a washline or tarp. They can also help retrieve bear-bagged food.

My efforts to convert others to using staffs have been largely unsuccessful. Most people interpret my using one as a sign of aging (now that I use two I've become resigned to people asking me where my skis are). On a two-week trek in the Pyrenees, I managed to persuade one companion to borrow my staff after he wrenched his shoulder and found walking with a pack painful. I pointed out that with the staff in the hand opposite his sore shoulder, he would lower that shoulder and take some of the weight off it. (This is why you should alternate the hand holding the staff if you use only one—otherwise, you may develop an aching shoulder.) He was impressed enough with the result to buy a cheap ash staff when we reached Gavarnie a couple of days later. Because he praised the staff so highly, another companion bought one as well. Both ended the walk convinced of its value.

The obvious material for a staff is wood, and it's easy to find a suitable piece in any woodland (don't try to find one in Iceland, though—it's virtually tree-less). As long as it's reasonably straight, solid, and at least elbow height (so it can be held with the lower arm at a right angle to the body, the most comfortable position), any strong stick will do. Most tourist stores in popular mountain areas sell wooden staffs, usually inexpensively. But you can't always buy or find a staff when you reach an area, and wooden staffs aren't easy to transport. You can't put them in your pack, and they're awkward to take on trains, buses, and planes.

The answer to this problem is the *adjustable aluminum staff.* Modeled after adjustable ski poles, these staffs are lighter, yet stronger, than wooden sticks, and can be carried in or on a pack. Many Alpine ski-pole manufacturers began to make them once they noted that skiers in the Alps often use their poles when walking in the summer. Indeed, a ski pole, especially an old one, makes a perfectly functional staff if you don't need an adjustable one—after all, many staffs are only slightly modified ski poles.

If you don't want to look like a skier on a day off, the Tracks Sherlock staffs (successors to the Chief of Staffs I recommended in the last edition) are excellent. The two-piece Sherlock Walking Staff adjusts from 41 to 56 inches by means of a button that clips into holes in the shaft. The handle is soft foam topped by a wooden knob that is removable to reveal a useful camera tripod mount. The steel point has a removable rubber tip. The Sherlock Travel Staff is similar, but is three-piece construction and measures 22 inches long when dismantled. Weights are 16 ounces for the Walking Staff and 18½ ounces for the Travel Staff. I've used the latter extensively and found it excellent. It's my choice when I use only one pole.

Since I usually use a pair of staffs, any adjustable ski-touring poles will do, though large baskets can be awkward in dense brush or rocky terrain. On the best sticks, the baskets can be changed to suit the season; that way your summer hiking sticks can also be your winter ski poles.

Leki probably makes the widest range of trekking poles, as well as some of the most technically advanced poles. The Super Makalu, my favorite, is a good example. These poles have three sections, and are easily adjusted by twisting the shafts and telescoping them. Between the top two sections is a concealed spring that absorbs shock and provides cushioning. The rubber grip is softer material than most (there is a version with even softer cork-and-latex grips) and is carefully shaped for comfortable handling. The straps are easily adjusted—you just pull the strap upward to free it, then tug the loose end. Pulling down on the strap locks it in place. The Makalu has a sharp and tough tungsten carbide tip. The standard tip is quite short; longer ones are available for snow and ice. The tip is designed to break before the shaft if too much leverage is put on the pole. It telescopes from 58 to 26 inches and will fit inside most large packs. A pair weighs 22 ounces.

There are plenty of other hiking/ski poles, of course. The Black Diamond Expedition Probe

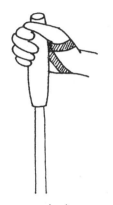

normal grip

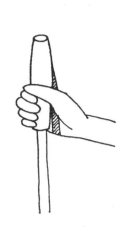

pole shortened

pole lengthened

Holding the pole.

poles have external flick-locks for adjusting the length that are very easy to use and can't slip. They telescope from 57 to 26 inches and weigh almost 20 ounces a pair.

To gain the most from hiking poles, though, you need to use them properly. Nordic skiers already know how to do this. First, gripping the handles firmly hinders proper use of the poles and can quickly tire your arms. Instead, use the straps to support your hands; by doing this you can flick the poles back and forth without having to jerk your arms around. Then, place the poles by swinging one in front, pressing down on it, then walking past it while the other pole is swung forward. On even terrain you can get a good rhythm.

When descending steep ground you can lengthen a pole by placing your hand over the top of the grip for greater support. When traversing steep slopes you can slip your hand out of the strap on the upper pole and grasp it lower down the shaft so it doesn't push you away from the slope. Don't put all your weight on the downhill pole, however, or even lean on it; if it breaks or suddenly collapses—as can happen—

you have no way of stopping a possibly dangerous fall.

I can't imagine backpacking without poles now, but I have heard a couple of stories that suggest there may be environmental problems with poles. The first report comes from the Alps, where ski poles have been used for hiking for many years. Apparently the edges of some of the neat, carefully made trails are being damaged by poles. I've also heard that increasing use of poles on the Appalachian Trail is leading to visible scratches on rocks. The answer to the latter would be to use rubber tips, provided with some poles, such as those from Tracks.

ICE AX

Whenever you're likely to encounter slopes of hard snow and ice, you need an *ice ax*. Winter would seem the obvious time to expect such terrain, though the snow then is often deep and soft. It's in spring and early summer, after the surface of the snow has melted and refrozen, perhaps several times, that ice axes are needed. I often pack an ice ax until June, and I have had

But It's Still Summer

An unexpected early September blizzard had blanketed the mountains with fresh snow—deep, soft, and wet. I struggled up to the 11,900-foot Farview Pass in the Never Summer range in the Colorado Rockies with the aid of a thick stick I'd picked up in the forest below. I had no ice ax and this was in the days before I carried a staff or hiking poles. My feet, in running shoes, were quickly sodden and chilled. At the pass, where the view was all of 50 yards, I wiped the snow off a trail sign, then followed the directions down into the Parika Lake basin, where I camped in the slight shelter of some stunted spruce. Once in the tent I stripped off my wet shoes and socks, pulled dry wool socks over my frozen feet, and slid into my sleeping bag. After several hot drinks and a steaming bowl of curry, my feet began to warm up. The temperature in the tent was a damp 40°F (4°C). Thankfully, the next day arrived with sunshine and a clear sky, and my feet felt only slightly cool as I followed the Continental Divide Trail across the snowy slopes of the Cloud Peaks and into Rocky Mountain National Park.

With the rest of Colorado to cross in the next few weeks, I needed more than running shoes and a stick, however. In the little mountain resort of Grand Lake I did a round of the stores. But it was still summer, and no one stocked gaiters or ice axes. (Outside, the mountains shone white with new snow.) Boots were available, of course, and I continued my walk in a sturdy pair of mid-weight leather Pivettas, good for stomping steps in snow. But it was 19 days and 320 miles of snowy trails later before I finally managed to find gaiters and an ice ax in the town of Creede—just in time to deal with a blizzard in the San Juans. The lesson from this was to have items I might need mailed ahead just in case. I could always send them on if they weren't required.

to seek out an alternative route as late as September when a steel-hard bank of old snow blocked the trail to a high pass.

A staff or ski pole, very useful for balance in soft snow, is inadequate when crossing steep, hard-packed snow or ice. On such surfaces, a slip can easily become a rapidly accelerating slide. The only way to stop such a fall is by a method known as *self-arrest,* which requires an ice ax. For instruction, take a course in snow and ice skills at an outdoor center or learn how from a competent friend. *Mountaineering: The Freedom of the Hills,* edited by Don Graydon (The Mountaineers), is a useful source for all aspects of snow travel other than skiing, but I'm not convinced that self-arrest can be learned from a written description. Practice is essential; in a real fall you have to react immediately and automatically, and you must be able to stop yourself,

whether you fall with your head downhill or on your back. On slopes where you may have to self-arrest, carry your ice ax with the pick pointing backward so that it's in position for self-arrest. On easier slopes I prefer to walk with the pick pointing forward so that if I stumble I won't impale myself.

Ice axes also can be used to cut steps in ice and snow too hard to kick your boot into (though wearing crampons would make this unnecessary), and to replace a staff for balance on snow. If you do slip on a snow slope, thrusting the ax shaft into the snow can often prevent you from sliding. (A staff can do this too, but it can't be used for self-arrest if it fails to hold you.) Other uses I've found peculiar to an ice ax include pulling stakes out of frozen ground or hard-packed snow, chopping holes in frozen streams or ponds to get water, chipping ice off

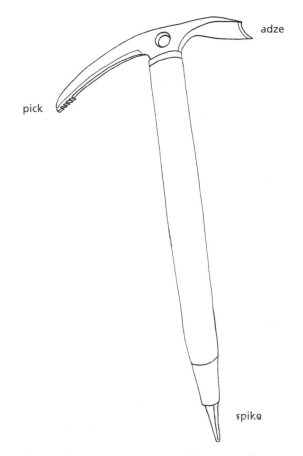

adze

pick

spike

An ice ax. Always carry an ice ax and crampons if you're likely to encounter steep, snowy areas or ice.

rocks I want to stand on without slipping when fording streams, and digging toilet holes.

There are many complicated and even bizarre ice ax styles available; most are specialty designs for climbing frozen waterfalls and iced-up vertical cliffs. All a backpacker needs is a simple, traditional ice ax, usually described as a "walking" or "general mountaineering" ax. The head of the ax should have a wide adze, useful for cutting steps and possibly for self-arrest in soft snow, and a gently curved pick. Two-piece heads are

perfectly adequate for walking use. The shaft can be aluminum alloy, reinforced fiberglass, or wood—the first is the lightest. Wrist loops are useful and worth attaching if your ax doesn't come with one. Length is a matter of debate; the conventional wisdom is to choose an ax whose spike is a half-inch or so off the ground when the ax is held by the side. However, my advice is to go for an ax 2 inches or longer than this if you intend to use it as a staff on easy ground.

Weights of axes run from 12 to 28 ounces. The lightest models are adequate for backpacking. Makes to look for include Climb High, Cassin, Salewa, Stubai, SMC, Mountain Technology, Charlet Moser, REI, Lowe Alpine/Camp, Camp High/Grivel, and Black Diamond.

For well over a decade I used a 25-ounce, 55 cm (metric measurements are standard for ice axes), fiberglass-shaft Stubai model, originally bought for climbing rather than backpacking. This replaced a 70 cm Simond ax weighing 27 ounces I carried the entire length of the Pacific Crest Trail. The pick on the Simond eventually broke when it was used to help change a car wheel on returning from a ski-mountaineering trip in the Alps. (This use is not recommended!) Those axes were state of the art when I bought them in the early 1980s. Now, stronger materials mean that axes can be much lighter; I have changed to a 70 cm Lowe/Camp HL250 model that weighs just 12 ounces—less than half the weight of my old axes. This ax has an alloy rather than a steel head and isn't suitable for serious climbing—it actually has "not for ice climbing" stamped on the pick—but for backpacking it's perfectly adequate. If you want an ax for easy climbing as well as hiking it should have a steel head, but it needn't weigh more than 16 to 20 ounces.

Ice axes are dangerous implements and

An ultralight ice ax suitable for hiking on steep, snowy terrain.

are traveling by public transport. You may not even be allowed on board without covering your ax in this way. The alternative, which I've now adopted, is to transport the ax inside my pack.

CRAMPONS

If conditions warrant carrying an ice ax, *crampons* will probably be useful as well. These metal spikes strap or clamp onto the soles of your boots and enable you to cross ice and hard snow without slipping. I rarely use them, but when I do, they are essential, so I also rarely leave them at home. Flexible crampons—ones with a hinge in the middle—can be fitted to most medium-weight boots for walking. Rigid crampons are strictly for climbers.

The number of points on a crampon doesn't matter much for walkers; 8-, 10-, or 12-point models are available. Points that angle out from the front of the boot are useful for climbing steep slopes because you can use the toe of the boot. I prefer crampons with angled toe points to those with vertical points.

Most crampons fasten to walking boots with straps, but some use ski-type bindings, which require boots with a prominent welt. The best straps are neoprene, which doesn't freeze. Fitting

demand care when used or carried. Use rubber head and spike protectors when transporting the ax to and from the mountains, especially if you

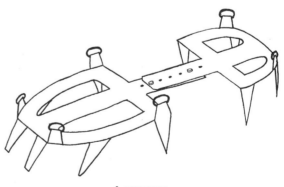

A crampon.

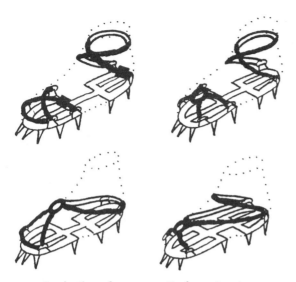

A selection of crampon attachment systems.

crampons to boots is a complicated business the first time, and finding the right size can be difficult. First-time buyers should take their boots to the store and have the salesperson demonstrate the fit and how to do up the straps.

I have a pair of Salewa 12-point, articulated crampons that weigh 2 pounds, but I am thinking of changing to one of the lighter models now available. Because my crampons spend more time in my pack than on my feet, I'm particularly interested in one of the new light alloy crampons, such as the 10-point, flexible Grivel GRL Crampons, which weigh just 18½ ounces. Like alloy ice axes, these aren't suitable for climbing, but for backpacking they're ideal. Good general-purpose crampons are made by Charlet Moser, Stubai, SMC, Simond, and Lowe/Camp, as well as Salewa and Climb High/Grivel. Like ice axes, crampons are potentially dangerous, so if you strap your crampons to the outside of your pack you should cover the spikes with rubber protectors. The tangled rubber strands of these can be a nuisance, however;

I long ago abandoned using them, and carry crampons inside the pack in a side pocket with a side zipper bought specifically for the purpose. Outdoor Research makes a Crampon Pouch with a heavy plastic bottom and end that can function as a side pocket. You can also wrap crampons in a length of tough cloth such as heavy-duty canvas, neoprene, or PVC.

Walking in crampons involves a change in gait and special techniques on steep slopes. You need to keep your feet flat on the snow or ice so that all the points bite. On steep slopes you can kick just the front points into the snow and walk up on your toes. I find the least-tiring way to climb moderately steep ground is to front-point with one foot while keeping the other flat on the ground, alternating my feet as they start to ache. It's best to take a course or learn how to use crampons from a competent friend.

SKIS AND SNOWSHOES

Walking through snow more than ankle-deep can be very difficult; once you sink in to your shins and deeper, it becomes an exhausting and slow process, aptly known as "postholing." The Scandinavians answered the problem some 4,000 years ago: Strap something to your feet that spreads your weight and allows you to ride on the snow's surface. After years of slogging through soft, wet snow I discovered this for myself when I traveled with three hikers who used snowshoes in the San Bernardino Mountains. I bought a pair to use in the snowbound High Sierra, where I watched enviously as two in our party swapped snowshoes for Nordic skis, swooped down snowfields and slid through the forest, leaving two of us on snowshoes to plod along in their wake. I determined to learn to ski.

Snowshoes have their uses, though. They are more maneuverable than skis in thick forest, and the largest ones will keep you on the surface of deep powdery snow into which the widest skis will sink. You also can use them with ordinary walking boots. Wooden snowshoes are still available, but they need careful maintenance. Better are the more durable, modern aluminum-framed ones with pivoting foot straps for use on steep slopes. The ones I used in the Sierra were Sherpa Featherweight Sno-Claw models that weighed a little over 3 pounds with straps. The Sno-Claw, a serrated edge that fits under the boot for grip on icy slopes, worked well on moderate slopes, but I changed to crampons for the steep slopes. Walking in snowshoes is hard, slow work compared with skiing, but far easier than walking in deep snow without them. Snowshoes have become popular for winter recreation, and there are now several good ranges available, including some lightweight models, such as the 2-pound Redfeather Redtails. Other well-regarded brands include Atlas, Northern Lites, Ramer, and Yuba. If you're interested in pursuing this subject, consult Gene Prater's *Snowshoeing* (The Mountaineers).

I abandoned snowshoes after just one three-week-long trial because the skiers in our party pulled way ahead time after time. Snowshoeing seemed a functional but tedious way to travel in the snow; skiing looked fun. Crossing the High Sierra in May with a 100-pound pack was not the time to learn how to ski, however. The next winter I took a Nordic ski course in the Scottish Highlands, and have since been on ski backpacking trips every year in places as far afield as the High Sierra, Greenland, the Alps, Lapland, the Norwegian mountains, and the Canadian Rockies. Much to my astonishment, since writing the first edition of this book I have also spent several months every winter leading ski tours and teaching people to ski. It is, in my view, the only way to travel in snowbound wildernesses.

Skiing is a complex subject. Alpine (downhill)

skis are strictly for lift-served skiing and ultra-steep mountain descents. Even with special Alpine ski mountaineering bindings and boots, progress on the flat and uphill is painfully slow and the weight of the gear tiring. Backpackers needn't consider these skis; they won't be carrying a winter backpacking load down the sort of descents that require such gear.

Nordic (backcountry, mountain touring, or cross-country) skis are best suited to ski backpacking. Avoid heavyweight skis designed for lift-served telemark skiing and lightweight ones designed for cut-track and low-level touring with light packs. For carrying a heavy load and breaking trail in snow that ranges from deep powder to breakable crust, *mountain skis* with metal edges are needed. These are narrower at the waist than at the tip and tail. For heavy-duty touring, look for around 10 mm of *sidecut.* Typical dimensions are 63-54-58 (shovel, waist, tail). More sidecut is fine, less isn't. The length should equal your height plus 20 to 25 cm (ski lengths are always in centimeters). Such skis will weigh 4½ to 6½ pounds. My favorite for rolling terrain are the Merrell Karhu XCDGTs, which have dimensions of 62-54-59 and weigh 5½ pounds. For steep mountain touring I use Asnes Mountain Extremes, which measure 73-56-63 and weigh 6½ pounds. There are numerous other makers. Whatever the skis, you need strong bindings, such as the Riva Cable Binding or the Rottefella Super Telemark, since they'll have to undergo the stress caused by your body weight plus a heavy pack.

You need only moderate skill to travel the wilderness on skis, and the enjoyment of ski touring far outweighs the effort required. Beginners will benefit from a course at a Nordic ski school; I did. For more specifics on wilderness touring, see my book *Wilderness Skiing and Winter Camping* (Ragged Mountain Press).

Poles are essential with skis and are a great

Ski backpacking is the ideal way to explore mountains in winter and spring.

help with snowshoes. Since lightweight fiberglass ones break easily, I recommend a metal pair. I like adjustable ones (long for the flat, shorter for uphill, shortest for downhill). Many models are available—see the discussion of hiking poles above. My Leki Lawisonds weigh 22 ounces.

FOOT CARE

Keeping your feet in good condition is a prerequisite to pain-free hiking. Keep toenails cut short and square; long nails will bruise, cut into the toes on either side, and inflict pain on descents. Also remember to dry your feet well to avoid softening the skin too much. Skin-hardening methods vary; some people douse their feet in rubbing alcohol prior to or even during long treks. I've never tried this, but I do go barefoot around the house and outside as much as possible. By going barefoot and wearing sandals without socks, I usually manage to achieve hard feet by the end of the summer.

It's important to stop walking and immediately attend to the first sign of a sore spot, covering the affected area to prevent further rubbing. Failure to do this may result in a blister. This is easy to preach, hard to practice. All too often I ignore warning signs, telling myself that I'll have a look when I next stop. When I do, I find a plump blister.

Blister remedies and cures are legion. What is common to all is that the blister must be covered to prevent infection, and cushioned against further rubbing. You can cover a blister with ordinary plaster, moleskin, micropore tape, or a more specialized material such as Spenco 2nd Skin or Compeed, the treatments I currently favor. 2nd Skin is a gel that is applied to a sore spot or blister, then held in place by a piece of sticky tape or plaster. It's a slimy substance, difficult to hold. You have to remove backing film from both sides before use and store it in an airtight foil bag, but for preventing blisters from forming and anesthetizing existing ones, it works far better than anything else I've tried except Compeed. Spenco markets a half-ounce Blister Kit consisting of a plastic wallet containing instructions, 2nd Skin in a resealable bag, adhesive tape, and foam padding for really painful blisters. I prefer to buy just the 2nd Skin for long walks because I don't use the foam pads, and the kit has only six 1¼-inch squares of 2nd Skin. Compeed is a similar gel but it's already bonded to an oval piece of fabric with sticky edges, so applying it is simple—just like applying an adhesive bandage. It seems to work just as well as 2nd Skin, but it is more expensive and can't be cut to the exact size needed. Even so, the ease of use makes it my first choice for blisters.

Some experts advise against lancing a blister before covering it, but if you continue to walk after a blister forms, you'll have to remove the fluid built up inside to minimize the pain. To do this I sterilize a needle in a match flame, pierce the blister at one edge, then roll the needle over the blister until all the fluid drains out. A piece of tissue (from the toilet roll if necessary) can absorb the fluid and wipe the area dry. Large blisters may need several holes to expel all the fluid. I know from painful experience that, however long it takes, the blister must be fully drained before being dressed. Otherwise your first steps will hurt so much you'll have to stop again. Antiseptic wipes can be used to clean the area, though 2nd Skin seems to do this well by itself.

Friction causes blisters, so it's best to try to find and remove the cause, which may be a tiny speck of grit or a rough sock seam. Often the cause isn't obvious, and you just have to hope that covering the blister will solve the problem. Mysteriously, footwear that has never given problems before can cause a blister one day, yet be fine again on future trips. However, I would suspect footwear that repeatedly causes sore spots. Either it doesn't fit properly or something inside needs smoothing.

I like to remove my footwear and socks several times during the day, weather permitting, in order to let my feet cool down and air. Pouring cold water over them provides even more relief on really hot days. Some people also like to apply foot powder to help keep their feet dry, but I've never noticed that powder makes a difference.

CHAPTER FOUR

Carrying the Load: The Pack

Unwisely we decided to carry loaded rucksacks. "To toughen ourselves up," as we optimistically put it. "About forty pounds should be enough," Hugh said, "so that we can press on."

Our drivers were aghast. It was difficult to persuade Abdul Ghiyas that we were not out of our minds. With the temperature around 110°, carrying our forty pound loads and twirling our ice axes, we set off from Jangalak.

—*A Short Walk in the Hindu Kush*, Eric Newby

The heart of the backpacker's equipment is the pack. Tents, boots, stoves, and rain gear may be unnecessary in a given time and place, but your pack is always with you. It must hold everything you need for many days' wilderness travel but still be as small a burden as possible. To do this, a pack must be more than the bag with shoulder straps that is adequate for day walks.

Ever since aluminum frames and hipbelts were introduced in the 1940s and 1950s, designers have tried to make carrying heavy loads as comfortable as possible. Internal and external frames, adjustable back systems, sternum straps, top tension straps, side tension straps, triple-density padded hipbelts, lumbar pads—the modern pack suspension system is a complex structure that requires careful selection and fitting. In terms of comfort, only your boots are

as important as your pack, so you must take the time to find a pack that fits.

TYPES OF PACKS

Walk into any outdoor equipment store and you'll be confronted by a vast array of packs. Any could be used for backpacking; the problem is to determine which ones are right for *your* kind of backpacking. Most people use one pack for all their hiking. If you do, then you need a pack with enough capacity for the bulkiest loads you are likely to carry. Overstuffing a too-small pack is not the way to achieve a comfortable carry. If

Walking Before Dawn

Under a soft gray light, mountaintops lie black and brooding, draped in pale wraith-like clouds. The last stars still shine in a dark sky, though far to the east a faint tinge of pink spreads along the horizon. As the light strengthens, the dark lines of peaks beyond the flat lake water stand out as if etched onto the sky. The pink intensifies into red and orange, then a spot on the horizon darkens and flares, a shaft of light cutting the air. The spot becomes an arc, then the sun. The reeds on a tiny islet out in the lake are transformed from black shadows to green life. I must turn my eyes from the brightness.

you go on trips ranging from summer over-nighters to winter through-hikes, you may be better off with more than one pack. That way you can tailor the load to the capacity and weight of the pack. I now use a lightweight, 3,500-cubic-inch pack for short summer trips and ultralight trips of any length; for any trip where the load will exceed 60 pounds I stick to a 7,200-cubic-inch heavyweight monster. Because I test gear regularly, I also use 4,000- and 5,000-cubic-inch packs for 35- to 55-pound loads. But I don't suggest backpackers need three or four different packs.

Daypacks and Ultralight Packs

Small packs designed for day walks can be dis-counted immediately for backpacking, except by a runner or ultra-lightweight fanatic pre-pared to compromise comfort for lightness and low bulk.

Packs made from ultra-lightweight nylon need weigh no more than 10 to 16 ounces. If you want one you'll probably have to make it yourself, however, as the Jardines do, because the only commercially available one I know of is made by the British company Karrimor. It's called the KIMM Sac. It weighs 16 ounces, has an 1,800-cubic-inch capacity, is constructed of ripstop nylon, and has lightly padded shoulder straps, padded hipbelt with zipped pockets, a single buckle-fastened lid, four mesh pockets, and a compression cord. For loads up to 25 pounds it's surprisingly comfortable.

Add a little more weight and a few more fea-tures and there are plenty of daypacks in the 1,800- to 2,500-cubic-inch range weighing 1½ to 2½ pounds.

Overnight Packs

Next up in size are packs in the 2,500- to 3,500-cubic-inch capacity range, often called *rucksacks*.

There are two styles: with fixed side pockets (for hut-to-hut hiking) and without side pockets (for Alpine climbing and ski touring). Both types are suitable for one- or two-night trips. Ultra-lightweight hikers often use them for summer-long walks. The most basic rucksacks have a padded back and shoulder straps, and a webbing waistbelt. More sophisticated ones, usu-ally larger, have an internal frame and a padded hipbelt. Weights run from 2 to 5 pounds.

The advantages of rucksacks are their light weight, simple design, and excellent stability, which is why they are popular with climbers and skiers. If you never carry more than 30 pounds, a pack from this category will probably be ade-quate. Most pack makers have several packs in this range, so the choice is large.

Backpacking Packs

These packs are designed for carrying heavy loads. They are sophisticated, complex, expen-sive, and marvelous. Without them, backpacking would be much more arduous and less pleasant. This category subdivides into two suspension systems based on frame type. Each system has its dedicated, vocal proponents.

First came the welded, tubular aluminum alloy *external frame*, its ladder-like appearance common on trails worldwide in the 1950s, '60s, and '70s. It's a simple, strong, and functional design, good for carrying heavy loads along smooth trails, but unstable in rougher, steeper terrain. It's easy to lash extra items to the frame, and capacities can be enormous.

Mountaineers, who wanted packs that could carry heavy loads comfortably but which retained the stability of the frameless Alpine rucksack, inserted flexible, flat metal bars down the back of the latter. Thus, in the late 1960s, the *internal-frame* pack was born. Development of the design has been rapid, and today most backpackers

Key Features: Packs

- A good fit. A badly fitted pack can give you sore shoulders and hips and a sore back, and can be very unstable.
- A well-designed hipbelt. A good hipbelt should support up to 90 percent of the pack weight without rubbing or causing sore hips.
- Curved, padded shoulder straps with top tension/load-lifter straps to take pressure off the top of the shoulders.
- A frame/framesheet to help transfer weight

to the hips and prevent lumpy gear from poking you in the back.
- A capacity and design suitable for the gear to be carried. A small pack for summer weekends doesn't need ice ax loops, ski slots, or room for a four-season sleeping bag—a pack for a winter ski backpacking trip does.
- Light weight. It should be as light as possible for the weight to be carried—about 10 percent of the total load weight.

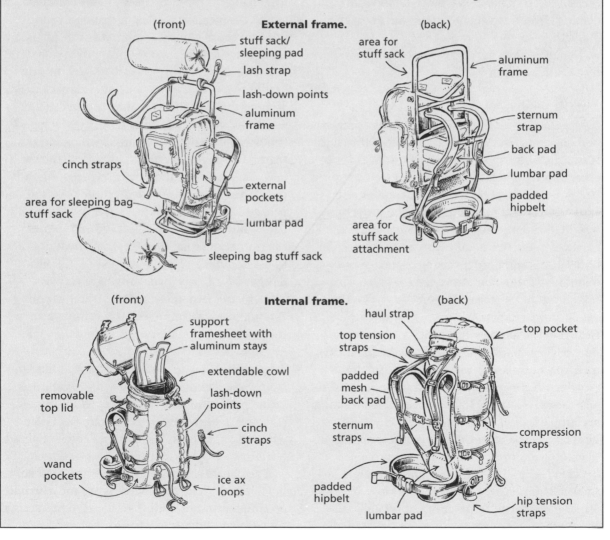

(front)   **External frame.**   (back)

stuff sack/ sleeping pad

lash strap

lash-down points

aluminum frame

cinch straps

external pockets

area for sleeping bag stuff sack

lumbar pad

sleeping bag stuff sack

area for stuff sack

aluminum frame

sternum strap

back pad

lumbar pad

padded hipbelt

area for stuff sack attachment

(front)   **Internal frame.**   (back)

support framesheet with aluminum stays

extendable cowl

removable top lid

lash-down points

cinch straps

wand pockets

ice ax loops

haul strap

top tension straps

top pocket

padded mesh back pad

sternum straps

compression straps

padded hipbelt

lumbar pad

hip tension straps

choose internal-frame packs. Ranging in capacity from 3,500 to 9,000 cubic inches, they serve just about any sort of backpacking, from summer weekend strolls to six-month expeditions. Internal-frame packs require careful fitting and adjustment, but for those prepared to take the time for proper fit, they are an excellent choice.

Just as the external frame seemed obsolete, new designs have appeared, featuring alloy frames with extreme curvature, as well as flexible synthetic frames designed to match an internal frame's body-hugging fit, which has given the old standby a new lease on life.

Details of internal and external frames are discussed later in this chapter.

Travel Packs

These are derived from internal-frame packs, and developed as a growing number of travelers realized that internal-frame packs were easier to carry and fit in vehicles than were external-frame packs. Large travel packs have the same suspension systems and capacities, and about the same weight, as internal-frame ones. Smaller travel packs have just shoulder straps and hipbelts. On both, frame and harness can be zipped away behind a panel when unneeded (or when you don't want to risk the suspicion that packs engender in some officials and in some countries). Covering the harness also protects it from airport baggage handlers. With the harness hidden, travel packs look like soft luggage, with handles, zip-around compartments, and front pockets, and they can be used like suitcases when packing and unpacking. I can't vouch for their effectiveness as backpacks, but the consensus seems to be that, while they're okay for the occasional overnight trip, they don't compare with real internal-frame packs for serious hiking. The larger ones with internal frames probably are adequate for long treks with moderate loads

(40 pounds or so) as long as you don't mind the panel zippers.

SUSPENSION SYSTEMS

The suspension system is the most important feature to consider when choosing a pack—it supports the load and it's the part of the pack that comes in direct contact with your body. A top-quality, properly fitted suspension system will enable you to carry heavy loads comfortably and in balance. An inadequate or badly fitted one will cause you great pain. As with boots, time is needed to fit a pack properly.

Frames

To hold the load steady and help transfer the weight from the shoulders to the hips, the pack needs some form of stiffening. For loads less than 30 pounds, a simple, foam-padded back is adequate, but once the weight exceeds this, a more rigid system is needed. In the past, the gear packed inside provided this rigidity to some packs, but these old designs required so much care in packing that they were very awkward to use and have all but disappeared. All packs designed for heavy loads now have frames.

As mentioned, there are two frame types: external, on which the packbag is hung on a frame by straps or clips or clevis pins, and the internal, which fits inside the fabric of the pack, often completely integrated into it and hidden from view. There are currently more internal-frame packs available, though external frames still have a following, especially among those who walk mainly on trails in forested and gentle terrain.

The debate centers on which frame best supports a heavy load and which is the most stable on rough ground; the answer used to be external for the first and internal for the second. Today,

A typical internal-frame pack—this one is from Lowe Alpine.

however, the best new designs and materials have made the distinction less clear cut.

For most purposes, I would choose internal-frame packs: They're more stable than all but a few externals, easier to carry around when you're not on the trail, less prone to damage, and comfortable with medium loads (from 30 to 45 pounds). If you carry more weight than that, pack choice becomes more critical. Before a Canadian Rockies walk in 1988, I would have

said that internals won hands down, with the Gregory Cassin being the best heavy-load carrier I had used. However, on that walk, I used a Lowe Holoflex external-frame pack and found it carried 65 to 85 pounds at least as well as the Gregory. Although both those packs have long since been discontinued, developments have continued, and the very best packs, whether externally or internally framed, handle heavy loads well.

External Frames: As noted earlier, the external frame has been around since the early 1950s. New designs introduced in the late 1980s and early 1990s have ensured it will be around for many more years. The traditional frame is made of tubular aluminum alloy and consists of two curved vertical bars to which a number of crossbars are welded. Kelty introduced such frames— they are still made in barely altered form by Kelty, Camp Trails (the other originator of this design), REI, and others. These non-adjustable frames come in three sizes, have padded shoulder straps and hipbelts, plus backbands and frame extensions. External frames are easy to fit; the weight transfers directly through the rigid frame to your hips, a vast improvement over earlier, unframed packs. Because of their rigidity, it is easy to keep the weight close to the center of gravity, enabling you to walk upright. Another argument for external frames is that, because they stand away from the back, they allow sweat to dissipate, unlike internal-frame packs, which "hug" the body. (I've always found that when I work hard carrying a heavy load I end up with a sweaty back, whatever the type of frame.)

External frames have balance and stability disadvantages, however. Because of their rigidity, external frames do not move with you; on steep downhills and when crossing rough ground they can be unstable, and can make walking difficult or unsafe. They also tend to be bulkier than

The Limits of External Frames

The trail was steep and rough, a direct line up the rocky mountainside. Just below the summit, two rock bands had to be surmounted. Climbing them wasn't difficult—just easy scrambling—but for a few yards the broken rock was very steep and I needed to steady myself with my hands. The only problem was that the tubes of my external-frame pack towered above my head and pushed my face forward into the slope, preventing me from looking up to see where the trail went. The rigid frame made balancing difficult, too, and forced me to lurch sideways when I made high steps. The situation wasn't dangerous, just awkward, but the experience was one of the main reasons I soon changed to an internal-frame pack, a design I've preferred ever since.

internal-frame packs, making them awkward for plane, car, or bus travel and difficult to stow in small tents. Their rigidity also makes them more susceptible to damage, especially on airplanes. For these reasons, I haven't used a traditional external frame since the early 1980s.

It's worth noting, though, that externals are generally considerably less expensive than internals.

Some new external-frame packs try to mimic the advantages of internals without the disadvantages. This has been achieved by modifying the frame and by using flexible plastic instead of rigid alloy. Kelty's Radial Frame has an exaggerated S-curve to hold the frame closer to the body, and a three-layer hipbelt and lumbar pad with a polyethylene plastic outer attached to a backband, intended to allow independent movement between it and the pack. Radial frames also telescope to fit a wide range of body heights. JanSport frames have crossbars attached to the side bars by flexible joints, which, JanSport claims, allow the frames to twist and flex with

body movement. A more recent development is the Evolution external-frame pack from internal-frame maker Gregory. This has an oversized tubular aluminum frame with flexible nylon crosspieces, and the same pre-molded foam shoulder straps and hipbelt as Gregory internals. Other developments are evident in Camp Trails' Comfort Flex polypropylene frames, and in Coleman's Peak 1 Kevlar-reinforced nylon frames.

Not having used any of these frames, I can't comment on how effective they are, but it seems that the key to better balance with an external frame is the freedom of movement of the hipbelt in relation to the pack, plus an increased curvature that molds the frame more closely to the body.

Internal Frames: The basic internal frame consists of two flat aluminum alloy stays running vertically down the pack's back (see illustration on page 75). This original design, introduced in the late 1960s by Lowe Alpine Systems, addressed the instability of external-frame packs on rugged terrain, and the difficulty of designing a frameless pack to carry a heavy load comfortably. The bars, or stays, are usually parallel, though in some designs they form an upright or inverted V.

Many internal frames now have flexible plastic *framesheets* as well as stays to give extra rigidity to the pack and prevent hard bits of gear from poking you in the back. There are many variations on the framesheet/parallel stays theme, using aluminum, carbon fiber, thermoplastic, Evazote and polyethylene.

In Gregory's top-of-the-range Summit Series packs, the carbon fiber stays are stronger and lighter than those made of aluminum. They're also vertically stiff but flexible from edge to edge. Dana Design's packs use carbon fiber stays but added a single aluminum stay down the center of the framesheet. Osprey packs have a curved ther-

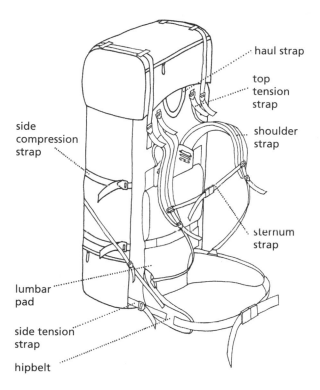

side compression strap

haul strap

top tension strap

shoulder strap

sternum strap

side tension strap

lumbar pad

hipbelt

The suspension system of internal-frame backpacks.

moplastic rod running over the shoulders from hip to hip around the perimeter of the pack, instead of a framesheet. vauDe packs have a plastic frame that looks like a cut-out framesheet. And McHale makes an unusual-looking Bayonet Frame pack, made from the usual twin alloy stays with an Evazote/polyethylene framesheet. The difference here is that each stay is a two-piece part. The top sections can be removed along with the framesheet when you want to turn the full-size backpack into a rucksack for day use.

Whatever the style, internal frames are light, and with use conform to the shape of the wearer's back, allowing a body-hugging fit that gives excellent stability. A few packs come with pre-bent stays that can be bent further, fine-tuning the frame to your particular shape.

Because internal frames move with your body and allow the weight to be packed lower and closer to your back, they are excellent for activities where balance is important, such as rock scrambling, skiing, and hiking over rough, steep terrain. A disadvantage of this is that it can lead to a forward lean to counterbalance the low weight. Careful packing with heavy items high up and close to the back is a partial answer when you are walking on a good trail, but is no panacea when the pack is poorly designed (see "Packing" later in this chapter).

On many packs, the stays are removable; this is one way to lighten the pack for a side trip or an ultralight trip. In snow, the stays could be used as tent stakes or even an emergency snow saw.

The Hipbelt

Your back and shoulders are not designed for bearing heavy loads for long. In fact, the human spine easily compresses under the pressure of a heavy load, which is why back injuries are so prevalent. Furthermore, when you carry a load on your shoulders, you must bend forward to counterbalance the backward pull of the load. This is uncomfortable and bad for your back, and the pressure on sensitive muscles and nerves in your shoulders can cause them to ache and go numb.

The solution is to lower the load to the hips, a far stronger part of the body, and one designed to bear weight. The *hipbelt* is by far the most important part of any pack suspension system designed for carrying heavy loads, and the part of the pack I always examine first. A well-fitting, well-padded hipbelt transfers most of the pack weight (at least 75 percent, and preferably 95 percent) from the shoulders and back to the hips, allowing the backpacker to stand upright and carry a properly balanced load in comfort for hours.

The first hipbelts were unpadded webbing. Today's are complex, multilayered creations of foam, plastic, and even graphite. A good hipbelt is well padded, with two or more layers of foam, at least a half-inch thick. The inner layer should be soft, so that it molds to your hips and absorbs shock; the outer layer should be stiff, so that the belt doesn't distort under the weight of a heavy load. Many companies add a third outer layer of stiff but flexible polypropylene or polyethylene in the belts on their largest packs to minimize twisting under a heavy load. A recent development, used by Gregory, has thermal-molded foam pads that create a hipbelt with a firm conical shape designed to hug the body without sagging.

As always, somebody disagrees with the prevailing wisdom. McHale, a custom pack maker in Seattle, claims stiff belts are uncomfortable and unnecessary; their belts, McHale says, made from Evazote foam with double buckles, wrap round the hips so well that they create their own firm structure. (They do this by being attached to the pack only at the bottom edge, and by being in front of, rather than behind, the lumbar pad, unlike most belts, so the belts mold to the shape of the body.) I haven't used a McHale hipbelt, but they look interesting; I haven't found any problems with conventional, stiffened belts, though.

An unusual way of stiffening the hipbelt comes from Vortex, whose belts have optional inflatable sections and a built-in air pump. I had a pack with an inflatable hipbelt in the early 1970s made by a long-gone British company. It worked well— until it burst. Unlike that pack, Vortex models have padding in the hipbelt as well, and will still be functional in the event of a puncture.

In addition to being thickly padded, a hipbelt should be at least 4 inches wide where it passes over the hips, narrowing toward the buckle. Conical or cupped belts are less likely than straight-cut ones to slip down over the hips; most belts on top-quality packs are shaped. For the heaviest loads, continuous wrap-around belts perform better than those sewn to the side of the pack; again, most top models have these. To provide support for the small of your back, the lower section of the pack should be well padded. This can be a continuation of the hipbelt (as in most external-frame packs), a special lumbar pad (as in most internal frames), or part of a completely padded back. The *lumbar pad* is important for supporting the load and spreading the weight over your lower back and hips. A too-stiff or too-soft lumbar pad can lead to pressure points and sore spots.

Belts that are attached only to the frame or the lumbar pad at or near the small of the back need side stabilizer or *side tension straps* to prevent the pack from swaying. These straps pull the edges of the pack in around the hips, which increases stability. Most internal-frame packs have them. A few models (such as some from Dana Design and Mountainsmith) also have *diagonal compression straps,* which run downward across the side of the pack to the hipbelt and help pull the load onto the hipbelt. They work well.

Many hipbelts are nylon-covered inside and out. Although adequate, a smooth covering like this can make the belt slip when it's worn over smooth, synthetic clothing, a problem that worsens as the load increases. Cordura or other texturized nylon is better; some companies use special high-friction fabrics. These may cover the whole inside of the belt or just the center of the lumbar pad.

Most hipbelt buckles are three-pronged Fastex. These are tough and easy to use, but they can slip. A more-secure buckle traps webbing between two overlapping halves; Kelty uses these. Also good are cam-lock buckles, such as those used by McHale.

Hipbelt size is important. The padded part of the belt should extend at least 2½ inches in front of the hipbone, and after you tighten the belt there should be enough webbing left on either side of the buckle to allow for weight loss on a long trek, and for adjustments over different thicknesses of clothing. Most packs come with permanent hipbelts, so you have to check the size when you buy. Packs that come in two or three sizes often have correspondingly sized belts. Companies that make packs with removable belts may offer a choice of belt sizes—as do Dana Design, Gregory, Kelty, and McHale. Such modular systems are the best way to achieve the optimum fit, especially if you're not an "average" size.

How big a belt you need depends on the weight you intend to carry. I've found that moderately padded belts handle loads up to 40 pounds adequately. Heavier loads, however, cause these belts to compress and press painfully on the hipbones, or they twist out of shape, making it difficult to put most of the load on the hips. For big loads, wide hipbelts with thick layers of padding and stiffened flexible reinforcements on the outside work well. My current favorite is the Dana Design Contour Hipbelt. I've carried 60-pound loads for weeks at a time using this belt and never had bruised or sore hips.

Finally, consider what you wear *under* a hipbelt as well, because this will be pressed against your skin. Pants with thick side seams, belt loops, rivets, and zippered pockets can rub painfully. Wide, elasticized waistbands or bib styles are better. If you do find a sore point under a hipbelt, check to see if it's caused by your clothing before you curse the pack.

Shoulder Straps

Most of the time, shoulder straps do little more than stop the pack from falling off your back.

However, because there are times when you have to carry all or some of the weight on your shoulders (for example, river crossings when you've undone the hipbelt for safety, and rock scrambles and downhill ski runs where for balance you've fully tightened all the straps to split the weight between shoulders and hips), these straps need to be foam-filled and tapered to keep the padding from slipping. This design is now standard on most good packs. Many straps are also curved so that they run neatly under the arms without twisting. For fit, the distance between the shoulder straps at the top is key.

Shoulder Stabilizer Straps

Packs designed for moderate to heavy loads (30 pounds and up) should have shoulder stabilizer straps (sometimes called top tension, load-balancing, or load-lifter straps) running from the top of the shoulder straps to the pack. These straps pull the load in over your shoulders to increase stability, and lift the shoulder straps off the sensitive nerves around the collarbone, transferring the weight to the much-tougher shoulder blades. By loosening or tightening the straps, which can be done while walking, you can shift the weight of the pack between the hips and the shoulders to find the most comfortable position for the terrain you're on.

On most packs, these straps are sewn to the shoulder straps, which means that altering the tension of one changes the other; so when you tighten the top tension straps for better stability, you also pull the shoulder straps down onto your shoulders. If they then feel too tight, you slacken off, which also loosens the top tension straps and causes the pack to fall backward. To maintain stability, you tighten the top tension straps. Repeating the process over and over can mean that by the end of the day the top tension straps can be at their minimum length, and therefore not as effective as they should be, while the shoulder straps have crept down your back and the shoulder-strap buckles are pinching your armpits. I've always put up with this, trying to get the adjustment about right at the start of the day and keeping any alterations to the minimum. Even so, I end some days with a pack that is very badly adjusted. Now there may be a simple solution to this problem in the form of McHale's Bypass shoulder system, in which the stabilizer straps aren't sewn to the shoulder straps. This means the shoulder straps can slide along the stabilizers when adjusted without the latter moving at all. I expect to see similar systems on other packs.

Sternum Straps

Sternum, or chest straps, are found on most packs, attached to buckles or webbing on the shoulder straps. These straps pull the shoulder straps into the chest and help to stabilize the pack. I don't use them all the time but find them helpful when skiing or scrambling, and for varying the pressure points of a heavy load during a long ascent. Most are simple webbing straps, but some have stretch sections that prevent over-tightening. Fully elasticized straps can't be tightened at all and are useless. Sternum straps can be purchased separately if they aren't a standard feature on your pack.

Pads and Padding

In addition to a padded hipbelt and lumbar pad, most packs have padded backs. If the entire back isn't padded, then the shoulder straps should run far enough down the back to protect the shoulder blades. As much of the pack never contacts the wearer's back directly, over-padding is unnecessary; too little, though, and sharp objects can poke you in the back.

External frames need something to hold the frame off the back, usually a wide band of tensioned nylon; mesh is better for ventilation than solid nylon. The tensioning cord or wire should be easy to tighten if it works loose.

FITTING THE PACK

Modern packs are so complex that you can't just walk into a store, sling one on your back, and walk away. A good pack must be fitted, and it is important that this is done properly. A poorly fitted pack will prove unstable, uncomfortable, and so painful and inefficient that you may never want to go backpacking again. The best way to avoid this is to buy from a store with expert staff who can fit the pack for you.

If you don't want to take the time to fit a pack properly and adjust it as necessary while walking, choose a simple, non-adjustable rucksack with a padded back, or a basic external-frame pack that needs less fitting. Rucksacks usually come in only one length, while traditional external frames often come in two or three sizes. A precise fit isn't essential (or indeed possible). Find a pack whose shoulder straps join the pack roughly level with your shoulders when the hipbelt is taking most of the weight comfortably on your hips. However, such packs can't compare to the comfort more sophisticated models offer for heavy loads and rough terrain.

The first task in fitting a pack is to find the right *frame size*. This can be done initially by finding the size the maker says is right for your height. You should be wary, however: It's *back (torso) length* rather than overall height that matters. I'm 5 feet 8 inches tall, but I have a long torso; packs designed for a taller person fit me perfectly.

The key measurement for fitting a pack is the distance between the top of your shoulders and

An adjustable harness system—this is Lowe Alpine's APS in a women's fit.

The most common way to achieve a good fit with an internal-frame pack (and some externals) is with an *adjustable harness,* which allows the shoulder straps to be moved up and down the back of the pack. On a few packs, such as those from vauDe, the positions of both the shoulder straps and hipbelt are adjustable. Hipbelt adjustments change the position of the base of the pack in relation to your body, which causes the load to press on the backside when the effective back length is shortened, and to ride too high on the back when it is lengthened. Both interfere with stability and comfort, so hipbelt adjustments should be made only in conjunction with shoulder-strap adjustments.

Lowe Alpine was first with an adjustable shoulder harness system. In its much-copied Parallux system, the shoulder straps are fitted into slots in a webbing column sewn down the center of the pack's back. Variations employ hook-and-loop straps or a slotted, plastic adjustment "ladder." These systems demand some fiddling; easier are stepless systems that use a locking slider, screw, or similar device to slide the shoulder straps up and down the central column. Even simpler are systems in which the shoulder straps are attached to a stiffened plastic yoke that slides up and down the stays; these can be adjusted while wearing the pack by simply pulling on two straps attached to the base of the plate. Whichever you choose, find the right length for your back and then forget about it.

Some companies, notably Dana Design, argue that adjustable backs are a compromise in packs designed for heavy loads, so instead they produce several size frames. Thus, the crucial distance between the hipbelt and the shoulder straps is always correct—you just have to make sure you get the right size. I bought my Dana Astralplane by mail order and I got it wrong the first time. The company quickly exchanged my pack,

your upper hipbone. This is because the hipbelt should ride with its upper edge ¾ to 1 inch above the hipbone, so that the weight is borne by the broadest, strongest part of the hips when the shoulder straps are in their correct position. Most pack makers tell you how to measure your back length and which of their frame sizes go with which back lengths. Pay attention to this. A correctly sized internal frame should extend 2 to 4 inches above your shoulders.

All packs come with fitting instructions, some more detailed than others. Instructions differ according to the specifications of the suspension system, of course, but there are some general principles that I'll outline here.

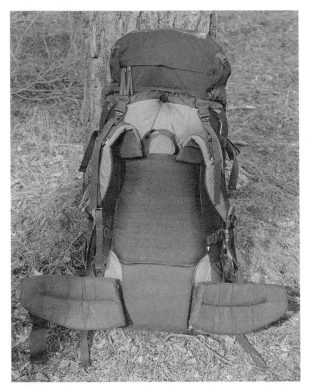

Fixed-length back systems like this one from Dana Design come in different sizes.

however, and I've found the Arcflex the most comfortable suspension system I've used.

For more advanced fitting, some manufacturers advise removing the stays of internal frames and bending them to the shape of your back before you start fitting the pack, but I've never been able to do this successfully, and pre-bent stays are the devil to reinsert in their sleeves.

Obviously, any system has a limited range over which it can be adjusted. At either end of this range a pack won't carry as well as it does if adjusted to a position nearer the middle. To overcome this, many manufacturers offer packs with different-length internal frames and a shorter back adjustment range than in packs with just one frame size. (Dana Design's ArcLight and Killer B packs fall into this category.)

Before you try on a pack, load it with at least 35 pounds of gear (most stores will have items available for this) and loosen all the straps. The next stage is to put the pack on and do up the hipbelt until it is carrying all the weight and the upper edge rides about an inch above the top of your hipbone. Next, adjust in the hipbelt stabilizer straps. Then tighten the shoulder straps and pull in the shoulder stabilizer straps. These should leave the shoulder straps at a point roughly level with or just in front of your collar bone, at an angle between 20 and 45 degrees (roughly level with your ears). If the angle is smaller than that, the harness needs lengthening; if it is larger, it needs shortening. The aim is to achieve a back length whereby most of the pack weight rides on the hips and the pack hugs the back to provide stability. Too short a back length causes the weight to pull back and down on the shoulders; too long, and—although the weight will be on the hips—the top of the pack will be unstable and will sway when you walk.

Once you find the right back length, most of your fitting problems are over. The shoulder straps themselves should curve over your shoulders a couple of inches before joining the pack. The lower buckles should be several inches below the armpits, but with enough webbing to allow for adjustment over different thicknesses of clothing.

Finally, make sure the sternum strap is in its correct position, just above the part of your chest that expands most when you breathe.

You know when you have a good fit by the way the pack carries when you walk. It should feel snug and body-hugging, almost as if it's been stuck to you. If it feels awkward or uncomfortable, keep adjusting until you get it right, or until you decide that this particular pack will never fit you correctly.

Once I have the best fit I can obtain with an internal-frame pack, I usually bend over and

Fitting the pack. 1. Adjust the back length. 2. The top tension straps should be at an angle of 25 to 40 degrees. Note how the shoulder straps wrap over the shoulders. The top of the frame should be 1½ to 2 inches above the shoulders. For maximum stability, the top tension straps should be pulled tight. 3. The top of the hipbelt should ride about an inch above your top hipbone. Tighten the side tension straps to pull in the load around the hips for maximum stability. This should be done each time you put on your pack.

stretch the pack on my back so that the frame can start to mold to my shape, a process that is usually complete after the first day's walk.

Minute adjustments to the harness will be necessary every time you use the pack. Loosening the top stabilizer straps, tightening the shoulder straps, then retightening the stabilizers cinches the pack to the body for maximum stability, but it also shifts some of the load onto the shoulders. This is necessary for steep descents or when skiing or crossing rough ground—anywhere balance is essential. For straightforward ascents and walking on the flat, the shoulder and stabilizer straps can be slackened off a touch so that all the weight drops onto the hips, after which the stabilizers should be tightened a little again until you can just slide a finger between the shoulder and the shoulder straps.

Every time you put on the pack you have to loosen the side stabilizer straps, then tighten

them after you've done up the hipbelt—otherwise the latter won't grip properly. While on the move, whenever the pack doesn't feel quite right or you can feel a pressure point developing, adjust the straps to shift the balance of the load slightly until it feels right again. I do this frequently during the day, almost unaware that I'm doing it.

If you want or need a custom fit, McHale, which sells through its own store or by mail order, will make a pack to your measurements. If you always seem to be between sizes with fixed-length packs, or at the ends of the adjustment systems of adjustable ones, a McHale pack might be the answer.

Women's Packs

Although makers don't usually say so, most packs are designed for the "average" man. However, women normally have shorter torsos, narrower shoulders, and wider hips than men do.

This means that men's packs usually have frames that are too long (leading to an unstable carry and too much weight on the shoulders), overly wide shoulder straps that slide off and have to be held in place by a tight sternum strap, and hipbelts that dig in at the lower edge and don't touch at the top.

Since the 1980s, packs specifically designed for women have become available from several companies (including Gregory, McHale, Lowe Alpine, The North Face, Osprey, and Kelty). On these designs, the shoulder straps are closer together, the frames are shorter, and the hipbelts are angled to suit women's hips. On some, like those from Gregory, the cant of the hipbelt is adjustable for fine-tuning the fit. Companies that don't make women's packs may offer shoulder straps in several sizes, hipbelts with different degrees of flare, plus different frame lengths.

Do these packs make a difference? My partner, Denise Thorn, a backpacker and hiker for many years, says they do. After over a decade of using "standard" packs, she tried one with a shorter frame and found it far more comfortable than any she'd used previously. Since then, she's found some fit her well, while others don't. The angle of the hipbelt seems to be a key: Belts with little flare are prone to pressing down on the hip, while those that are more angled (even if they are less padded) distribute weight more efficiently. The ones that do fit, she says, are far better than any man's pack.

PACKBAGS

Compared with the intricacies of frame and suspension systems, packbag design is straightforward. The choice is purely personal—the type of packbag you have has little effect on the comfort of your pack when it's on your back. How many pockets, compartments, and external attachment points you want depends on how you like to pack and the bulkiness of your gear. Tidy folk like packs with plenty of pockets and at least two compartments so they can organize their gear. Those less neat tend to go for large, single-compartment monsters into which everything can be shoved quickly.

There are a couple of points to consider, however. To maintain balance and comfortable posture, the load needs to be as close to your center of gravity as possible. This means keeping it near to your back and as high up as is feasible without reducing stability. While a good suspension system is the key to this, a packbag that extends upward, and perhaps out at the sides but not away from the back, helps. For this reason, if your pack has large rear pockets, you should only pack light items in them. Indeed, I used to avoid packs with such pockets, but my current Dana Design Astralplane has them, and I find that if I pack them with light items such as hats, gloves, and windshirts they don't affect the carry. Many packs have a strap running across the packbag at the top. When tightened, this strap pulls the load in toward the back. They work well and I look for one on a large pack.

The packbag is an integral part of an internal-frame pack—the frame may be embedded in a foam-padded back, encased in sleeves, or just attached at the top and bottom of the bag. Whatever the method, the frame and pack work together and cannot be used separately. Packbags may be attached to external frames in various ways, but the most common is with clevis pins and split rings. One frame conceivably could be used with several different packbags (although I know of no backpacker who does this).

Size

How large a packbag is necessary is a matter of some controversy among backpackers. I seem to be in the minority—I say "big is best," preferring packs that *Backpacker* magazine has called "load monsters." I like to pack everything (including my insulating mat when possible) inside the pack, and I like to know I can cram everything in quickly and easily, even in the dark after the tent has just blown down in a storm. Those who favor small packs say that a large pack equals a heavy pack because you'll always fill it up. I say this clearly applies only to the weak-willed! If I had only one pack, it would be the largest model I could find. A large pack cinched down when half full is far more comfortable than an over-loaded small one.

Packs in the 5,500- to 8,000-cubic-inch range suit me fine for long hikes in remote wilderness and winter expeditions; 3,500 to 5,000 cubic inches is adequate for summer weekends and lightweight trips. Note, though, that different manufacturers seem to have different ideas of what constitutes a cubic inch, so one maker's 6,000-cubic-inch pack may carry less than another's 4,500-cubic-inch model.

One advantage of internal-frame packs is that they usually have *compression straps* on the sides or front that you can pull in to hold the load close to the back when the pack isn't full. Traditional, external-frame packs lack these, though they do appear on some new designs. Packs with compression straps and removable, *extendible lids* are often specified with maximum and minimum capacities; to achieve maximum volume may require raising the lid so high that the top of the pack becomes unstable, so it's wise to check this before you buy.

External-frame packbags that run the length of the frame tend to be very large, with capacities up to 8,000 cubic inches. The more common three-quarter-length bags can have capacities as small as 2,500 cubic inches, though most average around 4,000 cubic inches. Extra gear (sleeping mat, tent, sleeping bag) can be strapped under the packbag without affecting how the pack carries, and, if necessary, even more gear can be

lashed on top. However, *if you strap extra gear under or above an internal-frame pack, you ruin its balance and fit.* Therefore, for carrying loads of differing size, a three-quarter-length packbag on an external frame is as versatile as an internal-frame pack with compression straps. If you need to carry a really awkward load, you can remove the packbag from an external frame and replace it with whatever you have to carry.

Internal Compartments

Most large packs come with zippered lower compartments, though packs with one huge compartment are still available. I used to prefer the latter because the lower compartments usually were too small and the zippers too short. Over the years, though, compartments have been designed larger, and zippers now run around the packbag or curve down to the lower edges, providing easy entry. I now prefer two-compartment packs because they provide better access to my load. Since the material separating the two compartments is held in place by a zipper or drawcord on most packs and can be removed to create a single compartment, I see no reason for not having the option. A few pack makers offer packs with more than two compartments, though I suspect this would make packing difficult.

Lids and Closures

You need to be able to cinch down the lid of your pack easily, both to keep the contents in and to prevent them from moving around. Most pack-bags have large lids, sometimes with elasticized edges for a closer fit, that close with two straps fastened by quick-release buckles. These are easy to use and a great improvement over the cord-and-toggle fastening still found on some external-frame packs.

Some packbags have a *floating lid* that attaches to the back of the pack by straps, and can be extended upward over a large load or tightened down over a small one. (A similar, though less-effective design is a lid that extends when you release the straps, but is sewn to the back of the packbag. When the lid is fully extended, it tends to restrict head movement, interferes with easy access to the lid pocket, and fails to cover the load.)

Most detachable lids contain large pockets (up to 1,260 cubic inches) and can be used as fanny packs or even small daypacks by rearranging the straps or using ones provided for that purpose. They can be useful for carrying odds and ends (film, hat, gloves, binoculars) for short strolls away from camp. I've used a detachable pack lid as a daypack for day-long treks away from camp, managing to pack in rain gear, warm clothing, and other essentials.

The lower compartments of packs are always closed by zippers. Extra, buckled straps that close over the zipper protect it from too much pressure and reduce the likelihood of it bursting. This has never happened to me, but I still like large zippers, whether they are toothed or coil; lightweight zippers, protected by straps or not, worry me. Top compartments usually close with two drawcords, one around the main body of the pack, which holds the load in, and one on the lighter-weight extension, which completely covers the load when pulled in. The only access to the load is through the top opening, so items packed at the bottom of the top compartment cannot be reached easily. (A vertical or diagonal zipper in the main body is a feature now available on many of the largest packbags. I find it useful, especially in bad weather, when I can extract the tent, including the poles, through the open zipper without unpacking other gear, opening the main lid, or letting in much rain or snow.)

Not long ago, many packs had zip-around front panels for suitcase-type loading, which gave access to the whole interior of the pack-bag. This was less than ideal for backpacking, because the pack had to be laid down to pack and unpack—not a good idea in the rain, or on mud or snow. A less-than-full load couldn't be pulled tight either, and it would move around in the pack. Panel-loading bags are now primarily for general-travel packs, though Gregory uses the design on the new Evolution external-frame packs, as does JanSport on many of its externals.

Many of the largest packs, however, have both top- and panel-loading main compartments. This has the advantages of both, and is an alternative to the main-compartment zippers. I would look for one or the other in any pack of more than 5,000-cubic-inch capacity.

Pockets

Pockets increase the capacity of a pack and are useful for stowing small, easily mislaid items and those that may be needed during the day. Lid pockets are found on virtually all packs except traditional external-frame models. The best pockets are large and have either curved zippers or zippers that run around the sides; some packs also have a second flat pocket in the lid for storing documents, money, permits, and similar items, accessible through an external or internal zipper.

External-frame packs usually come with one, two, or (rarely) three fixed pockets on each side. Internal-frame packs, usually designed for mountaineering as well as backpacking, usually don't have fixed side pockets, since these can get in the way when climbing. Instead, they may feature detachable side pockets, which attach to the compression straps and add 500 to 1,000 cubic inches per pair to the pack's capacity, and 7 to 12 ounces to the weight. I like these—they can be removed if I want to reduce the capacity of the pack, or if I want to use the pack for skiing or scrambling, when side pockets are a nuisance. Some side pockets have backs stiffened with a synthetic plate, which makes them slightly easier to pack, but also heavier. A few makers also offer large pockets that can be attached to the back of packs.

An alternative to a detachable pocket is an integral, pleated side pocket with side-zipper entry, which folds flat when not used. I've found pleated pockets more difficult to use than detachable pockets. They are narrow at the top and bottom and can be impeded by compression straps. They can impinge on the volume of the main compartment when full, as well. And you still have to carry the weight of the material when the pockets aren't needed. On the other hand, they are always there when you need them—you can't forget one.

Packs without side pockets usually have open pockets at the base of each side. These are known as *wand pockets* and are designed to hold the ends of long, thin items such as tent poles, hiking poles, or skis. Wand pockets are usually permanently attached; some, like those from McHale, are detachable and can be replaced with a larger open pocket that will hold a quart water bottle. Some wand pockets have elasticized edges and can be stretched to take a small water bottle. I often carry a map in the wand pocket for easy access.

Straps and Patches

Side compression straps can be used for attaching skis and other long items (walking sticks, tripods, tent poles, foam pads) as well as pockets. Most packbags come with one or two sets of straps for ice axes, and straps (and maybe a reinforced panel) for crampons on the lid. If straps don't come with the pack, there are usually several patches provided so you can thread your own. Many packs come with far too many exterior fastenings, but you can always cut off those you'll never use.

MATERIALS

Modern packs are made from a variety of coated nylons and polyesters; cotton canvas bags have disappeared. The synthetics are hard-wearing, light, non-absorbent, and flexible. *Texturized nylons*—made from a bulked filament that creates a durable, abrasion-resistant fabric—are often used for the pack base or bottom, sometimes with a layer of lighter nylon inside; some makers use this fabric for the whole packbag. The most common is Cordura, though a few companies have their own proprietary fabrics. *Packcloth* is a smoother, lighter nylon often used for the main body of the pack. All of these materials are strong and long-lasting.

The weight of fabric is a major part of the weight of a pack, so one way to keep the weight down is to look for lightweight fabrics. Packcloth and 500 denier Cordura are lighter than 1,000 denier Cordura, but not by enough to make a big difference in weight. There are, though, some *really* lightweight fabrics available. For small packs up to 2,500 cubic inches, *ripstop nylon* is adequate, but it's not stiff or strong enough for larger models. One fabric that is strong is *Spectra Cloth,* used by Kelty and McHale to make very light large packs—4-ounce Spectra Cloth is claimed to be both stronger and more abrasion resistant than 12-ounce 1,000 denier Cordura. With it, Kelty makes a 6,475-cubic-inch internal-frame pack, the White Phantom, that weighs just 3 pounds 1 ounce, and a 4,050-cubic-inch pack, the White Cloud, that weighs a mere 2 pounds 13 ounces. Unfortunately, there are penalties for these low weights: Spectra Cloth is very expensive (the White Phantom costs well over twice as much as a similar design made from packcloth; McHale packs increase in price by 50 percent for a Spectra model), and it's available in white only—it can't be dyed.

The North Face Alpine Light ultralight pack, front and back views.

There is a new, less-robust but much less-expensive fabric that could well appear in many packs in the future: *Dynamous,* a Kevlar-reinforced polyester that's half the weight of 500 denier fabric. It was apparently developed for snowboarding suits. The North Face utilizes it in two stripped-down, frameless Alpine packs designed for mountaineering: a 3,355-cubic-inch pack weighing 2 pounds 7 ounces (the Alpine Light), and a 4,270-cubic-inch pack weighing 2 pounds 12 ounces (the Himalayan Light). These weights reflect the minimalist design and suspension system as well as the fabric; I've tried the Alpine Light and found it adequate for loads

up to 30 pounds. At present, however, these packs are available only in Europe, which seems astonishing given that The North Face is an American company. If you're interested in these ultralight packs, I'd suggest writing to the company and asking why you can't buy them in the United States. These packs will be of interest only to ultralight backpackers due to the lack of a frame and the minimal hipbelt.

While most of these modern fabrics are fairly waterproof when new, the coating that makes them so is usually soon abraded, and the seams will leak in heavy rain, even if taped. Some manufacturers advise coating the seams with sealant, but the process is too involved for me to even contemplate. I rely on liners and covers (discussed later in this chapter) to keep the contents of the pack dry.

Weight

For many years I used a large, heavy, complex pack for all my backpacking, thinking that the pack was the one item of gear whose weight wasn't of major significance. I'm not quite so convinced of this now. For loads of 50 pounds and more, a pack with a sophisticated suspension system is certainly far more comfortable than one with a more basic design, despite the extra weight. With loads over 30 pounds, I find a framed pack more comfortable than a frameless one. Looking through the current catalogs, it seems that most packs weigh at least a pound for every 1,000 cubic inches of capacity—about 62 cubic inches per ounce. Many packs are heavier. The heaviest I've come across is a 5,700-cubic-inch external-frame model that weighs just an ounce under 9 pounds—only 40 cubic inches per ounce. But a standard 6,000-cubic-inch internal-frame pack I had in 1982 weighed less than 5 pounds.

Why have packs gotten heavier? More complex frames, thicker padding, heavier fabrics— which most packs are still made from, detachable pockets, detachable lids, more straps, zippers and buckles—all of these add weight. Are heavy packs necessary? Well, it depends on the weight of your load. Carrying 70 pounds on a winter trip requires a tough pack with a supportive suspension system. The 30-pound load you carry for a summer weekend or a lightweight, long-distance summer trail hike doesn't require the same ruggedness or support. If you like to walk in to a scenic campsite, stay a few days, then walk out, a few extra pounds hardly matter. However, for the distance hiker intent on a through-hike

of a long trail or on a climb, every ounce saved is important.

A good rule of thumb for estimating pack weight is that the pack shouldn't weigh more than 10 percent of the maximum total load likely to be carried in it: For a 70-pound winter load, a 7-pound pack is acceptable, but for a 30-pound summer load, a 3-pound pack would be better. (Of course, if you use the same pack year-round, as many backpackers do, the 7-pound pack would have to be adjusted for the 30-pound load.)

Acceptable weight can be roughly determined by the volume-to-weight ratio—divide the capacity by the weight in ounces. The average ratio for most modern packs is 60 to 65 cubic inches per ounce, so any figure lower than this means the pack is heavy for the capacity. There are enough packs in the 70- to 90-cubic-inch-per-ounce range to make it worthwhile seeking one of these out if weight is critical. Packs above 90 cubic inches per ounce are stripped-down, frameless packs, or made from expensive, lightweight Spectra Cloth. (Another quick calculation is to allow 1 pound of weight for every 1,000 cubic inches of capacity: A 5-pound something ounce, 5,000-cubic-inch pack is about average.)

I still count durability and support as the crucial factors for carrying heavy loads, though. When you're humping 60 pounds or more, a pound or two of additional pack weight is worth it if you get a more comfortable carry. However, for lighter loads, especially ones under 40 pounds, I look for packs with a volume-to-weight ratio of about 75 cubic inches per ounce or better.

DURABILITY

Top-quality packs are very tough, but many won't last for a walk of several months. I've suffered broken internal frames, snapped shoulder straps, and ripped-out hipbelts on long hikes. On my first solo walk in 1976 along the Pennine Way in England, the hipbelt tore off my new external-frame pack after just 200 miles. But I've also had packs last 2,000 miles and 4½ months of continuous use with loads averaging 60 to 70 pounds. My old Gregory Cassin, now discontin-ued, survived a three-month Yukon walk with a similar load when it was five years old, and had already been on several two- to four-week hikes, as well as numerous weekend walks. The only damage was to the top of one framestay sleeve, which ripped out. (A bandage of duct tape held it in place for the rest of the walk.) This degree

Packs: My Choices

My ideal pack for heavy loads would have a suspension system that enabled me to carry 75 pounds as though they were 30; would be superbly stable for skiing and crossing steep, rough ground; and would allow me to walk upright on the flat. Internal or external frame? I don't care! It's the performance, not the type of frame, that matters.

I would want a packbag with a capacity of at least 6,000 cubic inches; two compartments; detachable side pockets; an extendible, detach-able lid with a large pocket; and straps for ice axes and skis. The total unloaded weight shouldn't be more than 4 pounds. This pack would also see me through a 3,000-mile, six-month walk without anything breaking!

However, I backpack regularly with friends who don't like side pockets or lower compart-ments, and others who never use skis or ice axes. One trail companion swears that traditional external frames carry heavy loads better, despite having used top-quality packs for snow travel, where he concedes internals are better for bal-ance. Not everyone would want my ideal.

I haven't yet found my ideal large pack, but the Dana Design Astralplane comes close. It's cer-tainly more comfortable with a 70-pound load than any other pack I've tried, and also very stable. It's a bit heavy, but I've no other com-plaints. I can't say I've found anything approach-ing an ideal lightweight pack in the 3,000- to 4,000-cubic-inch range. The North Face Alpine Light comes closest—but it could do with a bet-ter hipbelt. Because weight is critical here—40 pounds would be the most I'd carry in such a

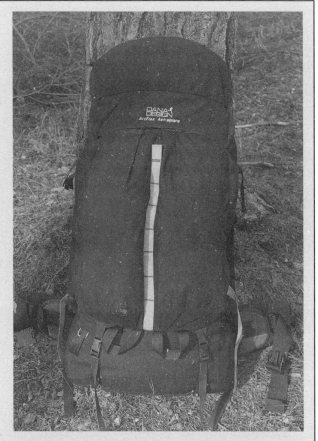

The Dana Design Astralplane—a 7,000-cubic-inch internal-frame pack—the author's favorite.

pack—4 pounds is the maximum weight for such a pack; I'd prefer one under 3 pounds. If it wasn't so expensive, the Kelty White Phantom would be a good choice.

of use is comparable to years, if not decades, of backpacking for those who, like most people, go out for several weekends a month and perhaps a couple of two- or three-week trips a year.

Of the three people I know who hiked all or most of the Pacific Crest Trail the same year I did, each one broke at least one pack. After months of constant use and harsh treatment, it seems something is almost bound to fail, which is hardly surprising when you consider how complex a modern pack is and how much can go wrong. The heavier the load, the more strain on the pack—another reason for keeping the load weight down.

Crude repairs can, and often must, be made to equipment in the field, but I'm loath to continue backpacking in remote country with a pack that has begun to show signs of wearing out, at least not before it's had a factory overhaul. After replacing broken packs at great expense in both time and money on my Pacific Crest Trail and Continental Divide walks, I had a spare pack ready and waiting when I set off on the 1988 length of the Canadian Rockies walk. On that hike, I replaced my pack early because it wasn't able to carry the weight. The replacement pack broke two weeks before the end of the trek, and I had to nurse it, bandaged with tape, to the finish. Perhaps I'm unlucky or particularly rough with packs, but I plan to have a spare pack for future lengthy ventures and would advise anyone else to do the same.

Reputable pack makers stand behind their products and most will replace or repair packs quickly if you explain the situation, though this isn't much comfort if you're days away from the nearest phone when your pack fails. Even a spare pack is no good until you can pick it up. It's important to be able to effect at least crude repairs; items to carry in a repair kit are covered in Chapter 8.

PACKING

Where you pack gear in your pack depends on the sort of hiking you are doing, and which items you're likely to need during the day. For walking on level ground on well-maintained trails, heavy, low-bulk items should be packed high and near to your back to keep the load close to your center of gravity and to enable you to maintain an upright stance. For any activity where balance is important, such as scrambling, bushwhacking, cross-country hiking on steep, rough ground, or skiing, the heavy, low-bulk items should be packed lower for better stability, though still as close to your back as possible. Women tend to have a lower center of gravity than men do, and they may find packing like this leads to a more comfortable carry for trail hiking, too. Whatever packing method, it's important that the load is stable. The items you'll need during the day should be accessible, and you should know where everything is.

I normally use a packbag with side or rear pockets, lid pocket, and lower compartment, so my packing system is based on this design. I don't like anything on the outside except winter hardware (ice ax and skis), and a closed-cell sleeping mat; everything else goes inside, and I pack most items in individual stuff sacks to keep everything organized.

The first thing to go into the lower compartment is the sleeping bag (in an oversize stuff sack inside a pack liner); this fills out the corners and enables an internal-frame pack to wrap around the hips. Next go my spare clothes (in another stuff sack) and my rain gear, which pads any unfilled spaces and is accessible if it rains. If I'm carrying a bivouac bag, it too goes in the lower compartment. I slide tent poles down one side of the upper compartment next to my back, and, if they are very long, through the cutaway corner of the lower compartment floor. Down the back of the pack goes my Therm-a-Rest mattress, folded into three sections. This protects it from abrasion and anything piercing the pack, which is unlikely. It also ensures that hard objects can't protrude into my back, which can be a problem with packs that don't have a plastic framesheet.

In the bottom of the top compartment I put cooking pans; stove and fuel; and small items such as candles, boot wax, and repair kit, with the heaviest items (such as full fuel bottles) close to my back. Once I have removed my lunch and the day's trail snacks, next to go in the top compartment is my food bag or bags, which I put toward the back of the pack because they're heavy. In front of the food bags go the tent, separated into two stuff sacks, and my camp footwear. At the top of the pack I put books, spare maps, perhaps a second camera, and, if there's room, a windshirt or warm top I've been wearing while packing to ward off the early morning chill. If I can't fit this in the top of the pack, I squeeze it into the lower compartment.

The lid pocket is filled, in no particular order, with hat, neck gaiter, gloves, mitts, writing materials (in a nylon pouch), tube of sunscreen, camera accessories bag, insect repellent, thermometer, and any small items that have escaped packing elsewhere. When I'm using a pack with side or rear pockets, one of them holds water containers and food for the day; the other holds fuel bottles if I'm using a white-gas or alcohol stove, plus tent stakes, headlamp, and first aid kit. Any items that didn't fit into the lid pocket or that I've overlooked also go in an outside pocket.

If I'm using a fanny pack around my waist, I carry in it the relevant map, compass, mini binoculars, camera lenses, dark glasses, and perhaps gloves and hat. Otherwise, these go in the outside pockets of the pack. My camera, in its padded case, is slung across my body on a padded strap.

Then, once I've shouldered the pack, tightened up the straps, and picked up my staff, I'm ready for the day's walk.

PUTTING ON THE PACK

This action, repeated many times daily, requires a great deal of energy and not a little finesse. With most loads, the easiest way to do it is to lift the pack using the shoulder strap (or the nylon loop attached to the top of the pack back on nearly all models), rest it on your hip, and put the arm on that side through the shoulder strap. With loads of less than 25 or 30 pounds, you can then simply swing the pack onto your back.

With heavy loads (50 pounds or so), I swing the pack onto my bent knee rather than my hip, then from a stooped position I slowly shift, rather than swing, the load onto my back. Heavy loads make me aware of how much energy putting on a pack requires; whenever I stop on the trail, I try to find a rock or bank to rest the pack on so I can back out of and into the harness. Such shelves are rare, though, so I usually sit down, put my arms through the shoulder straps, and then slowly stand up if I feel I haven't the energy to heave the pack onto my back. If there's no other support, my staff props the pack up while I do this. I also try to take the pack on and off less often when it's heavy; I keep items I need for the day in my fanny pack and rest the pack against something when I stop.

In camp, when the pack is not on my back, I sometimes keep it in the tent—if I'm not in bear country and there's room—but usually I leave it outside and put the pack cover over it to protect against precipitation. Items I don't need overnight are left in the pack, whether in or out of the tent.

During rest stops on the trail, the pack can be used as a seat if the ground is cold or wet. One

Putting on a heavy pack.
1. Grab your pack by the top of the shoulder straps.

2. Lift it onto your bent leg.

3. Swing it slowly around . . .

4. . . . onto your back.

5. Tighten all the straps.

6. You're ready to go!

advantage of an external frame is that it can be propped up with a staff and used as a backrest— its rigidity keeps it from twisting out of position and falling over, as happens with most flexible internal-frame packs. This backrest is so comfortable that I've tried to make an internal-frame pack perform the same function, and I've had a measure of success by wedging the staff into the pack's top hand loop. Unexpected collapses occur frequently, however.

PACK CARE

After a trip, I empty the pack, shake out any debris that has accumulated inside, and, if it's wet, hang it up to dry. You can try to remove stains with soap or other cleanser; I regard such marks as adding to the pack's character, and I'm also wary of damaging or weakening the fabric in any way, so I don't bother.

Before a trip, I check all the zippers. I also look for signs of any stitching failure if I didn't do so the last time I used the pack.

PACK ACCESSORIES
Liners and Covers

No pack is waterproof, whatever claims the manufacturer makes about the fabric. Water trickles in through the zippers, wicks along drawcords, seeps through the seams, and, when the waterproofing has worn off, leaks right through the fabric. My answer is to cocoon those items that must be kept dry (down-filled gear, maps, books) in waterproof liners or stuff sacks (ordinary stuff sacks aren't usually waterproof—the seams aren't sealed). In heavy rain, I place a cover over the pack as a backup to the liners.

I don't use a large liner that fills the pack because often there are wet items in the pack (such as the tent fly sheet and rain gear) that I want to separate from dry items. Instead, I place my sleeping bag in its stuff sack inside a waterproof stuff sack or liner and use another liner for clothes. I used to use cheap, lightweight, thick-mil plastic bags, but these tear easily (after a couple of days' use, unless you're lucky), and I became concerned about throwing so many away. For a number of years I used neoprene-coated nylon pack liners with taped seams. They came in 3,000- and 4,275-cubic-inch sizes but aren't easy to find now, because waterproof stuff sacks have replaced them. I now use Black Diamond Sealcoat stuff sacks instead of pack liners; they give better access to gear and are easier to use. They're made from elastomer-coated nylon and have tape-sealed seams. I've used one for my sleeping bag for three years now and it's still waterproof. There are eight sizes. Outdoor Research also offers waterproof stuff sacks with taped seams in seven sizes, and capacities from 300 to 2,500 cubic inches.

I also use a *pack cover*. It's made of urethane-coated nylon and weighs 7 ounces. The elasticized outer edge allows it to cover a wide range of pack shapes and sizes and prevents it from flying off in high winds. I also use it to cover the pack when it's left outside the tent overnight.

The only time I don't take a cover is when I'm carrying skis or an ice ax on the pack, or when I'm visiting an area in which rain is highly unlikely. Covers are widely available from many pack makers.

Fanny Packs

With a lot of equipment in a heavy pack, accessing all the odds and ends that are needed during a day's walk can be difficult; taking off the pack every time you need to check a map, apply sunscreen, nibble some trail mix, or scan the route ahead through your binoculars is simply too much of a chore and requires far too much energy. I often avoided doing these things—preferring to risk sunburn, feel hungry, and wonder if I was really on the right route than to constantly remove and reshoulder the pack—until I began to use a fanny pack. Now I wear a fanny pack or waist pack the wrong way around, and put all these items and more in it.

Fanny packs range from simple ultralight ones of thin nylon, to complex models complete with compartments, pockets, and padded hipbelts. Which you choose depends on how much you will carry and how often you will use it on side trips. Capacities run to as much as 915 cubic inches.

The fanny pack I've used most is just one refinement removed from the most basic design: It has side compression straps, which allow me to pull the pack tightly over any load to prevent movement. Otherwise, this polyurethane-proofed nylon pack is a one-compartment, zip-closed, 4-ounce bag of about 300-cubic-inch capacity with a simple waist strap. I used this one on a Continental Divide walk, and it just survived the full 3,000-mile, six-month trip, finishing with a zipper that kept pulling open and only ragged remnants of waterproofing. But it did the job, and I took another one—which is still in service—on the Canadian Rockies walk. On my Yukon walk, I used a 500-cubic-inch fanny pack with a padded base, zipped front pocket, zipped main compartment, two compression straps, padded hipbelt with side tension straps, and a grab handle. It was made from Cordura and weighed a hefty 10½ ounces. At first I worried that the wide padded belt and large Fastex buckle would feel uncomfortable under my pack, but they didn't. This pack can comfortably carry heavier items, such as camera lenses, than can

the simpler bag. The padded base provides more protection, too. For these reasons, it has become my first choice. Fanny packs are available from most pack makers—the choice is large.

Belt and Shoulder Pouches

Most pack makers and many other outdoor companies offer small zipped pouches and wallets designed to be fitted to the pack hipbelt or shoulder straps. I've tried these and find that they impede putting on and taking off the pack. I prefer a separate fanny pack for carrying small, frequently needed items. However, there are plenty of small pouches, with capacities of a few hundred cubic inches and weights of around 4 ounces, to consider if you're interested.

Duffel Bags

Transporting packs by car usually isn't a problem—you just sling them in the trunk and set off. If you fly, however, your pack is at the mercy of airport baggage handlers, and it can be damaged easily. The airline may ask you to sign a waiver releasing it from any liability for your pack.

The first thing to remember if you fly regularly is that internal frames are less prone to damage than externals. (When I flew home from Los Angeles after a hike, my external-frame pack came off the luggage carousel with a permanent bend and a couple of cracks in the frame.) You can further minimize the chances of damage by tightening all straps, tucking loose ends away, wrapping the hipbelt around the front of the pack and threading it through the ice ax loops or lower compartment compression straps to keep it in place. A long strap or length of thick cord can be wound round the pack and then tied into a loop to give the baggage handlers something to grab. Make sure you have nothing fastened to the outside of the pack.

A duffel bag offers more protection than the above measures. But you'll need a very large duffel bag if you have a large pack. Duffels don't have to be heavy, though; mine, from Dana Design, is called a Travel Pocket. It even doubles as a pack cover. Made of coated Cordura, it has an 8,000-cubic-inch capacity and weighs 28 ounces. I've transported my pack, along with other items, including several ice axes, many times—and nothing has suffered any damage.

You can get duffels that are fully waterproof, ideal for canoeing trips but unnecessary for getting gear from airport to airport, and ones that are padded, which are necessary only if you carry fragile items inside. (I always carry items like cameras, binoculars, and headlamps in my hand luggage.)

A duffel needs a couple of top compression straps, a grab handle, and perhaps a shoulder strap, but that's it. Many pack makers make duffels, as do companies like Eagle Creek, Fish Products, Mark Pack Works, and Sun Dog.

CHAPTER FIVE

Keeping Warm and Dry: Dressing for the Wilderness

A fine rain fell, while higher up the mountain was shrouded in mist. Showers of water dripped from every branch, so that it was not long before I reached the comparatively happy state of being unable to get any wetter. It is the long-drawn-out process of getting wet that is unpleasant, and when saturation point is reached one ceases to care.

—*Snow on the Equator,* H.W. Tilman

When the clouds roll in, the wind picks up, and the first raindrops fall, you need to know that your clothing will protect you from the coming storm. If it doesn't, you may have to stop and make camp early, crawling soggily into your tent and staying there until the skies clear. At the worst, you could find yourself in danger from hypothermia. While the prime purpose of clothing is to keep you warm and dry in wind and rain, it also must keep you warm in camp when the temperature falls below freezing, and cool when the sun shines. Choosing lightweight, low-bulk clothes that do all of this requires care. Before looking at clothing in detail, it's useful to have some understanding of how the body works when exercising, and what bearing this has on clothes.

HEAT LOSS AND HEAT PRODUCTION

The human body is designed for a tropical climate, and it ceases to function if its temperature falls more than a couple of degrees below 98.4°F (37°C). In non-tropical climates, the body needs a covering to maintain that temperature, because the heat it produces is lost to the cooler air. Ideally, clothing should allow a balance between heat loss and heat production, so that we feel neither hot nor cold—easy if we are sitting still on a calm, dry day, regardless of the temperature. Maintaining this balance when we alternate sitting still with varying degrees of activity in a range of air temperatures and conditions is much more difficult: when active the body creates heat and moisture, which has to be dispersed, but it seeks to conserve heat when exercise stops.

The body loses heat in four ways, which determine how clothing has to function to keep the body's temperature at an equilibrium:

Convection, the transfer of heat from the body to the air, is the major cause of heat loss. It occurs whenever the air is cooler than the body, which is most of the time. The rate of heat loss increases in proportion to air motion—once air begins to move over the skin (and through your clothing), it

> **Entering the Wilderness**
>
> The switchbacks ease. Suddenly we are in the defile surmounting the pass, gazing upon a wild new horizon. Below sprawls a tangle of bare rocky spurs and lake-strewn benches, split by curving valleys that gradually darken into green forest as they sink toward the black slash of a deeper, wider canyon. Beyond that, waves of rugged peaks are dotted with small white glaciers and remnant patches of snow. There is no mark of human hand. This is what we have come to find.

can whip body warmth away at an amazing rate. To prevent this, clothing must cut out the flow of air over the skin; that is, it must be windproof.

Conduction is the transfer of heat from one surface to another. All materials conduct heat, some better than others. Air conducts heat poorly, so the best protection against conductive heat loss is clothing that traps and holds air in its fibers. Indeed, the trapped air is what keeps you warm; the fabrics just hold it in place. Water, however, is a good heat conductor, so if the clothing next to your skin is wet, you will cool down rapidly. This means that clothing has to keep rain and snow out, which isn't difficult—the problem is that clothing must also transmit perspiration to the outer air to keep you dry, known as *breathability*, or moisture-vapor transmission.

Evaporation occurs when body moisture is transformed into vapor—a process that requires heat. During vigorous exercise, the body can respire as much as a quart of liquid an hour through the skin. Clothing must transport it away quickly so that it doesn't use up body heat. Wearing garments that can be ventilated easily, espe-

cially at the neck, is as important as wearing breathable materials through which moisture vapor can pass.

Radiation is the passing of heat directly between two objects without warming the intervening space. It is the way the sun heats the earth (and us on hot, clear days). Radiation requires a direct pathway, so wearing clothes—especially clothing that is tightly woven and smooth-surfaced—solves most of that problem.

THE LAYER SYSTEM

As if keeping out rain while expelling sweat and trapping heat while preventing the body from overheating were not enough, clothing for walkers also must be lightweight, durable, low in bulk, quick-drying, easy to care for, and it must perform in a variety of weather conditions. The usual solution is to wear several light layers of clothing on the torso and arms (legs require less protection), which can be adjusted to suit the conditions and activity. The *layer system* is versatile and efficient if used properly, which means constantly opening and closing zippers and cuff fastenings, and removing or adding layers. I also use layers on my legs, hands, and head in severe conditions.

A typical modern layer system consists of an inner layer of thin, synthetic wicking material that removes moisture from the skin, a thicker fleece mid-layer to trap air and provide insulation, and a waterproof/breathable outer shell to keep out wind and rain while allowing perspiration to pass through. Alternative or additional layers could be a thin shirt or sweater over underwear; a windproof shell for dry, windy conditions; and a down- or synthetic-insulation-filled garment for camp and rest stops in cold weather. If the weather will be wet as well as cold, another

Worst-Case Plan

I came close to finding my own worst-case plan inadequate when I spent a week battling through the high winds, lashing rain, and melting snow of an Icelandic June. I had with me a wicking, synthetic T-shirt; a thin, wicking synthetic shirt; a thin, low-loft polyester-insulated sweater; a single-layer synthetic windshirt; and a waterproof/breathable rain jacket—but I was barely warm enough when walking, because the shell layer couldn't cope with the wet, cold conditions, and I was permanently damp. Luckily, I'd taken a vapor-barrier suit as backup, so I was able to stay warm in camp, but a thicker warm layer would have been a welcome addition.

pile or fleece jacket could substitute for the latter garment. On trips where a wide range of weather conditions could be expected, the layers might include thin underwear, a medium-weight shirt, warm top, windproof top, waterproof top, and insulated top—six layers in all.

How many layers you plan to take on a particular trek depends on the conditions you expect. I take clothing that should keep me warm in the worst likely weather. If I'm in doubt as to what is enough, I sometimes take a light, insulated vest, or an even lighter vapor-barrier suit, just in case.

What I don't do is carry spare clothing, because this adds weight. Even on a summer-long walk, I carry only one base-layer top and one pair of trousers. If my inner layer gets cold and clammy, I wear a pile top next to my skin. If my trousers are wet, I wear long underwear or rain pants. The only spare items I carry are underpants and socks.

One alternative clothing system disputes the prevailing wisdom; it claims that breathable garments don't work. It involves a waterproof vapor-barrier lining that prevents moisture from leaving the skin, instead of removing it as quickly as possible. This is discussed in detail later in this chapter (see "Vapor Barrier Theory"). But first, let's look at the conventional, breathable three-layer approach.

The Inner Layer

Sometimes described as "thermal" underwear, the prime purpose of the inner, or base, layer is to keep the skin *dry* rather than *warm*. If perspiration is removed quickly from the skin's surface, your outer layers keep you warm more easily. Conversely, if the layer of clothing next to your skin becomes saturated and dries slowly, your other clothes, however good, have a hard time keeping you warm. No fabric, whatever the claims made for it, is warm when wet.

While on the move, your body can generate heat even if your inner layers are damp, as long as your outer layer keeps out rain and wind and your mid-layer provides enough warmth. But once you stop, wet undergarments will chill you rapidly, especially if you've been exercising hard. Often—after a climb to a pass or a summit—we want or need to stop. Once you stop, however, your body heat output drops rapidly, just when you need that heat to dry out your wet underwear. But your undergarment's warmth-trapping properties are impaired because its fibers hold less air and more water—which conducts heat from the body much more rapidly than air. The result is known as *after-exercise chill*. The wetter the clothing, the longer such chill lasts, and the colder and more uncomfortable you will be. Thus, the inner and outer layers are important because they can minimize after-exercise chill; what goes on in between these layers matters far less, and this is where compromises can be made.

The one inner material to avoid is cotton, since it absorbs moisture very quickly and in great quantities. It also takes a long time to dry, using up a massive amount of body heat in the process. To make matters worse, damp cotton also clings to the skin, preventing a layer of insulating air from forming. I haven't worn cotton underwear for years—not even on trips in sunny weather when some people like to wear light cotton or cotton-mix tops. I find short-sleeved, wicking, synthetic fabric works as well as cotton in the heat, and allows me to carry one top instead of two. Although I recommend some inner-layer fabrics, and am not so polite about others, they are all far superior to cotton.

Fabrics remove body moisture in two ways: They either transport or *wick* it away from the skin and into the air or the next layer of clothing, or they *absorb* it deep into their fibers to leave a dry surface next to the skin. Generally, wicking is a property of specially developed synthetic materials; traditional, natural fibers absorb.

Synthetics wick in four ways: by being non-absorbent (hydrophobic) and having an open weave through which the moisture quickly passes, pushed by body heat; by having hydrophilic (water-attracting) outer surfaces, which "pull" moisture through the fabric and away from the skin; by absorbing moisture and passing it along the fibers to the outside; and by both pushing and pulling moisture along blends of hydrophobic polyester and hydrophilic nylon, known as *push-pull fabrics.*

Although the best-wicking fabrics are very good, they can become overloaded with sweat and end up very damp on the inside. How long they take to dry when you're not producing body heat to push the moisture through the fabric is an important factor. The best are those that have brushed or raised inner surfaces so that there is a minimum of material in contact with the skin. If the outer surface can absorb moisture, it will draw it from the inner and then allow it to spread out through the fabric or over its surface, where it will evaporate more quickly. This can be achieved by using different materials on the inside and outside, as in push-pull polyester/nylon fabrics, or by having one piece of fabric with different inner and outer surfaces, as in Malden Mills' BiPolar Technology and Paramo's Parameta S clothing.

Other requirements influence fabric selection, however. All these modern fabrics are fairly lightweight. Most come in three weights or thicknesses, some in four. Lightweight fabrics are thin and fast-wicking, ideal for aerobic pursuits such as running, but also good for warm-weather backpacking and under other layers in cold weather. Mid-weight underwear is slightly heavier and thicker, and usually has a tighter weave. It's warmer, but often slower-wicking—good for all but the warmest weather. The heaviest weight and thickest constructions are known as *expedition* or *winter weight.* Some of these don't wick moisture or dry as fast as the lighter-weight fabrics, and are better suited as mid-layers. A few of the latest expedition fabrics work even better than thin ones, however. Most lightweight and mid-weight underwear is reasonably inexpensive, certainly when compared with mid- and outer-layer garments.

Designs are usually simple; most tops are available as either crew neck or crew- or turtle-neck with zipper, button, or stud fastenings at the neck. Most have long sleeves, though some short-sleeved tops, usually crew necks, are available. I prefer short-sleeved crew-neck T-shirt designs for warm weather, and long-sleeved zippered turtlenecks for colder weather.

Figure-hugging "tights" are the norm for long pants. Briefs made from wicking synthetics are also available, and are far superior to ordinary cotton or nylon. Close-fitting garments help trap air and wick moisture quickly, and also offer an easy fit under mid-layer clothing. Long under-pants need to have a particularly snug fit—there's nothing worse than baggy long johns sagging down inside other layers; elasticized waists are essential. Wrist and ankle cuffs need to grip well to keep them from riding up under other garments. Stretch fabrics often wick fastest due to the close fit. They're generally more comfortable, too. Seams should be flat-sewn to avoid rubbing and abrasion. Colors are usually dark, probably because dirt and stains show up less, but it is worth your time to consider white or pale-colored garments because they reflect heat better when worn alone in warm weather.

Choosing a wicking synthetic fabric can be difficult because there are so many, each claiming to work best. Actually, there are only a few base fabrics, and they're all derived from petrochemicals. Regardless of the fabric, open-knit garments absorb less moisture, wick faster, and dry more quickly than close-knit ones. The three main choices are *polypropylene* (polypro for short), *polyester,* and *chlorofiber.* Blends of these materials are also available.

When I reach a town during a long hike, I like to throw all my clothes in a laundromat washer and dryer. Underwear fabrics that require special care are a real pain at such times. It's worth checking washing instructions.

Polypropylene: Polypro is the lightest and thinnest of the three wicking synthetics. Introduced by Helly-Hansen in its Lifa Super line, it dominated the market for a while; now a host of specialty manufacturers make polypro garments. Polypro won't absorb moisture, but quickly passes it along its fibers and into the air or the next layer. It wicks away sweat so fast that after-exercise chill is negligible. However, after a day or so, polypro stinks to high heaven—a stench that can be hard to get rid of. Apart from the odor, if you don't wash it every couple of days polypro ceases to perform properly, and it will leave your skin feeling clammy and cold after exercise. So you have to carry several garments or rinse out one regularly and learn to live with the smell of stale sweat.

Polypro's drawbacks are mostly overcome in Helly-Hansen's Lifa Prolite. This has a softer, less "plastic" feel than the early polypro, and it can be washed at 200°F (93°C), a heat that rids it of noxious aroma. Lifa Prolite polypro comes in three types: thin, stretchy Lifa Super; slightly thicker Lifa Super Net, a fishnet weave; and Prowool, a polypro/wool blend. In warm weather I like Lifa Super. I've frequently worn my crew-neck top for several days without washing it, and although it smells faintly musty I can bear to have it in the tent, something I wouldn't do with old polypro after even one day's wear. After two weeks it really reeks, though. It still wicks moisture efficiently and, I suspect, faster than standard polypro. My crew-neck Lifa top weighs 4½ ounces, my bottoms 3¾ ounces.

Polyester: Polyester repels water and has a low wicking ability—not ideal for underwear. However, it can be treated with a chemical so that the outer surface becomes hydrophilic. The result is that moisture is drawn through the material to the outer surface, where it spreads out and quickly dries. The drawback is that after repeated washings the treatment wears off. When this happens the material stops wicking. Most polyesters are treated with an antibacterial agent to prevent odor.

Patagonia's Capilene was the first treated polyester. It was quickly followed by others, including REI's MTS, Acclimate, Comfortrel, and the very popular Malden Mills' Polartec 100, available in plain and BiPolar constructions, which is used by many companies.

Unlike polypro fabrics (except for Helly-Hansen's Lifa), treated polyester can be washed and dried at relatively high temperatures. I've used Capilene and Polartec 100, and both work as well as polypro and are effective for weeks at a time. It takes a week or so before treated polyester really reeks—though once it smells it's nearly as bad as polypro.

Polyester fabric structure can be altered so that it absorbs moisture, drawing water from the skin through the fabric to the outer surface. Weights and performance are much the same as for treated polyester, though with these fabrics there is no chemical that can wear off. I have tops made from DuPont's Thermax and Thermastat (both made from hollow-core polyester), and Thermal Dynamics (used by The North Face and other companies), and I've found they can all be worn for several days before starting to smell, and they all wick moisture, even when dirty. I have underpants made from CoolMax, also a DuPont fabric, which I've found very efficient and not as clammy as polypro. Another structurally altered polyester is BTU, from Hoechst-Celanese.

Weights for both tops and bottoms in the lightest polyester weaves range from 5½ to 6½ ounces; mid-weights can run up to 12 ounces for zippered turtlenecks.

I haven't yet used any of the polyester-based push-pull fabrics, such as Hind's Drylete or Nike's Dri-F.I.T., but those who have speak highly of them. I have used Malden Mills' BiPolar Power Stretch, which seems to work on a similar principle; it wicks moisture faster than any other material I've tried except Parameta S, and it dries extremely quickly. Power Stretch is used by many companies; my top and tights are made by Lowe Alpine and weigh 10 and 7 ounces, respectively—less than some expedition-weight underwear that isn't as warm or as efficient at removing moisture. There are other lightweight stretch fleeces, including Patagonia's Activist Fleece and Helly-Hansen's nylon ProStretch, which probably perform much like Power Stretch. They all have soft, brushed pile inners that wick moisture rapidly, and smooth tightly woven outers that spread the moisture so it evaporates quickly.

Chlorofiber: Chlorofiber is made of polyvinyl chloride (PVC), and like polypro and treated polyester, it absorbs little water and wicks well. Chlorofiber garments are comfortable and efficient, but they shrink to doll's size if put in more than lukewarm water or draped over a hot radiator. The most well-known chlorofiber is Thermolactyl, from Damart. Rhovyl is another brand name. (I haven't used pure chlorofiber since I washed a set of tops and bottoms in a machine set on a cool wash and had them shrink to half their size, leaving me with 17 days of snow travel along the Pacific Coast Trail with no long underwear.) Chlorofiber isn't as bad as old-style polypro—nothing is—but it still smells after a few days' wear. For strength, it's usually blended with nylon or polyester in an 80/20 mix.

Wool: Wool, the traditional material for thermal underwear, is not as popular now as it once was, yet it still has much to recommend it. Rather than wicking moisture, wool absorbs it into its fibers, leaving a dry surface against the skin. Wool can absorb up to 35 percent of its weight in water before it feels wet and cold, so after-exercise chill is not a problem unless you've been working harder than most backpackers normally do with a heavy pack. I've worn wool next to my skin for winter ski tours and not overloaded it. On those tours I've also worn the same shirt for a fortnight with no odor problem. Wool's only limitation is its insulating capability, which makes it a cold-weather-only material. I don't usually take it if I'm expecting temperatures to be above 50°F (10°C). Wool also is relatively lightweight; I have a crew-neck wool top that weighs 7 ounces, only a little more than a synthetic one.

What puts many people off wool is its reputation for being "itchy." I once said as much in several magazine articles after wearing thin, department-store wool sweaters next to my skin when I started backpacking, but a manufacturer of wool underwear quickly responded. Very fine wool designed to be worn next to the skin doesn't itch, he said. To prove it, John Skelton sent me a set of his K2 underwear (now unavailable), which I still have and use, and I had to admit that I was wrong.

Many wools *do* cause itching, though, and people with sensitive skin may be dubious about even the highest-quality, finest wools. However, there are now several synthetic/wool, two-layer, mid-weight garments that keep the wool off the skin. I have a Duofold Thermax/wool three-button crew-neck top that weighs 9.7 ounces. I've found it effective at wicking and very warm for a garment of this weight—too warm for summer, in fact. For the rest of the year, though, it's a good garment. Norwegian company Devold also makes Thermax/wool garments; Helly-Hansen makes polypro/wool combinations.

Silk: Silk is the other natural material commonly used in outdoor underwear. It can absorb up to 30 percent of its own weight in moisture before it feels damp. Silk's best attribute, however, is its luxurious texture; it's light, too—a long-sleeved top weighs just 3½ ounces. A silk top I wore on a two-week walk across the Scottish Highlands kept me warm and dry, and at the end the odor was negligible. It was badly stained with sweat and dirt, though. When I rested after strenuous exercise, the top felt cold and clammy for a few minutes, but then warmed up. I would not take silk on a longer trek, however, because it demands special care; it has to be hand-washed and dried flat, and it doesn't dry quickly, so it won't dry overnight in camp unless the air is very warm.

Hot-Weather Alternative Base Layers: Cotton or cotton-combination shirts have always been popular with backpackers for warm-weather wear, though I find a lightweight wicking synthetic top better because it gets less clammy and dries more quickly. When it's really hot I often walk without a top, anyway. If the weather turns unexpectedly cold, a wicking synthetic also works better than a shirt under other layers.

However, there are a growing number of both cotton and synthetic undershirts designed specifically for hot weather from companies like Sportif, Ex Officio, and Sequel. I have shirts in both fabrics and have found that the 100 percent synthetic ones work best because they dry quickest when damp. They're also lighter (around 8 ounces) and feel more pleasant next to the skin than cotton or cotton mixes when damp. Because cotton takes longer to dry than synthetic fabrics, I only wear it on trips where weight isn't crucial and I can carry more than one item for

---

Fabric: My Choices

Having used Prolite polypropylene, Polartec 100, Capilene, Thermal Dynamics, DryFlow, Thermax, Thermastat, and CoolMax extensively, I have a hard time choosing among them. They all work well. The choice comes down to style, fit, color, and price, rather than material. The lightweight and mid-weight versions of all of them are excellent for summer and mild-weather use, and adequate for winter. For cold conditions (wet or dry), however, Polartec Power Stretch stands out.

the next-to-the-skin layer. Overall, I think the windshirts described below are better choices—they can be used next to the skin and also as windproofs over other layers in cooler weather.

The best hot-weather shirt I've used is Sequel's Solar Shirt, made from CoolMax on the top half and WickNet, a wicking mesh, on the lower half and under the arms. It has a deep front opening that is closed by snaps; two snap-fastened, mesh-lined chest pockets that double as vents; a stand-up collar; and long tails. It's available in long- and short-sleeved versions that weigh 7.2 and 8 ounces, respectively. This shirt works as a wicking inner layer as well as a cool outer layer. I wore my long-sleeved one for two weeks in the Grand Canyon and found it superb in the heat, never feeling sticky or clammy, and drying very quickly. At the end of the late-fall trip, the weather became cold and windy, with frequent rain and hail showers; despite its accumulation of 10 days' sweat, dust, and sunscreen, the Solar Shirt performed well as a base layer underneath a micro-fleece top and lightweight rain jacket. It's now my favorite shirt for three-season use.

The Middle Layer

The middle layer of clothing keeps you warm. Mid-layer clothing also has to deal with the body moisture brought up from the inner layer, so it needs to wick that moisture away or absorb it without losing much of its insulation value.

Mid-layer clothing can be divided into two types: *trailwear,* and rest or *campwear.* The first category includes garments made from wool and light- and medium-weight pile. In above-freezing weather, one or two of these garments may be all you need while walking and in camp. Once temperatures fall, I carry heavyweight pile and down- or synthetic-filled garments.

Mid-layer shirts, sweaters, smocks, anoraks, and jackets come in every imaginable design.

Garments that open down the front at least part-way are easier to ventilate than polo- or crew-neck styles—and ventilation is the best way to get rid of excess heat and to prevent clothing from becoming damp with sweat. Far more moisture vapor can escape from an open neck than can wick through a material. Conversely, high collars keep your neck warm and hold in heat. I used to avoid pullover designs, fearing they would cause me to overheat, but as long as I can open up the top 8 or 10 inches, I've found I can cool off when necessary. Pullover tops tend to weigh less than open-fronted ones, so I now use them regularly.

Shirts: For years I relied on just a pile or fleece top for warmth, but after a number of trips on which I was too cool without my pile jacket but too warm with it, I started taking a lightweight shirt, usually made from a heavyweight wicking synthetic, as well. Of course, you can wear two layers of light- or medium-weight synthetics, but these will generally be heavier than a single expedition-weight one. I prefer very lightweight pile tops, because these weigh no more than expedition-weight underwear and are more versatile.

The traditional alternative to a synthetic shirt is a conventional wool or cotton one. Because I prefer pile for warmwear, it's been years since I carried a wool sweater or heavyweight wool shirt. I see no point in carrying a garment that is heavier than pile for the same insulation. Wool absorbs moisture, making it even heavier, takes ages to dry, requires special care, and isn't as durable as pile. Other people like wool shirts and sweaters, which are widely available. If you already have wool sweaters, you might as well wear them for backpacking and spend your money on good-quality inner and outer layers, where specialty fabrics are more necessary. You can replace your woolens with pile garments when they wear out.

I don't like cotton because of its poor performance when wet, but I'm not convinced that it's inappropriate for mid-layer use. I took a brushed chamois cotton shirt on a two-week walk to remind myself of just how cotton shirts perform. Worn over a silk inner layer, it was comfortable and warm; worn under a breathable shell, it never became more than slightly damp, despite wet and windy weather. I suspect that this was partly because the silk inner took up much of my sweat. (With a synthetic inner layer, the cotton shirt likely would have become damper.) But at 17½ ounces, the cotton shirt is heavier than a much-warmer fleece or pile top, and twice the weight of my other shirts.

Pile and fleece can be regarded as the synthetic equivalent of animal fur and work much the same way. Pile and fleece insulate well, wick moisture quickly, are lightweight, hard-wearing, almost non-absorbent, warm when wet because the surface next to the skin dries rapidly, and quick-drying. These properties make them ideal for outdoor clothing. I have carried a pile top on almost every trip since I first tried pile in the 1970s. When low-loft polyester insulations like Thinsulate came along, I switched to them for a short time, but they don't provide the almost instant warmth of pile, and don't perform as well in cold, wet weather, since they absorb more moisture and dry more slowly. Neither do they last as long or cover the same wide temperature range. Using them taught me just how good pile is.

There are many different types of pile and fleece. Generally, pile describes the more loosely knit, thicker, furrier fabrics; fleece is a denser fabric with a smoother finish. Manufacturers use both terms for the same fabric, so they are, in effect, interchangeable. (Since pile came first and fleece is a variety of it, I'll use "pile" when discussing both fabrics.)

Most pile is made from polyester, though a few types are made from nylon. Neither material has advantages over the other. Polypropylene and acrylic piles can be found, but neither has become popular.

Worn over a synthetic, wicking inner layer and under a waterproof/breathable shell, a pile top will keep you warm in just about any weather while you are on the move. Pile is most effective in wet, cold conditions, which is exactly when other warmwear doesn't work so well. A pile top can wick moisture as fast as synthetic underwear, so it will quickly pull sweat through its fibers. At the end of a wet, windy day, I've often found the outer of my pile jacket to be damp, but the inner layer dry. If you feel cold, nothing will warm you up as fast as a pile top, even a damp one, next to the skin.

Of course, pile has a few drawbacks, albeit minor ones. Most pile garments are not windproof, which means you need windproof layers over them even in a cool breeze. Although this is a disadvantage at times, their lack of wind resistance means that pile garments are effective over a wide temperature range—without a shell when it's warm or calm, and with one when it's cold or windy. Windproof pile clothing is available, but it's heavier, bulkier, and less breathable than ordinary pile, and you can't wear the two layers separately. Another drawback is that pile clothing doesn't compress well, so it takes up room in the pack, far more than a down jacket, for example.

Pile comes in different weights and in single and double versions—that is, either one or both sides has a raised or plush surface to trap air. After some use, little balls of fluff appear on the outside of single piles, making them look scruffy; this is known as *pilling*. It can be partly prevented by coating the outside of the fabric with resin or other material, but this makes garments stiff, and adds weight and bulk. If you are bothered by pilling—I am not—use a double-pile fabric, which won't pill, or put the smooth side, which is the one that pills, inside, out of sight. Most piles are double-sided. All pile fabrics work in a wide range of temperatures, but obviously the lighter ones aren't as warm as the heavier ones.

Pile garments need to be close-fitting to trap warm air efficiently and wick moisture away quickly. They are prone to the *bellows effect*—when cold air is sucked in at the bottom of the garment, replacing warm air—so the hem should be elasticized, have a drawcord, or be designed to tuck into your pants. Wrist cuffs keep warmth in best if they are close-fitting, as do neck closures. The broad, stretchy ribbing found on the cuffs and hem of many pile tops works well at keeping in warm air, but it absorbs moisture and then feels cold, and it takes a long time to dry. Better is the nonabsorbent and quick-drying stretch Lycra now found on many garments. Damp cuffs are only an inconvenience, not a serious problem. I have noticed an occasional touch of cold from wet rib-knit cuffs on a cold day, but they didn't cause much heat loss.

Most pile garments are hip-length, which is just about right to keep them from riding up under your pack hipbelt. A high collar will help keep your neck warm. Pockets are useful, especially lower hand-warmer ones, for around camp and at rest stops. Unlined pockets are warmer than lined ones, which also add a tiny smidgen of weight and absorb moisture. Hoods aren't necessary; a hat will do as well and doesn't restrict head movement and vision as some hoods will. I prefer pullover tops with zipper or snap closures at the neck, and chest and hand-warmer pockets, or zip-front jackets with lower pockets. Fancier designs simply add more weight.

Pile was first used in clothing from Helly-Hansen and tested in Norway's wet, cold climate, for which it proved ideal. It soon became popular in Britain, another country with wet, cold weather, and throughout the 1970s British climbers and walkers on jaunts abroad could be identified by their navy blue, nylon pile Helly tops.

In North America, pile became popular after Malden Mills made a smoother pile called Polarfleece for Patagonia in 1979. In 1983, this was replaced by the first of the Polartec fleeces, introduced as Synchilla by Patagonia, and the takeover of outdoor warmwear by pile clothing was under way. There are other manufacturers of pile, including Dyersburg, which now makes the pile Patagonia uses.

These newer pile fabrics provide the same performance for less weight than the originals. They also have smarter styling, don't pill, and are available in bright, cheery colors. Pile comes in various weights and finishes; different makers and companies use different systems for grading weight. Malden Mills lists its pile fabrics as Series 100, 200, and 300.

In warm weather I find the lightest pile garments, weighing from 10 to 16 ounces, provide all the insulation I need. Mid-weight pile, including Polartec 200, Lightweight Synchilla, and Mid-weight Propile (finished garment weights of 14 to 25 ounces), is arguably the most versatile, usable as campwear on cool summer evenings and as mid-wear while on the move in cold weather. Heavyweight piles, like Polartec 300, Original Synchilla, Patagonia's Retro Pile and Heavyweight Propile, are fine for winter conditions but too warm for general use. (You could carry this weight of pile instead of a filled garment as an extra-warm layer in wet, cold weather.) Weights for heavy pile garments run in the 16- to 30-ounce range.

Microfleece (sometimes called *microdenier fleece*), is an extremely comfortable, soft, dense, velvet-like, non-stretch microfiber fabric.

Although often promoted for next-to-the-skin wear, microfleece doesn't wick. It does make excellent mid-wear, and I find that when worn over stretch pile the combination is warm under a windproof shell for all but the bitterest winter weather. Weights run about 11 ounces. Microfleece also takes up little room in the pack. I use a microfleece top year-round, finding it a good substitute for a wool shirt.

Until recently, the only way to make a pile garment windproof was to add an outer, or lining, of windproof material, usually nylon. Shelled and lined pile garments are bulkier and heavier (20 to 40 ounces) than standard pile, less comfortable, and not quite as breathable. The best are surprisingly water resistant, though they won't keep out heavy rain; a waterproof/breathable shell is still needed. When snow rather than rain is expected, these garments are more useful. An ordinary pile top and a separate windshell are far more versatile, however.

The latest development in pile clothing consists of an ultralight, windproof membrane sandwiched between two layers of lightweight pile, which gives a fully windproof pile. (There are several versions, including Malden Mills' Polartec Windbloc 1000 and W.L. Gore's Windstopper fleece. Duofold and Columbia Sportswear have their own proprietary versions, while Patagonia has a variation called Performance Enhancing Film, in which the membrane is sandwiched between a Capilene mesh inner and a Light or Retro pile outer.) Weights run from 18 to 40 ounces.

Windproof pile is very warm. I've tried several types, and in all of them I've quickly overheated when walking uphill, even in very windy and very cold weather. I know backpackers who can walk in them all day without getting sweaty, though, so if you feel the cold, windproof pile could be the answer for winter backpacking.

Even though pile is non-absorbent and quick-drying, moisture can be trapped between the fibers, especially in thicker piles like Polartec 300 or the windproof types, which slows the drying time and makes the garments feel damp. Some pile fabrics have water repellency built in during manufacture; these shed water and snow from the surface quickly and don't hold moisture in the fibers, which speeds up drying time. You can improve the water repellency of any pile by treating it with a wash-in waterproofing agent such as Nikwax TX.10 Polarproof.

Increasingly, pile is being made from recycled polyester and plastic soft-drink bottles, which, according to many reports, significantly reduces the use of oil and natural gas (used in manufacturing polyester), and keeps plastic bottles out of landfills. Recycled pile was first introduced by Dyersburg Fabrics in 1993 in association with Patagonia, which made the first recycled pile garments. The first recycled pile actually contained about 50 percent virgin polyester, but the amount of recycled polyester is increasing. Malden Mills' Polartec Recycled Series now contains 89 percent recycled polyester; Dyersburg makes some 100 percent recycled pile. Malden Mills is testing 100 percent recycled pile, too, so it may appear soon in Polartec garments. Currently, the choice of recycled pile is limited to mid- and heavyweight standard double-sided pile, but both Malden Mills and Dyersburg intend to incorporate as much recycled pile in their fabric as possible. Dyersburg calls its recycled pile E.C.O. Fleece; Patagonia calls its PCR (Post-Consumer Recycled) fleece; Draper Knitting Mills makes recycled pile under the name Eco-Pile. It appears in many ranges under makers' own names.

Insulated Clothing: Whenever or wherever a pile garment won't keep you warm on its own, you need a second insulating layer. I carry one when

Down clothing and warm hats are good for keeping warm when cooking and eating in the snow.

I think I'm likely to wear my pile top while walking so that I can have extra warmth at rest stops and in camp, and also on any walk in bear country where I cook and eat outside without the warmth and shelter of my tent and sleeping bag. This garment could be a second, perhaps thicker, pile one; in cold, wet weather, Retro Pile or a windproof pile is a good choice, but there are warmer items that take up less space in the pack. I prefer down-filled clothing because it's warmer than pile and less bulky when packed.

If the need for a second layer seems marginal or weight is a factor, I carry a sleeveless top because it's most critical to keep the torso warm. On both the Pacific Crest Trail and the Continental Divide walks, I backed up my main warmwear with down- and polyester fiber-filled vests, respectively. These were just enough to keep me warm in combination with a midweight pile top when the temperature occasionally fell well below freezing. Generally, though, I carry a jacket or sweater, which doesn't weigh much more than a vest and provides much more warmth.

Waterfowl down is the lightest, warmest insulation there is, despite all attempts to create a synthetic that works as well. Garments filled with down pack small and provide much more warmth weight-for-weight than pile. They are too hot to wear when walking, but ideal when resting. Down is also durable, but *it must be kept dry.* When it is wet, down completely loses its insulating ability, and it dries very slowly, unless you can hang it out in a hot sun or put it in a machine dryer. Down can absorb vast amounts of water, so a sodden down garment is very heavy to carry, as well as useless. Nonetheless, down is my first choice for a second layer of insulation. Keeping it dry is easy, since I only wear it in camp or at rest stops in freezing temperatures.

For backpacking purposes, a lightweight down jacket or simple sweater is all you need—complex constructions, vast amounts of fill, and heavy, breathable, waterproof shells are for Himalayan mountaineers and polar explorers. Garments suitable for backpacking need no more than 6 to 9 ounces of down and should weigh no more than 25 ounces. The lightest I know of is the Feathered Friends Helios jacket, which weighs a mere 14 ounces. Lightweight nylon with sewn-through seams is adequate for the shell. Although a hood isn't necessary, a detachable one can be useful in bitter cold. Even lighter are down vests, which can weigh as little as 8 ounces, with 3½ to 4½ ounces of down fill. Most makers of down clothing offer one light-weight garment and perhaps a vest among expedition-weight models. I have a down vest weighing 10 ounces that I carry when weight is critical and the temperature probably won't dip much below freezing, and a 17-ounce down sweater for colder weather. Makers of good light-weight down clothing include Feathered Friends, The North Face, Marmot, Mountain Hardwear, and REI, among many others. (For a more thor-ough discussion of down and the construction of down-filled items, see the section on sleeping bags in this chapter.)

If you are allergic to feathers or nervous about garments that won't work when wet, polyester-filled jackets are an alternative. Although they too are cold when wet—despite manufacturers' claims—they dry quickly, so they perform better in wet weather than down does. Few jackets weigh much under 2 pounds, however, and most weigh more. Packed, they are bulkier than pile garments, and more than twice the size of comparable down ones. Synthetic-filled vests make more sense, as they weigh between 16 and 25 ounces. High-loft synthetic fills include Quallofil, Hollofil, and Polarguard. Again, see the sleeping bag section for more details.

While high-loft fills expand like down when uncompressed, and produce thick, warm-looking jackets, *microfiber synthetic insulations* provide warmth without the bulk. These now dominate synthetic-filled clothing, especially Alpine ski-wear, because of their slim looks and easy fit. First in the field was 3M's Thinsulate; there have since been a mass of others. The fill is made from very fine polyester and polypropylene fibers that are able to trap more air in a given thickness than anything else, including down. The result is garments that are warm but not bulky. On the other hand, microfiber-insulation garments weigh more than a comparably warm down jacket—well over 2 pounds—and are as bulky

---

Backpacking Terms Defined

- *Microporous:* a material with microscopic holes that allow moisture vapor through but keep liquid water (rain) out.
- *Hydrophilic:* a solid waterproof material with chains of water-attracting molecules built in, along which moisture vapor can pass through to the outside.
- *Membrane:* a very thin breathable water-proof film. *Gore-Tex* is a microporous mem-brane; *Sympatex* is a hydrophilic membrane.
- *Laminate:* a membrane stuck to a more durable fabric, usually a form of nylon. In *two-layer laminates,* the membrane is glued to the outer fabric, the lining hanging free. In *three-layer laminates,* the membrane is glued between an outer fabric and a light-weight inner scrim, so the finished material appears as just one layer. In *lining laminates,* the membrane is glued to the lining and the outer hangs free. In *drop liners,* the mem-brane is bonded to a light scrim and hangs free between the inner and outer layers.
- *Coating:* polyurethane applied to the inside of a fabric, usually nylon or polyester. Many makers have their own coatings, though they may come from the same source and there is often little difference between them.

to pack as equivalent high-loft insulated jackets. Most microfiber-filled tops, therefore, are not useful for backpacking.

An exception to the above are some very lightweight, low-bulk garments using the latest synthetic fills such as Primaloft, a high-loft insulation, and Microloft, a microfiber. These garments are alternatives to pile rather than down in terms of insulation. In fact, they're lighter than the heaviest piles and just as warm. They're also windproof and less bulky than pile. I haven't used them, but I'd guess they'd be a good alternative to windproof pile for wet, cold conditions. Typical are those from Patagonia (which uses Microloft in the Puffball Pullover and Vest; these weigh 14½ and 8½ ounces, respectively) and Marmot (which uses Primaloft in the Alpinist Sweater; this weighs 16 ounces).

The Outer Layer

Keeping out wind, rain, and snow is the most important task of your outer clothing. If this layer fails, it doesn't matter how good your other garments are—wet clothing exposed to the wind will chill you quickly, whatever material it's made from. In a wet outer garment, you can go from feeling warm to shivering with cold and on the verge of hypothermia very, very quickly, as I know from experience. I now take great care in selecting my shell clothing.

There are two types of shell garment: ones that are windproof but not waterproof, and ones that are both. A windproof/waterproof shell is essential; a windproof shell is optional. Any fabric that is waterproof is also windproof. The belief that some waterproof fabrics are not windproof is based on the misunderstanding that the reason a garment feels chilly in windy weather is because it's not windproof. There are several reasons why you might feel cold under a waterproof garment, but letting in the wind isn't one of them.

Don't, however, expect too much from rain gear. In heavy showers you can expect to remain pretty dry. At the end of a day of steady rain you'll probably be a little damp, even in waterproof/breathable rain gear, because the high humidity will restrict the fabric's breathability. In non-breathable rain gear you'll be soaked with your own condensation. If rain continues nonstop for several days so that you can't dry out any gear, you'll get wetter and wetter, however good your rain gear. This is where synthetic, wicking inner layers and pile mid-wear are important—they don't absorb much moisture and are still relatively warm when damp.

If rain keeps up for more than a few days, heading out to where you can dry your gear is a good idea. The wettest walk I've ever done was an 86-day, south-to-north trek through the mountains of Norway and Sweden. It rained most days and on several occasions rained nonstop for a week. The only way I could keep going was to spend the occasional day in a hotel drying out myself and my gear.

Waterproof/Breathable Fabrics: The moisture vapor given off by your body eventually reaches the outer layer of your clothing. If it can't escape from there, it will condense on the inner surface of that layer and eventually soak back into your clothes. The solution is to wear fabrics that allow water vapor to pass through, while keeping rain out. These are known as *moisture-vapor-permeable* or *waterproof/breathable* fabrics. Most, but not all, rainwear now is made from breathable fabrics, but this was not always the case. Until Gore-Tex came along in the late 1970s, you could either be wet from rain or wet from sweat, unless you went out only when it was sunny. The first is far more unpleasant and potentially dangerous than the second, so standard rainwear was made of non-breathable fabric.

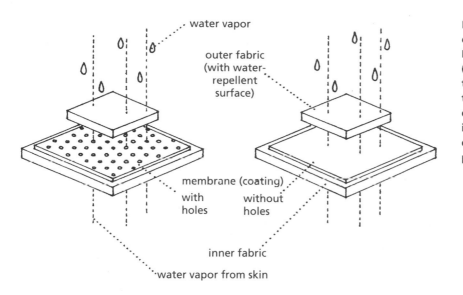

water vapor

outer fabric
(with water-
repellent
surface)

membrane (coating)
with   without
holes   holes

inner fabric

water vapor from skin

Breathable materials are either coated or laminated. In microporous coated fabric (left), water vapor passes through microscopic holes in the membrane. In hydrophilic coated fabric, water vapor is absorbed by, and then evaporated from, a nonporous membrane.

Since the advent of Gore-Tex, a host of water-proof fabrics claiming to transmit moisture vapor have appeared. Such fabrics work due to a pressure differential between the air inside and outside the jacket. The warmer the air, the more water vapor it can absorb. Since the air next to the skin is almost always warmer than the air outside your garments, it contains more water vapor, even in the rain. Condensation forms on the inside of non-breathable fabrics as the cooler air away from your skin becomes saturated with vapor that cannot escape. Water vapor can pass through a breathable fabric as long as the outside air is cooler than that inside. (Theoretically, waterproof/breathable fabrics can work both ways, but in conditions where rain clothing is needed the outside air temperature is always lower than your body temperature.) Breathable garments need to be relatively close-fitting to keep the air inside as warm as possible, because this enables the fabric to transmit moisture more effectively. However, ventilating any garment by opening the front, lowering the hood, and unding wrist fastenings is still the quickest

and most efficient way to let out moisture.

Breathable fabrics aren't perfect, of course, and they won't work in all conditions. There is a limit to the amount of moisture even the best of them can transmit in a given time. When you sweat hard, you won't stay bone dry under a breathable jacket, nor will you do so in continuous heavy rain, despite manufacturers' claims. When the outside of any garment is running with water, breathability is reduced and condensation forms. With the best breathables, once your output of energy slows down and you produce less moisture, any dampness will dry out through the fabric. The same happens after heavy rain.

In very cold conditions, especially if it's also windy, condensation may form on the inside of an outer garment. It might even freeze, creating a layer of ice. This seems to occur whether or not the garment transmits water vapor. The dewpoint—the point at which air becomes saturated with water vapor—is reached inside the clothing in freezing temperatures. Icing is a particular problem if a windproof layer is worn under the outer garment, probably because warm air is trapped inside the windproof layer, leaving the air between the two outer shells very cold. It also occurs with windproof, non-waterproof garments that transmit water vapor faster than the best breathable rain gear. On a spring ski tour in Lapland when the air was still and the temperature 20°F (−7°C), I wore a microfiber-insulated top with a polyester/cotton outer shell and jacket. After a few hours' skiing, I stopped and discovered a sheet of ice lining my outer jacket, which I removed. I stayed just as warm, and no more ice or condensation formed.

The best thing to wear under a shell garment when it's really cold seems to be a pile top, which keeps the air warmer throughout the clothing layers. If the clothing is too thick, though, breathability is compromised. Nick Brown of Paramo has calculated that more than $\frac{1}{15}$ inch of insulation is enough to significantly reduce breathability. Many heavyweight pile garments are thicker than this. They perform better when worn outside your rain jacket than inside.

There are two main categories of breathable materials: coatings and membranes. New coated fabrics appear constantly, though many garment makers assign their own names to the same fabrics. Generic fabrics include Entrant and Ultrex; proprietary ones include Triple Point Ceramic (Lowe Alpine), Helly-Tech (Helly-Hansen), H2NO Storm (Patagonia), Drytec (MontBell), Elements (REI), Microshed (Solstice), MVT (Moonstone), Texapore (Jack Wolfskin), Omni-Tech (Columbia Sportswear), and Camp-Tech (Campmor).

Coatings used to be inferior to laminates in terms of breathability, though just as waterproof. Now, however, the best coatings are as breathable as the best membranes, and are less expensive. The real differences are in the water repellency of outer fabrics, garment ventilation, whether the garment is lined, and what the lining material is.

The thickness of the coating matters: The thinnest coatings are the most breathable but least waterproof; the thickest are most waterproof but least breathable. Of the coated fabrics I've used, Triplepoint Ceramic works best. It's available in two specified weights, 1200 and 1600. I have a Lowe Alpine Northwind Jacket in 1200, with 1600 on the shoulders and arms for greater durability. It weighs 19 ounces and is excellent as a year-round rain jacket.

Membranes are arguably the most effective (and most expensive) breathable fabrics. There are far fewer of them than there are coated fabrics, with just one generally available—Gore-Tex—although Sympatex is becoming more widely distributed. There are a few proprietary membranes, such as Sierra Designs' Amino Acid Laminate and Marmot's MemBrain, as well as several proprietary laminates that usually use a Gore membrane (Alpine Designs' Weatherstop and Patagonia's Gridstop and Super Pluma are examples).

Gore-Tex, which started the breathable waterproof revolution, is a microporous membrane made from polytetrafluoroethylene. Sympatex is a hydrophilic membrane made of polyester. Both membranes can be laminated to a wide range of fabrics, mostly nylons, though sometimes to polyester or polyester/cotton. The thicker the fabric, the more durable the garment, but the lower its breathability. In three-layer laminates, the membrane is glued between two layers of nylon to produce a hard-wearing, somewhat stiff material. The glue dots used to stick the layers together reduce breathability. However, the latest three-layer laminates with ripstop nylon outers are lighter, more flexible, and more breathable than earlier ones that used Taslan and Taffeta nylons. More breathable, but less durable are two-layer laminates, in which the membrane is stuck to an outer layer while the inner lining

Methods of laminating waterproof fabrics.

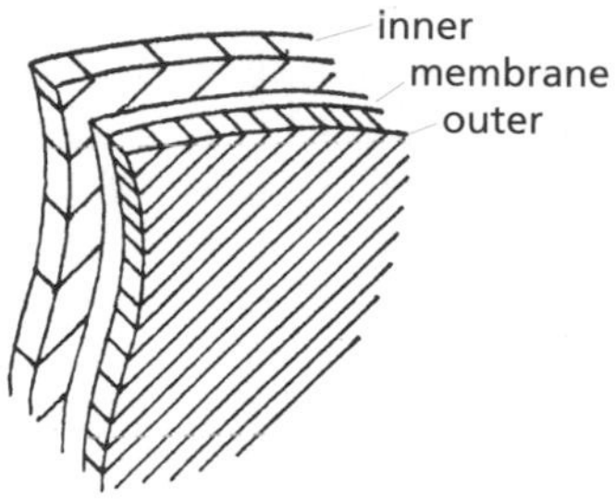

inner
membrane
outer

Two-layer laminates
Outer laminate

The waterproof membrane is
laminated to the back of the
outer fabric.

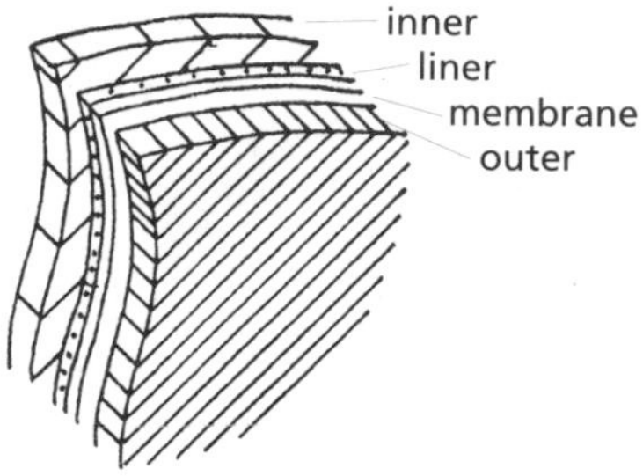

inner
liner
membrane
outer

Drop liner

The membrane is
laminated
with an interlining
material.

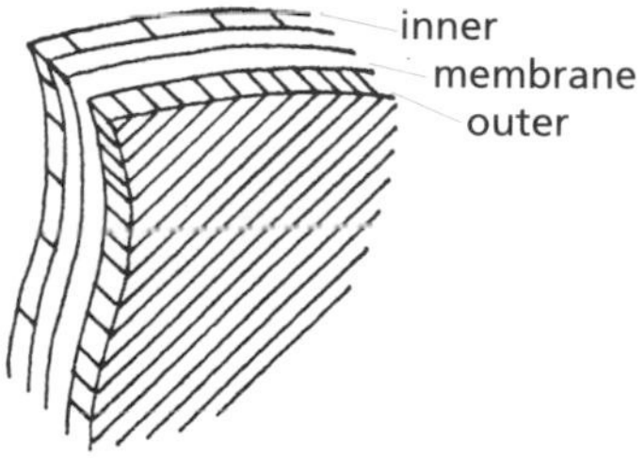

inner
membrane
outer

Lining laminate
(Laminated to drop liner: LTD)

The membrane is laminated
with the inner lining.

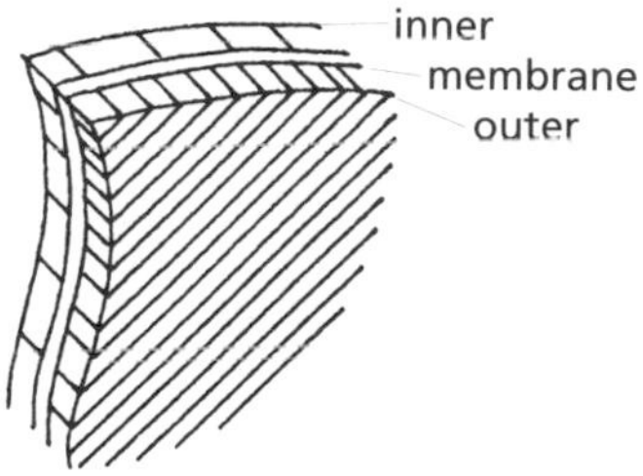

inner
membrane
outer

Three-layer laminate

The membrane is laminated
with both the inner and the
outer fabrics.

hangs free, or drop liners, in which the membrane is left loose between an inner and outer layer. Finally, there are *inner-lining laminates,* also called *laminated to the drop,* where the membrane is stuck to a very light inner layer.

This design minimizes the number of seams, which is a bonus.

The problems with both coatings and membranes are that they aren't very durable, can't be reproofed when they start to leak badly, and they

The Pick of the Breathables

Which breathable fabric is best? It depends on the membrane and the materials used for the inner and outer layer, so there is no easy answer. There's also a big trade-off between breathability and durability. Based on my extensive use of several garments, I've found that three-layer Gore-Tex performs slightly better than three-layer Sympatex. Surprisingly, I've also found that three-layer laminates breathe better than two-layer or drop-liner constructions, despite the many laboratory tests showing the opposite. The reason, I think, is that the tests are done on the two-layer laminate without a lining—but all finished garments have a lining, which impedes breathability. The best performer in terms of breathability is the inner-lining laminate because, I think, the membrane is kept warmer than in other constructions, making moisture vapor less likely to condense on it. There are still times, of course, when condensation will occur, whatever the construction.

For durability, however, Sympatex has the edge. I've twice worn out Gore-Tex three-layer garments on walks lasting several months, and three times had Gore-Tex jackets fail during heavy rain. I've given Sympatex garments more use than the Gore-Tex ones that failed, and have not yet had one leak.

How the latest coatings compare with membranes in terms of durability I haven't yet found out. Gore-Tex garments are widely offered in many styles. The North Face, REI, Patagonia, Mont-Bell, Moonstone, Solstice, Mountain Hardwear, Marmot, Sequel, and many more all make top-quality Gore-Tex garments; Sympatex is restricted at the time of writing to vauDe garments.

If I were buying a Gore-Tex garment, I would choose a three-layer one with a ripstop nylon outer; weights should be in the 16- to 22-ounce range. In Sympatex, I'd go for a lining-laminate garment; weights range from 16 to 30 ounces. The performance of coatings such as Triplepoint Ceramic are now so good that I'm no longer sure that membranes are worth the extra money.

allow passage of moisture vapor only through to the outside, not sweat. A recent development solves these problems. Paramo clothing, from Nikwax, is very durable, can be reproofed, and will allow sweat through to the outside. It does this without coatings or membranes. Instead it mimics the way animals stay dry—a unique waterproof/breathable system inventor Nick Brown calls the Nikwax Biological Analogy.

The fabric is said to mimic the way animal fur guides perspiration away from skin toward the outside and keeps rain out. Paramo utilizes a very thin polyester fleece, called Parameta, with fibers that are tightly packed on the inside but become less dense toward the outside, like animal fur. To replicate the animal oils that keep fur water repellent, Parameta is coated with

TX.10. Like fur, Parameta pumps water in one direction—away from the body. It does this at a faster rate than rain can fall, so moisture is always moved away from the body faster than it arrives, keeping you dry.

To be effective on its own, Parameta would have to be very thick, however. In order to keep it thin (and therefore not too warm), Paramo garments have an outer layer of windproof polyester microfiber, also treated with TX.10, which deflects most of the rain. The resulting material allows more moisture through, including condensed perspiration, than any membrane or coating. It's not dependent on humidity levels outside the garment, nor on temperature inside the garment. The fabric can be reproofed with TX.Direct if it starts to leak. In finished garments, all components, such as zippers and cords, are also treated with TX.10, so they won't wick moisture into the garment.

All this sounds wonderful, but is it true? I'm glad to say it is. I've been using Paramo garments since the early 1990s and have found them very comfortable and efficient. Reproofing with TX.10 works, so Paramo garments should last a long time. There is one limitation: These garments are quite warm due to the two-layer construction. They are too warm for summer. From late fall to spring, however, I wear Paramo trousers or bibs as my standard legwear, and have never had any condensation or rain penetration. The jackets, which weigh 25 ounces and more, can be used year-round in wet and windy places, though they're a little too warm and heavy to carry as a backup in drier areas.

Non-breathable Rain Gear: Non-breathable clothing is made from nylon or polyester, usually coated with polyurethane or PVC, though occasionally with silicon. Its greatest advantage is that it's far less expensive than waterproof/breathable fabrics. Polyurethane is much more durable than PVC—but both eventually crack and peel off the base layer. Both will also leave you soaked in sweat after a hard day walking in wet weather, and the only way to remove that moisture is to ventilate the garment. One way to limit the soaking is to wear a windproof layer under the waterproof one and trap some of the moisture between the two layers, which is what I did before waterproof/breathable fabrics were available.

While moving you will still feel warm, even if your undergarments are wet with sweat, because non-breathable rainwear holds in heat as well as moisture. Therefore, since rain is colder than perspiration, it's better to wear a non-breathable waterproof shell than a breathable non-waterproof one. When you stop, though, you'll cool down rapidly unless you put on extra clothes.

Non-breathable garments are worth considering only if you wear a windproof top most of the time, and rain gear only in continuous, heavy rain, or when prolonged rain is unlikely. Those on a tight budget should consider it, though. Remember, until the late 1970s all rain gear was non-breathable, and people still hiked the Appalachian Trail in the rain and slogged through the wet forests of the Pacific Northwest.

Designs are much the same as for breathable garments, and include the old standby *poncho,* still popular with some backpackers and quite versatile—it can double as a tarp or groundcloth. Ponchos are easier to ventilate than jackets, though they tend to act like sails in strong winds, making them unsuitable for use above the timberline.

Weights of non-breathable rain tops range from 4 ounces for a thin top, to 2 pounds for a tough, long-lasting one. Cheap vinyl rain gear is available, but it lasts about as long as it takes to put on and isn't worth considering, despite the price.

Garment Design

Material alone is not enough to ensure that a garment will perform well—design is nearly as important. The more ventilation, the fewer condensation problems there will be, so all closures and fastenings should be adjustable. The two basic choices are between *zip-front* and *pullover* garments. I've tried both and I always go for the zip-front jacket, because pullover jackets can be difficult to put on in a strong wind. The exception is with the ultralight rain gear I carry "just in case"—a pullover design that's lighter than a front-opening one, important when weight is critical.

Key Features: Rain Gear

- Waterproof/breathable fabric to allow some body moisture out.
- Taped seams; the fewer seams the better.
- An adjustable hood with a peak that gives protection and allows side-to-side vision.
- Adjustable cuffs.
- A full-length front zip with a storm flap.
- Zippered chest pockets big enough for maps.
- Low weight and bulk. (I always hope my rain jacket will spend most of its time in the pack!)

adjustable hood

minimal seams (all sealed)

pit zips

front pockets positioned out of the way of pack harness system

adjustable cuffs

full-length zipper with storm flaps

Length is a matter of personal choice. I like hip-length garments because they give my legs greater freedom of movement, but many people prefer longer ones so they don't need rain pants as frequently.

Aside from the fabric, *seams* are the most

A good hood will give protection and move with your head.

critical feature in a waterproof garment. Unless these are waterproofed (or you have a Paramo garment), they will leak. In waterproof/breathable garments and the more expensive nonbreathables, seams are usually taped, the most effective way of making them watertight. In cheaper garments, seams may be coated with a special sealant instead. If you have a garment with uncoated seams, buy a tube of sealant and coat the seams yourself. You also can do this when the original sealant cracks and comes off—which it will. Taped seams can peel off, though this is very rare. Even so, the fewer seams the better, and where the seams are located is important, too. The best garments have seamless yokes or capes over the shoulders to avoid abrasion from pack straps.

The front zipper is another major source of leakage. This must be covered with a single or, preferably, a double waterproof flap, closed with snaps or Velcro. Even so, after facing into driving rain for any length of time, you may find a damp patch inside the zipper where water has found its way in. Often it's at the neck, which a high collar helps prevent. The covering flap should come all the way to the top of the zipper. Most zippers open from the bottom as well as the top. These are slightly more awkward to use than single ones, and have no advantages that I can see except perhaps to allow ease of movement in very long garments.

Hoods are clearly potential leak points. Good ones fit closely around the face when the drawcords are tightened, without leaving a gap under the chin. Fold-away hoods that wrap around a high collar often provide better protection than fixed hoods, though they are more awkward to use—I find the slight inconvenience worthwhile, though. Detachable hoods need to have a large overlap of material to prevent rain running down your neck; most are very difficult to attach in strong winds. A wired or otherwise stiffened peak or visor helps keep off hail or driving rain, and people who wear glasses tell me that such a peak is essential. The best hoods move with your head so that you can look to the side without staring at the inner lining, which is the case with too many designs. Clearly, the best way to check this is to try the hood on, but you can make a quick assessment by looking at the hood seams: A single seam running back to front over the hood generally means it won't move with you; if there are two seams, or a single seam that runs around or across the hood from one side to the other, the hood is more likely to allow good visibility. Unfortunately, the hoods that limit vision most are the ones that give the best protection. I prefer protection to visibility, especially where the rain drives down for hours and swirling mists hide the view.

In cold weather, I usually wear a pile-lined, waterproof/breathable cap with a large peak instead of a hood during light showers, and under a hood in storms and blizzards for better protection than any hood alone can give. This combination is too warm outside the snow season, though I suppose an unlined cap might work as well. Whether or not you wear such a cap, your jacket hood must be big enough to allow you to wear warm headwear underneath, whether a full balaclava or a lightweight knitted hat. (Many hoods now have a drawcord or adjustable tab at the back so they can be expanded to cover a bulky hat, or reduced in size so that the peak doesn't flop in your eyes when you take the hat off. These work well.) Front hood drawcords can lash you in the face in strong winds; some jackets have tabs to hold drawcords down or cords that tuck into the jacket at each end. These can be fiddly to use but are welcome in storms.

Sleeves need to be cut full under the arms to allow for free movement. Trying on a garment is the best way to find out how well the sleeves are cut. *Articulated sleeves* with a built-in curve at the elbow are available. When I wrote the last edition of this book I said I doubted whether these had any advantages over ordinary sleeves

for backpackers. I've now used a jacket with these—and I was right. Some garments have underarm zippers, which allow better ventilation, but they tend to leak in heavy rain. They can also be extremely hard to use—I wonder if designers have ever stood on a mountaintop in a blizzard with one arm raised in the air while the other hand gropes under pack straps to try to do up a zipper. The cuffs on sleeves need to be adjustable to aid ventilation. I like simple, external, Velcro-closed ones rather than the neater but more awkward internal storm cuffs, and I abhor non-adjustable elasticized ones because they make my arms overheat and run with sweat. Wide sleeves provide the most ventilation and can even be rolled up when it's warm. They're also easy to pull over gloves or mitts.

Pockets are undoubtedly useful, but making them waterproof is difficult, if not downright impossible. My preference is for two chest pockets only. Hem pockets are usually inaccessible under a fastened hipbelt; I don't carry anything in them anyway, because they then flap irritatingly against my legs. However, since shell jackets, particularly the more expensive ones, are often used as general-purpose garments, people want plenty of pockets. Zippered or not, pocket openings should always be covered by flaps, and the seams should be taped or sealed on the inside. The most water-resistant hem pockets hang inside the jacket, attached only at the top.

The best compromise between waterproofness and accessibility for chest pockets is a vertical-zippered entrance under the front flap, but outside the jacket's front zipper. (Pockets inside the jacket stay dry, but you let in wind and rain when you open the jacket front to use them.) Pockets on the outside of the jacket that have angled flaps and zippers are the best for access, but the first to leak in heavy rain. Zippers that close upward are best because small items in the pocket are less likely to fall out when you open them. One advantage of pullover garments is that they usually have a single large "kangaroo" pouch on the chest, which is the easiest to use and very water resistant.

Pockets don't need to be made from the same material as the rest of the garment. A lightweight, un-proofed nylon is adequate (avoid cotton—it absorbs moisture). However, mesh is the best material for chest pockets because it adds minimum weight and you can ventilate the garment by opening the pockets. Mesh is particularly effective on a garment with two outside angled chest pockets, because with both pockets open but protected by their flaps you can ventilate the whole chest and armpit area. Mesh is also the best material for the inner lining that most two-layer laminates and coated garments have, again because it's lightweight and because it helps moisture reach the breathable layer as quickly as possible. If the mesh is made from a wicking fabric, as many now are, all the better. Woven linings, even nylon ones, become wet with condensation, however breathable the outer layer.

Drawcords are needed at the collar for tightening the hood. They are also often found at the waist, but these are unnecessary, since the pack's hipbelt cinches around the bottom of the jacket. Self-locking toggles are a boon on drawcords; trying to untangle an iced-up tiny knot with frozen fingers in order to lower your hood is not easy or fun.

Finally, a note on the trend toward shell garments with extra zippers for attaching warm-wear: I hate them. The zippers add weight for no practical purpose, and increase the cost. I've only used such garments briefly, but as far as I can see, it's done purely so that the combined garment can be worn as a warm raincoat. I don't find the effort of donning two garments so great that I can't manage it.

Lightweight Rain Jackets: My Choices

My current favorite lightweight rain jacket is the 19-ounce Lowe Alpine Northwind Jacket, which has a Triplepoint Ceramic 1200 coating with a Triplepoint Ceramic 1600 yoke over the shoulders, a wrap-around fold-away hood with volume adjuster and visor, mesh lining, half-elasticized Velcro-closed cuffs, and two large, angled chest pockets. It's not perfect, though. I'd like more stiffening in the hood peak, no elastic in the cuffs, mesh rather than solid pockets, and upward-closing pocket zips. But the design offers a good combination of performance, durability, and weight, and the fabric is soft and comfortable.

In cold weather, I wear a Paramo Alta jacket that weighs 29½ ounces. This has a roll-away, wire-stiffened hood with volume adjustment, wide Velcro-closed cuffs that are easy to ventilate (you can roll up the sleeves), an extra-large map pocket, and two hand pockets. It deals easily with the worst winter storms and is very comfortable. I justify the weight by not carrying a separate windproof shell, because the high breathability of the Alta makes one unnecessary.

Weight: Most shell garments weigh from 6 to 32 ounces. Those at the lower end are too light, except for trips when you don't expect to need rain gear but want it just in case, or when you regularly use an "almost-waterproof" windproof top or an umbrella, and they won't last long if worn often. Those above about 26 ounces are just too heavy (except for Paramo tops, where the warmth means you won't need other garments). Most rain gear with reasonable durability is in the 16- to 25-ounce range, and it's where you'll also find the biggest selection.

Fit: Rain jackets are more comfortable if they fit properly. When they were simply baggy waterproof sacks with sleeves this hardly mattered,

A good rain jacket will keep you dry in wet weather. Look for one with a good hood, like this one.

but today's garments are more tailored and much closer-fitting. The jacket should be roomy enough to cover a pile top and still feel unrestricted. Remember, a close-fitting jacket will have better breathability, but a slightly large garment is far better than a slightly small one. I also like sleeves that are long enough to pull over my hands so that I won't need gloves if the weather turns unexpectedly cool. Until recently, women had to put up with ill-fitting garments—the so-called unisex sizes were really just men's sizes in disguise. These days, though, many companies make jackets specifically designed for women.

Rain Pants: Rain pants used to be uncomfortable, restrictive garments that sagged at the waist, bulged at the knees, and snagged at the ankles. Like most hikers, I wore them only during the heaviest downpours.

The introduction of waterproof/breathable fabrics made rain pants slightly more comfortable, but it was only when designers got to work on them that they really changed. In part this is due to changes in legwear in general. Traditional rain pants had to be big and baggy because they had to fit over heavy wool knickers or trousers, which were also big and baggy. Modern legwear is made from lighter, thinner fabrics and is more slim-fitting, so voluminous rain pants are simply not needed. Softer fabrics have helped, too.

The changes have been so dramatic that the best waterproof legwear is comfortable enough to be worn instead of normal outdoor trousers, either next to the skin or over long underwear.

There are two basic designs of waterproof legwear: simple pants, and bibs with a high back and chest and suspenders. For most walking, pants are best, especially if they will spend much of the time in your pack. Bibs are heavier and bulkier. Bibs, however, are excellent in cold weather, especially for ski touring—they are warmer than pants, prevent gaps at the waist when you stretch, and minimize the chances of snow getting into your clothes. They're difficult to put on in a wind, though. Because of their weight and bulk, they're best worn all day rather than carried.

Synthetic long underwear or, in really cold weather, stretch fleece pants are the best garments to wear under rain pants. Synthetic trail pants are good too, but cotton/nylon and cotton trousers tend to feel damp and cold.

Features to look for are adjustable drawcords at the waist and knee-length zips to allow you to get them on over boots. Pockets, or slits to allow access to inner legwear pockets, are useful. If you intend to wear rain pants all the time, then full-length side zips are benefits because they can be opened at the top for ventilation; they also allow rain pants to be put on over crampons or skis, though handling long zips in a strong wind can be difficult. A drawback is that it's very difficult to make full-length side zips fully waterproof. Velcro-closed overflaps help, but they make putting the garment on even more difficult. I still prefer this design, though; I'd rather have good ventilation and suffer the occasional leak. Gussets behind knee-length zips help to keep rain out, but they tend to catch in the zips. For men, pants with flies are worth considering. Elasticized ankle hems are a feature I don't like—I find they ride up over the boot top, letting water in; non-elasticized hems with drawcords or Velcro-closed tabs are better.

Weights of rain pants run from 4 to 32 ounces, depending on design and fabric. As with rain jackets, heavier garments will outlast lighter ones. Rain pants suffer more hard wear than jackets, though, so if you plan to wear them all or most of the time, extra weight could be better. However, if they'll spend most of their time in your pack, the lighter the better. Heavier garments might be too hot in summer. Conversely, in severe winter conditions, the lightest rain pants don't give much protection.

Try legwear on before you buy, preferably over the underlayers you will wear with them—you need to be sure they don't bind anywhere when you move. Length is important, too. Unfortunately, few makers offer different leg lengths in the same waist size (REI, Moonstone, Patagonia, and Paramo do in some models). Alterations are possible, though zipped legs make this difficult (ones where the zips start a little way above the hem are easier to shorten). It's better to find a pair that fit to begin with.

> ### Legwear: My Choice
>
> In continuous rain I keep my legs warm and dry by wearing wicking synthetic long underwear under my rain pants. In bitter weather with strong winds, I add a pair of trail pants between. However, *synthetic legwear* will keep you reasonably warm when wet and dries quickly, so I often don't bother wearing rain pants at all in summer. In summer I always carry an ultralight pair of coated waterproof/breathable pants with zipped lower legs that weigh 4½ ounces. These are quite fragile and wouldn't stand up to continuous use, but because they spend most of their time in the pack, weight is my main concern. On the few occasions I've worn them they've kept my legs adequately warm and dry. In winter, I wear Paramo pants with full-length zips for ventilation and side pockets; they weigh 18 ounces. The weight is justified because I wear them all the time and don't carry additional trail pants. For ski backpacking, I prefer the Paramo bibs, which weigh 32 ounces, but give greater protection to the chest and midriff. Both of these garments are so warm that I've never worn long underwear with them.

Water Repellency. Eventually, the water repellency of the outer, or face, fabric begins to wear off and the material starts to absorb moisture. When this happens, damp patches appear on the outer of the garment, a process known as *wetting out.* This usually occurs first where pack straps have rubbed on shoulders and around hips. Moisture absorption adds to weight and drying time and impairs breathability, leading many wearers to think their garment is leaking. Fabric manufacturers are very aware of this problem and much work goes into creating better durable water repellent (DWR) treatments. They certainly last much longer now than when they were first introduced. Then, they lasted only a week or so.

One way to maintain water repellency is to clean rain gear only when it really needs it; even the most gentle wash removes some of the DWR. It's best to sponge off dirt. When you finally decide you can't stand to wear your rain gear again until it's clean, it should be washed with a pure soap powder or a special treatment such as Loft Tech Wash (Nikwax). *Never* have these garments dry-cleaned—the solvents strip off all DWR.

Reviving water repellency can be done by machine-drying or ironing the garment on a low- to medium-heat setting. This will melt the original DWR and spread it over the outer surface. If you tumble dry your rain gear, make sure all zippers are done up and flaps closed to minimize damage. I know one expert whose tests show that tumble drying often damages the coating or membrane, leading to eventual leakage—enough to stop me from doing it. Ironing is much safer.

So much of the original DWR will eventually wear off that it can't be revived. The best way to replace it is with a wash-in treatment such as TX.Direct, from Nikwax. This not only replaces the DWR but also seals minute cracks in the membrane or coating without affecting the breathability. Spray-on treatments aren't as effective and don't last as long.

Umbrellas: I first met a hiker carrying an umbrella on a rainy day on the North Boundary Trail in Jasper National Park. It's much more comfortable than a rain jacket, Stu Dechka told me. His Gore-Tex jacket was draped over his pack to keep it dry. I was surprised, but thought no more of it until five years later when I read *The Pacific Crest Trail Hiker's Handbook,* in which Ray Jardine extols the virtues of umbrellas. My hiking apprenticeship took place in the windy, treeless British hills, and I'd never given

umbrellas serious consideration, sure that severe winds would tear them apart. However, I could see that for hiking in forests and areas where gales are unusual, an umbrella could have great advantages.

When I had the opportunity to hike for a few days with Ray Jardine, we took umbrellas, and I discovered that in the woods they are excellent. It was wonderful to stride through the forest in heavy rain with my hood down and my jacket wide open and stay dry. The sealed-in, closed-off feeling of being enveloped in a rain jacket was absent. At stops, the umbrella provided shelter and protected the pack. Above the timberline—this was late October and we were in the Three Sisters Wilderness in the Cascades—a gusty

Even in summer, mountain passes can be breezy—a light windshirt and windpants will cut the wind.

wind was blowing and Ray showed me how to point the umbrella into the wind and close it down slightly to protect it and also keep the rain out of my face. As we climbed higher, however, the wind grew stronger and gusted from every direction; eventually both our umbrellas inverted and ripped apart. Such severe conditions would be unusual during the summer hiking season, but I'm too cautious to hike without rain clothing, even with an umbrella (though Ray and Jenny Jardine have hiked both the Appalachian and Pacific Crest Trails with umbrellas and without rain gear). I'll certainly use one again for forest walking, though. An umbrella also makes a good sunshade for desert travel.

Small umbrellas are best for hiking. My current one is 31 inches long closed and 38 inches in diameter open; it weighs 12½ ounces. In his book, Ray details how he customizes his umbrellas.

Windproofs

The advent of waterproof/breathable fabrics was hailed as a weight-saving boon, since one garment served to protect from both wind and rain. This is true, but even the best fabrics are far less breathable than non-waterproof windproof ones, and waterproof jackets are never as comfortable as lightweight windproof tops. Paramo garments are the only exception to this. I usually carry a windproof top as well as a waterproof one, unless weight is a real concern.

One combination setup is a double layer, water-repellent, windproof jacket plus an ultralight rain jacket; another, more common combination is a single-layer, lightweight, windproof top and a standard-weight rain jacket.

Double-layer windproof jacket designs are similar to waterproof ones, and weigh 16 to 50 ounces, which is why you wouldn't want to carry a full-weight rain jacket as well. The lightest are made from various polyester, cotton, and

---

Wind Top: My Choice

The top I use is Patagonia's Pneumatic Pullover, which weighs 9½ ounces and has a roll-up hood with peak and volume adjuster, a large chest pocket, and a long neck zipper. The fabric consists of a treated ripstop polyester backed with a water-resistant breathable barrier made by W.L. Gore, of Gore-Tex fame. It's comfortable to wear and the packed size is minimal. The water resistance is very good, as I found on a two-week ski tour in the High Sierra during which several spring storms dumped snow that was so wet that it was closer to rain at times. The Pneumatic Pullover worn over a lightweight pile top and a lightweight synthetic inner layer kept me warm and dry throughout, and I never wore the rain jacket I carried. The breathability was excellent, and although there was slight condensation at times, it was far less than I would have expected in a fully waterproof jacket.

---

nylon combinations, which dry quickly and are very comfortable, but not very water-resistant. The standard is the hard-wearing 60/40 cotton/nylon cloth.

Single-layer windproof tops, sometimes called *windshirts,* make much more sense, since they can double as a mid-layer shirt to keep a cool breeze off the inner layer, and as a shell to keep stronger, colder winds off your warmwear. They aren't as water-repellent as double garments, so you must also carry a fully waterproof top.

Lightweight nylons and polyesters, especially microfibers, are the best materials for windshirts; they're windproof, water-repellent, quick-drying, low in bulk, and durable.

Manufacturers of single-layer and even double-layer microfiber garments include Patagonia, Sierra Designs, Marmot, Lowe Alpine, Sequel, Mountain Hardwear, Columbia, REI, and The North Face—and the ranks are increasing constantly. Fabric names to look for include Pertex, Supplex, Hydrenaline, Versatech, Gore Activent (called Pneumatic by Patagonia), Climaguard, Tactel, Bergundtal, Perfecta, Silmond, and Dri-Clime. If worn over a pile jacket, single-layer garments made from these fabrics will keep out rain surprisingly well. At the same time, they are more breathable than any fully waterproof fabric.

Most windshirts are pullover designs, which I prefer because they are lighter in weight than jackets and more comfortable when worn as a shirt in camp. They're usually short, so they won't extend below a rain jacket if one is worn over the top. The size should be adequate for wearing over all your warmwear. Useful features are hoods, map-size chest pockets, and adjustable cuffs. Windshirts can be worn next to the skin, but they may feel a little clammy when you're on the move. There are windshirts with wicking linings, however, that should overcome this.

THE VAPOR-BARRIER THEORY

As always there is a view that challenges the accepted wisdom, in this case the concept of "breathability." Our skin is always slightly moist, however dry it may feel; if it really dries out, it cracks and chaps, and open sores appear. Our bodies constantly produce liquid—either sweat, or, when we aren't exercising hard, insensible perspiration. The aim of breathable clothing is to move moisture away from the skin as quickly as possible and transport it to the outside air where it can evaporate. This inevitably causes heat loss. And as we have seen, maintaining breathability is difficult in severe weather conditions.

The vapor-barrier theory says that, instead of trying to remove this moisture from the skin, we should try to keep it there so that its production and attendant evaporative heat loss will cease. This will enable us to stay warm and our clothing

to stay dry, because it won't have to deal with large amounts of liquid. To achieve this, one wears a *non-breathable waterproof layer* either next to or close to the skin, with insulating layers over it. Because heat is trapped inside, less clothing need be worn.

Because of the way they work, vapor barriers are most efficient in dry cold—that is, in temperatures below freezing—because when humidity is high, heat loss by evaporation lessens. Vapor-barrier clothing also prevents moisture loss by helping stave off dehydration, a potentially serious problem in dry, cold conditions.

When I first read about vapor barriers, I thought that anyone using one would be soaked in sweat. However, when several reputable outdoor writers said vapor barriers worked, I decided to give the idea a try rather than reject it out of hand.

Apparently, if you have a hairy body, waterproof fabrics feel comfortable worn next to the skin. However, I'm fairly hairless, and the vapor barriers I've tried make me feel instantly clammy unless I wear something under them. Thin, non-absorbent synthetics, such as polypro, are ideal for wearing under vapor barriers. Initially, I used old polyurethane-coated lightweight rain gear as a vapor-barrier suit, but I overheated rapidly when walking and started to sweat even when the temperature was several degrees below freezing. It was superb as warmwear in camp, however. I was as warm wearing my vapor-barrier top under a pile jacket as I was when wearing a down jacket over it. Wearing the vapor barrier in my sleeping bag added several degrees of warmth to the bag, and since the barrier was thin and had a slippery surface, it didn't restrict me or make me uncomfortable.

I was impressed enough with these first experiments to change my waterproof suit for a lighter, more comfortable, vapor-barrier design made from a soft-coated ripstop nylon that weighs just 7 ounces. The shirt has a zipper front and Velcro-closed cuffs; the trousers have a drawcord waist and Velcro closures at the ankles. Although they perform well, I have rarely used them since the first winter, because every time I walked in them I quickly overheated. I've never used them in temperatures below 14°F (−10°C), which probably means I haven't tried them in cold enough conditions. Another reason I don't wear them is because, although I know they will keep me warm, I somehow don't have any real confidence in them. A down jacket looks warm, and carrying one is psychologically reassuring; two thin pieces of nylon just don't have the same effect. Nowadays I tend to carry the vapor-barrier suit as an emergency backup for winter sleeping in unexpectedly low temperatures, but I very rarely use it.

Plastic bags, or thin plastic or rubber socks and gloves, can be worn on feet and hands as vapor barriers. I've tried both and they work, but again, I usually don't bother. If your feet become very cold and wet, however, an emergency vapor barrier worn over a dry, thin sock with a thicker sock over does help them warm up. I used this combination near the end of the Canadian Rockies walk, when I had to ford a half-frozen river seven times in a matter of hours, and then walk on frozen ground in boots that were splitting and in socks with holes. Dry inner socks and plastic bags made a huge difference.

Few companies make vapor-barrier gear. The main one is Stephensons, of Warmlite tent fame, which offers shirts, pants, gloves, and socks made in a fabric called Fuzzy Stuff. This is a stretchy, brushed nylon glued to a urethane film. The inner is said to feel like soft flannel and be far more comfortable against the skin than ordinary coated nylon. It wicks moisture and spreads it out for rapid drying. It sounds as though it should be far better than simple coated fabrics and is probably the stuff to try if you want to see what vapor-barrier clothing is like.

LEGWEAR

What you wear on your legs is not as important as what you wear on your upper body, but you still must consider comfort and protection from the weather. Legwear needs to be either loose-fitting or stretchy, so that it doesn't interfere with movement when walking.

Shorts

Shorts are my favorite legwear. Nothing else provides the same freedom of movement and comfort. If the upper body is kept warm, you can wear shorts in surprisingly cold conditions. I carry them on all except winter trips, though strong winds, insects, and rain often keep them in the pack. Any shorts will do, as long as they have roomy legs that don't bind the thighs. Many people wear cut-down jeans, a good way to use up worn-out clothing. (Some people, like Ray Jardine, recommend close-fitting stretch Lycra shorts. He says they prevent rashes caused by your thighs rubbing together. I don't suffer from this, but if you do, these shorts could be the answer.) Running shorts are the cheapest and lightest types available (my 100 percent polyester Nike ones weigh just 2 ounces), but they are flimsy and don't stand up well to contact with granite boulders, rough logs, and other normal wilderness seats. I carry them on trips when I doubt I'll wear shorts but want a pair in case the weather is gentler than expected.

When I'm planning to wear shorts, I prefer more substantial ones, preferably with pockets. For years I used polyester/cotton blend ones (8 ounces) with lots of pockets and a double seat. They are very hard-wearing—I have pairs that survived both a Pacific Crest Trail and a Conti-

An outfit for desert and hot-weather hiking—shorts, a synthetic wicking shirt, and a hat that shades the face.

nental Divide walk. There are dozens of models, some made from pure cotton, some from cotton/nylon, some from 100 percent synthetics. Weights range from 8 to 16 ounces. However, such shorts don't feature a built-in brief, so underpants have to be worn, or at least carried for wearing under long pants. This makes such shorts bulky and uncomfortable under trousers, and this is further complicated by pockets and fly zippers. This is a minor point, but I like to be able to pull trousers on over my shorts when the weather changes. Having a built-in brief lets me keep my shorts on when I do this, plus saves the snippet of weight of underpants.

At the start of the Canadian Rockies walk, I found nearly ideal shorts. I had brought along a pair of polyester/cotton shorts that I hadn't tried until the first day's walk, a stroll along Upper Waterton Lake with just a daypack. This was enough to show me that the shorts were too tight

in the leg, so I spent a few hours browsing and trying on shorts in the outdoor stores in Waterton, on the edge of Waterton Lakes National Park. I bought a pair of Patagonia Baggies shorts (5 ounces). I wore them for most of the next 3½ months and found them comfortable and durable. The wide-cut legs made them easy to walk in, while the material dried quickly when wet. Since then I've worn them for short trips in the British hills and two, two-week treks in the Pyrenees, after the last of which I had to throw them out because they'd torn along the side seams. Four months of heavy wear is, I think, quite reasonable for such a lightweight garment. I bought another pair for the 1,000-mile Yukon walk, and they also lasted through the 1,300-mile Scandinavian mountains walk. I still wear them, though with a bit of patching. When they wear out I'll buy another pair.

Trousers

Unfortunately, the weather does not always allow you to wear just shorts. Indeed, during some summers I've hardly worn them at all. I always carry trousers in case the weather changes or insects make wearing shorts masochistic; bushwhacking in shorts can be painful, too. Around camp and in cold weather, synthetic long underwear can be worn under shorts. They don't repel wind or insects, though, and I rarely wear them, since I have to remove my shorts to don the long underwear. It's much easier to pull trousers on over shorts for extra warmth—and simpler to remove trousers rather than long underwear when you warm up.

Trousers fall into two categories: those that will be worn mostly in mild conditions but occasionally in storms, and those strictly for cold, stormy weather. Whether to wear full- or knicker-length trousers is a matter of personal choice. I used to wear knickers all the time, but for many years now I've preferred full-length trousers, perhaps because I feel less conspicuous entering a strange town alone and on foot in trousers. The same applies to air or train travel. I no longer wear them for ski trips, either. There are few knickers available in the shops now, so it would seem I'm not alone in my preference.

Many people hike in jeans, despite the fact that they are cold when wet and take an age to dry. These are potentially dangerous attributes in severe conditions, but wearing rain pants minimizes them. Other objections to cotton jeans are that they are heavy, too tight, and not very durable. I find them so uncomfortable that I no longer own a pair, even for everyday wear.

For three-season use, I favor the *trail pants.* These generally weigh from 5 to 25 ounces. Features may include double knees, double seats, and multiple pockets, many of them zippered. Some versions, usually called *wind pants,* have full-length side zips so they can be pulled on over boots and vented in warm weather. A few, like Marmot's DriClime Windpants, also have wicking linings. The traditional and heaviest material for trail pants is 100 percent cotton. Cotton/polyester or cotton/nylon blends such as 65/35 cloth are better; best are 100 per cent synthetics, especially microfibers, because they are much lighter and faster-drying, though just as hard-wearing, windproof, and comfortable. I've worn such pants on all my long walks, changing from polyester/cotton blends to microfibers when they became available.

When buying a pair of pants, the main thing to check is the fit. These pants are now popular everyday wear, so some are styled for fashion rather than function. Many of the newer designs feature elasticized waistbands rather than conventional belt loops. I like these because I don't wear a belt under a pack hipbelt, and I appreciate the stretchy waist when I feast in a restaurant

after a long trip on dried food. I like to have at least one pocket with a snap or zipper for my wallet and money when traveling to and from the wilderness; large thigh pockets can carry maps.

Trail pants with zip-off legs for conversion into shorts seem to be gaining in popularity. Examples are the Sequel Solar Shants (100 percent ripstop cotton, 12 ounces), Sportif 2-in-1 Pants/Shorts (Supplex nylon, 11.1 ounces; 100 percent cotton, 20 ounces), REI Convertible Pants (100 percent cotton or 100 percent nylon), and Woolrich Ripstop Fatigue Pants (100 percent ripstop cotton, 16 ounces). I haven't tried any of these, but the idea is intriguing. Stephensons' Converta Pants, made from tough, fire-resistant Nomex nylon, are a variation. They have zippers in the seams so the legs can be folded up and tucked into the waistband.

I wear lightweight pants any time shorts would be too cool. If the weather turns really cold or mornings are frosty, I wear long underwear under them. With rain pants on top, the pants/long underwear combination can cope with all but the worst winter weather while I'm on the move. Three layers are more versatile than one thick pair of pants when large variations in weather can be expected. In *really* cold conditions, thicker long underwear or vapor-barrier pants could be worn.

An alternative to trail pants/long underwear is a separate, single pair of warm pants. I used to prefer these for constant wear in cold conditions, since two layers are more restrictive and less comfortable than one. The obvious material is pile, which is warm, light (typically 8 to 22 ounces), non-absorbent, and quick-drying. I don't like thick pile pants, however, because they're not windproof, not very light, and are bulky to pack. I've owned a pair of Helly-Hansen nylon pile Polar Trousers (17 ounces) for many years, but rarely use them because they require a pair of windproof pants over them in even the gentlest

The simple watch cap is the only headwear needed most of the year. Thicker versions are good for winter wear.

breeze, which makes them too hot. Power Stretch pile pants are far better, however. My Lowe Alpine pair weighs 6.8 ounces. They're very warm, very comfortable, repel breezes and light rain or snow, and can be worn under rain pants in cold, wet weather or under trail pants in strong winds. They function well over a wider temperature range than any other warm pants I've tried.

Pants padded with microfiber insulation, such as Thinsulate, may be fine for Alpine skiing or winter mountaineering, but the few pairs I've tried are too warm for hiking and too bulky to carry for campwear. Thick, stretch nylon pants are better. These shed snow and rain and are reasonably windproof and very hard-wearing. I wore these for years for winter backpacking and ski touring. However, the current popularity of rain pants or bibs combined with pile pants for winter wear means stretch nylon pants are less common than they once were. Patagonia makes some from nylon/acrylic/Lycra called Talus Pants that weigh 12 ounces. Similar and even harder-

wearing are stretch pants made from Spandura, a combination of Cordura nylon and Lycra. Outdoor Research uses this in its Flex-Tex Pants. Spandura is expensive, though.

Wool or wool-blend pants used to be common; my first winter walking trousers were of Derby Tweed. They were warm, but heavy, itchy, and very absorbent. When wet, they rubbed my inner thighs raw, and they took days to dry out. After my first weekend in stretch nylon knickers, I never wore wool trousers again. Perhaps it's no wonder wool pants are now hard to find.

For severe weather, down-filled trousers are available. I've never been out in conditions cold enough to warrant even considering these, but you might like to know they exist. Not surprisingly, there isn't a wide choice; examples are The North Face's Himalayan Pants (28 ounces) and Marmot's 8000 Meter Pants (33 ounces). These have as much goose down in them as the lightest down sleeping bags! Vapor-barrier trousers worn over long johns and under fleece or pile-and-shell trousers would probably prove as warm as down ones.

HEADWEAR

"If your feet are cold, put on a hat." This adage was one of the first pieces of outdoor lore I ever learned. It's also one of the most accurate.

When you start to get cold, your body protects its core by slowing down the blood supply to the extremities—fingers, toes, nose—first. However, your brain requires a constant supply of blood in order to function properly, so the circulation to your head is maintained. If it's unprotected in cold weather you can lose enormous amounts of heat through your head— anywhere from 20 to 75 percent, depending on whose figures you read. The capillaries just below your scalp never close down to conserve heat the way they do on hands and feet, so *you must protect your head in order to stay warm.*

But which hat? Not so long ago the choice was simple: The only material was wool and the only styles were bob hats and balaclavas. Then came synthetic fabrics—nylon, polyester, acrylic. Designs didn't change, though, until pile and fleece became the main material for warmwear and outdoor companies began employing designers to make their clothing more stylish.

Now, outdoor hats come in a wild variety of colors and styles and every sort of material, including pile, wicking synthetics, wool, and mixtures of everything. All of these fabrics are warm, but I prefer fleece or a synthetic—wool makes my head itch, takes much longer to dry if it gets wet, doesn't have the same temperature range, isn't as durable, and is slightly heavier. Wool hats lined with a synthetic are available, though, and I have a 3-ounce REI Ragg wool hat with polypro lining that I used on the Scandinavian mountains walk; by the end of that trip

A fleece-lined, waterproof/breathable hat is useful in cold weather.

holes were beginning to appear in it, though. Fleece and knitted synthetic hats tend to keep their shape better than wool ones do, although they can stretch and occasionally need a hot wash to shrink them back to size.

Whatever the style, hats can be divided into two categories: those that are windproof and those (the majority) that aren't. Windproof hats are made from windproof fleece such as Polartec Windbloc or Gore Windstopper, or have an outer made from a waterproof/breathable or windproof synthetic material. In a cold wind, any hat that isn't windproof will feel cold unless you put your hood up. Non-windproof hats are more breathable, though, and they're better for milder weather than windproof hats.

How warm a hat will be is determined by both thickness and style. Whether it can be pulled down to protect the ears is an important feature. As with other clothing, the warmest hat isn't always the best—one that will keep your ears warm in a blizzard will be too hot for a cool

Hats: My Choices

I use different hats for different weather conditions and times of year. Most of the year I carry a simple fleece hat with ear flaps, a style known as Peruvian or Andean. It weighs just 1.8 ounces. This hat is warm and comfortable (but it doesn't perform any better than the less-expensive knitted acrylic and polyester hats I used to wear). In winter and cold weather, and on long trips, I carry a spare hat in case I lose one (as I did on the Canadian Rockies walk, when I foolishly tucked it into my pack hipbelt rather than a pocket while bushwhacking.)

Instead of a spare hat, I often carry a lightweight neck gaiter. This can be pulled over the head to form a thick collar or scarf; it also can be worn as a balaclava or rolled up to make a hat. I have two, one wool (4½ ounces), and one polypro (2½ ounces), which I prefer because the wool one is rather hot. The polypro neck gaiter combined with the fleece hat provides the protection of a full-weight balaclava without the bulk or restrictiveness. They're also available in silk, which is probably excellent, and pile, which probably would be too warm for me. The Snowcap, made by Sequel, is a Polartec 300 fleece hat

Fleece hats are very warm. Ones with ear flaps are good in winter and won't blow off in a wind.

evening at a summer camp. How much you feel the cold matters, too. I know people who are happy bareheaded when I need a thick hat; others wear balaclavas pulled down in what feels like warm weather to me.

There are currently four main styles, all available in windproof and non-windproof fabrics. The basic *bob hat* (also called a *watch cap, stocking cap,* or *tuque*) is still with us, though it may have ear flaps. The *balaclava* still survives, too. A newer design consists of a tube of material open at each end. This style, known as a *neck gaiter,* can be combined with a hat to form a balaclava. Some have a drawcord at one end and can be worn as a hat when this end is closed. The final

style is the *peaked cap,* with ear flaps and a pile lining. This is the most weatherproof design; it protects the face from rain, snow, and sun, and can be used in place of a jacket hood. There are also warm *headbands,* useful for when a full hat isn't needed but your ears feel chilly.

Some hat styles are available in several sizes, though many aren't. Because most pile doesn't stretch the way that knitted wool or acrylic does, it's important to get a good fit if you choose pile headgear. Hats that are a bit tight will be very uncomfortable after a few hours' wear. However, if the fit is too slack the hat will blow off in every breeze; chin straps are useful to prevent this.

(Left) A polypro neck gaiter worn as a hat. (Middle) A polypro neck gaiter worn as a neck warmer—more secure and warmer than a scarf. (Right) A polypro neck gaiter worn as a balaclava. It may look silly, but when you need it, you won't care!

with a rigid visor and a Polartec 300 neck gaiter that can be attached to each other by Velcro strips to form a balaclava. It weighs 4.8 ounces.

Because I don't like hoods on my warmwear and prefer not to wear the one on my rain jacket or windshirt, in cold weather I wear a pile-lined waterproof/breathable cap. This keeps my head and ears warm and dry in the worst winter storm; on sunny days the ear flaps can be folded out of the way. There are many such hats available. I have two: a Lowe Alpine Mountain Cap with Triplepoint Ceramic outer and Polartec 200 lining, and an Extremities Ice Cap with a Gore-Tex outer and Eco-Pile inner. Both work very well. An interesting cap is Outdoor Research's Hat For All Seasons. This has a pile inner hat and a Gore-Tex shell with a large stiffened peak and a wicking synthetic lining. The inner and outer can be worn separately; total weight is 5 ounces. Down caps exist, too. Years ago I bought one, but it's too hot and its ear flaps cut out all sound when they are down, so I never use it. I also find hats made from windproof fleece hot and far less breathable than lined waterproof caps. If you feel the cold, this could be a good choice, however.

Sun Hats

I never used to wear a sun hat, not even when I crossed the desert regions of Southern California and New Mexico in baking temperatures. I thought my thick head of hair shaded my head from the sun. However, while I still have the hair I now find a sun hat adds greatly to my comfort in hot, sunny weather. I was simply ignorant of the benefits of a hat. (I used to wear a bandanna headband to prevent sweat from dripping into my eyes, and I discovered that soaked in cold water it helped keep me cool. You can do the

Wearing a wide-brimmed hat is the best way to protect your face and neck against the sun.

same with a hat, of course. One trail companion used to resort to the old handkerchief-knotted-at-the-corners when his head felt too warm; he now wears a proper sun hat.)

Oddly enough, it was in the far north on the 1,000-mile Yukon walk that I found a sun hat essential. I discovered a good hat not only kept off the sun, which in July was painfully hot (hotter than I remember it being in the desert), but it also repelled light rain, kept leaves and twigs out of my hair when I was bushwhacking, and held my head net in place when the bugs were bad. While in the Yukon, I discovered the Canadian-made Tilley Hat. This is a cotton duck hat with a wide brim and a fairly high crown, reminiscent of an Australian bush hat. The instructions (it comes with a detailed leaflet!) say the fit should be loose—the double cords for the chin and the back of the head hold it in place in windy weather. Loose fit is the key to comfort; I actually liked wearing the Tilley Hat, so much so that I

wore it when I didn't really need to. It warded off light showers, was far less restrictive than a jacket hood, and, sprayed with insect repellent, kept bugs off my face without a head net. The Tilley weighs 5¾ ounces and comes with a lifetime guarantee. After a hard summer's use mine was still in good condition, although battered. I've since replaced it with a new, darker one (the original was an off-white) that has had lots of use, including the 1,300-mile Scandinavian mountains walk. I think the Tilley Hat is vastly superior to any other cotton-brimmed hat available. The latest brimmed hats are made from synthetic materials and often have reflective foil in the crown. Examples are Sequel's Desert Shield and Outdoor Research's Sonora Sombrero.

Since I discovered the Tilley Hat, new sun hats have appeared, many of them based on the French Foreign Legion-look, with a peaked cap linked to a loose cape. Tucking a bandanna under the rim of a baseball cap gives much the same protection, though it's difficult to keep in place. The advantages over the Tilley and other wide-brimmed hats is that these hats don't catch on the top of the pack, they can be folded flat, they give complete protection to the neck regardless of the angle of the sun, and they stay on in high winds and when moving fast. (I tried my Tilley for skiing and it just wouldn't stay on.)

One of the first of these new sun hats was the Sequel Desert Rhat, made from breathable mesh lined with a reflective foil, with a cotton front and a terry sweatband. The extra-large, stiffened visor has a black underside to absorb reflected light. The cape is made from cotton and attaches with Velcro strips. It's now my alternative to the Tilley Hat—it's lighter (at 4 oz.) and easier to pack. They're both excellent.

Outdoor Research makes a sun hat called the Safari Cap from a soft Cordura/nylon mix called Solarplex. Patagonia's Vented Broadbill Hat has a double-mesh crown and a back flap to cover the neck; Lowe Alpine's polyester/cotton Wilderness Cap is similar.

I must mention Outdoor Research's Modular Hat. This combines features of the Safari Cap and the Hat for All Seasons. It's based around a visor and headband. To this can be added a Solarplex crown to make a high-tech baseball hat, and a Solarplex cape to make a Safari Cap. Alternatively, you can add a Gore-Tex crown to create a waterproof/breathable baseball cap, then some lined ear flaps for more warmth, and finally a pile liner for cold-weather use. It sounds a bit over the top, but I've been on trips where I could imagine wearing all the combinations, especially in the spring, when the weather can change from blizzard conditions to near heat wave in a few hours.

GLOVES AND MITTS

Cold hands are not only painful and unpleasant, but they make the simplest task, like opening the pack or unwrapping a granola bar, very difficult. I always carry at least one pair of gloves, except at the height of summer. These are liner or inner gloves made of synthetic wicking material, thin enough to wear while doing things like pitching the tent or taking photographs, but surprisingly warm. At about 1 to 2 ounces per pair, they are hardly noticeable in the pack. They don't last long if worn regularly, though; I go through at least one pair every year. Wool and silk versions are available, which may be more durable but probably not as quick-drying as synthetics.

In cold temperatures, thicker mitts or gloves are needed. For many years I used ones made from boiled wool. Boiling shrinks the wool fibers to make a dense fabric that increases wind and water resistance. Dachstein is the commonest brand; weights are 4 to 5 ounces. I've had both mitts and gloves and have worn both out between the thumb and forefinger, a major wear point if you use trekking poles or ski poles. For no rea-

son other than to try a new fabric, I replaced them with gloves made from Polartec Windbloc fleece. I found these more windproof but not as warm. I could do much more with my hands while wearing them, though, because they were thinner. But they wore out at the base of the fingers and thumb even faster than the wool ones did. There are now several windproof fleece gloves available (such as Outdoor Research's Windstopper Gripper Gloves and REI's Windbloc Gloves) that have extra-strong material here.

Another debate centers on whether to wear gloves or mitts. Gloves aren't as warm as mitts because they have to keep each finger warm separately, but mitts decrease dexterity and you have to pull them off for all sorts of fine tasks. Those who suffer from cold hands usually prefer mitts, though. I like gloves because I can do most things with them on. (If your hands do get very cold, by the way, a good way to warm them up is to windmill your arms around as fast as possible—this sends blood rushing to your fingertips and quickly, if a little painfully, restores feeling and warmth to them.)

Another feature to look for is whether handwear has gauntlet-type wrists designed to go over jacket sleeves, or elasticized cuffs designed to go inside sleeves. Gauntlets are best if you use hiking or ski poles because snow and rain can't be blown up your sleeves. If you don't use poles, cuffs are better—water running down your sleeves can't run into your handwear.

In bitter, stormy weather, wool and pile handwear, whether gloves or mitts, doesn't keep my hands warm, so I also wear a pair of waterproof/breathable overmitts. They work well, but you can't do much with them on.

I originally put together my own layering system of gloves and mittens from separate sources, but many companies offer two-layer systems consisting of pile or fleece inners and waterproof/breathable overmitts. The great advantage of these is that the two layers are designed to fit on top of each other. I now have two systems—one for moderate cold, one for extreme cold. The first set is Manzella's 3-Way HandGear: fleece gloves with outers made from a waterproof/breathable polyurethane laminate with a nylon shell. They have pre-curved fingers and a fabric grip on the palms. The weight is just 2½ ounces, incredibly light for overmitts or gloves. They're not fully waterproof, however, and don't cover much of the wrist, nor will they fit over really thick gloves. When severe cold is expected, I use Black Diamond Shell Gloves with thick Retro Pile inners—bought because of the latter, the thickest pile gloves I've seen. They weigh 9½ ounces and have long, gauntlet-type wrists. They've kept my hands warm in a bitter, if windless, −30°F (−34°C). I use them mainly in short stints of up to an hour or so if my hands are feeling very cold, changing to lighter gloves once my hands warm up. The outers of the Black Diamonds are waterproof but not breathable, which means they can get a bit damp. Current models come with waterproof/breathable Entrant-coated outers. They're also available as mitts.

I've also tried using insulated Alpine ski gloves on the trail. My pair of Gates Thinsulate-lined Gore-Tex gloves (6 ounces) are warm and allow good dexterity, but unfortunately the first two pairs I owned split at the base of the fingers. The second replacement pair lasted several winters, though they're not as warm now because the fill has compacted. There are plenty of ski gloves around, but I still prefer a two-layer system for its versatility.

Losing a mitten or a glove in bad weather can have serious consequences. Once, while getting something out of my pack, I dropped a wool mitt that I'd tucked under my arm. Before I could grab it the wind whisked it away into the gray, snow-filled sky. Luckily I was about to descend into the warmth of a valley a short distance away. Even so, my hand, clad in just a liner glove, was very cold by the time I reached shelter. Since then I've adopted two precautions. One is to attach wrist loops (often called "idiot loops") to my mittens so that they dangle at my wrists when I take the mitts off. I use thin elastic shock cord for this. Many mittens now come with D-rings or other attachments for wrist loops; others come with the loops already attached. On my wool mittens, I simply push the shock cord through the wool about ¾ inch from the cuff. My second precaution, unless weight is critical, is to carry a spare pair of mittens or gloves. I always do this on ski tours, when it's inadvisable (or impossible) to travel with your hands in your pockets.

In an emergency, you can wear spare socks on your hands. I used this ploy at the end of the Canadian Rockies walk during a bitterly cold blizzard, when my hands weren't warm enough in both liner gloves and wool mittens. With thick socks added, my hands went from achingly cold to comfortably warm, almost hot. Unfortunately, if your feet are cold, the reverse is not possible!

BANDANNAS

While not really clothing, a bandanna is an essential piece of equipment. This 1-ounce square of cotton can be a headband, brow-wiper, handkerchief, pot holder, dishcloth, flannel, towel, and cape for protecting the back of the neck from the sun. I usually carry two—one threaded through a loop on my pack shoulder straps so I can wipe sweat off my face whenever necessary. I rinse them frequently, and tie them to the back of the pack to dry.

CARRYING CLOTHES

Nylon stuff sacks are ideal containers for clothing, especially compressible down- and synthetic-filled items. Stuff sacks weigh from 1 to 4 ounces, depending on size and thickness of material—thin ones are fine for use inside the pack. I usually carry spare clothing in a stuff sack in the lower compartment of the pack, with my down jacket in its own stuff sack inside the larger one for extra protection. Dirty clothing usually languishes in a plastic bag at the very bottom of the pack. Rain gear and clothing I may need during the day (windshirt or warm top) moves around according to how much space I have, sometimes traveling at the very top of the pack, other times at the front of the lower compartment. These garments aren't put in stuff sacks because they must always be accessible quickly. Head- and handwear go in a pack pocket, usually the top one, or in the fanny pack if I expect to need it during the day.

FABRIC TREATMENT AND CARE

At home I simply follow the washing instructions sewn into every garment. Note these carefully—many fabrics that are tough in the field are vulnerable to detergents, softeners, and washer and dryer temperature settings. Polypro, other synthetics, and pile function best if they're kept as clean as possible. Pile and brushed synthetics should be washed inside-out to minimize pilling and to help fluff the inner fabric. Some materials can be damaged by too much washing, however. Down in particular will lose some loft every time it's washed; wool loses natural oils. I sponge stains and dirty marks off the shells of down garments, but have never washed one. Frankly, I'd rather send my down jacket away for professional cleaning than risk damaging it by doing it myself. Your local outdoor store should know of companies that do this. If not, ask the garment maker. I suspect washing shortens the life of waterproof garments, so I rarely wash them.

Special soaps for high-tech clothing are available. Nikwax makes two liquid soaps: Loft Down Wash (for down clothing); and Loft Tech Wash (for wool, polyester, and waterproof/breathable materials, which leaves water-repellent qualities intact). Nikwax recommends Loft Tech for cleaning Gore-Tex. I've used it and it seems to work. I avoid harsh detergents anyway, and use washing powders (like Ecover), which neither strip away water-repellent treatments and natural oils nor harm the environment.

During a trip, garment care is minimal; it is nonexistent in cold and wet weather. On walks of a week or less, I never wash anything; on longer ones, I rinse out underwear, socks, and any really grubby items every week or so, as long as it's sunny enough for them to dry quickly. I don't wash laundry in a stream or lake, of course, but in a cooking pot, using water from my large camp water container. Since I'm only removing sweat and debris, I don't use soap. Garments can be hung to dry from a length of cord strung between two bushes or on the back of the pack while walking. On walks lasting more than a few weeks, I try to find a laundromat when I stop in a town to pick up supplies. If I find one, I wear my rain pants and wash everything else. I try to avoid carrying fabrics like silk that require special care, because I want to do one wash (at 100° to 125°F [38° to 52°C]) and then tumble it dry on a high heat setting.

Most outdoor clothing can be stored flat in drawers, but down- and synthetic-filled garments should be kept on hangers so that loft is maintained; prolonged compression may permanently affect loft. Check zippers and fastenings before you put garments away, and make necessary repairs. It's irritating to discover that a zipper needs replacing when you are packing hastily for a trip.

CHAPTER 6

Shelter: Camping in the Wilderness

It is raining hard, and we have no shelter . . . We sit on the rocks all night, wrapped in our ponchos, getting what sleep we can.

—The Exploration of the Colorado River and Its Canyons, J.W. Powell

Silence. A ragged edge of pine trees, black against a starry sky. Beyond, the white slash of a snow-slope on the distant mountainside. A cocooned figure stirs, stretches. A head emerges from the warm depths, looks around in wonderment, then slumps back to sleep. Hours pass. The stars move. An animal cry, lonely and wild, slices through the quiet. A faint line of red light appears in the east as the sky lightens and a faint breeze ripples the grasses. The figure moves again, sits up, still huddled in the sleeping bag, then pulls on a shirt. A hand reaches out and the faint crack of a match being struck rings around the clearing. A light flares up, then a sudden roar breaks the stillness. A pan is placed onto the blue ring of the stove's flame. The figure draws back into its shelter, waiting for the first hot drink and watching the dawn as the stars fade slowly away and the strengthening sun turns the black shadows into rocks and, farther away, cliffs, every detail sharp and bright in the warm light. The trees turn green again as warm golden shafts of sunlight

illuminate the silent figure. Another day in the wilderness has begun.

Nights and dawns like that, when the wind rattles the tent and the rain pounds down, are what distinguishes backpacking from day walking and touring from hut to hut, hostel to hostel, or hotel to hotel. On all my walks I seek those moments when I feel part of the world around me, when I merge with the trees and hills. Such times come most often and last longest when I spend several days and nights living in the wilderness.

A backpacker needs shelter from cold, wind, rain, insects, and, in some places, sun. The kind of shelter you need depends on the terrain, time of year, and how Spartan you are prepared to be.

> **Dawn**
>
> My campsite is near a lake backed by pale talus slopes and steep cliffs. The night sky is alive with stars and edged by the deeper blackness of surrounding forest and silhouetted mountains. I awake to the first rays of sunlight catching the highest peak. The lake shines green and gray, reflecting rocks and trees in its cool depths. How many other mornings have I waited, warm in my sleeping bag, for the sun? The joy does not diminish.

In a breathable-fabric bivy bag you can seal yourself in against the weather. This is a Gore-Tex model.

Some people like to sleep in a tent every night; others use one only in the worst conditions. Robert Peary, who reached the North Pole in 1909, never used a tent or a sleeping bag, but slept outside in his furs, curled up beside his sled. Most mortals require a little more shelter than that, though. In ascending order of protection, shelters include bivouac bags, tarps, tents, and huts and bothies; snowholes are a winter option.

BIVOUAC BAGS

Sleeping out under the stars is the ideal way to spend a night in the wilderness. The last things you see before you fall asleep are the stars and the dark edges of trees and hills. At dawn, you wake to the rising sun and watch the return of color and movement to the world. These most magical times of day are lost to those inside a tent.

Of course, since the weather can be unkind and is often changeable, instead of sunlight you may wake up to cold raindrops on your face. The simplest way to cope with weather changes is to use a *bivouac* (or *bivy*) *bag*. This is a waterproof "envelope" into which you slip your sleeping bag when the weather turns wet or windy. More sophisticated designs have short poles at the head to keep the bag fabric off your face. (Ones with poles at each end are really mini-tents, so I'll consider them under that heading.)

The least-expensive bags are made from nonbreathable waterproof materials such as plastic or "space blanket" metalized fabrics. These are light—from 4 to 12 ounces—but they're suitable only for emergency use because they keep in all your body moisture. I carry one on dayhikes and occasionally on backpacking treks when I expect to make a lot of side trips away from camp; the blanket doubles as a groundsheet.

Breathable bivy bags, however, work well. Most are made from Gore-Tex, though there are a few that use other waterproof/breathable fabrics, including proprietary ones like Bibler's Todd-Tex. Highly breathable but not fully waterproof fabrics like Gore's Dryloft are also used; these are better than waterproof fabrics in dry cold or to keep drips off your sleeping bag inside a tent or snowhole, but they won't keep out a night of heavy rain. Many bivy bags have non-breathable, coated undersides. Obviously, with these you need to place your sleeping mat inside the bag to avoid problems with condensation. Some bags have straps inside to hold your mat in place. All bags have hoods of some sort, closed with a zipper or drawcord. The bigger bivy bags also can hold some of your gear. Weight depends on the fabric and the design, but generally runs from 12 to 28 ounces.

Straight-across zippers or drawcord-closed entrances are adequate for occasional use. Complex entrances with vertical, diagonal, or curved zippers—or even arm openings like the REI Cyclops Bivy Sack (28 ounces)—are only worth considering if you intend to bivouac regularly. Even better for heavy use are bivy bags with

poles at the head that keep the fabric off your face, plus mesh to keep out insects. These weigh in the 30- to 40-ounce range. (Makers include Outdoor Research, Integral Designs, and Feathered Friends.) One spacious option is to combine a small tarp with a bivy bag, using a hiking pole or poles for support. This isn't as stable as a bivy bag with integral poles, but the setup can allow you room to cook under cover.

Bivouacking offers the practical advantages of a light pack and the convenience of sleeping where a tent could not be pitched, such as in the lee of a boulder or under a spreading tree.

While a good bivy bag will keep out rain and wind, there are times when you don't want to be cocooned in one, particularly when cooking. Even if the weather is good, biting insects can make bivouacking a nightmare—although some bags come with insect netting. Thus, unless the night will be calm, dry, and insect-free, I prefer to sleep in a tent and cook, eat, read, write, and

In dry weather, shelter isn't needed—just a sleeping bag, mat, and groundsheet.

contemplate the world in comfort. This doesn't mean I never carry or use a bivy bag; there are situations, even when tent camping, when one can come in handy.

The bivy bag I use is a standard, 19-ounce Gore-Tex bag with a simple horizontal zippered entrance covered by a flap. It once kept me and my down sleeping bag dry during several hours of heavy rain—after I'd realized that to prevent leaks the zipper should be under rather than over me. That was many years ago. I rarely carry it on summer trips now—I just sleep out in my sleeping bag and move into a tent if the weather changes. I infrequently use a bivy bag on ultra-light overnight trips when the forecast is for fine weather. The last time I did this was to try out a prototype waterproof/breathable, coated poly-urethane bivy bag. I was high on a bare mountainside and the summer night was clear and starry. There was just a slight breeze, which I avoided by sleeping in a small hollow. By dawn, a thick, damp mist covered the ground. The outside of my bivy bag was wet, and there was a lot of condensation on the smooth inner surface and the outside of my sleeping bag. This isn't unusual, though bags with a soft, slightly furry inside (like most Gore-Tex ones) are less prone to condensation.

It's advisable to air your sleeping bag as soon as possible after a night in a bivy bag in order to get rid of any moisture it may have absorbed. In damp weather I always remove my sleeping bag from the bivy bag and pack it away as soon as I get up so it won't absorb more moisture than it already has. Condensation is another reason for using bivy bags only on short trips.

In winter I sometimes use the bivy bag inside my tent to protect against condensation drips and for extra warmth—a bivy bag adds several degrees to the range of a sleeping bag. This system can be used on long-distance walks where great variations in night temperatures can be expected.

I've also used the bivy bag when snowholing, and in damp shelters. Waterproofness deteriorates with use, and as my bivy bag is 14 years old, I wouldn't rely on it on a wet night anymore.

TARPS

Constructing your own shelter from sheets of plastic or nylon (tarps) and cord is something hardly any backpacker does these days—lightweight tents provide much greater protection against wind, rain, and insects. Because it's so cheap, torn polyethylene sheeting is too often found littering the wilderness. Even when they are carried out, poly sheets are still a solid-waste problem; in my view, they should not be used at all.

Tarps are useful, however, in parts of the world where the presence of bears means that you shouldn't eat or store food in your tent. On both the Canadian Rockies and Yukon walks, I carried a 9-by-8-foot silicone elastomer-coated ripstop nylon tarp, with grommets for attaching guylines along each side, to use as a kitchen shelter in wet and windy weather. I used it often enough to defend carrying its 16 ounces of weight. On the many occasions that I made camp in cold, wet, windy weather, the protection it provided while I cooked and ate was essential. I usually pitched it as a lean-to, slung between two trees on a length of cord. Occasionally I made more complex structures, using fallen trees and branches as makeshift poles, or I used my hiking pole. At sites with a picnic table, I found I could string the tarp over the table and create a sheltered sitting and eating area.

I've never used just a tarp in lieu of a tent on a long walk, though I can imagine doing so where I could camp under trees every night and where biting insects weren't a problem, or where rain was unlikely and I expected to sleep under the stars.

A tarp can be battened down to give almost as much protection as a tent. Note use of staff as center pole.

Another use for a tarp is as an awning for your tent. I've done this occasionally and it can provide a large under-cover cooking, storage, and drying area that also allows you to leave your tent door open in rain with no danger of leakage. I drape the tarp over the tent door, peg out the sides, then use a hiking pole or poles to support the front.

Lightweight tarps used to be hard to find, but no longer—some tent makers now offer coated nylon groundsheets, cut to the shape of their tent floors, that could double as adequate tarps. Campmor also makes a series to fit many popular tents. Weights range from 8 to 25 ounces and measurements from around 4 by 7 feet to 7 by 12 feet. Most have multiple grommets. Those from The North Face, called Tent Footprints, have elastic attachment loops, while Wild Country's Shadows have webbing pullouts. When I replace my current tarp, I'll probably get one of these.

The tarp I have now was specially made for me. Anyone with a sewing machine could make one by hemming a sheet of coated nylon and adding a few grommets for guylines and stakes.

Traditional rectangular coated nylon tarps are available from Campmor and Outdoor Products. These weigh from 12 to 50 ounces and measure from 5 by 7 feet to 12 by 16 feet.

There are a few sophisticated ripstop nylon tarps available from companies like Moss. These are expensive, but worth considering if you're thinking of using a tarp as your main shelter. These multi-sided tarps have many tie points. The larger ones, designed for groups, come with poles and weigh up to 15 pounds. Of more interest to most backpackers will be ones like the Moss Tentwing, which has an area of 35 square feet and weighs 28 ounces.

Bridging the gap between tarps and tents is the Black Diamond Megamid, described as a "three-person tarp tent." The Megamid is a pyramid-shaped ripstop nylon tarp with an adjustable shock-corded aluminum central pole. The total weight is 3 pounds 6 ounces, but the pole can be left behind and a staff, ski pole, or long stick substituted. The tarp also has integral loops, so it can be hung from a branch. The inside is 9 feet square—ample room for three people and

A tarp pitched as a lean-to is good for light rain, dew, and breezes, and as a shelter for short stops.

gear—and this sounds like an interesting design that should resist storms better than most tarps.

Netting

Insects can be a real problem if you use a tarp shelter. Some experienced backpackers I know drape pieces of no-see-um netting over the head of their sleeping bags. Edko makes a 34-by-34-inch Sleepscreen that weighs 10 ounces. If you want more room, the Edko Sleepscreen II measures 35 by 35 inches and weighs 23 ounces—this is a mini dome tent made of mesh that fits over the head of your sleeping bag.

If you want enough room to cook and store gear, then a large piece of netting—an "inner tent"—hung under a tarp would keep out all insects while giving reasonable living space. Simple nets are light and roomy. I haven't tried this myself, but it seems like a good idea.

GROUNDSHEETS

When sleeping out, with or without a bivy bag or tarp, a *groundsheet* protects the sleeping bag,

especially if the ground is wet. It's also handy if you want to spread out items that need to be kept clean and dry. I also carry a groundsheet when I stay in basic mountain huts, because the floors in these are often wet and muddy, and when I sleep in a snowhole. Now that tent floors are more durable, I no longer use one under my tent.

Most groundsheets are designed for car camping and are far too heavy for backpacking. Polythene sheets are lighter but don't last long, and they can't be staked out, which is necessary if it's windy. Waterproofed nylon is better, but is relatively expensive and it needs to be heavier than a tarp if it is to last. The coated nylon, tent-shaped groundsheets described on page 138 are probably the best ones currently available.

Before the new tent groundsheets appeared, the best ready-made groundsheets I'd come across were the laminated aluminized polyethylene, polyester, and 4 × 6½-foot fiberglass sheets available in various thicknesses under names such as Sportsman's Blanket and All Weather Blankets (12 and 17 ounces, respectively). They usually are blue or red on one side and silver on the other. Don't confuse them with the similar-looking but thin and useless "space blankets," which are often stacked with them in stores; these won't last one night as a groundsheet without tearing. Both blankets are far superior to plastic sheeting. One drawback is that they tend to crack and then leak at the fold points long before they are punctured or torn. When I replace the one I have, I intend to roll the new one rather than fold it to see if it lasts longer.

You can use one of these blankets as a tarp in an emergency, though they are a bit small for this. I used mine this way once during a thunderstorm in Yellowstone National Park. I wasn't carrying a full-size tarp, but I didn't want to cook in my tent because of bears, nor did I want to sit outside in the cold storm. So I slung my Sportsman's Blanket, carried as a groundsheet, between two trees as a lean-to, and used my pack as a seat while I cooked, ate, and watched the lightning flashes light up the forest and the rain bouncing off the sodden earth. I've also used one of these blankets, silver side out, as a sunshade when resting in shadeless desert.

TENTS

For most backpackers, shelter means a tent. A tent provides more protection from the weather than a bivy bag. It also provides space to sit up, cook, and eat in comfort, read, make notes, sort gear, play cards, and watch the world outside. A tarp provides more space, ounce-for-ounce, of course, but it doesn't give the same protection against windy weather or, especially, biting insects.

Selecting the right tent isn't easy. They come in all shapes and sizes, and few stores have the space to display many. There are, therefore, limited opportunities to see pitched tents and to crawl in and out of them to assess how well one suits your needs. Public tent displays are held in various places in many countries (the biggest is in Holland in September), but most people cannot get to these. However, a good store should be prepared to erect a tent you are considering buying so you can have a look at it. Good advice from a salesperson and careful study of catalogs and magazines will help you narrow the field.

But it's useful to have an idea of the type of tent you're looking for before you go shopping. When and where will it be used? How many must it sleep? How critical is weight? How do you feel about the color? Is the shape attractive? Price and personal choice also are important—this will be your home on many wilderness nights.

Because the main purpose of a tent is to protect the occupants from wind, rain, and snow, it must be wind- and waterproof. For wilderness use, it must also be lightweight and low in bulk when packed, while at the same time strong and durable.

Condensation

Like shell clothing, tents must repel rain while letting condensation out. The moisture constantly given off by your body is considerable over a night, to which may be added that from wet clothes and cooking. There is no perfect solution, but the problem is minimized by having two layers—a breathable, non-waterproof inner wall and a sealed waterproof *fly sheet.* The theory is that moisture passes through the inner fabric and is then carried away by the flow of air circulating between the two layers. Any condensation will be on the fly sheet and will run down it to the ground, with stray drips repelled by the inner wall.

To some extent this works. However, moist air is carried away only if there is a breeze and if it can escape. Since warm air rises, a vent high up on the fly sheet could create a chimney effect,

Key Features: Tents

- Easy pitching. Check for minimum stakes or freestanding design.
- Shock-corded poles that can be quickly fitted to the tent via clips or wide sleeves.
- Waterproof, UV-resistant fly sheet.
- Uncoated inner tent to allow condensation to escape.

- Good space-to-weight ratio.
- Insect net doors. (When the mosquitoes or black flies are abundant, this is more important than any other feature.)
- A roomy vestibule.

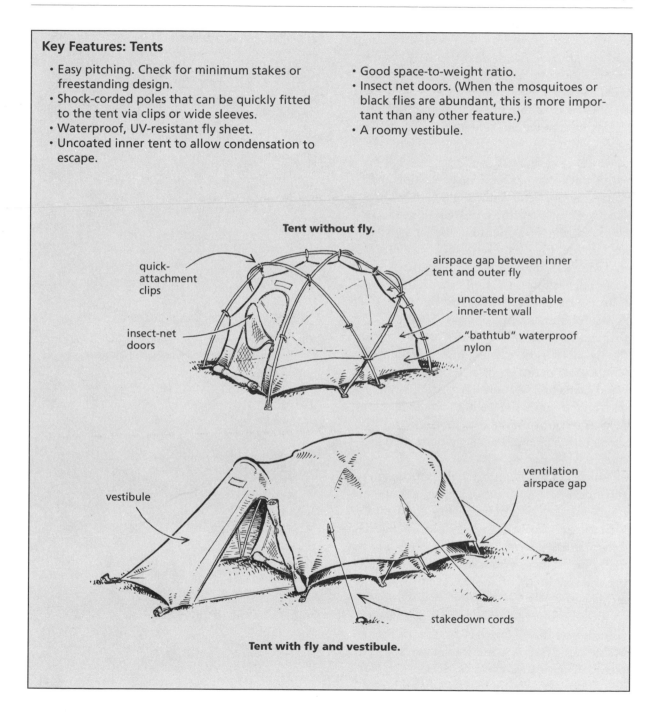

Tent without fly.

quick-attachment clips

insect-net doors

airspace gap between inner tent and outer fly

uncoated breathable inner-tent wall

"bathtub" waterproof nylon

vestibule

ventilation airspace gap

stakedown cords

Tent with fly and vestibule.

drawing cool, dry air in under the bottom edge and expelling damp air out the top. Vents are more common than they used to be, but most tents still don't have them; they are expensive and can be hard to make fully waterproof.

Instead, many tents have two-way door zippers. I always leave at least the top few inches open unless rain starts coming in through the gap—if it's a choice between protection and condensation, I close up the tent and let the fly sheet become soaked. To prevent this moisture from reaching the inner tent, the gap between the tent and the fly sheet must be big enough so that wind cannot push the two together.

Condensation is worst in calm, humid conditions. Nothing short of sleeping under the open sky—not even leaving all the doors open—can then prevent streams of water running down the fly sheet. Where biting insects are a problem, I've sometimes felt as though my tent was a sauna as I've cooked inside the vestibule with all the doors shut tightly, producing clouds of steam that promptly condensed on the fly sheet. I prefer being warm and damp to being eaten alive, however.

Condensation is a more serious problem in sub-freezing temperatures, when the inner tent can become so cold that moisture condenses on it and then drips back on the sleeper below. If temperatures drop even more, the moisture can freeze on the tent. When you wake in the morning and start to move about, creating heat, the ice melts.

If you camp regularly in damp, humid climes—on the Olympic Peninsula, or in the Maine woods—it's worth looking for tents with plenty of ventilation options, such as hoods over door zippers or covered vents. I'd avoid tents where the inner tent door is angled outward at the bottom—condensation on the fly sheet can drip onto the groundsheet or your sleeping bag when the door is open.

Double-Walled Tent Fabrics

Most two-skin tents are made of nylon or polyester. These are undoubtedly the best fabrics—they're strong, lightweight, quick-drying, and durable. Cotton, the traditional tent material, is not strong enough at the weights needed to make lightweight tents. The few all-cotton traditional (ridged) tents that are available are heavy—10 pounds minimum—which is fine for base camps or where you have pack animals or porters, but not for backpacking. Some people claim that very fine cotton, which is sometimes used as the inner in tents with nylon fly sheets, helps reduce condensation and feels pleasant. But even the lightest cotton inners are heavier than nylon ones and absorb condensation, which makes them heavier still, and they take a long time to dry. And if you touch a wet cotton inner, you will get wet and perhaps cause a drip at that spot.

A semi-geodesic dome with a properly fitted fly sheet: Ideally, it should be taut enough to enable water to run off and away from the tent but loose enough to allow air to circulate between the tent and the fly, limiting condensation.

Non-waterproofed nylon inners, in contrast, absorb no moisture, dry quickly, and are very light. Tents designed for warm weather usually have large mesh panels for ventilation, to keep out insects, and provide views of the stars when the fly sheet isn't being used. Anywhere that insects are a problem, mesh door panels (in addition to solid ones) are a good idea.

Fly sheets may be polyurethane- or elastomer silicone-coated; both keep out the rain. Elastomer silicone-coated nylon is the lightest and strongest and has the best ultraviolet light resistance. However, it doesn't meet fire-retardant standards and can't be sold in several states. Weights for tough inner and outer nylons are in the 1- to 2-ounces-per-square-yard range, the lighter ones needing slightly more care than the heavier. To prevent leaks, fly-sheet seams should be sealed. Many tents come with taped seams; others come with tubes of sealant that you must apply.

The double-skin tent design is the standard for lightweight tents. An intriguing alternative promoted by Stephensons-Warmlite tents is to have both layers made of coated fabric, permanently linked so they are pitched together, with an insulating layer of air between the two. The inner layer also has an aluminized coating on the inside to block radiant heat. There are low and high vents to create a chimney effect. This design minimizes condensation, according to the mak-

---

Testing a Single-Skin Tent

I used a Gore-Tex tent (a cross-over pole dome no longer available) on the Pacific Crest Trail, a walk that lasted more than five months, and I have a good idea of how single-layer tents work in different conditions. In the snowbound High Sierra, where the temperature fell to around 14°F (−10°C) every night and the humidity was low, I had no problems with condensation, whereas my companions in two-skin tents found their fly sheets frozen solid each morning. However, in wet weather in September in the Cascades, condensation was a real problem, with moisture running down the taped seams of the tent and forming pools on the groundsheet. On many rainy mornings I had to pack a wet tent and then pitch it, still sodden, in the evening, by which time the moisture had spread all over the groundsheet. I kept my down sleeping bag dry by sleeping in a Gore-Tex bivy bag inside the tent.

In theory, the efficiency of waterproof/breathable fabrics depends on the variation in pressure between the inside and the outside of the material, but I found levels of condensation related solely to the outside humidity, not whether I closed or opened the tent doors. I also found that ventilation was the best way to minimize and clear condensation. If I were to buy another single-skin tent, I would look for a good vent system.

But even then, I would use a single-skin tent only where prolonged wet weather and high humidity were unlikely. On a spring ski crossing of the vast Columbia icefield in the Canadian Rockies, our group of four had two similar-size tunnel tents—one a two-skin model, the other a Gore-Tex single-skin. Instead of four days, our crossing took eight because of blizzards, and we spent several days trapped in the tents. The temperature never dropped below 24°F (−4°C); most of the time it was within a degree or two of 32°F (0°C). This meant there was a slow thaw much of the time, which made conditions damp, with wet spindrift blowing constantly into the tents. The two of us in the two-skin tent stayed warm and comfortable, if bored. The condensation that formed on the fly sheet and in patches on the inner at night dried out during the day. The pair in the Gore-Tex tent had a rough time: Their down sleeping bags were wet with condensation, barely providing any insulation. Their tent was sodden inside and dripped on them constantly from the first night on. If we'd been trapped by the weather for many more days they could have been at serious risk of developing hypothermia.

ers, because the inner tent is warmer than in standard designs. I've not tried this approach, but it makes theoretical sense and has been reviewed positively.

Breathable Fabric Tents

Tents made from waterproof/breathable fabrics are easy to pitch, wind resistant, and lightweight because they have just one layer. Gore-Tex is used by many makers, but there are tents made from proprietary waterproof/breathable fabrics such as ToddTex (Bibler), Byrotex (Garuda), and Vertex (The North Face).

The advantages of single-skin tents are great, but there are disadvantages, too. It's generally agreed by makers that breathable fabrics don't work very well in larger tents, apparently because there isn't enough temperature and humidity differential between the interior space and the outside air for moisture vapor to pass through the fabric. Therefore, most single-skin models are small tunnels or domes.

Floors

Tent floors are usually made from urethane-coated nylon in weights from 1.9 to 4 ounces per square yard. The first nylon floors didn't stay waterproof for very long and ripped easily, which meant using a groundsheet under them. Now, the nylons used are tough enough not to need a groundsheet, though some people still do so. The tent I used on the Canadian Rockies walk was still waterproof after 80 nights without any protection under it.

The best floors are tray-shaped, without ground-level seams. Side walls prevent puddles outside the tent from splashing into the tent. Tiny puncture holes are the most likely damage to occur to floors. Covering them with spots of nylon tape prevents further leaks.

If you use a groundsheet with your tent, be sure the edges don't extend beyond the edges of the fly sheet, or rain can collect between it and the tent floor. Even when it's tucked well under the tent this can still happen. When I use a groundsheet (which I do only when a tent floor is worn and no longer waterproof and I haven't yet returned it to the maker to be replaced), I place it *inside* the tent.

Poles

These days, most tent poles are flexible, though some traditional tent designs still use rigid poles. The latter are always made from aluminum, flexible ones usually so, though some are made from fiberglass. I've never used a tent with hollow fiberglass poles, but makers claim they are stronger than aluminum ones; they're certainly lighter. I have used flexible aluminum poles extensively, and have found them excellent. Easton 7075 tempered aluminum is generally regarded as the best for poles and it's used by many of the leading tent makers. The latest material is Magnum Helix glass/epoxy, which is said to be 50 percent stronger than the same weight of aluminum or fiberglass. Kelty uses it.

Some flexible poles come pre-bent (that is, they are curved when new). If they are not prebent, they often develop a curve with use. This is not something to worry about—just don't try to straighten them because they may break. Poles with the sections linked by elastic shock cord are the easiest to use, especially in tents where they are threaded through sleeves.

I avoid tents that have solid fiberglass poles because the sections can come apart inside the tent sleeve—a real nightmare. With shock cord–linked poles, it's almost impossible to lose sections (though I managed it once after a shock cord snapped). You also don't have to fiddle around putting the right pieces together every time you pitch the tent. Some rigid poles "nest" inside each other. The only advantage is lower bulk, though not enough in my view to counteract the lack of shock cord, especially since inner sections can be difficult to remove.

Most flexible and some rigid poles are attached to the tent, either the inner or the outer, by threading them through nylon or mesh sleeves and then fixing the end in a grommet or loop. However, a growing number of makers use clips, D-rings, or shock cord to hang the tent from the poles; some use flexible hubs at pole intersections. These are quicker to pitch than sleeved poles, and allow better airflow between inner and fly sheet. I don't think there's enough difference between the various methods to choose a tent because of it, though. Weight, size, design, and overall quality are far more important.

Poles are strong when the tent is pitched but vulnerable when lying on the ground. This is especially so with long, thin, flexible ones. Be careful not to step on them! And don't use them as hand-holds when entering and leaving the tent. A companion once broke one of my flexible poles by putting all his weight on it as he left the tent. This was during a winter gale in a remote area of Norway, so I had to scramble out of my sleeping bag, throw on some clothes, and repair it before the storm caused any damage. (I fixed it by slipping a short alloy sleeve over the break and binding it in place with tape. Such sleeves are supplied with most flexible pole tents. I always carry one, though that's the only time I've used it.)

Stakes

Regardless of advertisements and catalog photos, every tent requires some staking to hold it down in wind. How many staking points are needed is another matter—15 to 20 is reasonable, though some tents require fewer. Long, heavy steel stakes aren't necessary. I usually use 7-inch, round alloy stakes (⅓ ounce each), which hold in most soils; for softer ground, I always carry a few 6-inch alloy V-angle stakes (½ ounce each). Stakes are easy to misplace, so I take two or three more than needed to pitch the tent. I've returned on many occasions with more stakes than I started out with, having found ones others have lost. I keep stakes in the small nylon stuff sack supplied with most tents, and carry them in a pack pocket so that they're easy to find when I pitch the tent.

Guylines

Depending on the design, tents need anything from two to a dozen or more guylines to keep them taut and stable in a wind, though more than 10 is too many for a tent that will be pitched daily. Most tents come supplied with a full set of guys, but some only have the main ones, plus attachment points for others. It pays to attach these extra guys because they're usually needed in a storm. I'd rather have plenty of guylines and leave them tied back when it's calm than not have enough.

To avoid confusion and to help when sorting out tangles, different-colored guylines are useful, especially when several are attached to the tent at the same point. If the guylines are tied back in loops when packing your tent they are less likely to tangle. I always try to do this, though when packing in a hurry during a storm I often forget and end up cursing myself the next night as I undo knots with numb fingers. Metal locking sliders come with most guylines, but you can also buy them separately. It's useful to know how to tie the tautline hitch (see accompanying illustration) in case you need extra guylines and have no extra mechanical sliders. Nylon stretches when wet, so guylines should be staked out tightly. If it's wet and windy, I generally retighten them before going to sleep.

The tautline hitch

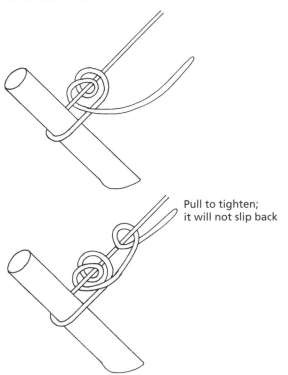

Pull to tighten;
it will not slip back

Size and Weight

The weight of a tent is directly related to its size. Tents come in a wide range of sizes—from tiny bivy tents barely big enough for one person to monsters that will sleep four Himalayan mountaineers and all their gear. The minimum space needed is enough to lie down and stretch out without pushing against the walls or either end— and this is all the space the smallest tents have. They don't have the room to allow you to sit out a storm in comfort (which means having enough headroom to sit up), nor space to lay out gear inside, nor a vestibule big enough for safe cooking. How much space two people need depends on how cramped they're prepared to be and how friendly they are. (Many tents described

in catalogs as sleeping two assume very close friendships!)

Most tent makers give the floor areas of their tents, as do some retailers, and all give length and width so you can compare sizes. As a rough guide, I'd look for at least 27 to 30 square feet of floor area in a three-season tent for two, and 30 to 35 square feet or more in a winter tent. For solo use, 25 to 27 square feet is plenty of room. The width for twosomes should be at least 54 inches at the widest point; for soloists, 36 inches. The length for each should be 7 to 8 feet, longer if you're taller than 5 foot 10 inches. Those over 6 feet tall need to consider length carefully; in many tents, they'll find their feet pushing against the end.

For summer use below timberline or in desert areas where storms are unlikely and you just want a bedroom to keep out bugs or the occasional shower, the smallest, lightest tents may be fine. If you venture above timberline or into winter, however, more room is needed because you may have to cook under cover or sit out a four-day blizzard.

Being able to sit up in a tent makes a huge difference to how "roomy" it feels. This is so important to me that I don't use tents, however lightweight, that don't allow me to sit up straight, because they make me feel uncomfortably confined. The key factor here is the distance between the floor and the top of your head when you're sitting cross-legged. If you know that, you can determine from catalogs which tents will be roomy and which will give you a crick in the neck. I always look for a tent with at least 35 inches inner height. If two of you want to sit up, that height should run the entire length of the inner.

You also should consider the size of the vestibule, if any. If you expect to cook and store gear in the vestibule, it needs to be roomy enough for you to do so and still allow you to

A cross-over pole dome tent with two entrances is excellent for access, ventillation, and views.

enter and leave. It must also be high enough to prevent the fabric from catching fire or melting when a stove is used under it. Tents for two often have double vestibules, and although they are heavier, they make tent living much easier. For areas where you usually live outside and only use the tent for sleeping, vestibule size isn't crucial. In bear country you never cook, eat, or store food in the tent, so you don't need a vestibule for that purpose.

I also like vestibules with large zippered doors that can be rolled out of the way to give me a view. It's not quite the same as bivouacking, but lying with my head by the door is far better than spending a fine evening or night encased in a nylon cocoon. This is why I also prefer tents in which the whole front or side of the tent can be opened up.

Making a big, roomy tent is no problem. Making a big, roomy, lightweight tent is, even with modern materials. I was surprised once to find that my tents were 20 to 25 percent *heav-*

ier than ones I'd used a decade earlier—I had been seduced by complex designs and masses of room. I decided I would no longer carry a tent that weighed more than 4½ pounds for solo use, and I've stuck to that, the only exceptions being when I've tested heavier tents for magazine reviews. Keeping the weight down when you share a tent is easier. I've used a 5½-pound tent for snow camping with two and not felt cramped, and there are plenty in the 5- to 8-pound range that provide ample room.

Some tent makers include the weight of the stuff sacks, poles, and stakes in the specs, but most only give the weight of the tent, fly sheet, and poles (apparently believing that stuff sacks, guylines, and stakes are optional items you might leave behind on some trips). Conveniently, this just happens to lead to lower catalog weights for tents. Few backpackers leave stakes behind except by mistake, and guylines and stuff sacks are normally carried too, so what is important is the *pack weight,* sometimes called the *field* or

Vestibules are useful as windbreaks.

trail weight. The difference is significant—up to 12 ounces in a solo unit, as much as 1½ pounds in a two-person winter model. Some retailers give the pack weights of tents. If you're unsure, weigh the tent yourself before purchase.

Stability

The stability of your tent becomes a matter of great concern once you've struggled alone in the dark, cramming gear into a pack under a thrashing sheet of nylon after the wind has snapped one of your tent poles—which happened to me in the English Lake District one August. It was pouring rain and I had to make a long night descent to the valley, where the only shelter I could find was in a public toilet. If it had been a more remote location in winter, I could have been in serious trouble.

Over the years, three tents have collapsed on me—twice because of the wind and once because of a heavy, wet snowfall. And on two occasions I've camped with others whose tents have been blown down. I've also slept peacefully in a well-designed tent during a gale that blew down less-stable tents nearby and shook others so hard that the occupants had little sleep. If you spend the night expecting your thrashing tent to collapse at any minute, you'll be too exhausted to enjoy the next day.

The importance of tent stability depends on where and when you use your tent. For three-season, low-level, sheltered camping, it's not a

Snow camping can be comfortable. Note the seat inside the vestibule and the sunbathing slot.

Some tents won't withstand high winds.

major concern. For high-level, exposed sites and winter mountain camping, stability should be a prime factor in tent choice.

Tent shape, the materials it's made of, the number of supporting poles and how they are arranged, and the number and position of guy-lines all contribute to stability. Makers describe tents as three- or four-season models, which give a general indication of stability. The best three-season tents generally are as stable as four-season ones; often what they lack is extra space, snow-shedding ability, and large vestibules.

Stability is relative: Gales that strip roofs off buildings and blow down trees can certainly shred even the strongest four-season mountain tent. In strong winds, your experience and ability to select a sheltered site are as important as the tent you have. In storms, if pitching the tent seems impossible, it's better to go on, even after dark, in search of a more sheltered spot. You rarely have to camp in storm-force winds, but if you do, seek out whatever windbreaks you can—piles of stones or banks of vegetation—and consider sleeping out in a bivy bag, if you are carrying one, or even wrapped up in your tent. It may be uncomfortable, but it beats having your tent destroyed in the middle of the night.

Careful pitching is important, too. A taut tent with no loose folds of material will resist wind much better than a saggy mass of nylon. The best mountain tents will still thrash around in a storm if badly pitched. When pitched properly, a stable tent should feel fairly rigid when you push against the poles.

DESIGN

Since the advent of dome tents in the early 1970s, designers have created a bewildering array of tent shapes, some of them quite bizarre. Overall, though, these developments have led to a superb range of tents that are lighter, roomier, tougher, and more durable than ever before.

Ridge Tents

Before flexible poles appeared, most tent designs were variations on the standard ridge tent, a solid structure still popular with many backpackers. The general floor shape is rectangular, but the lightest ones often taper in width and height at the rear. The simplest, but least stable and most awkward to use, are those with upright poles at either end. Except for some budget models, the few tents in this category still available have A-poles, which make a far more stable tent and also leave entrances clear. Many have ridge poles as well, which make the tents free-standing and more wind resistant. A-pole tents don't have good space-to-weight ratios, however, and the angled walls mean a lack of headroom compared with other designs.

Domes

As good as the best traditional tents are, flexible-pole dome models are vastly superior. Dome tents are those in which the flexible poles cross each other at some point. They are the roomiest tents available, and they are self-supporting, so they can be pitched and then picked up and moved to another position—if there's no wind.

Tent types.

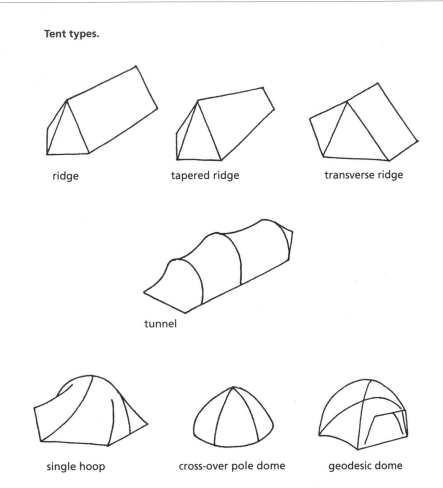

ridge   tapered ridge   transverse ridge

tunnel

single hoop   cross-over pole dome   geodesic dome

(One does hear stories of tents taking off in a wind like giant balloons, never to be seen again.)

The two most common domes are the *geodesic* and *cross-over pole,* though there are many variations. Geodesic domes are highly complex structures in which four or more long poles cross each other at several points to form roomy, stable tents. Cross-over pole domes are simpler: two or three poles cross at the apex to make a spacious tent that is lighter than a geodesic, though not as stable. Weights for either start at about 5½ pounds. Both geodesics and cross-over pole domes are popular, so the choice is large. Makers are legion.

Neither geodesic nor cross-over pole designs can be scaled down efficiently to make solo tents, but geodesic domes are the most stable, roomiest two-person tents available. Because of this, geodesics have developed a good reputation for mountaineering and polar expedition use, but at 9 pounds and more, full-size ones are too heavy for summer backpacking trips. Elongated, low-profile domes are lighter, however, and are excellent for mountain camping in winter. My favorite winter camping tent (when I'm not going solo) is a four-pole, low-profile Wild Country Quasar, a "stretched geodesic" design. It has large vestibules at each end and enough room for two to sleep, live, and cook under cover. Being rectan-

A cross-over pole dome tent at a high mountain camp.

Headroom is excellent. I've had four playing cards in it during a storm! It has sleeved poles and goes up on 14 stakes very quickly. The inherent shape is so stable that only two side guys are needed. I've used it in storms and blizzards everywhere from the Halingskarvet Mountains in Norway to the Pyrenees and the Isle of Skye, and never felt insecure in it. When other tents are shaking like jelly, it just sways slightly from side to side. I've also lived in it for 36 hours at a stretch without feeling cramped or falling out with my tent partner.

Corporate changes mean it's currently available from two companies—under its original name of Quasar from Terra Nova (at 8 pounds 2 ounces), and from Wild Country as the Mountain (at 8 pounds 12 ounces). Its success can be judged by the number of similar tents from other makers, including The North Face, Mountain Hardwear, Sierra Designs, Bibler (whose single-skin Fitzroy is the lightest low-profile geodesic, at 6 pounds), and Eureka.

gular, it offers more usable floor space (33.8 square feet) than the usual hexagonal geodesic.

An elongated low-profile geodesic dome—probably the best design for high mountain winter camping.

Three-pole semi-geodesic domes are roomy, lightweight, and freestanding.

Lighter are three-pole semi-geodesics, cross-over pole domes with a third pole added at the front. In some models—the better ones in my experience—the back of the tent is tapered to the ground to give a very stable wedge shape. On the Continental Divide walk, I used a tent of this design (a Wild Country Voyager weighing 6 pounds; the current version, the Terra Nova Ultra Voyager, weighs 5½ pounds), and found it roomy, durable, and good in gales and heavy snowfalls, when the flat roofs of these designs can be a problem. It's described as a two-person, three-season tent. I enjoyed the space, but I wouldn't carry such a heavy tent on a long solo walk again. Few semi-geodesics are light enough for solo use, in fact, and those that are use lighter materials to achieve lower weights. The North Face's popular 4¼-pound Lunar Light (formerly the Tadpole) is probably the lightest. It has mesh side walls and doors on the inner. It's ideal for warm-weather use (it has a three-season rating),

but cold breezes can blow under the fly sheet and through the mesh, so it's not for the cold.

For two, though, the semi-geodesic design is an excellent choice—it's stable, freestanding, and light for the space provided.

Tunnels

In tunnel tents, the poles form a series of parallel hoops along the length of the tent. The great advantage of tunnels is that they have a better space-to-weight ratio than any other design. They're also very easy to pitch, though they're not freestanding. This category includes the tiniest tents—such as single-skin bivy tents, some with just one pole—weighing only 2 to 3 pounds. I've never tried one because they are so low and narrow that I get claustrophobic just looking at them. The simplest models that can be called real tents have two hoops and weigh upward of 3½ pounds.

If the support poles are far apart, leaving large

A two-pole tunnel tent—
light enough for one, roomy
enough for two.

areas of material between them to catch the wind, tunnel tents aren't very stable. However, tunnels with poles that are close together and with tension stakes at each end are much more wind tolerant. I used a 4¾-pound, two-pole tunnel—the Swedish-made Hilleberg Nallo 2—on a 1,300-mile Scandinavian mountains walk, and found it highly stable as long as I pitched the rear into the wind. (Cross-winds shake tunnels, and one night the tent was shaking so much I got up around midnight and dashed out into the lashing rain to turn the tent 90 degrees into the wind. The difference was astonishing.)

The lightest tunnel tents, indeed the lightest tents for the size of any design, are the Stephensons-Warmlite models. They are made of ultralight fabrics and the weights are astounding—the smallest model, the 2R, weighs an ounce under 3 pounds, yet is 60 inches wide at the front, 48 inches wide at the rear, 134 inches long, and 40 inches high at the apex. Standard are inside *stabilizer straps* for use in high winds.

I've used these in British-made tunnel tents and found they improve stability.

There are several tunnel tents suitable for three-season solo use, including the popular Sierra Designs Clip Flashlight, at 3 pounds 10 ounces. Larger tunnel tents often have three

Large three-to-four-person three-pole tunnel tents at an exposed camp on the Greenland ice cap.

poles, sometimes of different sizes, with the largest one placed in the middle. These are excellent for two or more people. The high center pole creates a great deal of living space. Two of us found one such tent adequate for the several days we spent trapped by a blizzard on the Columbia icefield.

Like domes, tunnel tents are very popular, and most tent makers have at least one in their catalog.

Single-Hoop Tents

The problem with solo tents is that weight and size are related. Length has to remain constant, of course—one person needs the same space to stretch out as two—which means that width and height have to be reduced to cut the weight. A slimmed-down version of a ridge, dome, or tunnel tent usually results in a tent you can barely sit up in. One answer is the single-hoop tent, a style that really only works for solo tents. As the name suggests, this design features one long, curved pole that may run across the tent or along the length of it. Single-hoop tents can be remarkably stable for their weight if the guying system is good.

I know of only one North American single-hoop tent—the single-skin Garuda Jalan Jalan, which weighs 3 pounds 7 ounces and has a

Single-hoop tents are ideal for solo backpacking.

floor area of 27.4 square feet. In Europe there are more models, the lightest of which is the Swedish Hilleberg Akto, which weighs 3 pounds 10 ounces. I used the Akto for a 15-day fall trip to the Grand Canyon and found it excellent.

PITCHES AND PITCHING: MINIMUM-IMPACT CAMPING

One of the pleasures of backpacking is sleeping in a different place every night. This can also be one of the horrors if you are stumbling around in the rain looking for a site long after dark. In areas where there are prepared backcountry sites that must be used, as in some of the national parks, finding a pitch isn't a problem. In other popular areas, especially along long-distance

Siting in the Dark

One day toward the end of the Canadian Rockies walk, I picked a small lake on a watershed for a camp, only to find when I reached it a half hour or so before dark that the area around it was a quagmire, beyond which were steep slopes. Circling the lake, I saw there was no place to camp, so I continued on down into the forest, my headlamp picking out the trail ahead. For some time, I descended a steep hillside where it would have been a waste of time to even look for a site. Eventually, the trail, which was not marked on my map, reached the valley bottom, crossed a creek, and started up the other side. There was no flat ground, but there was water—the first since the lake—so I stopped and searched for a site. I found one between two fir trees. There was barely enough room for the tent, but the ground was flat enough for me to sleep comfortably. In the morning, my site looked as makeshift as you could imagine, the sort of place no one would dream of selecting in daylight, but it had served its purpose.

On forested hillsides, flat ground may be hard to find.

trails, you will find plenty of well-used sites. If you take time to look at such places and work out why they have been used so much, you'll soon learn what to look for when selecting a site.

There are both practical and aesthetic criteria involved in selecting a good campsite. For a good night's rest you want as flat a site as possible on ground that is fairly firm and dry. Often, however, you must make do with a slight slope; most people then sleep with their head uphill (if I don't, I develop a bad headache and cannot sleep). Sometimes the slope can be so gentle that it's unnoticeable—until you lie down and try to sleep. If it's very windy, a sheltered spot makes for a more secure and less noisy camp, though I often head uphill and into the breeze if insects are a problem.

Water nearby is a necessity, unless you carry it to what you know will be a waterless pitch, as I sometimes do. It's best not to camp right next to a creek or pool, however; you could damage the banks, you'll be highly visible to other visitors, and you may deter wildlife. In many national parks and wilderness areas in the United States, camping within a few hundred feet of water is illegal as well. Siting well away from water and trails whenever possible is best.

When I'm in unfamiliar country where there are no "official" sites, I generally work out over

Short grass withstands camping impact better than longer vegetation. A camp in the Colorado Rockies.

breakfast each morning where I want to be that evening and select from the map a probable area for a site. Usually I find a reasonable spot soon after I arrive. If an obvious one doesn't present itself within minutes, I take off my pack and explore the area. If this doesn't produce a spot I'm happy with, I shoulder the pack and move on. At times, especially when daylight hours are short, this can mean continuing into the night.

When a selected site turns out to be unusable and I have to continue, tired and hungry, into the night, I remind myself that a site always turns up; it just may require a little imagination to make the most of what seems unsuitable terrain. Perfect pitches are wonderful, yet many of those I remember best are the ones, like that in the northern Rockies (see sidebar), that were snatched almost out of thin air.

Minimum-impact camping is necessary if we are to preserve wild lands. The rules I give may not seem to accord with the freedom of backpacking, but I'd rather follow them and be able,

in most areas, to choose where I camp than to have my sites selected for me.

All sites, whether previously used or not, should be left spotless, which means no trenching around tents, no cutting of turf, and no preparation of the tent site. Previously unused sites should always—*always*—be left with no sign anyone has been there. This means camping on bare ground or forest duff, or on vegetation such as grass that will be least damaged by your stay—which shouldn't be longer than one night. If you will be staying more than one night on a site that is easily damaged, move your tent or tents each day. Paths from tent to water are easily created by groups, though solo campers can make them, too. You can reduce the number of trips by carrying a water container big enough to supply your camp and by using a different route each time you go to the water. Fires should be lit only if you can do so without leaving any sign of them when you depart. Rocks moved to hold down tent stakes—rarely necessary though often

Stone walls built to protect tents from the wind should always be dismantled.

done—should be returned to the streams or boulder fields from where they were taken; I've spent many hours removing rings of stones marking regularly used sites everywhere from the Scottish Highlands to the Rocky Mountains. When you leave a wild site, make sure you obliterate all evidence you've been there, roughing up any flattened vegetation as a last chore.

Of course, you will often camp on sites that have been used before. If possible, I pass by what looks to be a site that is used only occasionally, perhaps stopping to disguise further the signs of its use. A well-used site, however, should be reused, because doing so limits the impact to one place in a given area. This doesn't give you license to add to the damage, however. Use bare patches for pitching and any existing fireplaces or rings. Tidying up the place may encourage others to use the site rather than make new ones. As with every site, leave nothing and alter nothing.

What can the minimal-impact camper do about flooding, since trenching around tents is not an option? Flooding does happen, albeit rarely; I've only been swamped three times. On the first occasion I was able to move to a higher, drier site nearby, but the second time there was nowhere to go, and a lengthy thunderstorm was sending streams of rain running under the groundsheet. This had my companion and me running around barelegged, draped in rain jackets, digging shallow diversion ditches with our ice axes. I wasn't happy doing this—even though it was because the site was so well used that the hard-packed soil wouldn't soak up the water—but I was less happy at the thought of the tent being flooded. After the storm, we tried as well as we could to replace the earth and minimize the signs of our trenching. On the third occasion, again camping on a well-used, hard-packed site, I woke to find the groundsheet floating on a pool of water. A short, shallow trench dug with my toilet trowel allowed this to drain off, and there was little damage to repair.

My view now is that, while trenching should never be done on a pristine site or before it is absolutely necessary, a minimum of digging is justifiable if there is no other choice, the site is well used, and the soil is replaced afterward.

Safe Camping

Wilderness camping is generally a safe activity as long as you have the right gear and necessary skills. However, there are some external dangers—what climbers call "objective" dangers—that need considering at times.

In forests, dead trees and branches can fall on your tent; it's always wise to look up when selecting a site and not camp under dead limbs. If there are dead trees nearby, I like to ensure they are leaning away from the tent. Trees don't just fall in storms, either—the only time I've seen a tree come down was on a calm day in Yellowstone National Park. I heard a loud crack and looked up to see a large pine topple over and crash to the ground.

Lightning is a potential hazard at certain times of the year. Camping out in the middle of a large open area or above timberline isn't advisable during summer thunderstorms. On a two-week trip I took in the Colorado Rockies there were thunderstorms every evening, often lasting well into the night, and on several occasions I reluctantly passed up scenic timberline campsites and descended to camp in the security of the forest. When a deafening crack of thunder right overhead woke me up, and the flashes of lightning lit up the tent, I was glad to be deep in the trees.

Big storms can cause a different and potentially serious problem in desert areas: flash floods. Heavy rainfall in mountains far away can cause walls of water to roar down desert

A single-hoop tent in a side canyon of the Grand Canyon. Be wary of flash floods at such sites.

canyons, sweeping away everything in their path. If there are signs of distant storms, I'd be very careful about camping in narrow canyons or at the bottom of drainages that are regularly swept by floods. In many desert areas, summer months bring frequent storms that make camping in any canyon bottom hazardous. I've never seen a flash flood, though I have seen the destruction these floods can cause. There is a dramatic and sobering description of a flash flood in George Steck's *Grand Canyon Loop Hikes II* (Chockstone Press) that is well worth reading if you are going backpacking in desert canyons. Steck narrowly escaped when his camp was overwhelmed by flood water. He lost his tarp, groundsheet, pad, sleeping bag, boots, spare clothing, eating implements, and walking stick, many of which were found downstream the next day. (The book, with its companion volume, *Grand Canyon Loop Hikes I*, is entertaining and informative and recommended reading for anyone venturing off the main trails in the Grand Canyon.)

High mountains with permanent snowfields and glaciers present another problem: avalanches (of snow rather than water). This isn't much of a problem except in winter and spring, but there are a few canyon bottom campsites I know of—one of them on the Pacific Crest Trail in the Glacier Peak Wilderness in the North Cascades—which can be swept by avalanches even in summer. Signs to watch for are treeless corridors below snowfields, bent and flattened vegetation, and large areas of willows and alder—the latter often called "slide alder" because it occurs so often in avalanche zones. These shrubs are flexible enough to survive repeated avalanches.

Making Camp

Compared with finding a site, setting up camp is easy. I don't have a set routine—it all depends on the time and the weather. In cold or wet weather, when I'm exhausted or if darkness is imminent, I pitch the tent immediately and chuck in the gear I'll need overnight. I then fill my water bottles, crawl into the tent, change into warm or dry clothes if necessary, set up the stove, and sort out my gear in comfort while the water boils for a hot drink. (This assumes I'm not in an area where bears could be a problem, of course). By the time the water has boiled, I'm comfortably in my sleeping bag. The whole operation from starting to pitch the tent to taking the first sip can be done in 10 minutes, though I usually like to do it in a more leisurely 15 or 20. The key is knowing your tent so well that you

Staking out a tent.

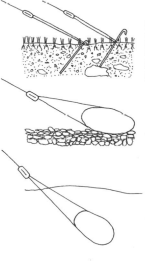

Drive stake into ground at 45 degrees, buried to the head if possible. Otherwise, guyline should go around it at ground level.

On stony ground or loose gravel it may be necessary to tighten the guyline around a large boulder.

On snow, tie guyline around a buried stuff sack filled with snow. Stamp down snow on top of it.

Alternatively, put the guyline around the middle of a stick or long stake that is buried horizontally.

can pitch it even when you're too tired to think. For greatest weather resistance and strength, pitch your tent very taut and tighten guylines until, in Phoenix's words, "you can play a tune on them." This also minimizes flapping and noise. When there's plenty of daylight and it's warm and sunny, I may just sit and relax for a half hour before I do anything.

In some places and at certain times, though, setting up camp is not so easy. In rocky terrain where stakes won't go in you may have to attach loops to the staking points and tie them and the guylines to rocks to hold down the tent. I've only done this a couple of times, but when I have had to, it's been essential—it's one reason why I always carry a length of cord. In deep snow, tent stakes are nearly useless. However, in total snow cover, you'll be carrying items such as ice axes, crampons, skis, and ski poles—all of which can be used to support the tent, through extra guylines tied to the staking points if necessary.

In soft snow, I use skis or snowshoes to stamp out a hard platform first; a snow shovel is also

A wall of snow blocks protects a winter camp from the wind. Note the use of skis and poles as stakes for guylines.

useful for this, especially when it comes to the final leveling of the site. If you use stakes, loop the guylines around them, then bury them lengthwise and pack the snow down on top. Once the temperature falls below zero, they'll freeze in place. Come morning, you'll probably need an ice ax to dig them out. Sticks could be used instead of stakes. An alternative, which I've never tried, is to fill stuff sacks with snow, attach guylines to them, and bury them. There are special, wide snow stakes available for snow camping that work well. However, they're bulky and relatively heavy, so I've only used them with groups on trips where we camped on snow every night. I'd rather improvise.

Whatever the surface, pitching a tent is easy—except in wind. You just follow the instructions that come with it. With a new tent, do a practice run in the garden or on open ground near your home to familiarize yourself with how it goes up and to check that all the pieces are there. There are so many different ways of putting up tents that detailed advice is impossible. If it's windy, I generally stake out the end of the inner or outer, whichever pitches first, that will face into the wind, then thread or clip the poles into position before raising the tent off the ground. In a strong wind, you may have to lay on the tent while you do this. The more the tent thrashes in the wind, the more vulnerable it is to damage, so speed is important. Once the basic shape is established, the rest of the staking can be done in a more relaxed manner. If the site allows, rectangular or tapered tents should be pitched with the tail or end into the wind; keeping the door in the lee of the wind is a good idea for cooking, too. Rain is not as much of a problem as wind, though you'll want to get a double-skin tent up quickly.

When striking camp, I usually pack the tent last so that it can air out and any condensation can dry. In rain, I pack everything under cover.

In very heavy rain, you can collapse the inner tent, leaving the fly sheet staked out, withdraw the poles, and then stuff the inner into its bag from under the fly sheet so that it stays dry. Shock cord–linked poles must be pushed out of their sleeves. If you pull them, they're likely to come apart. In very cold conditions, pole sections may freeze together—don't try to force them apart, as they may break. Instead, rub the joints with your hands until the ice melts. In bitter cold, I wear liner gloves to do this so the metal doesn't stick to my skin. If poles are frozen together, the chances are that any condensation will have frozen to the fly sheet. If the fly sheet is coated with ice on the inside and frost on the outside, shake as much of it off as you can before you pack it. If the day is sunny and you have time, you could wait for it to thaw and evaporate.

TENT CARE

Tents look after themselves when you're out walking. On sunny mornings, I try to dry off any condensation, spreading the tent over bushes or dry ground or hanging it over a length of cord or branch. If stakes are particularly dirty, I wipe them clean. Most tents come with two stuff sacks for poles and stakes, but only one for the fly sheet and inner. I always use an extra stuff sack for the fly, because two small units are easier to pack and it keeps the dry inner tent separate from the fly sheet if the latter is wet. The easiest way to pack tents is, appropriately enough, to *stuff* them into their stuff sacks—the waterproofing may crack along crease lines if you habitually fold the tent the same way. I always put my tent near the top of the pack so it's accessible for quick pitching the next night. I slide the poles down one of the corners of the pack between the sides and back. (Some people strap poles to the outside of the pack, but I'm afraid they might be damaged there, or even fall off and be lost. Stakes tend to work their way down to the bottom when kept in the main pack, so I put mine in a pocket.)

After a trip, I hang the tent up to dry before storing it in its stuff sacks. Nylon won't rot, but a tent stored wet will mildew, which leaves a stain and an unpleasant, musty smell and may damage the proofing. Single-skin waterproof/breathable tents need plenty of drying time; they often appear dry even when damp, as moisture can remain in the slightly absorbent inner material. If you want to wash your tent, use mild soap and warm water, never detergent, as this can damage the proofing. Poles will corrode if not dried before storage. Salt corrodes poles very fast, so if you have been camping near the sea, wipe them down before you dry and store them.

WILDERNESS SHELTERS

Many wilderness areas have unlocked shelters for walkers to use. These usually provide shelter from the elements but no more, so you'll still need a sleeping bag, mat, stove, and warm clothing. On certain long-distance routes, such as the Appalachian Trail, walkers can use shelters almost every night. The most luxurious I've found are in Scandinavia, where pinewood huts contain wood-burning stoves with supplies of logs, bunk beds, cooking utensils, and food supplies. There is a charge for these huts—payment is made via an honor box on the wall—and many are wardened in the summer. Most mountain shelters are primitive; some are just lean-tos. I generally prefer the freedom and solitude of a tent or bivouac, but in bad weather such shelters can be a blessing. I always like to know where they are in case I need them.

SNOW CAVES

In deep snow, you can dig a shelter rather than pitch a tent. Snow is a good insulator and cuts out all wind; inside a snow cave, it is calm and quiet even when a blizzard rages outside. To dig a proper one takes at least several hours, so you

Snow holes can be surprisingly comfortable. Denise Thorn revising some theory during a storm.

Snow domes are easy to build—first just pile up a large heap of snow.

Once the dome is built, simply tunnel into it and dig out the center.

need to consider this if you're planning to dig one. Ice axes, cooking pans, and toilet trowels can all be used as digging tools, but a proper snow shovel speeds up the process considerably.

Whatever tool you use, digging snow is hot work; strip off your warmwear so it doesn't become soaked with sweat. Start by digging a narrow, horizontal trench into a bank of snow

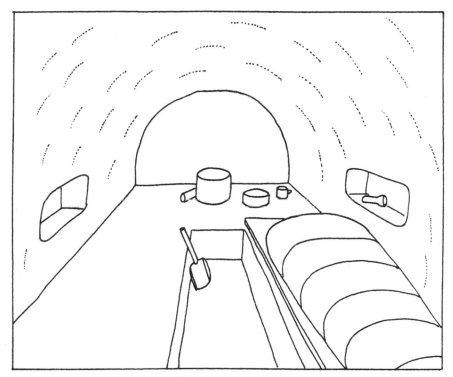

Sleeping benches and cooking area inside a snow cave.

A snow trench with a tarp roof held in place by ski poles and with a ski as a center pole.

Stages in excavation of a snow cave.

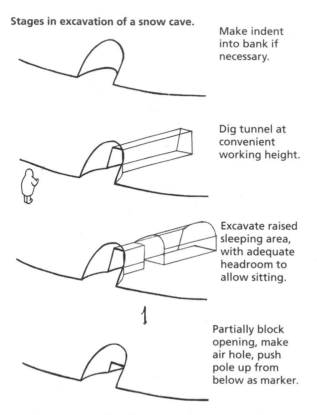

Make indent into bank if necessary.

Dig tunnel at convenient working height.

Excavate raised sleeping area, with adequate headroom to allow sitting.

Partially block opening, make air hole, push pole up from below as marker.

that is at least 6 feet deep. Once you are well into the snow bank, you can dig out the area around it to form waist-level sleeping platforms. (These are raised so that cold air will sink into the trench.) The roof should be curved and as smooth as possible to minimize drips.

How big you make the cave depends on how many it must shelter, how much time you have, and how much snow there is. The entrance should slope upward out of the cave and be kept small to prevent snow and wind from blowing in. Make sure you include an air inlet to prevent carbon monoxide buildup when you are cooking. Where there are no steep slopes, a snow dome can be built. To do this, simply pile up a huge mound of snow, then dig out the center.

If you have little time to dig a snow shelter because of a storm, any structure will do. Mountaineers high in the Himalayas have survived for several days and nights in body-size "snow coffins" when necessary. A simple trench can be roofed with tilted snow blocks or with skis, over which are spread fly sheets or tarps, the edges held down with snow. The aim is to get out of the wind.

Be careful where you put things, especially small items, in a snow shelter (and when digging it), indeed whenever you're camping on snow—it's easy for them to become buried. My book, *Wilderness Skiing and Winter Camping* (Ragged Mountain Press), contains much more detail on snow shelters.

SLEEPING BAGS

Whether you sleep out under the stars, in a tent, or in a bivy bag, you need to keep warm at night. For most people this means using a sleeping bag. I've heard stories of people who just pile on extra clothes at night, but I've never met anyone who does this by choice (an enforced bivouac when you aren't carrying a sleeping bag is another matter), and it sounds both uncomfortable and inefficient.

A sleeping bag traps warm air to prevent the body from cooling down. In general, the sleeping bag must allow perspiration to pass through it (unless a vapor barrier is used) while it retains body heat, which means both fill and shell should be breathable. If you intend to sleep out in your bag without shelter, you also need a wind-resistant bag with a quick-drying shell, or a bag with a waterproof/breathable shell.

Fill

Choosing a sleeping bag is much easier than choosing a tent. There are far fewer designs, though many models. The biggest decision is which kind of insulation or fill to go for. The ideal material would be lightweight but very warm, low in packed bulk, durable, non-absorbent, quick-drying, warm when wet, and comfortable. Unfortunately, this ideal doesn't yet exist, so compromises have to be made in terms of which properties are most important—determined in part by when and where you'll camp, and what shelter you'll use. The basic fill choice is between synthetic fibers or waterfowl down.

Synthetics: Prior to the mid-1970s, when DuPont launched Fiberfill II, synthetic-filled sleeping bags were far too heavy and bulky to consider carrying in a pack. Since then, a host of good polyester synthetic fills have appeared, and backpackers can now choose from a wide selection of reasonably lightweight bags. There are two basic types: *short staple fibers* and *continuous filaments.* Short staple fibers consist of short sections of fill; continuous filaments are endless strands of fiber. Both produce fine webs of material that trap air when uncompressed and keep the sleeper warm, but will pack down to a small size for carrying. Polarguard, from Hoechst-Celanese, is the best-known continuous-filament fill, though there are well-regarded proprietary versions, like Wiggy's Lamilite. The latest version of Polarguard is Polarguard HV, which has hollow fibers that are said to be 20 percent lighter than the earlier version. There are many versions of short staple fiber fills, with new ones frequently appearing. The latest ones are DuPont's Microloft, Albany International's Primaloft, and 3M's Thinsulate Lite Loft. These are generally regarded as the top-quality short-staple fills, supplanting Quallofil and Hollofil, which now appear mainly in low-cost and entry-level bags. There are proprietary

short-staple fills, too, including Gold-Eck's Loft Technology and MontBell's ExcelLoft.

Synthetic fills cost less than down, are easy to care for, and resist moisture. They are not, however "warm when wet," as some manufacturers claim—nothing is. What matters is how fast something dries, and synthetic fills dry fairly quickly, since they are virtually non-absorbent. Because the fill doesn't collapse when saturated, much of its warm-air-trapping thickness is retained. When compared with a wet down-filled bag, a wet synthetic one will start to feel warm in a comparatively short time, as long as it's protected from rain and wind. You can't sleep outside in a storm in a synthetic-fill bag and stay warm, however. Reviews suggest that Primaloft is the most water-resistant synthetic.

The disadvantages of synthetic fills are short life, less comfort compared with down or pile, and more bulk and greater weight for the same warmth compared with down. The new synthetics are lighter, more compressible, and perhaps more durable than earlier ones, but they still don't compare with down. In the long run, down costs less: One company that makes both down and synthetic bags estimates that with average use, a down bag will last 12 years, but a synthetic one only four years.

Down: The lightest, warmest, most comfortable, most durable sleeping bags use down as fill. Down bags are the best choice when weight and bulk are critical factors, since nothing comes anywhere near down for compactness and low weight combined with good insulation. Down, the fluffy underplumage (not a true feather) of ducks and geese, consists of clusters of thin filaments that trap air and thus provide insulation. No synthetic fiber has down's insulating ability.

Unlike feathers, down has no stalks that can

poke through fabric. But it must be kept dry, as it loses virtually all its insulation when wet, and it's very absorbent, so it takes a long time to dry. Drying a down bag in bad weather is practically impossible—only a hot sun or a machine dryer can do the job. Therefore, keeping a down bag dry means packing it in a waterproof bag and always using shelter when it rains. Down bags also require frequent airing to remove any moisture picked up from humid air or your body during the night. Caring for a down bag need not be difficult or a chore, though; I've used down bags on almost all my long walks and never yet had one get more than a little damp.

Down comes in several different grades and two different types. Pure down is usually at least 85 percent down, the remainder being small feathers, which are impossible to separate from the down. Down-and-feather fills are at least 50 percent down (many are 70 percent or 80 percent), but feather-and-down fill is less than 50 percent down. Feather-and-down and all-feather fills have just about vanished, since they offer no advantages over synthetics, which are easier to care for. The more stalks you feel in down fill, the higher the percentage of feathers in it. *Goose down* is generally regarded as warmer, weight for weight, than *duck down;* it is also more expensive.

The more volume a given amount of down can fill, the higher its quality, because the thickness, or *loft,* determines the warmth. Measuring the volume filled by 1 ounce of down determines the *fill power.* The industry standard is 550 cubic inches per ounce (550 fill), but many makers use downs with a higher fill power than this. Most pure down fills usually have fill powers of between 550 and 750 cubic inches per ounce. Some makers, however, don't give fill powers for their down products, which makes comparison difficult. Of those that do, most offer two grades of bags, ones with 550 or 600 fill, and ones with 700 or greater

fill. Fill power higher than 700 is rare, though Feathered Friends offers 775 fill on special order; Marmot uses 725 fill in its top bags.

There are fewer manufacturers of down sleeping bags than of synthetic ones and, due to the cost of the fill, virtually all down bags are high quality, since it isn't worthwhile to cut costs. The North Face, Marmot, Feathered Friends, Slumberjack, Mountain Hardwear, REI, Sierra Designs, Western Mountaineering, and L.L. Bean make quality down-filled bags.

Shell Materials

Nylon and polyester are the best materials for shells—they're lightweight, hard-wearing, wind- and water-resistant, non-absorbent, and quick-drying. The latest, softest synthetics are comfortable against the skin, making them suitable for the inner as well as the outer shell. Because in the past synthetics felt cold and clammy, many people still prefer cotton or polyester/cotton inners, even though these are heavier, more absorbent, slower drying, and harder to keep clean. After several months of continuous use, a polyester/cotton inner feels sticky and unpleasant—I speak from experience—but because a synthetic liner won't absorb sweat or dirt, it stays fairly fresh as long as it's aired occasionally. Some bags use wicking synthetics, such as CoolMax or Thermastat, for linings.

The newest microfiber synthetics add a very pleasant feel and the ability to spread moisture rapidly over the surface, which speeds up evaporation. As a result, they make particularly good shell materials; look for Versatech, Super Microfiber, and Pertex.

Waterproof/breathable outer shells are virtually waterproof, though leaks can occur along the seams. The standard material for such shells used to be Gore-Tex, but this is now being replaced by a new Gore fabric called Dryloft, which is said to be twice as breathable. Although very resistant to wetting, such shells add weight and cost and can make drying a damp bag take longer (turning it inside-out is best). I find a separate waterproof/breathable bivy bag more versatile. On the Columbia icefield crossing in the Canadian Rockies, I used a Gore-Tex bivy sack with a down bag, while the others in the group used Gore-Tex–shelled down bags. We were pinned down for days by a storm, and the atmosphere in the tents became so humid that I slept in the bivy bag every night. Each dawn the outside of it was damp, but my sleeping bag was dry, which meant I could pack away the latter but leave the bivy out to dry. My tent companion had to turn his bag inside out to air it and had a much harder time keeping it dry.

Whatever the outer fabric, the shell should have a DWR (durable water repellent) treatment. As with clothing, this treatment will wear off in time; it can be restored by medium-heat tumble drying. (Ironing should work too, but I wouldn't risk ironing a sleeping bag.) Wash-in waterproofings also can be used, though drying the bag thoroughly—which is essential—can take a long time.

Shape and Size

The most efficient sleeping bag fit is the one that traps warm air closest to your body. A bag with lots of room in it is a bag with lots of dead air space to heat. Most bags reduce this dead space by tapering from head to foot. Most also have hoods to prevent heat from being lost through the head. The resulting shape is called a *mummy bag,* presumably for its resemblance to an ancient Egyptian corpse. It's the standard shape for high-performance, lightweight sleeping bags.

A sleeping bag that is too wide or too long will have extra air space to heat, so it won't keep you

as warm as a proper-size one could; the weight will be more than you need to carry, too. A bag that is too small will be uncomfortable, and won't keep you warm in spots where you press against the shell and flatten the fill.

For these reasons, bags come in different lengths and widths, and many companies offer two sizes in each model. Finding a reasonable fit isn't too difficult, although very tall people may find their choices limited, and short people may end up with a bag a little too long. It's worth climbing into a bag in the store to see how it fits before you buy it, even if you do feel a little conspicuous doing so.

As with much outdoor gear, most sleeping bags are designed for men, with women being directed to the shorter versions. However, as I've pointed out, the fit as well as the length is important for efficiency and comfort, and men's bags tend to be too roomy at the shoulders and too tight at the hips for many women. Makers are starting to notice this and are now designing bags for women. Sierra Designs and Kelty make LiteLoft and Polarguard HV bags that are shaped for women and have more fill for the same temperature rating, since, apparently, women generally sleep colder than men. Annie Getchell gave them a good review in the December 1995 issue of *Backpacker* magazine.

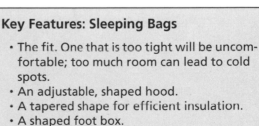

Key Features: Sleeping Bags

- The fit. One that is too tight will be uncomfortable; too much room can lead to cold spots.
- An adjustable, shaped hood.
- A tapered shape for efficient insulation.
- A shaped foot box.
- A two-way zipper for ventilation.
- A filled draft tube behind the zipper to prevent heat loss.

Construction

The method used to hold fill in a sleeping bag affects how efficient a bag is: Fill will migrate unless it's held in channels, which give sleeping bags their familiar ringed or ribbed look.

To create these channels, the inner and outer fabric is stitched together. The simplest and lightest way of doing this is with *straight-through* or *sewn-through* stitching, adequate only for bags designed for above-freezing temperatures. This is because heat escapes through the stitch lines, and the channels thus created don't allow the fill to expand fully or to remain spread throughout the

channel. Most of the lightest synthetic bags and a few down ones use sewn-through stitching.

To cut this heat loss, the inner and outer can be connected by short walls of material to make rectangular boxes, hence the name *box-wall construction.* If the walls are angled (offsetting the top and bottom stitches), it is called *slant-wall construction.* Virtually all cold-weather down bags use walled construction. Synthetic-fill bags can't use box-wall construction because the fill is fixed in layers. In *double-layer construction,* two or even three sewn-through layers are used, with each stitch line offset to avoid cold spots— a rather heavy but efficient method. In *shingle construction,* slanted layers of overlapping fiber are sewn to both the inner and the outer. This is reckoned to be lighter and to allow the fill to loft more easily.

Whatever the internal construction, a bag's channels are usually split in two by side baffles that prevent all the fill ending up on the top or bottom. Some bags (usually lightweight down ones) dispense with these side baffles on the premise that it might be useful at times to be able to shift the fill to the top or bottom of the bag to give more or less warmth. I distrust such a construction because the down could move even when I don't want it to. Another construction method I don't like, used in both down and synthetic bags, places side baffles at ground level so that more of the fill is in the upper section. The justification is that warm air rises, so by having the seams low, less heat will escape through them. Other makers simply put more fill in the upper half of the bag.

The problem with bags that have more fill in the top than the bottom is they don't account for sleepers who don't keep their bags the right way up, which includes me; I often wake to find the hood above me, having turned the bag completely over during the night. For that reason, I prefer

Sleeping bag construction.

Down-filled

Polyester-filled

sewn-through

box-wall

double-construction

slant-wall

shingle

overlapping tubes

to have the fill equally distributed. Unfortunately, the current trend is to have more fill in the top of bags. However, it's often the most-expensive bags that have this; ones with equal fill above and below being regarded as having "lower specifications" even though, in my experience, they perform better. This is another case where the most expensive gear is not necessarily the best.

To prevent fill compression, the outer shell on many bags is cut larger than the inner; this is known as *differential cut.* Bag makers debate the need for this construction. I've used bags with and without it and can't feel much difference.

Design Features

Hoods: A good hood should fit closely around the head and have a drawcord with self-locking toggles that permit easy adjustment from inside the bag. Most hoods fit well, though few are easy to adjust from inside. Bags for use in below-freezing temperatures should have large hoods in which you can bury all but your nose. Bags for warmer conditions sometimes have smaller hoods, or none at all, to save weight. In above-freezing temperatures, I often fold the hood under the bag.

Shoulder Baffles: A filled, drawcord-adjusted collar or neck baffle to prevent drafts is a feature of many bags, especially those designed for cold weather. I've only recently used one, but I like them because I can close the bag up around my shoulders while leaving the hood open.

Feet: To keep your feet warm, a sleeping bag should have a shaped or *boxed foot* section. If the two halves of the bag are simply sewn together at the foot, your feet will compress the fill when they push on it, reducing loft there. A boxed foot has an extra circular section, which could either

be channeled or a single unit. Cold-weather bags may have an offset double layer of fill in the boxed foot. In down bags, some boxed feet have internal box walls.

Zippers: Almost all bags, except for the lightest down ones, now have a side zipper. For years I distrusted zippers—they added weight, leaked heat, and were a source of potential disaster if they broke. I've now developed a grudging acceptance of them, though I still can see no real advantages. In theory, zippers allow you to regulate temperature and make getting in and out easier. Some bags can be zipped together to make one big bag.

Most bags have full-length zippers. To prevent heat loss, zippers must have filled baffles running down the inside. Unfortunately, these baffles are ideal zipper snags, so a stiffened, anti-snag strip is necessary. These are far from perfect, but they do lessen the number of times the zipper catches. When the zipper does jam, as it will, don't try to tug it free—you could tear the fabric. Instead, gently ease the fabric out of the zipper teeth. Two-way zippers let you open the bottom of the bag so you can stick your feet out to cool off if you overheat. It could even be possible to waddle around outside wearing your bag as a somewhat restrictive, but very warm coat, though I can't imagine when you would want to do that.

Warmth and Weight

Rating sleeping bags for warmth is difficult, because there is no standard rating system used by all companies. Most companies use *season ratings* or *temperature ranges.* The latter is more useful, since you don't know the area or altitude to which the general season rating applies. Usually five seasons are listed, the fifth meaning "extreme cold." Bags warm enough for deep-winter use are too hot in most summers, yet these are usually listed as four-season models. *Temperature ratings* give the lowest temperature at which the bag should keep you warm; more useful are data that give you a temperature range. Warm sleepers should note the lower temperature, cold sleepers the higher. A few makers, like Moonstone, give separate ratings for warm and cold sleepers. Another figure often given is the bag's loft—but what's important is the *loft over the body,* not the total thickness of the bag—check whether the manufacturer's figures are for the whole bag or just the top half.

Although there's no standard, most bags with comparable fills cover a reasonably close temperature range. I'd be very suspicious of any maker that rates a bag as vastly warmer than rivals with similar fill.

No rating system, however, can account for the different metabolic rates of different bodies. Warm sleepers, like me, can use lightweight bags at lower than their rated temperatures; cold sleepers may shiver a summer night away in a bag made for the polar conditions. (I have a friend who sleeps buried in a four-season mummy bag while I'm comfortable half-out of a summer model.)

Other factors also influence how warmly you'll sleep. Food is fuel is heat, so however tired I am at the end of a long day, I always eat before going to sleep on a cold night; if I don't, I wake in the early hours of the morning feeling chilly. (If it's warm and I don't eat, I wake because I'm hungry!) Putting on some clothes is an obvious thing to do when you wake in the night feeling chilly, but a carbohydrate snack can also help warm you up. Fatigue can keep you shivering long after you expect to be warm. The weather is a factor—high humidity means a damp bag (though it may feel perfectly dry), less loft, and conductive heat loss. Thus, you may feel colder

when the temperature's around freezing and the humidity is high than you do when it's below freezing but dry. Wind reduces a bag's efficiency, as does sleeping under an open sky with no barrier to prevent radiant heat loss. If you bivy regularly, you'll need a warmer bag than if you always use a tent. A sleeping mat of some sort makes such a big difference, especially if the ground is wet or frozen, that I always carry one.

High loft requires more fill, which means more weight. Down-filled bags are much lighter than synthetics across all temperature ranges, from around 1¾ pounds for ones rated to 20°F (−7°C) to 5¼ pounds for −60°F (−51°C) models. The lightest synthetic-fill bags check in at about 2¾ pounds for a 20°F (−7°C) bag, and 5¾ pounds for a −40°F (−40°C) one. On the basis of weight alone, I would choose a down bag.

Models and Choices

There are hundreds of sleeping bags available, but far fewer sleeping bag designs. However, it's fairly easy to reduce the choice to a handful of models that fit your specific criteria. I look for the lightest, least bulky bag, which means one with down fill, that will keep me warm when I sleep unclothed in a tent in the average temperatures for the time and place of my trip. If temperatures are cooler than average and I feel chilled, I wear clothes.

For many years I used two bags—one for above-freezing temperatures and one for below-freezing temperatures. But the late 1980s saw the introduction of ultralight down bags with around 10 ounces of fill, total weights of 25 ounces or less, and ratings around 40°F (4°C). I now use one of these for summer trips when I'm expecting temperatures to be mostly above freezing. This means that I now use three bags—an ultralight one for above-freezing temperatures, a three-season one for use in temperatures down to 15°F (−9°C), and a winter one for colder temperatures.

Ultralight bags use very light fabrics and may have half-zips or, like mine, no zips at all. Seams may be sewn-through and hoods small. The point is to keep the weight down. Top-quality fills—mine is 700 fill goose down—provide the warmth. There aren't many bags like this. The few include Feathered Friends Rock Wren, which has 10 ounces of 700 fill down, weighs 23 ounces, and is rated to 40°F (4°C); and Western Mountaineering's Iroquois, which weighs 25 ounces and is rated to 38°F (3°C). Such bags can be used as liners inside three-season bags for extreme cold-weather use, though I've never tried this.

There is much greater choice in three-season bags, and a much greater variation in weight—from 2 to 3½ pounds. Unless you're a cold sleeper, the ones at the lighter end (with 16 to 20 ounces of fill) are adequate. My current model weighs 2 pounds 1½ ounces and has 18 ounces of 700 fill goose down and an ultralight ripstop Pertex nylon shell. I've slept in it in temperatures down to 12°F (−11°C), when I was warm enough wearing base layers, socks, and a thin fleece top, and find it fine for the 20°F (−7°C) to 50°F (10°C) range; above that temperature it's too warm. Most quality makers have bags like this—it's the closest to being a general-purpose bag you can find.

My winter bag sees little use these days because I rarely venture into areas where the temperature will be below 15°F (−9°C) on many nights, and I'd rather wear clothes in my three-season bag than carry the extra bulk and weight. (My bag is typical of many winter bags: it weighs 3½ pounds, with 26½ ounces of 650 fill down. It's great at 5°F [−15°C] but too hot at 35°F [2°C].) Most makers offer similar bags, as well as ones designed

for much colder temperatures—right down to Edko's handmade, limited-edition Siberian Tiger bag, which weighs 5 pounds 5 ounces and is rated to −60°F (−51°C).

I only use synthetic bags when I'm sent ones for tests and reviews, but they're the ones most people buy. I find down softer and more comfortable, as well as lighter and less bulky. However, improvements in synthetic fills may soon mean bags that rival down warmth for weight.

The Unusual

The standard sleeping system for backpacking consists of a series of separate components—a tent, tarp, or bivy bag; a sleeping bag; and a sleeping mat. This allows for a huge number of variations.

Some makers, however, have looked at ways to integrate the various components in order to save weight and increase efficiency. Stephensons has combined sleeping bag and sleeping mat in its Warmlite triple bags, which include either a 2-inch foam mat or a goose down–filled air mat, both built in. The bags also have vapor barrier inners and two removable tops for different temperatures. The thin top is rated to 25°F (−4°C), the thick one to 0°F (−18°C), and the combination to an astonishing −70°F (−57°C). Different sizes are available, but weights for the complete system are around 6 pounds.

The idea of combining the bag and mat is used by other makers, including Cascade Designs, whose Polarguard and LiteLoft-filled Synergy bags have a sleeve for inserting a mat. I've tried this design in a bag from New Zealand company Macpac and found that though it made for a very light sleeping bag with low packed bulk, there were disadvantages. The main one was that you can't sit up easily in the bag because of the pad. I use my sleeping bag as an article of clothing in the tent in cold weather, pulling it up under my armpits and tightening the drawstrings. I couldn't do this with the integral mat, which meant carrying extra clothing, which cancels the weight saved by a lighter bag. The Macpac bag wasn't tapered, either—it had to have room for a rectangular mat, which led to cold spots in the lower half. (A bag with a built-in mat like the Warmlite can be tapered.)

Envirogear takes its Cocoon bags a step further: they consist of an inflatable down-filled mattress and a separate inflatable down-filled blanket that zip together. By varying the amount of air, the rating of the Cocoon 4 varies from 70°F (21°C) when compressed to −45°F (−43°C) when fully inflated. The Cocoon 3 is rated from 70°F (21°C) to 10°F (−12°C). The shells and linings of the Cocoon are waterproof but not breathable, so the down always stays dry. The ability to vary the warmth apparently prevents the problems of overheating possible with other vapor barriers (Envirogear says that the skin will re-absorb all the vapor given off). The Cocoon 3 weighs 6¼ pounds; the Cocoon 4 weighs 8 pounds for the smaller size, 9 pounds for the larger. The final pieces of the Cocoon system are an attachable canopy that protects the user's head and keeps out insects and rain, and a mesh enclosure that covers the whole bag. The weight of this addition is 1¼ pounds.

Does it work? I don't know, but it does sound interesting.

Carrying

Many people, especially those who use external-frame packs, like to strap their sleeping bags under the packbag. But however sturdy your stuff sack, this leaves your sleeping bag vulnerable to rain, dirt, and damage. I pack my bag at the bottom of the lower compartment, in an oversize waterproof stuff sack (like those made by Black Diamond and Outdoor Research). Ordinary stuff sacks usually aren't waterproof— the seams aren't sealed—so when I use one of these I pack it inside a heavy-duty garbage bag or waterproof nylon sack liner as well. The oversize stuff sack enables the bag to mold to the curve of the pack around the lower back and hips and to fill the corners. A round stuff sack packed to bursting is very hard to fit in a pack without leaving lots of unfilled space. This is especially so with compression stuff sacks.

Care

In the field, all sleeping bags benefit from being aired whenever possible to allow any moisture to evaporate. This is especially important with down bags, which can absorb a surprising amount of moisture overnight. It's also a good idea to remove down bags from their stuff sacks well before use to let the fill expand, and to give them a shake before climbing in, which helps distribute the fill. Neither of these actions make the slightest difference to synthetic bags.

Small cuts or holes in the fabric can be patched with ripstop nylon tape or duct tape to prevent any fill escaping. You can sew a patch on when you return home—just remember to coat the stitch lines with seam seal to make them downproof.

At home, *never* store down or synthetic bags compressed; eventually the fill won't be able to expand fully, reducing the bag's ability to keep you warm. This affects synthetic bags most; prolonged compression leads to a completely flattened fill. Bags should be stored so that the fill can loft, which means either flat (mine live on top of a wardrobe), hung up, or packed loosely in a very large bag. Moisture needs to escape, so don't store them in a waterproof bag; cotton or polyester/cotton is ideal. Many manufacturers provide a storage sack with each sleeping bag.

Sleeping bags should be aired every morning if possible.

This is all the precaution you need to take until the bag needs cleaning. Synthetic bags can be machine washed, although they shouldn't be dry-cleaned. Cleaning down bags is a very different matter, however, and one fraught with danger. First, down loses some of its insulating properties every time it gets cleaned, so it should only be cleaned when the fill is so dirty that it no longer keeps you as warm as it should. If only the shell is dirty, wipe off spots with something like Stergene.

Eventually though, every down bag needs to be thoroughly cleaned. The danger is that down absorbs vast amounts of water and the bag becomes very heavy; if it is lifted when wet, the baffles may tear under the weight of the wet down. Most instructions say bags should be hand-washed in a bath or large tub and dried quickly in a large tumble dryer to prevent the down from forming clumps. Finally, special soaps are needed, since standard washing powders strip the natural oils from down and shorten its life. I always send down bags away to be washed or dry-

cleaned by experts. This relieves me of the task and increases the likelihood that my bag will survive. Many experts think that improper cleaning ruins more down bags than anything else, including prolonged use.

If you decide to have someone else clean your bag, where do you go? To find local cleaners, if there are any, contact the store where you bought the bag or the manufacturer for its recommendations. Not all dry cleaners can handle down-filled items. It's very important that the bag be well aired afterward—the fumes from dry-cleaning chemicals are poisonous. Some dry-cleaning agents also ruin down, so be sure the company you use knows what it's doing. I prefer to have the bag washed rather than dry-cleaned because I think this is safer; however, it is harder to find someone who offers this service.

Reconstruction

The shell of your down-filled bag eventually may become so filthy it makes your skin crawl and no cleaning company will touch it. This happened to me with the bag I used on the Continental Divide walk. It had a polyester/cotton inner, which was in an appalling condition after 157 nights' use. Dry cleaners I approached wouldn't handle it, saying the inner was rotten and would disintegrate during cleaning. Since the expensive goose down fill still lofted well and kept me warm, I was loath to throw the bag away, so I had it remade. This cost less than half the price of a new bag and included washing the down. The resulting bag is not only a better fit, since I could specify the length, but it weighs just 2 pounds rather than 2 pounds 12 ounces, because the inner shell is now nylon.

Ask at your local outdoor store and check the classified ads in the outdoor press to find a company that will remake bags.

Liners

One way to improve the warmth—and cleanliness—of a sleeping bag is to wear clothes in it. A liner accomplishes the same but adds weight. Liners are available in cotton, polypropylene, silk, pile, and coated nylon. I'd disregard cotton entirely because of its weight, absorbency, and slow drying time. Polypropylene liners make more sense—a typical one weighs 16 ounces, which is still heavier than a set of polypro underwear. Pile liners can uprate a bag for colder conditions, but a pile suit is more versatile. Silk (at 5 ounces or so) is really light and low in bulk, and I have a silk liner that I sometimes use when weight isn't important. It's what I'd recommend if you really want a liner.

Coated nylon liners are a different matter; they form a vapor barrier that keeps moisture in and stops evaporative heat loss. In dry cold, especially when the temperature is well below freezing, a vapor-barrier liner can add a surprising amount of warmth to the bag. They weigh 6 to 8 ounces. Again, I prefer to wear vapor-barrier

clothing because of the versatility, so I've never used a vapor-barrier liner. There are a few available from companies like Marmot and Feathered Friends.

A lightweight sleeping bag can be used as a liner inside another bag for cold-weather use. I've tried this, though, and found that the two bags twist inside each other and aren't very comfortable. A few makers have looked at this problem and have come up with filled liners that zip or snap into place. Mountain Hardwear's Upgrade Bag Liners include ones with 550 fill goose down and Polarguard HV that weigh 32 and 33 ounces in the regular lengths. The down liner is said to add 25°F (−4°C) of warmth, the synthetic 20°F (−7°C). Moonstone's snap-in Advanced Concept Liners are similar but much lighter, as they only fit into the top half of a bag. There are versions with 700 fill down weighing 17 ounces, and a LiteLoft fill weighing 18 ounces. Each is said to add up to 25°F (−4°C) extra warmth. Still, I'd rather wear extra clothing.

MATS AND PILLOWS

Every bag needs the insulation of a sleeping mat under it to prevent ground chill from striking upward where the fill is compressed under your body weight. Mats also provide cushioning. In summer weather, some hardy souls manage without a mat by putting clothing (and even their packs) under their bags, but most people, myself included, use a mat year-round.

There are two sorts of sleeping mats in general use, *closed-cell foam* mats and *self-inflating, open-cell foam* mats. (Air beds and covered open-cell foam have just about vanished as far as backpackers are concerned.) Closed-cell foam mats are lightweight, reasonably inexpensive, and hard-wearing, but very bulky to carry. Although they are efficient insulators, they don't add

The author at a bivouac site in the Grand Canyon—dry ground meant a groundsheet wasn't needed.

much cushioning. These mats may be made from either pressure-blown or chemically blown foam; the first are warmer, more durable, and resist compression better than the second, but they look identical and manufacturers rarely tell you which is which. The synthetics they're made from don't affect performance—Evazote (EVA), Ensolite, and polyurethane are common ones.

Closed-cell mats come in different lengths, widths, and thicknesses. I find three-quarter-length (about 57 inches) adequate—I use clothes as a pillow and under my feet if necessary. This saves a little weight and packing bulk. A three-quarter-length, four-season, pressure-blown mat weighs 9 ounces or more.

I've found the most comfortable closed-cell mat to be Cascade Designs' EVA Ridge-Rest, which has a deep-ridged design that adds softness and traps air for greater warmth. Although it has more bulk than flat-surfaced mats, the three-quarter-length model weighs only 9 ounces.

Because of their bulk, closed-cell mats are normally carried on the outside of the pack, wherever there are convenient straps. In hiking through low, dense brush, however, attaching a mat to the side of a pack is a good way to get it ripped up, as I discovered when bushwhacking down an unmaintained trail in a side canyon of the Grand Canyon. Before it was totally torn apart, I transferred it to the top of the pack where it was above the bushes. In forests with low branches, the top of the pack is not where you want a mat, of course.

Cascade Designs is better known for introducing the first (and best) self-inflating mat, the Therm-a-Rest. I've used one now for more than a decade. The polyurethane-waterproofed nylon shell of these mats is bonded to an open-cell, polyurethane foam core that expands when the valve at one corner is opened; a few puffs of breath help. Once the mat has reached the desired thickness, the valve can be closed to prevent the air escaping. The comfort and warmth the Therm-a-Rest provides are astonishing. I've slept on stones

Sleeping mats and groundsheet. Top: Ridge Rest. Bottom: Therm-a-Rest Ultra Lite. Below: Sportsman's Blanket.

and not noticed, and have been comfortable on snow when others were using two closed-cell foam mats. Every time I've loaned one to dubious friends, they've gone out and bought one as soon as possible.

In an attempt to cut the weight of my load I went back to using a closed-cell foam mat for a while recently. I found I had to be much more selective about where I slept; even on the softest ground, the closed-cell foam was far less comfortable than the Therm-a-Rest. Proponents of minimal mats assured me that after a few nights I would get used to the hardness underneath me—I didn't—and after a year's trial I'm returning to a Therm-a-Rest except for short, ultra-lightweight trips.

Therm-a-Rests now come in six different styles with weights up to 3 pounds 13 ounces. My new mat of choice is the three-quarter-length Ultra Lite II, which weighs just 14 ounces. One of the original Ultra Lites lasted through both the Continental Divide and Canadian Rockies walks, plus all the trips in between, before finally puncturing around the valve, where a repair was impossible. I estimate that I'd have gone through at least four closed-cell foam mats in that time, which puts the initial high price of the Therm-a-Rest into perspective.

Although slightly heavier than most closed-cell foam mats, the Ultra Lite II is much less bulky and can be folded and packed down the back of the pack, where it is protected from damage. Therm-a-Rests require care, though; I don't throw it down on the bare ground and sit on it without checking for sharp objects that might puncture it. If I'm not using a tent, I always carry a groundsheet to protect it. In case the mat does spring a leak, a repair kit containing patches, glue, and a spare valve is available. It weighs very little and I always carry it. Finding a pinprick-size leak can be difficult, however—it must be immersed in a creek or pool and inspected for bubbles, the way one finds leaks in rubber tires.

Preparing for Bed and Coping with the Night

There is no right way to prepare for bed, but for those who are interested, this is what I do: Once a campsite has been selected and my shelter, if any, erected, I lay out my Therm-a-Rest and open the valve. If the ground is cold and I want to sit on the mat, I generally blow it up rather than wait for it to expand. Then I pull out my sleeping bag and lay it out on the mat. Depending on the temperature, I may lie on or in the bag while I cook, eat, read, make notes, study the map, watch the stars and the trees, daydream, or otherwise wile away the evening until I start to feel sleepy. Then I usually strip off my clothes, arrange a pillow, lie down, and adjust the sleeping bag until I feel warm enough. Spare clothes go in a stuff sack, which I place on or in the pack, which is either acting as a backrest if I'm bivouacking, or lying in or near the tent. Only if wildlife is a problem do I like being far from my pack at night; then the clothes I'll want in the morning are kept in a stuff sack by my side. My footwear stays nearby, too, as does my headlamp, candle lantern, notebook, pens, books, maps, and a water bottle. Again, except where wildlife is a problem, my stove, pans, and food stay beside me, ready for breakfast.

Most nights don't need coping with because I sleep right through. On the very rare occasions when the tent has collapsed, I've abandoned camp in the dark. Usually, though, storms mean only that I don't get quite enough sleep, and I am glad to see the first gray distorted edges of daylight through the fly sheet.

But what do you do when you wake feeling chilly long before dawn? First, if you haven't done up the hood of the sleeping bag or have the zipper partly open, adjusting those may do the trick. Nights grow colder as the hours go by, so you may need to adjust the sleeping bag often to stay warm. I'm so used to doing this that I barely wake at all, but just fumble with the drawcords and sink back to sleep. The next stage, if you're still cold, is to don some clothes and have a snack. If wearing all your clothes doesn't make you warm, then either you've seriously overestimated the capabilities of your sleeping bag and clothing or the temperatures are extremely cold for the area and time of year. In that case, all you can do is shiver until dawn, with the aid of hot food and drink, then get out, and not make the same mistake again.

Various copies of the Therm-a-Rest have appeared on the market, but they are heavier, bulkier, and don't look as well made or durable. I recommend sticking with the original. If punctures really worry you, a Wiggy's Groundpad could be worth considering—these self-inflating, non-absorbent mats are filled with "densified polyester fiberfill" and are immune to punctures. They're not light though; the shortest version (44 inches) weighs 20 ounces.

For a pillow, I simply use a pile or down top, sometimes packed in a stuff sack. I've tried using my boots, as some people do, but have found them uncomfortable. For those who prefer more comfort than folded clothing provides, there are a number of lightweight pillows available. Inflatable nylon or filled pillows can be found in many outdoor stores. They weigh 4 to 15 ounces and take up very little room when packed.

CHAPTER SEVEN

The Wilderness Kitchen

Up with another red dawn. Frozen dew crackles on my sleeping bag as I unzip and slide out of it. I build a fire and boil the last of my water; tea and Fig Newtons for breakfast.

—*Beyond the Wall,* Edward Abbey

FOOD AND DRINK

One of the joys of backpacking is taking the first sip of a hot drink at the end of a long day. Often it's the anticipation of that moment that keeps me going for the last hour or so. The tent is up, my boots are off, and I can lie back and start to unwind. I may eat and drink while lying in the tent, a gale raging outside, or while sitting outside, back against a tree or boulder, admiring the view. Either way, this period of relaxation and renewal is a crucial part of living in the wilderness, one of the aspects of backpacking that differentiates it from day walking.

Food plays a large part in how much you enjoy the outdoors. The possibilities and permutations are endless, so your diet can be constantly varied. Wilderness dining has two extremes: gourmet eaters and survival eaters. The first like to make camp at lunch time so they have several hours to set up field ovens; they bake cakes and bread, and cook multi-course

dinners. They walk only a few miles each day, and may use the same campsite for several nights. Survival eaters, on the other hand, breakfast on a handful of dry cereal and a swig of water, and are up and walking within minutes of waking. They pound dozens of miles every day; lunch is a series of cold snacks eaten on the move. Dinner consists of a freeze-dried meal "cooked" by pouring hot water into the packet, or more cold snacks.

Most people, of course, fall somewhere between these two extremes. I lean heavily toward being a survival eater, so you won't learn here how to bake bread or make soufflés. If you're interested in doing so I'd suggest having a look at *The Camper's Companion,* by Rick Greenspan and Hal Kahn (Foghorn Press), the follow-up to *Backpacking: A Hedonist's Guide* (a book I recommended in the first edition of *The Backpacker's Handbook*). Greenspan and Kahn's book is also good on fishing and fish dishes for those handy with a rod. Two excellent books of recipes for those gourmets who also favor whole foods and a less indolent form of backpacking are *Simple Foods for the Pack,* by Vikki Kinmont and Claudia Axcell (Sierra Club Books), and the more recent *Good Food for Camp & Trail,* by Dorcas S. Miller (Pruett). Other interesting cookbooks are June Fleming's *The Well-Fed Backpacker* (Random House) and the wonderfully

Reasons for Backpacking

The exact route doesn't matter; we have altered our original plans several times. Time passes. We hear the scolding of squirrels, screeching of jays, clicking of deer hooves, the delicate whisper of breezes in the aspens, the trickle of tiny creeks, and the roar of mighty waterfalls. Yes, and the whine of mosquitoes, the buzz of rattlesnakes, and unseen animals in the night that just might be bears. But beyond these sounds—or perhaps beneath them—is a profound silence. When I leave the roaring cataracts of a river to enter a thick grove of massive, ancient conifers, it is as though I've walked under a blanket—so all-embracing, so physical, is the silence.

named *Gorp, Glop and Glue Stew*, by Yvonne Prater and Ruth Dyer Mendenhall (The Mountaineers), in which more than 150 well-known outdoorspeople give their favorite recipes and tell some kitchen tales.

Which foods are best for backpacking, especially long-haul trips, is debatable. At one gathering I attended, a speaker denounced a certain popular candy bar as "not food," and said that hikers should head for the salad bar, not the all-you-can-eat pizza place, when they reach town. Conversely, a recent book by a professional mountain guide says that for breakfast "a good, old-fashioned fry-up is highly recommended." Ray Jardine swears by corn spaghetti for maintaining endurance over long distances; I find that lots of pasta of any sort keeps me going more than rice, potato, or other carbohydrates. What it comes down to, of course, is personal choice. If a certain food helps you enjoy backpacking, then take it with you, whatever anyone else says.

Here, I describe what I eat and why. I prefer less-processed, additive-free foods, and I am mostly vegetarian. I have been known to eat candy bars at times, however, and I can't resist pizza.

Many of the facts and figures quoted below have been taken from *Food Facts*, by David Briggs and Mark Wahlquist (Penguin), a fascinating volume that I recommend to anyone interested in pursuing the subject.

Hot or Cold?

Hot food provides no more energy than cold food, and cooking food can destroy some vitamins, though certain starches such as potatoes, beans, and lentils need to be cooked to make them more digestible and, in the case of the last two, to destroy substances that make utilizing their protein difficult. One way to cut the weight of your pack significantly would be to eat only cold food, and thus dispense with stove, fuel, and cookware. I've considered this, but I always

Hot drinks are welcome in cold weather. Metal vacuum flasks are heavy but unbreakable.

end up taking food that needs cooking because, on short trips, the extra weight is so slight that it doesn't matter; on long trips, the psychological boost of hot food is essential, especially if the weather turns cold and wet.

I wouldn't recommend trying to survive without a stove and hot sustenance in winter, when you may have to melt snow for water, and a hot meal can send waves of welcome warmth through your cold, stiff body. If anyone becomes really cold, wet, shivering, and perhaps on the verge of hypothermia, hot food and drink are possibly essential.

Fats, Proteins, Carbohydrates

Food consists of several components, each of which the body needs. The main ones are fats, proteins, and carbohydrates. All three provide energy but also serve other functions.

Fats release their energy slowly and can be stored in the body to be used when required. Because fats are digested gradually, they aren't a quick source of energy. Your body cannot easily digest food while exercising, either, so it's best to avoid eating a lot of fat during the day. Eating fats as part of your evening meal, however, enables them to release their energy during the night, which helps keep you warm. Sources of fat include dairy products, margarine, eggs, nuts, and meat. The current wisdom is that you should cut down on foods high in saturated fats (butter, animal-fat margarine, cheese, whole milk, lard, chocolate) and replace them with those high in polyunsaturated fats (vegetable margarines, low-fat spreads, vegetable oil) and monosaturated fats (olive oil). Nutritionists also recommend cutting down the total amount of fat in the diet, anyway, since fat can have other unwanted health effects. The body needs some fat, but nothing like the amount most people in developed countries eat. However, fats are an important part of the backpacker's diet, especially in cold weather.

Protein renews muscles and body tissue. During digestion, proteins break down into the amino acids from which they're made. The body then rebuilds these into muscle and tissue protein. Complete proteins contain a full complement of amino acids; they're most commonly found in meat, eggs, and dairy products. Incomplete proteins lack one or more amino acids, and are found in grains and legumes—however, these can be combined to create complete proteins. Thus, a stew with beans and barley provides all the amino acids you need. The body either burns protein as fuel or stores it as fat if it isn't immediately used for muscle regeneration, so protein is best eaten in small amounts at every meal.

The body quickly and directly turns *carbohydrates* into energy, so these are the foods most needed by the backpacker. Carbohydrates may be simple or complex. Simple ones are sugars (sucrose, dextrose, fructose, glucose, and honey); complex ones are starches (grains, vegetables, legumes). Generally, you should try to rely more on complex carbohydrates, because they provide more energy over a longer period of time. They also provide fiber, vitamins, and minerals. Fiber is essential in your diet to prevent constipation—a potential problem for the backpacker living on dehydrated food for a long period. Sugars give you a quick boost when you're tired, but it won't last, and can lead to feeling tired when the energy they supply is used up.

Determining what constitutes a proper proportion of these components in your diet is a nutritionist's basic reason for being. The current advice is to eat less fat and protein, and more carbohydrates. Most backpackers, especially those who undertake long walks, will have come to this conclusion, I suspect, because it's carbohydrates that speed you along the trail and that you crave when food runs low. My backpacking menu is probably 60 to 70 percent carbohydrates, the rest split equally between fats and proteins.

Vitamins and Minerals

Vitamins and minerals are also food components, but not ones you need worry about on trips of less than one month. Even if your diet is deficient in them for short periods, this is not likely to be harmful. On long trips, however, a lack of fresh food could mean that you need to add a vitamin and mineral supplement to your diet. I took a daily multivitamin with minerals supplement on both the Pacific Crest Trail and Canadian Rockies walks, but not on the Continental Divide walk. On the Yukon trek, I took 1 gram of vitamin C a day. The supplements made no obvious difference; I wasn't ill on any of the trips, except for a bad cold that lasted a few days on the Yukon walk. I may still take a vitamin supplement on future long walks because, at the very least, it does no harm, and it may prevent a deficiency.

Calories and Weight

A calorie is the measure of food's energy value. The calorie measurement used in reference to food is the *kilocalorie* (kcal)—it represents the amount of heat needed to raise 1 kilogram of water 1°C (34°F). (Kilocalorie, or Calorie, is the proper term; however, it's often referred to as "calorie" on food packets.) Sometimes *kilojoules* are used instead of kilocalories. There are 4.2 kilojoules to the kilocalorie.

How many kilocalories a person needs per day depends on his or her metabolism, weight, age, sex, and level of activity. Metabolism is an extremely complex process that is not fully understood, but it defines the body processes that transform foodstuffs into usable elements and energy; any surplus is stored as fat. If you eat more kilocalories than you use, you will put on weight; if you eat less, you will lose it. Putting on weight is not usually a problem for the backpacker, but losing it may be. The weight that most concerns the backpacker is that of the food he or she must carry in order to have enough energy.

	Kilocalories per Hour	
Activity	**128-pound woman**	**154-pound man**
Sleeping, resting, fasting	30–60	60–90
Sitting–reading, desk work	60–90	90–120
Sitting–typing, playing piano, operating controls	90–150	120–180
Light bench work, serving in store, gardening, slow walking	120–210	180–240
Social sports, cycling, tennis, light factory work, light farm work	180–300	240–360
Heavy physical labor, carrying, stacking, cutting wood, jogging, competitive sports	240–420	360–510
Very hard physical labor, intense physical activity, heavy lifting, very vigorous sporting activity	600+	720+

Food	Kilocalories per 3½ ounces	% fat	% protein	% carbohydrate
Dairy products, fats, and oils				
Margarine	720	81.0	0.6	0.4
Low-fat spread	366	36.8	6.0	3.0
Vegetable oil	900	100.0	—	—
Instant dried skim milk	355	1.3	36.0	53.0
Cheddar cheese	398	32.2	25.0	2.1
Edam cheese	305	23.0	24.0	—
Parmesan cheese	410	30.0	35.0	—
Eggs, dried	592	41.2	47.0	4.1
Low-fat cheese spread	175	9.0	20.0	4.0
Dried fruit				
Apples	275	—	1.0	78.0
Apricots	261	—	5.0	66.5
Dates	275	—	2.2	72.9
Figs	275	—	4.3	69.1
Peaches	261	—	3.1	68.3
Raisins	289	—	2.5	77.4
Vegetables				
Potatoes, dehydrated	352	—	8.3	80.4
Tomato flakes	342	—	10.8	76.7
Baked beans	123	2.6	6.1	19.0
Nuts				
Almonds	600	57.7	18.6	19.5
Brazil nuts	652	66.9	14.3	10.9
Coconut, desiccated	605	62.0	6.0	6.0
Peanut butter	589	49.4	27.8	17.2
Peanuts, roasted	582	49.8	26.0	18.8
Grain products				
Oatmeal	375	7.0	11.0	62.4
Muesli, sweetened	348	6.3	10.4	66.6
Pasta, white	370	—	12.5	75.2
Pasta, whole wheat	323	0.5	12.5	67.2
Rice, brown	359	—	7.5	77.4
Rice, white	363	—	6.7	80.4
Flour, plain	360	2.0	11.0	75.0
Flour, whole meal	345	3.0	12.0	72.0

Each person's metabolic rate differs, though generally the fitter and more active you are, the faster you will burn up food, whether you are working or at rest. Figures are available for the kilocalories needed for "everyday life" for people of different sizes. For someone of my height (5 feet 8 inches) and weight (154 to 161 pounds), it's around 2,500 kilocalories a day. Of that, 1,785

Food	Kilocalories per 3½ ounces	% fat	% protein	% carbohydrate
Baked products				
Granola bar	382	13.4	4.9	64.4
Crispbread, rye	345	1.2	13.0	76.3
Oat crackers	369	15.7	10.1	65.6
Bread, white	271	—	8.7	50.5
Baked products				
Bread, whole meal	243	—	10.5	47.7
Cookies, chocolate	525	28.0	6.0	67.0
Fig bar	356	5.6	3.9	75.4
Cake, fruit	355	13.0	5.0	58.0
Meat and fish				
Beef, dried	204	6.3	34.3	—
Beef, corned, canned	264	18.0	23.5	—
Salami	490	45.0	19.0	2.0
Salmon, canned	151	7.1	20.8	—
Sardines, drained	165	11.1	24.0	—
Tuna, drained	165	8.2	28.8	—
Sugars and sweets				
Honey	303	—	0.3	82.0
Sugar, brown	373	—	—	96.4
Sugar, white	384	—	—	99.5
Chocolate, milk	518	32.3	7.7	56.9
Custard, instant	378	10.2	2.9	72.6
Drinks				
Cocoa, mix	391	10.6	9.4	73.9
Coffee	2	—	0.2	—
Tea	1	—	0.1	—
Complete meals				
Pasta and sauce	384	4.7	13.1	77.1
Vegetable goulash and potato mix	375	11.9	15.9	54.4
Vegetable cottage pie	391	3.0	16.3	66.5
Thick pea soup	333	5.3	17.0	58.0
Bean stew mix	349	2.9	17.5	67.3
Fruit and nut bar	420	28.0	17.0	56.0

kilocalories make up the basal metabolism (the energy required simply to keep the body functioning), based on 1,100 kilocalories per 45 kilograms of body weight. To be able to expend more energy without burning body stores, I need to consume more kilocalories—it's clear that my backpacking menu must provide more than 2,500 kilocalories a day.

You can calculate roughly your kilocalorie needs based on figures that give kilocalorie demands of different activities. I had never done this until I wrote this book; I carried the same weight of food on each walk, believing it would provide the same number of kilocalories. However, I've made some calculations because I was curious to see how closely my field-based figures compared with scientific ones. This exercise could be useful for others in planning their food supplies. These figures are adapted from *Food Facts.*

If we include walking with a pack at the upper end of category 5 and the lower end of category 6, then men need 360 kilocalories per hour and women 240. If you walk for about seven hours a day, not including stops, as I do, that works out to 2,100 kilocalories for a woman, and 2,520 for a man (five and six per minute, respectively). Splitting up the rest of the day into nine hours of sleeping and resting (category 1), which requires 270 to 540 kilocalories (women) and 540 to 810 (men), and eight hours of category 4 (setting up camp, cooking, packing, "slow walking" around the site), which requires 960 to 1,680 kilocalories (women) and 1,440 to 1,920 (men), we end up with totals of 3,330 to 4,320 kilocalories (women) and 4,500 to 5,250 (men). These figures are very rough, of course, but they seem on the high side. You could argue, however, that a lot of backpacking activity falls into categories 6 and 7, and requires more energy than given here, not less.

Those figures seem high to me because I only need around 4,000 kilocalories a day on trips that will last no more than a few weeks. But these figures are for "average" people, and no one fits them exactly. Even so, such exercises are useful to those who would like to be precise about how much energy they use and where it comes from.

On longer walks, my appetite goes up dramatically after the first couple of weeks, and I now plan for more food from that time onward. I estimate that on long treks I average at least 5,000 kilocalories a day. In bitter weather, I may need more because of the cold, and more again on ski tours, because skiing uses up energy at a far greater rate than walking.

Many foods these days have the calorie content listed on the package, which is useful for making comparisons and compiling menus. I always check labels to see if the kilocalories are listed. Unlike many who count calories, I'm searching for *high-calorie,* not low-calorie foods. The figures in the table here are taken from a variety of sources, including *Agricultural Handbook No. 8: Composition of Foods* (U.S. Department of Agriculture), reproduced in *Mountaineering: The Freedom of the Hills* (4th edition); *Food Facts,* by David Briggs and Mark Wahlquist; and manufacturers' specifications.

Based on calories only, these figures suggest that you should live solely on margarine, vegetable oil, dried eggs, nuts, and chocolate in order to carry the least weight. But you wouldn't feel very well or walk easily, since all these are very high in fats. In fact, fats contain 9 kilocalories per gram, while proteins and carbohydrates have just 4.

The diet of complex carbohydrates (dried skimmed milk, dried fruit, dried vegetables, pasta, rice, oat crackers, muesli, and granola bars), plus a little fat (cheese, margarine) that I eat and recommend gives around 400 kilocalories per 3½ ounces. This works out to 2.2 pounds of food for 4,000 kilocalories per day, which is about what I carry. This diet should also provide enough protein. Only a sugar-based diet runs the risk of being insufficient in protein.

It's worth checking the caloric content of any food you intend to carry—there are significant variations between brands, and high-calorie carbohydrate-based foods mean less weight than low-calorie ones. For example, I'm glad I don't carry canned fish—as so many backpackers do—since, according to the chart, the weight per calorie (including the can) is very high. However, I really should give up my coffee in favor of cocoa!

On two- or three-day warm-weather trips, weight of food in the pack isn't a major concern, and I often take loaves of bread, fresh fruit, canned goods, and anything else I find in the cupboard. But in cold weather, and especially on long treks—when your basic load is much bigger and heavier, and at least a week's worth of food has to be carried—weight matters a great deal. Unfortunately, you need less food for short trips and more for long ones. I've read of people who get by on roughly 16 to 24 ounces of food per day without subsisting on margarine and nuts, but I can't—at least not for more than a few days.

I have to carry 35 ounces of food for each day on the trail. Powdered drinks, condiments, and other odds and ends are included in this total, which roughly divides into 5 ounces for breakfast, 14 ounces for dinner, and 14 ounces consumed during the day. The main evening meal usually weighs around 7 ounces, the other 7 ounces made up of soup, margarine, herbs and spices, milk powder, coffee, and sugar. These figures yield approximately 800, 1,600, and 1,600 kilocalories for the three meals.

Carrying 35 ounces a day equals 15 pounds a week; 30 pounds a fortnight. Two weeks' worth is the most I ever consider carrying, and I only do that if there's no other choice. On the Pacific Crest Trail I carried *44 pounds* of food on the 23-day crossing of the snowbound High Sierra, which made for a 100-pound load, because I also carried snowshoes, ice ax, crampons, and cold-weather clothing. My pack was too heavy for me to lift; I had to put it on while sitting down. The weight was ridiculous, and I only attempted to carry it because I had no idea what such a load would feel like. And I *still* ran short of food—probably because of the extra energy I needed to carry all that weight. Never again: Two weeks' food is the most that is reasonable for me to carry. If the total weight of my food comes to much more than 2.2 pounds a day, I know I've packed too much, so I jettison some.

On long walks and in cold conditions, I keep the weight down to 2.2 pounds a day by increasing the amount of fat, usually by adding more margarine and cheese to evening meals. Polar explorers often consume appallingly large amounts of fat daily, since it's the only way they can consume the 7,000 to 8,000 kilocalories they need. Eating that amount in carbohydrates would mean huge loads and never-ending meals.

Dried Food

Pack bulk doesn't matter much on one- or two-night jaunts, but it can be a problem on longer trips. Fresh, canned, and retort (cooked food vacuum-wrapped in foil) goods are bulky and heavy, so dried foods are the backpacker's staple for long-haul treks. By removing the moisture from foods, the caloric value of the food is maintained, while its weight and bulk are drastically reduced.

The simplest method of drying food is under a hot sun. Because this doesn't remove as much moisture as other methods, it's not used for many foods, though some fruits, such as bananas, may be sun-dried. Air-drying, where the food is spun in a drum or arranged on trays in a container through which hot air is blown, produces *dehydrated* foods. Commercial, reconstituted dehydrated foods have a reputation for being unappetizing, the result of damage to the cell structure during the process. In *spray-drying,* food is sprayed at high speed into a high hot air-filled cylinder. (This is used to dry milk, cheese, and coffee.) The most complex and expensive method of extracting the water from foods is *freeze-drying,* whereby food is flash-frozen so that the moisture in it turns to ice crystals that aren't large enough to damage cell structure. The food is then placed in a low-temperature vacuum, which turns the ice directly into vapor without passing through a liquid state (sublimation), again leaving the cells undamaged. Freeze-dried food is costly compared with dehydrated food, but it tastes better. Because the food can be cooked before being freeze-dried, it often just needs boiling water.

Home Dehydrating: Many backpackers dehydrate their own food, everything from dinners to fruit snacks. I've not done this myself, though I've eaten home-dehydrated food and been impressed enough to plan on doing it myself "one day." Home dehydrators consist of racks of trays through which heat from an electric motor is blown by a fan. There are several models, and some mail-order companies like Campmor sell them. You could also build your own or even use the oven—on low heat (around 140°F [60°C)]) and with the door slightly open. I've tried dried fruits—passion fruit is particularly tasty—dried tomato sauce, and dried tinned salmon and tuna. All were very palatable and quick to cook as long as they were soaked a little while first. Many outdoor cookbooks have sections on dehydrating. Alan Kesselheim's *Lightweight Gourmet* (Ragged Mountain Press) has comprehensive details, as does Dorcas Miller's *Good Food for Camp & Trail.*

Cooking Times and Methods

The time food takes to cook affects the amount of stove fuel you have to carry and the amount of time you have to wait for a meal at the end of the day. When you're crouched over a tiny stove, exhausted and hungry at the end of a long day with a storm raging all around, knowing your energy-restoring dinner will be ready in five rather than 30 minutes can be very important. Also, as you gain altitude and air pressure drops, water boils at a lower temperature. This means that recommended cooking times increase—times listed on food packets are for sea level. The boiling point of water drops 9°F ($-13°C$) for every 5,000 feet in altitude; cooking time doubles for every 9°F ($-13°C$) drop in the boiling point of water. So at 5,000 feet, the cooking time is twice what it would be at sea level; at 10,000 feet nearly four times as long; at 15,000 feet seven times; and at 20,000 feet an appalling 13 times. These cooking times are for fresh foods, of course; pre-cooked dried food takes only a little longer to cook at altitude. For cooking above 7,000 to 8,000 feet, quick-cook and pre-cooked foods are needed.

These figures are important because the majority of backpacking foods are cooked in boiling water. Frying requires carrying oil or cooking fat, and cleaning the greasy pan can be difficult, so I rarely fry food. You can bake and roast if you have a fire for cooking, but I've never done so. Anglers often carry foil to wrap trout in before placing them in the embers of a fire—the one type of roasting that makes sense to me. Baking is becoming more popular with the new, lightweight portable devices like the Outback Oven and the BakePacker. These are so easy to use that I occasionally bake in camp now, though only with prepared mixes (see pages 239–241 for more on this topic).

Many packaged foods—from soups to noodles—don't require any cooking, just boiling water and a quick stir. They usually taste inferior to meals that require a little simmering, but I generally carry a few for those times at the end of long, hard days when I want hot food quickly and I'm not too fussy. I also take them when bivouacking, in case I have to produce a meal in a gale. Most of my meals need five to 10 minutes' simmering, a good balance between tasty and fast food.

Cooking times can be reduced by pre-soaking some foods in cold water. This works with dried vegetables, dried meat, soya products, and legumes, but not with pasta or rice. Some people soak food in a tightly capped bottle during the day so that it's ready for cooking when they reach camp. Fuel—though not time—can be saved with most foods that need simmering by bringing the water to a boil, adding the food, and then turning off the heat. As long as a well-fitting lid is used, the food will at least partially, if not completely, cook in the hot water. I often do this when I make camp with plenty of time to spare, and reheat the food when I'm ready to eat.

What's Available

A list of foods suitable for backpacking would fill a separate book, so here are just a few suggestions heavily biased toward my own diet.

Suitable foods can be found in supermarkets, grocery stores, whole- or health-food stores, and outdoor stores. Prices are lowest in supermarkets, which actually have all the foods you need. Quite a few will be processed foods with additives, however, which may affect your decision. Check cooking times carefully; one packet of soup may take five minutes to cook while one next to it on the shelf takes 25. Health-food stores supply unadulterated foods and a wide variety of cereals, dried fruits, and grain bars, though the number of supermarkets selling these items is increasing. Outdoor stores are where you'll find foods specially made for backpackers and mountaineers. Lightweight, low-bulk, often freeze-dried, and expensive, these are fine if you have the money and don't mind the taste.

The best specialty backpacking meals I've found come from the California company AlpineAire, whose foods I ate on the Continental Divide walk. Even after 5½ months on the trail, I hadn't grown tired of the food. I tried vastly inferior British meals on the Canadian Rockies walk, but quickly returned to AlpineAire for the Yukon walk. AlpineAire foods are additive-free, use whole-meal pasta and brown rice, and include both freeze-dried and dehydrated items. The range includes dishes for breakfast and evening meals, plus soups and light meals for lunch. A company whose food has been highly recommended by other writers and by hikers I know, but which I haven't tried, is Uncle John's Foods of Colorado. Other brands are Backpacker's Pantry, my second choice after AlpineAire; Mountain House; Richmoor; and Harvest Foodworks. Offering a wide selection of specialty outdoor foods by mail order, including AlpineAire, are Trail Foods, which supplied my Pacific Crest Trail walk.

The latest specialty foods are designed for baking devices like the BakePacker and Outback Oven (for more on these, see "Ovens and Baking Devices," pages 239–241). Adventure Foods makes a range of meals for the BakePacker. I've tried the Gingerbread and the Honey Cornbread, and both are delicious. The dry weights are 7 and 9.6 ounces, and there is enough for two. More mixes are available, and Jean S. Spangenberg's *The BakePacker's Companion* (Sylva Herald Publishing) lists many more recipes. For the Outback Oven, Traveling Light offers a selection of just-add-water mixes. The ones I've tried—the Spinach, Mushroom & Cheddar Quiche and the Fudge Brownies—were also delicious. The dry weights are 12 and 16 ounces, and they make enough for two. When traveling solo, surplus baked goods can be carried and eaten the next day, something you would never do with dehydrated food.

The smell of fresh-baked foods emanating from these mini ovens is truly wonderful, but cooking times are long and some preparation is required. These are luxury foods for days when I have time to spare and trips where weight isn't important. (For more information on the manufacturers and suppliers listed here, see Appendix 3.)

Basic Breakfast

The only hot sustenance I normally have when I'm still bleary-eyed and trying to come to terms with being awake is a mug or two of coffee with sugar and dried milk (combined weight 0.3 ounce). I eat 4 ounces of muesli or granola with dried milk (0.3 to 0.6 ounce) and a few spoonfuls of sugar (about 0.5 to 0.6 ounce), unless the brand is pre-sweetened. I have no preference for any particular brand—there are many good ones. If it's cold enough for the water in the pan to have frozen overnight, I dump the cereal on top of the ice, then heat the lot on the stove to make a sort of muesli porridge.

For those who prefer a daily hot breakfast, oatmeal is a possibility, as are various dried omelet and pancake mixes. Of course, you can eat anything at any time of the day. One of my trail companions eats instant noodles for breakfast, though that's not a food I could face at the start of the day. I traveled part of the Pacific Crest Trail with an experienced hiker who ate trail mix for breakfast, which I have tried but find too dry. Another hiker I met on the same walk ate instant freeze-dried meals three times a day for the whole six-month walk, another diet I couldn't contemplate.

Lengthy Lunch

Walking with a pack requires a constant, steady supply of energy, so I eat several times during the day. I often eat the first mouthfuls of "lunch" soon after breakfast, before I start walking. Some people like to stop and make hot drinks during the day, or even cook soup or light meals—I don't. I rarely stop for more than 10 or 20 minutes at a time, and I'm happy to snack on cold foods and drink cold water. Also, the days when I'd most like something hot are those when the weather's so cold or wet that stopping for more than a couple of minutes is a bad idea. In such conditions, I'd rather keep moving and make camp earlier. On days when long stops are pleasant, I don't feel the need for hot food.

A staple snack food mixture of dried fruit, nuts, and seeds is known as *trail mix* or *gorp*, among a host of other names. At its most basic, it consists of peanuts and raisins, but more sophisticated and tasty mixes can include bits of dried fruit (my favorites are papaya, pineapple, and dates), a range of nuts, desiccated coconut, chocolate or carob chips, butterscotch chips, M&Ms, sunflower and sesame seeds, crunchy roasted cereal (granola), and anything else you fancy. I prefer trail mix to be on the sweet side; others prefer a more savory taste. I find I can easily eat 2½ to 3½ ounces a day. I generally add any dried fruit I buy to the trail mix. The exception is sun-dried bananas, which come in 8-ounce blocks; I eat them as an alternative to the mix.

I used to eat several chocolate and other candy bars every day, but following the recommendation to cut down on fat and sugar and increase complex carbohydrates, I no longer do so. Instead, I munch on cereal or granola bars, usually three or four a day.

I also often carry a more substantial cereal bar, usually some form of sweetened oat cookie. The best lunch foods I've discovered are the California-made Bear Valley Meal Pack and Pemmican bars, which I took on the Continental Divide and Yukon walks. They are filling, packed with kilocalories (415 to 470 per bar, depending on the variety), tasty, and surprisingly light, at just over 3½ ounces per bar. They are basically a compressed mix of grains, dried fruit, nuts, and soy products with various natural flavorings. They also contain all eight essential amino acids, which makes them a good source of protein. I ate at least one every day of the 5½-month Divide walk, and two or more a day in the Yukon, and never grew tired of them. If I ever do a trip where I eat only cold food, these bars will make up the main part of my diet.

All the above foods are, to a greater or lesser degree, sweet. Having some crispbread, crackers, and cheese or vegetable spread makes a pleasant contrast. I prefer tortillas or pita bread, both of which come in resealable plastic bags. Whole-meal tortillas are best for eating unheated; white-flour tortillas taste uncooked to me. If you carry breads, beware of them going moldy. I took enough pita bread for one a day on a two-week walk in the Grand Canyon. A few days before the end of the trip I was eating one in the dark when an appalling taste flooded my mouth—the next day I noticed the green patches of mold on the remaining bread.

Cheese or vegetable pate spreads that come in squeeze tubes are, for me, a necessity on breads. Meat eaters often carry pate or salami to go with crackers, while those with a really sweet tooth can take jam or honey, both of which are available in plastic squeeze bottles or tubs. I avoid spreads in tubs and foil—they ooze around the edges and smear themselves on your clothes and the sides of the plastic bags they have to be kept in.

Dehydrated Dinner

A one-pot dehydrated or freeze-dried meal is the basis of my evening repast. It's possible to concoct such meals at home from basic ingredients, but I prefer to use complete meals, which I doctor to suit my taste. As mentioned earlier, my favorites come from AlpineAire, all of whose meals now require only boiling water and a seven- to 10-minute wait. A typical meatless example (they make beef, turkey, seafood, and chicken dishes, too) is Mountain Chili (contents: cooked freeze-dried pinto beans, soy protein, tomato powder, cornmeal, freeze-dried corn, spices, bell peppers, onions, and salt), which has a net weight of 7 ounces. It makes two servings—maybe, if you're not hungry, haven't been walking all day, and have lots of other food to eat. I have no problem eating all 30 ounces and 680 kilocalories in one sitting. (When searching store shelves for evening meals, I look for dry weights of around 7 ounces and ignore the number of servings. If the amount is well below 7 ounces, I only carry it if I'm planning on adding extra food.)

When I don't eat AlpineAire meals, I live on pasta-based dinners. Lipton offers a host of pasta-and-sauce meals that are quick-cooking and tasty; I know people who've hiked the Pacific Crest Trail using Lipton's meals as their main dinners. The staple outdoor dinner, though, is that perennial hikers' favorite—macaroni and cheese. Kraft Cheesy Pasta is the most common brand (contents: pasta, cheese, dried skimmed milk, dried whey, salt, emulsifying salts, lactic acid, color). It cooks in six minutes and comes in 6¾-ounce packs, just right for a single meal (the pack says "serves 2–3"). The makers advise adding milk and margarine to the dish. I add extra cheese, too.

Oriental noodles with flavor packets—usually sold under the name Ramen—cook in about four minutes and are a good alternative to macaroni and cheese. Westbrae Ramens, made from whole-meal flour and found in health-food stores and some supermarkets, are my favorites.

Each of the half-dozen varieties weighs around 3 ounces and makes 9 ounces of cooked food. I use two packets of noodles per meal, and add a packet of dehydrated soup mix, cheese, and margarine to make a full meal. Supermarkets sell white-flour versions of these noodles, which I sometimes use.

If I do make up my own meals, they're usually based on macaroni or other pasta as a base, to which I add dehydrated soup mix, such as onion or tomato, plus cheese sliced up with my pocketknife. These are so easy to prepare that I do so in camp rather than at home. Almost every night of the 86-day Scandinavian mountain hike I dined on quick-cook macaroni mixed with packet soup, dried milk and cheese, plus flavorings.

There are various ways to enhance the taste of any meal. Adding herbs and spices, soup mix, or cheese are popular ways to "doctor" meals. I carry garlic powder (fresh cloves on short trips), curry or chili powder, black pepper, and mixed herbs (but not salt, which I dislike). Margarine, cheese, and milk powder add kilocalories as well as taste and bulk to meals. Packet soups can be flavoring agents or the base for a meal with pasta, rice, cheese, dried milk, and other ingredients added to increase the food value. I often mix foods on the last few evenings of a long trip, using up whatever I have left. If I am buying pasta or rice to add to soup I look for quick-cooking varieties.

I usually eat a bowl of packet soup before having my main meal, unless I'm very hungry. The ones that require simmering for five or 10 minutes taste best (I like Knorr), but instant soups require less time and fuel to prepare. The biggest problem with them is the serving size—a meager 7 ounces when rehydrated, and only 118 kilocalories. I solve this problem by eating two packets at a time (2 ounces total dry weight).

Again, adding margarine and cheese increases the energy content.

My staples are margarine, dried milk, and cheese. I use about 1¾ ounces of margarine every evening, so a 9-ounce tub lasts five days. Parkay and other liquid margarines in squeeze bottles weigh around 16 ounces, and are less messy and easier to use than tub varieties. (Margarine does come in tubes, but it's hard to find and tastes awful.) I plan on 2 ounces of cheese a day— twice that if it's a main part of a meal. On long trips I use up any cheese in the first few days, and so eat the lowest-calorie meals I'm carrying then. Instant non-fat dry milk adds taste and calories to any dish and is also good with breakfast cereal, and tea or coffee. I think the best is Milkman Instant Milk, which tastes more like fresh milk than any of the others; I prefer brands that contain nothing but milk powder rather than those with additives. A standard 7-ounce pack of instant milk will make 3½ pints, and lasts me at least four or five days.

Coffee and sugar make up the final course of my evening sustenance. Three or four mugs an evening means carrying ¾ ounce of sugar and 0.2 ounce of instant coffee per day. Despite being English, I don't drink tea, but those who do seem to find a large supply of tea bags essential—though an amazing number of mugs can be wrung from just one bag when supplies run low. Cocoa and hot chocolate supply plenty of kilocalories—unlike coffee or tea—and are available in convenient packets, but I rarely carry them. I have recently taken a liking to hot spiced cider drinks, available in mug-size sachets, and I now often drink one or two of these in the evening instead of coffee.

Variations

There are variations, of course, on what food can be taken on any backpacking outing. On two-

or three-day trips, I may carry bread rather than crackers. In fact, I sometimes make up a packet of sandwiches for each day's lunch. Retort foods are feasible then, too—they're lighter and tastier than canned goods, though heavier and bulkier than dried ones. As mentioned, I've started to carry the BakePacker or Outback Oven plus baking mixes on trips where weight isn't important. (I also tend to carry these on late fall and winter trips when there are long, dark evenings that can be passed baking goodies for the next day.)

Cold weather and winter treks in northern latitudes call for a big change in my diet. Short daylight hours mean more time spent in camp and less on the move, while increased cold means a need for more kilocalories—so I take slightly less food for daytime but more for the evening. In particular, I usually add some sort of dessert as a third course; hot instant custard with dried fruit is a favorite. A 3-ounce packet provides 378 kilocalories even before you add dried fruit. Cold instant puddings are also a good way to pile on calories; preparation time can be speeded up by burying them in the snow to set.

Emergency Supplies

For many years I carried a compressed block of foil-wrapped emergency rations, known as Turblokken, at the bottom of my pack, assuming that it would keep me going if I ran out of food. I finally ate it once when my supplies ran low and I wanted to climb some mountains, which I wouldn't have been able to do if I detoured to resupply. My journal records that it was "fairly tasteless but kept me going." Now I carry a little extra food, such as an 8-ounce block of dried bananas, for emergencies. I also bring one extra day's worth of supplies in case bad weather slows me down or keeps me in camp. If you can catch fish or know which insects and plants are edible, you can, of course, try to "live off the land."

I've only run out of food once in an area so remote that I couldn't walk out to a supply point in a day or two. My situation was complicated because I was a bit unclear about where I was (notice I didn't say "lost"). I had to ration my food severely for several days, and emerged from the forest extremely hungry, but without having run out of energy. I learned that, if you have to, you can get by on remarkably little food—at least for a short time. I would go to great lengths to avoid such a situation recurring, however. Once is more than enough.

Packaging

Plastic bags are essential for carrying food. I bag everything that needs repacking, including coffee, sugar, dried milk, trail mix, muesli, and meals such as macaroni and cheese that come in cardboard cartons. If I need the instructions, I tear them off and put them in the bag with the food. The only items I keep in their cardboard containers are oat crackers and other bread substitutes that are vulnerable to breakage. I also keep margarine tubs and cheese in plastic bags in case of leaks. Packets of soup, granola bars, and complete meals packaged in light foil containers don't need repacking, but can be bagged together so that it's easy to see what you have. Bagging also serves as extra protection against tears in the foil. The best bags I've found are Ziploc. I always carry a few spare bags in case one splits. Freezer bags with wire twist-tie closures are an alternative, but they aren't as easy to use.

Outdoor stores carry many plastic food containers, but I don't use them—they take up as much space empty as they do full; plastic bags compress to almost nothing. The only plastic containers I regularly use are empty plastic film canisters, which I wash out and use to carry herbs and spices. Flip-top lids with shake holes are available to fit these canisters; they work well.

I keep my food together in the pack in large, heavy-duty, transparent plastic bags, which I close with an elastic band. On long treks and in bear country, where food has to be hung from a tree at night, I use nylon stuff sacks, which are less convenient but far tougher and more durable. When I'm carrying more than a week's food I use two of these. I put day food, which tends to be the bulkiest of my rations, in one bag, and camp food in the other. Two smaller bags are easier to pack than one large one, and it's easier to find items.

Resupply

On trips of up to a week, resupplying isn't necessary; you carry all you need, unless your route passes through a place where you can buy food. On treks that last a month or more, you have to plan how to resupply. If you are prepared to live on whatever is available locally, you can visit a town or village once a week and resupply there. This can be quite interesting! Most small stores stock packet soups, crackers, bread, cheese, candy, chocolate bars, coffee, and tea, but dried meals and breakfast cereals can be hard to find. This can mean carrying more weight and bulk than you'd like in order to have enough kilocalories.

What I prefer to do on nearly all my long walks is to send supplies to myself to be collected along the way. This way, I know what is in each supply box and can plan accurately; I can also include items such as maps and camera film in the same boxes. The obvious places to send supplies to are post offices. Boxes should be addressed to yourself c/o General Delivery ("Poste Restante" in Europe) in the town scheduled for pickup. They should be marked "Hold for walker," and include the date on which you intend to collect them. I also write to the postmasters at the post offices to tell them what I'm

doing. It's also a good idea to phone them to check that the supplies have arrived; during the Canadian Rockies walk, one box went astray, causing me a week's delay.

Some mail-order food suppliers, such as Trail Foods and AlpineAire, will ship food to post offices along your route, a service I used on both the Pacific Crest Trail and Continental Divide walks. If there are no post offices where I need to resupply, I contact a park or forest service ranger or warden office, or the nearest youth hostel, lodge, or motel, to ask if they will hold supplies for me. I've never yet been refused, though some of the latter places request a small fee (I always offer payment when I write). Rangers or outfitters may also be prepared to take food into wilderness cabins or camps if you're on a long trip and you ask. When I walked through the Yukon Territory I found a commercial tourboat operator who was prepared to take supplies down the Yukon River for me—I was able to walk for 23 days without having to leave the wilderness to resupply.

You can cache food in advance, if you have the time or have someone who can do it for you, though I've never done this. Obviously, cached food has to be stored in an animal-proof container and hidden where only you can find it.

Another resupply alternative is to have food dropped by helicopter or brought in by bush plane. I considered this for the remote northern section of the Canadian Rockies walk, but rejected it, mainly because of the high cost, but also because I wasn't happy about bringing noisy machines into the wilderness unless it was absolutely necessary. Instead, I tried to carry all my food for this 300-mile section. I took 17 days' food, but spent 23 in the wilderness. Luckily, it was hunting season—the seasonal occupants of several remote outfitters' camps fed me as I passed through. Without them, I couldn't have completed the walk. Of course, I could and should have contacted them in advance and asked if they'd take supplies in for me, which is what I would do on a similar venture now.

Food Storage in Camp

On most trips I like to keep my food in the tent, which provides easy access and protection from small animals and birds. If you leave the tent door open, however, bolder creatures may venture in. (Camped on a quiet farm site in North

This post served as good place to hang food and packs at a popular site in the Grand Canyon, where wildlife may be a problem.

Wales many years ago, I was awakened abruptly during the night by something furry brushing against my face. I sat up with a jolt, just in time to glimpse a dark shape sliding under the fly sheet. A quick scan around revealed the muddy paw prints of the farm cat crossing the groundsheet to my food bag, out of which the animal had pulled and then gnawed a lump of cheese.)

Don't leave food outside on the ground, even if it's in the pack, as this is a sure way to feed local wildlife. Sharp teeth will quickly make holes in the toughest materials. Even food left in the tent vestibule may be pinched. I once led Outward Bound treks that used to finish at a coastal campsite on the Isle of Skye, where we could resupply with fresh food. On every trek, despite warnings, students would leave their supplies (usually bread and bacon) inside their fly-sheet doors, only to have seagulls—and sometimes even sheep—steal them.

The worst problems I've had with wildlife were in the Grand Canyon. Deer mice seem to raid even the remotest, least-used sites. Ravens, ring-tailed cats, and mule deer are all ready to eat your food as well. In the summer of 1995, rangers had to shoot 23 mule deer that were starving to death in the Grand Canyon; autopsies showed their stomachs were clogged with plastic bags, nylon cord, and other indigestible items. On popular backcountry sites in the Grand Canyon, posts are provided for hanging food bags and packs, and park regulations stress that all plastic bags and food must be kept packed away. When you feel like rebelling against the rules, remember those mule deer.

George Steck, who has hiked more miles in the canyon than most people have, says in his *Grand Canyon Treks* books that he has yet to find a sure way to keep mice out of his food. Putting it in a cookpot with the lid on is his favorite method, but this obviously only protects small amounts of food. One night, mice kept me awake from dusk until dawn by running over me and my gear and rustling through the pack, whose pockets and compartments I'd left open so creatures wouldn't rip their way in. My food—inside plastic bags in a heavy-duty stuff sack and hung from a branch—was untouched, however. I heard a story of another hiker at the same site who slept with a sock full of sand that he swung at the mice.

Such problems are common throughout the canyons and deserts of the Southwest. The best solution I've come across is one described by Betty Tucker-Bryan in the December 1995 issue of *Backpacker* magazine. She developed what she calls a "Baxter Bag"—a bag made of a large folded piece of wire mesh "hardware cloth" with two sides sewn together by copper wire. The third side is stitched shut once the food is inside. This would be awkward to open and close but should repel small mammals. Steck describes making a similar container from stainless steel screening, with the sides stapled shut. Animals couldn't gnaw their way in; instead, the container was stolen—filled with food—by rock squirrels.

Bearbagging: In areas where bears may raid campsites in search of food, food bags need to be hung at least 12 feet above the ground, 10 feet away from the trunk of a tree, and 6 feet below any branch. There are various ways of doing this, and all require at least 50 feet of nylon line and a tough stuff sack or two. Any stuff sacks will do, but Gregory offers ones specially designed for bearbagging. These Bear Bags (10 inches by 15 inches, and 15 by 20 inches; 7.6 and 8.8 ounces) come with sewn-in haul loops and a 40-foot length of parachute cord with an attached sack for a rock.

The simplest bearbagging method is to tie a rock to the end of the line, throw it over a branch at least 20 feet above the ground, haul up the food until the bottom of the bag is at least 12 feet up, then tie off the line around the trunk of the tree. This is not always as easy as it sounds.

Up near the timberline the trees are usually smaller, with shorter branches. Here, you will usually have to suspend food bags between two trees about 25 feet apart, which involves throwing one end of the weighted line over a branch, tying it off, and then repeating the process with the second tree. Keep the line between the two trees within reach so you can tie the food bag

Hanging food ("bearbagging") is the usual way of protecting it against bears.

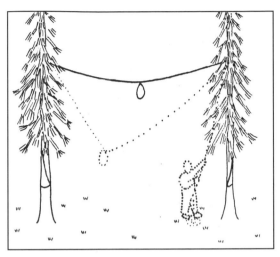

When bearbagging, pack food in plastic bags and place them in a strong nylon bag suspended 12 feet above the ground, 6 feet below any branch, and 10 feet away from any trunk.

Line is placed over branches before attaching food bag.

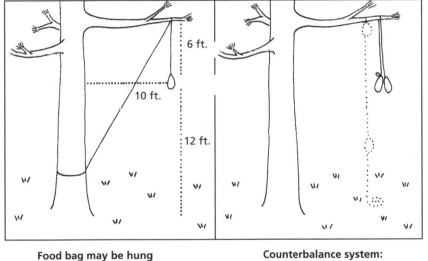

Food bag may be hung from a long, strong branch.

Counterbalance system: retrieve using a stick.

to it. Then haul the bag up until it is halfway between the trees and 12 feet off the ground. I only use this method, however, if I can't find a suitable single branch within reasonable distance of my camp. I've spent the best part of an hour hanging my food in this way, expending a lot of energy on curses as branches broke and rocks whirled off into space or spun around branches, leaving a tangle of line to unwind. But whenever I've felt like giving up, I've thought about losing my food to a bear and gone on until my food was secure.

In a few areas, such as in Yosemite National Park, bears have learned that breaking a line rewards them with a bag of food. In these places, standard bearbagging techniques don't work. Instead, you must use a counterbalance system, which involves throwing the line over a branch, tying a food bag to the end of the line, and hauling it right up to the branch; you then tie a second food bag (or bag of rocks) to the other end of the line, push any extra line into the bag, and throw the second bag so that both bags end up above the ground and away from the tree trunk. If you leave a loop of line at the top of one of the bags, you can hook it with a stick or your staff to pull the bags down the next morning.

In popular backcountry sites in some national parks, such as Yosemite, and Banff and Jasper in the Canadian Rockies, high wires between trees or poles with pulleys are provided for bearbagging. These make the procedure easier, though it can still be difficult if you are alone and have a heavy food bag.

All bearbagging complicates camp setup, and there is a tendency to forgo it at the end of a long, hard day or in bad weather. Certainly, when I make camp after dark, I often suspend my food somewhere I wouldn't be happy with in daylight. I *always hang it,* though.

Bearbagging protects bears as well as food, since a bear that finds food at a campsite may learn to raid it regularly, becoming such a danger that it has to be destroyed.

The safest bear-country campsite is near trees. If you end up far from any timber, store food well away from your tent in airtight plastic bags, which is what I did in the northern Yukon, where trees big enough to hang food from are few and far between. Habitual above-timberline bear-country campers may want to use bear-resistant plastic cylinders made by Garcia Machine. In certain areas, such as Denali

National Park in Alaska and the Slims River Valley of Kluane National Park in the Yukon, where grizzly bears are very common, these cylinders are compulsory and can be rented from park offices. They are also recommended by an increasing number of national parks. The last time I was in Yosemite I used the smallest Backpacker version, which weighs 3 pounds and holds five to six days' food for one person. These containers are made from hard plastic and have a round lid with a recessed catch that can be

Bear-resistant food containers are a requirement in some areas, and recommended in others.

opened with a small coin or screwdriver, but not by a bear's claws. They are awkward to pack and take up a lot of room due to the cylindrical shape. (My companion and I had one each; it took us a few days before deciding that the best way to pack them was to stand them up in the center of the top compartment of the pack and then pack gear around them.) Fitting six days' food into them, along with other items attractive to bears, such as sunscreen, was very difficult; for the first couple of nights on each leg of our two-week walk, we hung food out. However, it was wonderful not to have to hang food every night, and great to have easy access to food and drink at all times. I wouldn't carry a bear-resistant container (we nicknamed them "bear barrels" due to the shape) on a trip where weight or pack space was critical, nor would I take them on a trip in areas where bear problems aren't likely, but for Yosemite and those northern parks with high grizzly populations, they're much preferable to hanging food.

Bears are attracted to food by smell, so they may consider items such as toothpaste, soap, insect repellent, sunscreen, food-stained clothing, dish rags, and dirty pots and pans to be food—*keep them out of your tent* and hang them with your food.

Another way to avoid possible bear problems is to avoid popular backcountry sites. In Yosemite, steer clear of large lakes ringed by well-used sites and campsites where lots of people are camped. Bears will frequent those places where there is a regular and prolific supply of food.

If a bear does get your food *don't try to get it back.* The bear will defend what it regards as its own food.

"Wild" Foods

I'm often asked why I don't "live off the land" during long wilderness treks. The phrase conjures up the carefree image of a walker ambling along, munching on nuts and fruits plucked from trailside bushes and whisking tasty trout from every stream.

In fact, unless you hunt animals or spend a long time fishing, finding enough to eat in the wilderness is very difficult for most people, and does not allow time for walking all day. Then too, our wild lands are limited and fragile; we should take no more from them than we absolutely must, which means going into them with all the food we need. If every wilderness traveler relied on foraging plants for food, popular areas would soon be stripped bare.

Fishing, perhaps, is an exception. Mountain lakes and streams often seem prolific in trout or other fish, and the stocks usually are unaffected by regular fishing. I wouldn't rely on fishing for food, but anglers might carry light fishing outfits (and licenses) in areas known for fish, and thereby supplement their diets with some fresh food. *The Camper's Companion,* by Rick Greenspan and Hal Kahn, contains useful information for the would-be backcountry angler.

WATER

While you can manage without food for a surprisingly long time, this is not so with water. Dehydration can kill you in a matter of days—and long before you are in real danger you'll cease to enjoy what you're doing, as your mind dulls and your perceptions numb.

On any walk, you need to know where water sources are and what the condition of the water is likely to be. In many places water is not a problem—unless there's too much of it—but in others, especially desert or semi-desert areas, the location of water sources can determine your route. Water supply is one of the first things I want to know about a region new to me.

How much water you need per day varies from person to person and depends on the weather conditions, the amount of energy used, and the type of food you carry. I can walk all day without a drink in cool, damp conditions, though I don't recommend this. On the other hand, I may drink a quart an hour on a very hot day in an area where there is no shade. Estimating needs for camp is easier: With the dried foods I eat, I can get by with 2 quarts per night, but I prefer to have 4 or more—and that is just for cooking and drinking, not for washing utensils or myself. It also assumes I've had enough to drink during the day, and am either camping near water or expect to find a source fairly early the next day.

When you have to carry water, these calculations become important, because water weighs more than 2 pounds per quart. In desert areas of the Southwest, I've carried up to 18 pounds of water—a tremendous weight added to the weight of the pack. Luckily, it's rare to have to carry that much, at least for a whole day. "Dry" camps (ones away from water sources, often high up on mountain ridges or summits) may require you to carry 3 or 4 quarts of water, but often this can be picked up late in the day so you only have to carry it a few hours. Remember, you need enough water to get you to the next source, as well as for use in dry camps.

Snow-covered country is odd—everything is shrouded in solid water, but it is effectively a desert. Walking in snow can dehydrate you as quickly as desert walking, because the dry air sucks moisture out of your body. The thirstiest I've ever felt was when I skied all day in hot sunshine with no shade and not enough liquid. Eating snow cools the mouth, but provides little real

Warnings should be heeded. This one is in the Grand Canyon.

relief. The answer, easily given but not so easily carried out, is to melt enough snow in camp to keep you well supplied during the day.

Ideally, you should never allow yourself to become even slightly dehydrated. The best way to avoid this is to drink regularly, whether you feel thirsty or not. In practice, dehydration may creep up on you, and only when your mouth starts to feel sticky and your tongue swollen will you realize how thirsty you are. Warning signs of dehydration are a reduction in urine output, and a change in the color of the urine—the paler, the better. If it is dark, you need to drink a fair amount of water quickly.

Sources

Streams, rivers, lakes, and ponds are obvious sources of water, easily identified on a map. In areas dotted with these features, you won't need to carry much or to worry about running out. Check contour lines carefully, however, to see exactly where the water is. Often the high ridges that make for superb walking can be far above any water. In such places, it's better to carry full bottles than make long descents and re-ascents when you need a drink. Remember, too, that dotted blue lines on the map usually indicate *seasonal* water sources; the rushing stream in June, heavy with snowmelt, may have vanished completely by late September.

If large water sources are scarce, it may be necessary to hunt out tiny trickles and seeps. To find these, look for areas of richer, denser vegetation, and for depressions and gullies in which water may gather or run. You generally do better to rely on maps and guidebooks for information on the whereabouts of water.

In desert areas, locating water is critical to survival. My experience is limited to crossing the Mojave Desert and the semi-deserts of southern California on the Pacific Crest Trail, the deserts of New Mexico on the Continental Divide, and in the Grand Canyon. On the long trails I linked guaranteed water sources that were never more than 25 miles apart. Even so, I often carried 4 quarts of water at a time; in the Grand Canyon I had to carry up to 2 gallons at a time. On that trip I learned that it's important to check guidebooks for information on water sources, and, more importantly, to ask local rangers for current information on water sources. If a source seems problematic, carry enough water to get to the next one. For those intending more serious desert ventures and who want to know about caching water, desert stills, and similar solutions, I recommend a look at Colin Fletcher's *The Complete Walker III* (Knopf), which goes into this in great detail. Most "survival" books also cover desert travel but, unlike Fletcher's book, are not written specifically for the backpacker.

Treatment

A real problem with water is deciding whether what you find is safe to drink. Water clarity is not necessarily an indication of either purity or contamination. Even the most sparkling, crystal-clear mountain stream may not be safe to drink from.

The invisible contaminants include a wide variety of microorganisms that cause diarrhea and dysentery—sometimes mild, sometimes severe. The protozoa *Giardia lamblia,* which causes a virulent stomach disorder—giardiasis, or giardia—curable only by specific antibiotics, is the one that has received most attention. A fear of giardia swept through the backpacking world in the 1980s. While the parasite that causes giardia is indeed found in many wilderness streams and lakes, too many people are far too concerned about it. Giardia isn't fatal, and you're unlikely to be incapacitated. Although it makes some people feel quite ill, others, perhaps the majority, will hardly notice any effects. In many areas of the Third World, it's so common that it's hardly ever treated.

Giardia lamblia lives in the intestines of humans and animals. It gets into water as cysts excreted with feces, which is one reason always to site toilets well away from water. The symptoms of giardia appear a few weeks after ingestion, and include diarrhea, stomachache, a bloated feeling, nausea, and foul-smelling feces. However, these symptoms occur in other stomach disorders as well, and only a stool analysis can confirm infection.

The chances of catching giardiasis aren't that high, however, despite media coverage to the contrary. The understandable desire of park and forest agencies to avoid litigation adds to worries—they generally advise people that all water needs treating. However, the latest research, published in the journal *Wilderness and Environmental Medicine* and abstracted by *Backpacker* magazine, suggests that giardiasis and other stomach disorders are spread "by oral-fecal or food-borne transmission not by contaminated drinking water." The study's authors, who surveyed health departments in all 50 states, compare the likelihood of catching giardiasis from drinking water to the risk of a shark attack, and say that it's "an extraordinarily rare event to which the public and press have seemingly devoted inappropriate attention." If this study is correct, *it's far more important to wash your hands and keep your cooking utensils clean than to treat your water.*

What should you do? I've never treated water, as long as it looks clear and I'm above any habitations or livestock herds. I once had a serious bout of diarrhea after a wilderness trip, but the cause, although undiagnosed, wasn't giardiasis. If you're really worried about stomach disorders, you could ease your concerns by treating all water, but you should also, as noted above, take great care with personal hygiene and keep your cooking utensils clean.

Purifying all water poses its own dangers. In the Montana Rockies during my Continental Divide walk, I regularly met members of a large party doing the same trek. Most of them were very worried about giardiasis, and they filtered or boiled all water before drinking it. While restocking and resting in Butte after several weeks of very hot weather, I met one of this party walking down the street looking pale and thin. I was surprised to see him—when we'd last met, he'd been intent on taking a more roundabout route than mine. He told me that he'd staggered out of the mountains feeling weak and sick. He didn't have giardiasis—he was suffering from severe dehydration! He wouldn't drink unfiltered water and he hadn't time to filter the amount he should have been drinking.

Water can be purified by boiling it, treating it with chemicals, and by filtering it. Visibly dirty water can be filtered through a bandanna, as can glacier melt water, but this doesn't remove microorganisms—it should still be treated. Boiling is the surest way to kill dangerous organisms, but it's impractical because it uses fuel and takes time. However, it isn't necessary to boil water for the five to 15 minutes often advised. Just bringing it to a boil will do—harmful organisms, including *Giardia* cysts, are killed at temperatures below the boiling point.

Iodine and chlorine tablets are lightweight and simple to use; iodine treatment is regarded as the most effective. Both chemicals make the water taste foul, so if you use either one, I'd suggest carrying fruit-flavored crystals or powder to make the water drinkable. The most common brand of iodine tablets, Wisconsin Pharmacal's Potable Aqua, which comes in 3½-ounce bottles containing 50 tablets, is now available with neutralizing tablets (ascorbic acid) that remove the taste. I've tried these and they work. I used chlorine on the Pacific Crest Trail and Potable Aqua on the Continental Divide. I drank from filthy stockponds on both walks and never became ill, so presumably both treatments worked. Tablets have a limited life, so you should buy a fresh supply at least annually. Once a bottle is opened, it should be used within a few weeks or else discarded.

Iodine crystals, available at drugstores, are a long lasting alternative to tablets. These can be held in solution, and small amounts poured into water bottles when required, though you need to be sure no undissolved crystals enter the drinking water. The Polar Pure Iodine Crystal Kit (3 ounces dry weight; more, of course, when the crystals are in solution), available from REI, contains crystals, thermometer, and instructions, and will purify 2,000 quarts of water. It is safer to use than crystals alone; a filter cone inside the container prevents the crystals from accidentally falling into your drinking water. However, it's heavier than crystals or tablets, and involves carrying a glass container with liquid in it. I used it for a while, but have gone back to Potable Aqua. If I ever do a long trip where water will frequently need purifying, I'll take the Polar Pure however, due to its long life and number of quarts it will disinfect.

Despite what is often stated in outdoor literature, iodine isn't highly toxic. Apparently, if you do ingest too much you'll probably vomit, getting rid of most of the iodine in the process. Normal doses of iodine won't harm you. Wilkerson's *Medicine for Mountaineering* (The Mountaineers) reports that inmates of three Florida prisons have consumed water disinfected with iodine over a 15-year period with no ill effects. Only those with known thyroid problems or goiters need to be careful.

Filtration is the most popular method of water treatment. There are a number of filters on the market, most easy to use but heavy to carry compared with purifying tablets or crystals. I have no direct experience with any filters, but users report that they all clog up, usually within a short period. In my opinion, they are all too heavy, too complicated, and too inefficient for backpacking. Weights of filters start at 6 ounces for simple ones designed for occasional use to heavy-duty, 13-pound ones designed for large expeditions. Those designed for typical backpacking run in the 8- to 24-ounce range.

Filters can remove bacteria, organic chemicals, and protozoa, including *Giardia.* They can't remove viruses unless they also include chemical disinfection, in which case you might as well just use iodine.

Viruses are the most dangerous waterborne organisms—they can cause fatal diseases like polio and hepatitis. But viruses aren't a problem in most of North America. If you visit the Third World, however, they are a real threat. When I went trekking in Nepal, all vegetables and fruit were washed in iodine-treated water, and I used iodine to purify all water. Filters, the trekking company told me, were ineffective.

Flavorings

Clear, cold mountain stream water is the most refreshing drink there is, which is the main reason I'm reluctant to treat water unless absolutely necessary. Filtered water loses a little of its zest and sparkle, and tastes a little flat, but chemically treated water tastes so awful that you just have to add something to it. Kool-Aid and similar fruit-flavored powdered drink mixes are the obvious solution. Three versions are available: those to which sugar must be added, those containing sugar, and those containing artificial sweeteners. The pre-sweetened ones are the most useful— if you're carrying the stuff, you might as well have a few extra kilocalories along with it.

Healthier alternatives to sugar and chemical concoctions are electrolytic salt mixes, like Gatorade. The electrolytes are potassium and sodium chloride, which are depleted through heavy sweating. While electrolytic drinks may be necessary for running, they aren't needed for most backpacking—although they could be in desert regions. Such drinks have almost replaced salt tablets, though the latter are still available. I carried salt tablets across the Mojave Desert but never used them. Salt tablets are purported to help retain body fluids, but my answer to heavy sweating and walking in hot weather is to drink small amounts frequently.

Bottles, Bags, and Flasks

Even on trips in areas where water is plentiful, some form of water container is needed—in dry, hot country several may be essential. You need good-quality ones, too, because a container fail- ure could be very serious. For that reason, I always carry several containers, never just one large one.

Containers are available in a wide variety of shapes, sizes, and makes, in both aluminum and plastic. Aluminum keeps liquids cool in summer, but unless it's lacquered inside, it contaminates water to which drink mixes have been added. Plastic bottles warm up quickly, but the con- tents don't taint, at least when the bottles are new. When little water needs to be carried, pint bottles are adequate, but I prefer quart ones for general use, and carry at least two in desert areas, along with a collapsible, flexible waterbag.

The standard aluminum bottles are the Swiss- made round red- or blue-lacquered Sigg bottles (the uncoated silver ones are for stove fuel, as are the new red ones with "Fuel Bottle" written on the side in large letters, a sensible precaution). These come in pint and quart sizes, weighing

Water containers. From the left: a gallon waterbag, a 2-gallon waterbag, and a quart-size bottle.

4 and 5 ounces. Sigg bottles are durable and have screw-tops with rubber seals that don't leak—at least none of mine ever have. However, they also have narrow openings, which make them hard to fill from seeps and trickles.

I use Nalgene heavy-duty, food-grade plastic bottles, which are round, have screw-tops and wide mouths for easy filling, and come in pint and quart sizes. I find Nalgene bottles leakproof and hard-wearing, unlike some of the cheaper generic bottles that leak and crack along the seams after a relatively short time. Nalgene bottles are available in high-density polyethylene with unattached screw-tops, or in more durable Lexan polycarbonate with attached tops. I used to use the first, but, having twice spent an hour or more searching in a creek for a dropped lid, I changed to the loop-top style when I bought a new bottle. The quart size weighs 5 ounces. Whatever bottle I bring, I carry it where I can get at it easily, either in an outside pocket or right at the top of the pack.

Lighter, less-expensive alternatives to custom-made bottles are plastic soft-drink bottles. These have improved in quality in recent years and many are now strong enough for backpacking. When I needed extra bottles for a walk in the Grand Canyon, I bought two quart-size bottles of Gatorade. I drank the contents the first day, then used the bottles (which weigh 3 ounces empty) for the rest of the trip.

On most trips I only carry one rigid water bottle, so I need something else for camp. However, if you try to make do in camp with one water container plus your cookware, you will spend a lot of time fetching water. For years my camp container was a light, collapsible waterbag that holds 2 gallons, yet weighs only 3½ ounces. It consists of a double-layer flexible plastic inner bladder and a tough nylon outer, with a leak-proof spigot and two webbing handles. All the

parts are replaceable, and ripstop tape can be used for emergency repairs. Such waterbags are quite durable but can be damaged, especially by fire and ice. Hot sparks can melt holes in the fabric, and if the contents freeze, slivers of ice can pierce the bladder when the bag is folded up.

My choice is the Ortlieb Waterbag, made from coated nylon with welded seams. My gallon-size model weighs 2½ ounces and has proved much tougher than a standard waterbag. It's also easier to carry full in the pack because it is slightly more rigid than others. I also have a quart-size Liqui-pak bag with a flexible plastic inner and a nylon outer (weight: 4 ounces), with a quick-release buckle strap that I carry when I may need extra capacity; it folds flat when not needed. It can also be clipped to your hipbelt or side tension straps for easy access. Larger sizes are also available.

Of the other brands of waterbags, the best-quality and probably the most durable (but also the most expensive) ones are MSR's Dromedary Bags. These are made from laminated Cordura nylon and have brass grommets laced with webbing along each side. They're available to hold 2, 4, 6, and 10 quarts. They're not light, though— the 10-quart size weighs 6½ ounces.

Four quarts of water usually sees to all my needs in camp, so a gallon waterbag holds enough. Other uses of a waterbag are as a portable shower, and, so I'm told, as a pillow. They aren't, however, good for carrying water! The larger ones are especially awkward to carry in a pack. I've carried my 2-gallon one full a number of times, usually strapped to the top or back of my pack, and I've found the water in it sloshes about, altering the balance of the load in an unnerving way. For distances that take less than an hour to walk, I actually prefer to carry my waterbag by hand, by its strap.

The best way to carry a lot of water a considerable distance is in rigid bottles. At times, however, it may be necessary to carry so much water that all your containers are necessary. Twice in the Grand Canyon I carried three quart-size bottles (one Nalgene and two Gatorade), plus the quart Liquipak and gallon Ortlieb water-bags, all full.

The latest idea in water carriers is for ones with drinking tubes attached so you can sip as you hike. I've never used one of these, but they look like a good idea. On a ski tour in the High Sierra, two members of our party used 2-quart CamelBak carriers, which consist of long, narrow, flexible plastic bladders with attached drinking tubes. They carried the CamelBaks inside the top compartments of their packs. (The bags worked well until the tubes froze and cracked.) Other easy-access methods are to hold a water bottle in a belt holster or pack wand pocket, or buckle a Liquipak or similar container to your belt. Dana Design makes pouches called Ribs that attach to the lower webbing section of pack shoulder straps. The 6-ounce Bottle Rib will take a quart bottle.

Some water carriers aren't worth considering. Clear-plastic water carriers that roll up on a wooden bar are too fragile, as are collapsible plastic jugs. Both crack and leak very quickly.

In winter I often carry a vacuum flask that serves two functions. By filling it with hot water before I retire, I have warm water that soon comes to a boil in the morning, speeding up my departure on short winter days. If I fill it before leaving camp, I can enjoy hot drinks (usually coffee, but sometimes hot fruit juice or soup) during the day. This eliminates the need to stop and fire up the stove. The best flasks are unbreakable stainless steel. After having smashed several glass ones, I purchased a Coleman stainless steel pint flask, which weighs 18½ ounces. This has proved invaluable. Each of its many dents shows how many glass flasks I would have

broken. It is heavy, though, so I was interested to learn that Sigg is introducing an aluminum vacuum pint flask that weighs 12 ounces.

Another alternative is an insulated bottle cover. I have an Outdoor Research Water Bottle Parka that holds a quart-size Nalgene bottle. It weighs 4 ounces, so with the bottle the weight is still half that of the stainless steel flask, yet with twice the capacity. The covers won't keep liquids hot for long, however, so they aren't suitable for tea or coffee unless you like them lukewarm, but they are fine for fruit juice.

The best way to store plastic water containers is open, because they are less likely to taint water. If water starts to taste unpleasant, filling the container with a mild solution of bicarbonate of soda and leaving it to soak should clear it. Iodine, chlorine, or bleach can also be used for disinfecting bottles. Washing containers regularly is advisable to prevent the buildup of dirt, especially around the screw threads on the tops.

THE CAMPFIRE

Sitting around a campfire on a cold evening is, for many people, the ideal way to end a day in the wilderness. However, in many areas badly situated and constructed fires have left scars that will take decades and more to heal, and too many trees have been stripped of their lower branches, and even hacked down, to provide fuel. Even collecting fallen wood can damage the environment if not enough is left to replenish the soil with nutrients and provide shelter for animals and food for insects and fungi.

The alternative is to use a stove for cooking, and clothing and shelter for warmth. But an essential element of the wilderness experience would be lost if campfires could never be lit; although I cook on a stove 99 percent of the time, I do occasionally light a fire. It is necessary,

Kitchens should be sited on bare ground whenever possible to minimize impact.

however, to treat fires as a luxury, and to ensure that they have minimum impact on the environment. Landowners and land managers may ban fires in certain areas—for a few dry weeks when the fire risk is high, or for decades if a damaged area is being left to recover. In national parks, fire permits may be needed, and you may be required to carry a stove. Such regulations may seem restrictive, but they prevent further degradation of popular areas.

Fires, officially permitted or not, are inappropriate in some areas, anyway. They shouldn't be lit at and above the timberline, because of the slow growth rate of trees and woody plants, and the soils there need to be replenished by the nutrients from deadwood.

In other areas, fires can be lit even on pristine sites without significant harm to the environment, as long as you know what you're doing.

The ideal places for fires are below the high-water mark on the coast, and below the spring flood level along rivers—any traces will be washed away and there is usually plenty of wood to burn. Fires on beaches and riverbanks can be lit on shingle rocks and sand so that no scars are left.

Using mineral surfaces for fires whenever possible minimizes the impact in other spots, too. Alternatives are flat rocks, bare earth, or sparse vegetation. Meadowland should never be scarred—or threatened—by a campfire. If you use a rock as the base, heap 3 or more inches of fine sand and gravel on it to keep it from being blackened by the fire. On the ground, a shallow pit should be dug so that the fire is lit on soil, not vegetation or forest duff. Material that is removed should be piled to one side so that it can be replaced when you leave. I use my toilet trowel for such excavations, which take only minutes when I find a suitable spot.

Do not build a ring of rocks around a fire on a pristine site. Many people construct a fireplace this way, yet it really serves no purpose, although the concept is that it contains the fire. The best way to prevent a fire from spreading is to clear the area around it of flammable materials; a site 24 to 32 inches across is big enough. You should also make sure that there are no low branches or tree roots above or below the fire, and that you pitch your tent well away, preferably upwind, so that sparks can't harm it. Other gear, especially nylon, also needs to be kept well away from fires.

You should leave no sign of your fire. All wood should be burned to a fine ash that can then be scattered widely before the pit is refilled with the sod or duff removed when it was dug. Spreading duff and loose vegetation over the site helps conceal it. The remains of fires lit on rocks should be scattered too, and the soil used as a base should be returned to its source.

With a wind screen, a wall like this one needn't be built to shelter your stove.

If you camp at a well-used site with many rock-ringed fireplaces, use one of these rather than make a new one, even a minimum-impact one. If I have time, I dismantle the least-used fire rings, scattering any ashes and charcoal, in the

A badly sited fire pit that has blackened the rocks. A properly sited fire leaves no trace.

hope that they won't be used again. Some back-country sites in national parks provide metal fireboxes. Obviously, where this is done they should be used. Cut wood may also be supplied at such sites to prevent damage to the surrounding forest.

If you collect fuel wood, do so with care. First and foremost, do not remove wood—even deadwood—from living trees. Snags are needed by wildlife and also can add to the site's attractiveness. Nothing is worse than a campsite surrounded by trees and ground stripped of branches. In high-use areas, search for wood farther afield rather than along the edges of the site. Shorelines and riverbanks are good places to scavenge for wood. Only collect what you will use, and use only small sticks that you can break by hand, as these are easily burned to ash. Axes and saws are not required.

Lighting and Tending the Fire

There is a certain mystique to fire lighting, and pages of text are devoted to it in survival and woodcraft books, with many different types of fires described. Basically, the secret of fire lighting is simple: Start small, with dry tinder. Paper makes good tinder, but I wouldn't carry it just for this purpose. I lighten my load by burning pages from the books I read; food wrappings work well, too. If you have no paper, then the finest twigs, tiny pine cones, dry leaves, moss, and any other dry plant material can be used. When the weather is wet, look for kindling in dry spots under logs and at the base of large trees. Good kindling can be created by half-slicing small slivers off a dry twig to make a *feather-stick*. A candle stub or solid fuel tablet can help a fire start when you can find only damp kindling.

Once you have a small pile of kindling, build up a pyramid of small dry twigs around it, mak-ing sure that there is plenty of air space. Then light the kindling. When the twigs start to catch, slightly larger pieces of wood can be added. Don't overdo it—it's easy to smother a new fire. At this stage, the fire's shape is irrelevant; you can alter it once the fire is burning well. I try to arrange an area of hot coals at one end of a cooking fire—coals, not flames, provide heat. Small metal grills with short legs make balancing pans over an open fire easy. The Coghlan Fire Grill (11 ounces) I carried in the Yukon was worth the weight, because I cooked over fires often on that walk. Cake racks also make good lightweight grills—the ends can be balanced on rocks.

If lighting the fire proves difficult, dismantle it and start again; don't waste matches and kindling by pushing bits of paper into the fire and lighting them. People occasionally use stove fuel to get a fire going. This is highly dangerous and not recommended. *Never throw fuel onto a smoldering fire that won't light properly.* And you should never do something I once saw done in a shelter one damp December night: Having failed to light the pile of damp wood stacked haphazardly in the fireplace, the other occupant of the shelter attempted to ignite it by holding his lit cartridge stove in it. I was busy cooking over a stove at the time, so my companion hastily decided that she wanted to devote herself to getting the fire lit conventionally, and took over. Luckily, she succeeded.

Do not leave your fires unattended, and make sure the ashes are cold before you leave the next day—huge areas of forest have burned due to carelessness with campfires. If you're not scattering the ashes to the four winds because they're in a well-used fire ring and you've had a morning fire, douse them with water to make sure they're out. Foil or silver-lined food wrappings won't be consumed in a fire, so don't toss them in unless you are prepared to fish them out and

A folding grill is useful when cooking over a fire.

carry them with you when you leave. This applies to hut fires as well; I've spent many hours cleaning out shelter fireplaces blocked by foil.

STOVES

Stoves negate the need for campfires. A stove also ensures that you can have hot food and drink quickly whenever you want or need it. I always carry one. In foul weather, a stove enables me to cook hot meals in the warmth and shelter of my tent. There's nothing like waking up to the sound of wind and rain on the fly sheet and being able to reach out, light the stove—on which a pan of water was set the night before—and quickly have a hot drink to brace me for the weather outside.

There aren't many stoves to choose from, but the differences among them are significant. In some situations, a malfunctioning stove is merely a nuisance; other times it's a serious problem, particularly if you're relying on it for cooking dried food or if you need it to melt snow

for water, and lighting a fire is not an option. Some stoves work well in the cold and wind, others don't. A long wait for a stove to produce hot water when you're cold, wet, and tired is, at the very least, dispiriting, but if you are on the verge of hypothermia, it's dangerous.

A stove must be capable of bringing water to a boil under the most horrendous conditions you are likely to encounter; it must be small and light enough to carry; and it must be as simple as possible to operate. Stability is important too, particularly with stoves that will be used with large pans.

Charts and tables that compare the weights, rate of fuel consumption, and boiling times of various stoves can be misleading. Many factors that affect a stove's performance in the field can't be duplicated in a controlled environment; moreover, individual stoves of the same model can perform very differently. One error perpetuated by comparison charts is that alcohol stoves, like the Trangia, take longer to boil water than others. This may be so in still air, and if the time taken to set up and light the stove isn't taken into account. However, in the field, alcohol stoves can heat water faster than any other type. Indeed, they work best in the sort of stormy weather that makes many other stoves difficult to light, never mind bring water to a boil.

Weights aren't comparable, either—some models include wind screens and pan sets in the total weight. The amount of fuel you have to carry for a given period affects the total carry weight, as well.

I have carried out my own stove tests, so you can at least compare my findings with those of others. Please note all the caveats. My overall conclusions are that virtually all stoves are efficient and reliable; in general, a half-decent stove should bring a pint of water to boil within five minutes of being lit, as long as the burner is adequately shielded from the wind; and no stove should weigh more than 21 to 25 ounces, excluding pans and wind screen.

Fuels

The availability of fuel in the areas you visit may determine which stove you carry, especially on a long trek where you need to resupply fuel every week. The choices are solid fuel, liquid fuel (alcohol, kerosene, or gasoline), and cartridges (butane or butane/propane).

Different areas of the world favor different fuels, which is worth knowing if you range widely, as I do. In Scandinavia, alcohol is the common fuel; in the Alps and Pyrenees, it is butane/propane; in Africa and Asia, kerosene. This doesn't mean that you won't find other fuels in those places, just that you're more likely, especially in out-of-the-way places, to find fuels that local people favor. Automobile gasoline can be found everywhere, of course, though obtaining small amounts can be difficult. Filling a pint-size aluminum fuel bottle from a high-pressure pump at a gas station is not easy, and in my experience usually results in the fuel's spraying everywhere. (Three of us refueled this way during the Pacific Crest Trail walk, and I'd rather not have to do so again. The gas station staff thought the whole episode was hilarious, however, and only charged us for the amount in our bottles rather than the somewhat larger amount vaporizing off our clothes and their bays.)

How much fuel you use each day depends on the type of stove you have, the weather, and the type of cooking you do. If you cook three meals a day and use foods with long cooking times, you'll use more fuel than someone like me, who cooks just one meal a day and boils water only for a hot drink at breakfast. I based figures on how long fuels last for my cooking needs. If yours are different, you'll need to adapt them. Also, estimates should be doubled if you are melting snow, because it takes the same amount of energy to produce a given amount of water from snow as it does to bring that amount of water to a boil. The figures assume the use of a full wind screen with all stoves, whether supplied or not. My figures are for solo use—but it shouldn't be assumed that the amount of fuel per person is the same, regardless of the size of a group. In my experience, larger groups are far more fuel efficient. On ski trips in Greenland and the High Sierra, groups of 10 people used less fuel per person—including melting snow for water—than I would expect to use on a solo summer trip.

Beware! This table shows the results of one set of tests in benign conditions. To relate it to field use a number of factors need to be taken into account:

1. The fast boil time of the cartridge stoves was achieved using full cartridges. As the cartridges empty, boiling time increases.

Stove Performance			
Stove	Fuel	Weight (oz.)	Boiling Time (min./sec.)[1]
White-gas/multi-fuel stoves			
MSR XGK II Shaker Jet	White gas, leaded and unleaded gasoline, kerosene, diesel, and more	15.8 [2]	5" 25'
MSR WhisperLite Internationale	White gas, leaded and unleaded gasoline, kerosene	14 [2]	4" 50'
Peak 1 Apex II	White gas, leaded and unleaded gasoline, kerosene	18½ [3]	3" 50'
Peak 1 Feather 442 Dual-Fuel	White gas, leaded and unleaded gasoline	24	2" 55'
Peak 1 Multi-Fuel	White gas, kerosene	18½	4" 10'
Sigg Fire-Jet	White gas, leaded and unleaded gasoline, kerosene	12½ [4]	5" 30'
Optimus Svea 123	White gas	18	4" 30'
Cartridge stoves			
Camping Gaz Tristar	Butane/propane[5]	13	3"16'
MSR RapidFire	Butane/propane	12½	4" 50'
Coleman/Peak 1 Alpine	Butane/propane	13½	3" 30'

The colder it is, the quicker this occurs. The performance of the white-gas/kerosene and alcohol stoves stays the same until they run out of fuel, as long as pressure is maintained.

2. Wind can play havoc with stove performance. The MSR stoves, both the alcohol stoves, and the Markill Storm-Cooker come with adequate wind screens. The others don't—performance declines drastically in wind unless wind screens are added.

3. Alcohol stoves perform better in windy weather. The performance of the other stoves declines to some extent in wind, even when wind screens are used.

4. Other tests give wildly different results from mine. I cannot explain this. I suspect both minor but important differences in the testing procedures, and the fact individual stoves of the same model can perform quite differently. Slight design changes can affect the performance, too.

Stove	Fuel	Weight (oz.)	Boiling Time (min./sec.)[1]
Cartridge stoves			
Coleman/Peak 1 Micro	Butane/propane	5½	3" 30'
Markill Storm-Cooker	Butane/propane	33[6]	3" 55'
Primus 2263 Mini	Butane/propane	5½	3" 22'
Primus 3233 Spider	Butane/propane	13	3" 10'
Trangia 27K with Epigas burner	Butane/propane	6 (gas burner only) 42[6]	4" 35'
Alcohol stoves			
Trangia 27K	Alcohol	35[6]	15" 45'
Optimus Trapper	Alcohol	37[6]	6" 30'

NOTES: 1. The test consisted of bringing a pint of water to a rolling boil in a covered 1¾-pint stainless steel Trangia pan (except for the Markill Storm-Cooker and the Optimus Trapper, where I used the pans provided). The water temperature was 40°F (4°C), the air temperature 52°F (11°C). The test was conducted in windless indoor conditions. Coleman Fuel was used for the white-gas/multi-fuel stoves, and Coleman 250 butane/propane cartridges for the cartridge stoves, except for the Coleman Peak 1 Micro (Micro 3100 cartridge) and the Camping Gaz Tristar (CV270 cartridge).
2. Weight does not include fuel bottle/tank. MSR fuel bottles weigh 4½ oz. for the 22 fl. oz. size and 7½ oz. for the 33 fl. oz. size.
3. Weight includes 17 fl. oz. fuel bottle/tank, because this is provided with the stove and there are no alternatives.
4. Weight does not include fuel bottle/tank. Sigg fuel bottles weigh 4 oz. for the 21 fl. oz. size, and 5 oz. for the 31 fl. oz. size.
5. Will fit only Camping Gaz CV270 and CV470 cartridges.
6. Includes pan set.

Models

There aren't very many models of stoves; I've tried most of those suitable for backpacking. Here I've described all the models included in my test, plus a few new ones that weren't available for testing. Different features may be needed by different people, so I can't say that any one stove is best. For example, good simmer control is essential for those who cook complex meals, but those who only want to boil water will be more interested in maximum heat output.

Solid Fuel: Solid-fuel tablets and jellied alcohol, available under various names, aren't efficient enough to consider for most backpacking. On the Pacific Crest Trail, however, I met a hiker who boiled water three times a day for his instant, eat-from-the-bag, freeze-dried meals in a metal cup balanced on two stones or small earth walls over a large solid-fuel tablet. This is not the way I would do it, but it did help keep his pack weight down. If your cooking needs are minimal or you usually use a fire, solid fuel could be of interest to you. Names to look for include Caricook, Meta, and Esbit (tablets), and Firestar (alcohol). There are tiny metal stoves—just fuel holders, really—also available under the same names.

Alcohol Stoves: Fuel for alcohol stoves can be hard to find and expensive. It is available in most countries under various names, usually including the words *alcohol* or *spirit* (denatured alcohol, rubbing alcohol, or marine stove fuel in North America; methylated spirits in Britain; *alcool à brûler* in France; T or Rod spirit in Scandinavia). It can be found in drugstores and hardware stores as well as outdoor stores, but may not be available in small towns and mountain resorts. If you plan to use an alcohol stove on a long walk, I'd check for fuel availability in advance.

Alcohol is the only fuel not derived from petroleum, which makes it more environmentally friendly than other fuels. It's also the only one that burns unpressurized as a liquid, which makes it a safe fuel. It's clean, too, evaporating quickly when spilled. For these reasons, it's a good fuel any time you'll be cooking regularly in a tent vestibule. It's not a hot fuel, however—it produces only half as much heat as the same weight of gasoline or kerosene. A quart lasts me little more than a week, which makes it a heavier fuel than others to carry on long trips.

Alcohol is most popular in Scandinavia, and the Swedish-made Trangia Storm-Cookers are probably the safest and simplest stoves available—also the ones that work best in strong winds. They come as complete units, including burner, wind screen/pan support, pans, lid, and pot grab, which fit together to form a compact unit for carrying. The burner consists of a short, hollow-walled, open cylinder with jets around the top, into which you pour fuel—2 fluid ounces fills it. To light it, you simply touch a match to the alcohol. The burner rests inside a rigid aluminum wind screen, which contains fold-out supports onto which the pans are placed. With a lid over the top you have virtually a sealed unit, so heat loss is minimal. There are small holes in one side of the wind screen base, which can be turned into the wind to create a draft and a stronger flame—alcohol stoves are the only ones I know that boil water more quickly when it's windy. The flame can be con-

A Trangia alcohol stove with a stainless steel cookset.

trolled somewhat by dropping a simmer ring over the jets so that only the surface of the reservoir is burning, then partially covering this with a flat metal disc, which you knock into place with a spoon or knife until you achieve the required degree of heat. It's a crude system, and awkward to operate. Trangias are not designed for cooking meals that need long simmering.

The unit can be set up very quickly and has little that can go wrong; the only maintenance needed is to prick the jets occasionally. Trangias are absolutely silent—you can often hear the water coming to a boil. They are safe, too, though you need to be careful when using one in daylight because the flame is invisible then. Because a full burner only lasts a half hour at most (depending on the wind and use of the simmer ring), refilling while the stove is in use is often necessary, and inadvertently refilling a still-burning stove from a fuel bottle is the biggest danger alcohol stoves present— this could cause the fuel bottle to ignite. If the stove goes out during use, I refill it by pouring fuel into the burner lid, then into the burner. If the lid caught fire, I could simply drop it into the burner well, perhaps singeing my fingers. Trangias don't flare, however, so they are the safest stove for use under a tent fly sheet. They are also very stable. They do blacken pan bottoms, which many people don't like. This doesn't bother me; in theory, blackened pans should absorb heat faster than shiny silver ones, so I make no attempt to clean the exterior of Trangia pans. Packing them isn't a problem; they fit inside the wind screen, and once they've cooled the soot rarely comes off on your hands, unlike the soot from campfires.

When packing up the stove, I pour any unused fuel back into the fuel bottle after it's cooled; fuel tends to leak if carried in the burner. I also pack the burner in a plastic bag and carry it separately from the pans so that it doesn't dirty them and leave a lingering smell of fuel.

Trangias come in two sizes, each available with two pans, a lid, and an optional kettle. The cook kit comes in non-stick and Duossal (a laminate of stainless steel and aluminum) versions. For solo use, the Trangia 27 is ideal; including pans, lid, and pot grab, it weighs 35 ounces with non-stick pans, 33 with Duossal ones (without the pans and pot grab the unit weighs 15 ounces). Substituting the pint-size kettle for one of the pans brings the weight up by an ounce. The larger Trangia 25 models have larger pans and an optional quart kettle. The 25 weighs 31 or 45 ounces, depending on the pan material—too heavy for one backpacker but fine for two or three. There is also a Mini-Trangia consisting of the burner, a simplified wind screen, and a quart pan with lid that weighs 12 ounces. I've not used it, but it looks a good choice for ultralight solo trips.

I've had a Trangia 27 since the early 1970s. It was my regular stove for all treks—it has been all over Scotland, to Norway in summer and winter, to Iceland, and on my 1,250-mile walk from one end of Britain to the other. Although dented, it still works perfectly. There is so little to go wrong that it's just about indestructible. Indeed, I have heard of a Trangia being run over by a truck and simply beaten back into shape, then returned to use. I don't take it on long trips anymore, though, because of the weight, both of the unit itself and the fuel.

The Swiss company Sigg makes an almost identical stove to the Trangia called the Traveller (2½ pounds). Otherwise the only alternative to the Trangia is the more complex Optimus 81 Trapper, also made in Sweden, which is only available in a 2-pounds 2-ounce model. Fuel capacity is half a pint. It comes complete with two pans and a lid, and looks similar to a Trangia

The Optimus Trapper alcohol stove with cookset.

except that the burner is a felt-lined, open-ended tube that acts as a wick when soaked in fuel. When it's full, the felt is saturated with fuel, but there is no liquid alcohol to spill, even if the stove is turned upside down. (I've even seen a lit one rolled along the floor as a demonstration of how safe it is, but I don't recommend trying this!) The Trapper burns hotter than the Trangia, and its flame is far more controllable, so it also simmers better. The Trapper doesn't blacken pans, either.

The Trapper is too big and heavy for solo walkers, but just right for two people. Two experienced backpacking friends of mine, Chris and Janet Ainsworth, use a Trapper on winter trips and praise it highly. I concur with their view after seeing how fast their Trapper boiled more than a quart of water from snow. During a ski tour in the Norwegian mountains, an overnight storm had worsened by dawn, and we'd packed up and fled from our exposed campsite without bothering with breakfast. As soon as we found a boulder big enough to protect the four of us from the full force of the wind, we stopped for

some much-needed sustenance and a hot drink. The Trapper was set up, lit, and produced boiling water almost before we'd gotten the mugs ready. Few stoves could have matched it for speed, and many would have been difficult to use at all in such circumstances.

White-Gas and Multi-Fuel Stoves: White gas is probably the most efficient stove fuel, lighting easily and burning very hot. As automotive fuel, it's available everywhere, and, as far as stove use is concerned, it's very cheap. However, auto gas quickly clogs stove fuel lines and jets, which need frequent cleaning when run on it. Many makers state firmly that automotive fuel shouldn't be used in certain models, though newer models are often designed to run on unleaded gasoline. Generally, these stoves run better on specially refined white gas—sold under various names, the most common being Coleman Fuel, though MSR White Gas is increasingly available. White gas is available in outdoor, sporting, and hardware stores and often, especially in towns near popular parks or wilderness areas, in supermarkets. Whatever form it comes in, this is a volatile fuel, igniting easily if spilled; its use requires a lot of care. In North America, it's the only fuel you can find just about anywhere. Because it burns so hot, I find a quart lasts me at least 10 days.

Unlike alcohol stoves, white-gas models burn vaporized fuel, which means that the fuel has to be pressurized. Once stoves are lit, the heat from the flames keeps the fuel line hot so that the fuel in it expands and turns to gas. Multi-fuel stoves—included here because they are basically white-gas models that can be adapted to run on other fuels—enhance this process by looping the fuel line through the flame to ensure vaporization. This is particularly useful when they are used to burn kerosene. In the simplest stoves, the fuel is transmitted from the tank to the burner via a wick that leads it into the fuel line. These stoves have to be pre-heated or primed before they can be lit to ensure that the fuel vaporizes. Stoves with pumps are slightly easier to light, though priming is still usually necessary.

Because they burn pressurized fuel, all the stoves in this category can flare during lighting, so great care is needed if they are to be used in a tent vestibule. I don't recommend them for tent cooking. Some white-gas stoves have built-in fuel tanks; other, newer models use a fuel bottle as the tank. Both types operate best when the tanks are at least half full—they should never be totally filled, because then the fuel can't expand and you won't be able to pressurize the stove fully. Built-in fuel tanks are usually small, ⅓- to ¾-pint capacity, which means they may need refilling every few days. I find it best to top up the fuel tank last thing before packing away the

stove in the morning. That way I'm unlikely to run out while cooking the evening meal. If you run out of fuel while cooking, you must wait for the stove to cool down before you can refill it.

White-gas stoves have either *roarer* or *ported* burners. In the first, which is also used for kerosene stoves, a stream of vaporized fuel is pushed out of the jet, ignites, and hits a burner plate that spreads it out into a ring of flame. Roarer burners, as you might guess, are noisy. In ported burners, the flames come out of a ring of jets, just like a kitchen gas range. Ported burners are much quieter than roarer burners. Neither type seems more efficient than the other, though ported ones are easier to control and, thus, better for simmering.

The choice in these stoves is larger than with alcohol or kerosene stoves, although virtually all come from three makers: Optimus, MSR (Mountain Safety Research), and Coleman.

The Optimus Svea 123, a popular white-gas stove for many decades.

The Optimus Svea 123 has been around for decades; until the MSR and Coleman models took the market by storm in the 1980s, it was one of the most popular white-gas stoves. (For a while, Optimus called the stove the Climber, but they have reverted to Svea, perhaps realizing that this name was still in common use and that many people didn't recognize the new name.) The Svea was especially appealing for the solo backpacker because it was light, compact, and easy to use. At 18 ounces, it was the lightest white-gas stove until the MSR models appeared.

The Svea looks like a brass can with perforations. It's made up of a simple roarer burner unit screwed into a ⅓-pint brass fuel tank and a circular wind screen/pan support unit that fits around the burner. A small aluminum cup fits over the top to protect the burner when it is in the pack. The tank has a screw-on cap with a built-in safety valve designed to release pressure if the tank overheats. (If this happens, the jet of fuel that spurts out will almost certainly become a jet of flame, so it's wise always to use the stove with the tank cap pointing away from you and anything flammable—like your tent.) The Svea's burner is operated by a key that fits onto an arm jutting out from the burner. The key can be inserted through the wind screen but is placed inside it when packed.

To light the Svea, you must heat the tank slightly to make the fuel expand and to make some of it vaporize—there is no pump. The simplest way to do this is to fill the shallow recess at the foot of the burner tube with about a teaspoon of gasoline from the fuel bottle and light it. By the time the last of the flames are dying away, the tank should be sufficiently warm so that, as you turn the key and open the jet, the burner catches. If you miss this point, a quickly applied match will usually light the stove. The flame should be blue. If it's yellow, you did not pressurize the fuel enough and the stove is burning semi-liquid fuel. Turn it off and reprime it, though with less fuel. Once lit, the key can be used to control the flame, but the range of control is limited. The key also controls a built-in jet cleaner, which is operated by turning the key beyond the "on" position. This should be done infrequently to avoid widening the jet hole.

Although the Svea is quite powerful, it requires a separate wind screen in a strong wind; the one that comes with it is not adequate. Because the tank is below the burner, the stove must not be fully surrounded by a wind screen, in case the tank overheats. Its stability is adequate for small pans; large ones demand care, owing to the stove's tall, narrow shape.

Sveas are tough and long-lived. When I did the burn test, I hauled my blackened Svea—veteran of the Continental Divide Trail but not used for more than five years—out of the jumble of old gear it was tangled in, brushed off the cobwebs, filled the tank, and primed it. It lit straight away and boiled the water faster than some new white-gas models. This left me wondering why I hadn't used it for so long.

Optimus makes other white-gas and multi-fuel stoves. The Hunter (18 ounces) has been around for years, though it never achieved the popularity of the Svea. It offers better stability than the Svea because of a lower profile, but keeping the tank pressurized is apparently more difficult because it isn't directly below the burner.

The latest stove from Optimus is the No. 11 Explorer, a heavy-duty, multi-fuel stove designed for expedition use. It's the first Optimus stove to use a fuel bottle—Sigg bottles are recommended—as the fuel tank. It has a solid brass burner, stainless steel wind screen, built-in cleaning needle, and stainless steel hose. The flame control is on the burner rather than the fuel bottle. Optimus says it will run on most liquid fuels, including white gas, unleaded gaso-

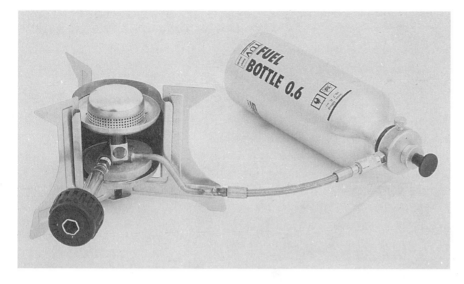

The Optimus Explorer Multi-Fuel Stove.

line, kerosene, and denatured alcohol. This looks a good stove for winter use, especially by groups.

The Coleman Peak 1 Feather 442 Dual-Fuel and Peak 1 Multi-Fuel stoves are high-tech constructions bristling with levers and knobs. Both have ported burners set atop 11-fluid-ounce fuel tanks, and built-in pumps, so they need priming only in very cold weather, at least in theory. The Feather 442 weighs 24 ounces and runs on white gas and unleaded gasoline. Lighting it without priming is possible, but the instructions need to be followed precisely, and flaring is likely—my success rate is about 25 percent. I find it easier to light the stove by priming with a little fuel around the burner, especially in cold weather. Once lit, the Feather 442 is a powerful stove, producing the fastest boil time in my test. Simmering is possible, but there isn't the fine control of some stoves. The Feather 442 is on the heavy side for solo backpacking, but a good choice for groups or base camp use.

The Multi-Fuel Stove is similar to the Feather 442, though slightly lighter, at 18½ ounces. As with the Feather 442, lighting the Multi-Fuel involves pressurizing the tank with 25 to 50 strokes of the pump, lighting the burner, then pumping 15 to 30 more strokes. For some reason, though, the stove lights without priming more easily than the Feather 442. It also lights better in the cold.

The Peak 1 Multi-Fuel Stove runs on white gas and kerosene.

The Peak 1 Apex II runs on white gas, auto gasoline, and kerosene.

The pentagon-shaped wind screen around the burner prevents the flame from extinguishing in a wind, but the stove still needs a wind screen to improve efficiency and cooking times. A tapered plastic ring around the base means the short legs can be adjusted to keep the stove level on uneven ground. The weight and bulk make it unsuitable for solo use, but it's a good choice for groups of two or more.

"Dual-fuel" would be a more accurate description of this stove than "multi-fuel," though. The unit can run on white gas or kerosene, but in order to use the latter the burner and generator must be changed. This complex task requires a small wrench that I would not like to carry in the field. The burner/generator and wrench add an extra 2½ ounces to the weight. The stove's instructions also clearly say "Never use regular or premium leaded automotive fuel."

The third Coleman liquid fuel stove, the Apex II, runs on white gas or kerosene as well,

but can also be used with unleaded gasoline. As with the Multi-Fuel, you have to change the generator to use kerosene, however, and I've always run mine on Coleman Fuel. It's the lightest Peak 1 model, weighing just 18½ ounces, including the 17-fluid-ounce standard fuel bottle. Though in theory it can be lit without priming, I've found this works only when the fuel bottle is full, there's no wind, the temperature is well above freezing, and the instructions are followed precisely. What I like about the Apex II is that there is a flame control on the burner, as well as a fuel control knob on the pump—this makes it the only white-gas stove on which fine flame control is possible, so simmering is easy. The weight and bulk make it suitable for solo use, yet the power is adequate for groups.

I used an Apex II along with an MSR WhisperLite to cook for 10 on a two-week ski-backpacking trip in the High Sierra. The Apex II was great for simmering. It's a bit fragile, though,

The MSR XGK II Shaker Jet—
the latest version of the
original multi-fuel stove.

and easily dented. Unlike other stoves that use fuel bottles as tanks, it can't be folded up for packing and so is slightly bulkier than other models. It's not field-maintainable either, which would worry me on a long hike, especially in a remote area.

The MSR XGK II deserves the name *multi-fuel*. It will run on white gas, leaded and unleaded gasoline, aviation fuel, kerosene, diesel, and more, though you may have to clean it regularly when using anything other than white gas. When you don't know what fuel you will find in remote areas, this stove seems to be a good choice. I once ran one on white spirits for a week when that was the only fuel I could get. The stove gave off appalling dirty fumes, but otherwise worked perfectly.

The XGK consists of a roarer burner (and it does!) with a long, rigid fuel tube that fits into a pump that, in turn, plugs into a fuel bottle. This setup obviates the need for a tank and enables the burner to be fully shielded from wind without danger of overheating. The XGK was the first stove to use this design, now the standard for lightweight backpacking stoves. The XGK was also the first stove to come with a folding foil wind screen and reflector. These work well—I'm surprised that other stove makers haven't adopted the idea. As it is, these seemingly crude bits of foil make MSR stoves the only white-gas models with adequate wind screens.

The latest version, the XGK II Shaker Jet, has a weighted cleaning needle built into the burner that cleans the jet when you gently shake the stove, which is much easier than using a separate jet pricker; it also pushes dirt out of the burner rather than down into the fuel tube. The new XGK also has improved pan supports that don't work loose like the old wires did. (These can be retrofitted to old models.) The weight is 15.8 ounces including the wind screen. Of course, you have to add the weight of a fuel bottle. These come in three capacities, weighing 3, 4½, and 7½ ounces. The XGK can be maintained in the field; a maintenance kit weighing 2 ounces is available.

The XGK II is easy to light, but simmering is difficult. I've also found the new Shaker version is less powerful than older models, though it's still adequate for year-round use. I think this is because the new supports hold the pan farther away from the burner.

MSR's other pressure stoves—the Whisper-Lite and WhisperLite Internationale—are in essence the same, the only difference being that the first will burn only white gas while the second will also burn auto gasoline and kerosene, and now has the same Shaker Jet as the XGK. Both are small, collapsible, spidery-looking stoves with ported burners—hence the name WhisperLite. Like the XGK, the WhisperLites save weight by having pumps that plug into fuel bottles, so tanks aren't needed. At 14 ounces each they are light enough for solo use, and powerful enough for group cooking. As mentioned earlier, I've twice used my Internationale for cooking

for 10 for two weeks at a time on spring ski trips, using both white gas and kerosene, and it's worked perfectly with both fuels. The weight includes the pump and the folding aluminum-foil wind screen and reflector supplied with each stove. Fuel bottles are the same as for the XGK.

To light these stoves, you pressurize the fuel by pumping it and then release a little of it into a cup below the burner by opening the valve on top of the pump. You light the fuel in the cup to prime the stove and, as the flame dies down, reopen the valve. The whole process takes only a few seconds. Flame control is limited, so simmering is difficult, but WhisperLites are as powerful as much heavier models. (If you want to use kerosene in the Internationale, you have only to change the tiny jet unit—which takes seconds.)

The wind screen allows both stoves to work efficiently in stormy weather, especially if you fold the screen so that no space is left between it and your pans. Both stoves are maintainable in the field; maintenance kits, which include spare parts, weigh 1½ ounces. I carried an Inter-

The MSR WhisperLite Internationale 600 runs on white gas, auto gasoline, and kerosene.

nationale on the Canadian Rockies and Yukon walks, and it has proved very reliable, performing as well now as when it was new. The only repair has been to the leather pump washer, which dried out; I regreased it with margarine and it worked perfectly. (I did, though, have the stove fully serviced between the two walks.)

Currently, the Internationale has replaced the Svea 123 as my first choice for long walks because it's easier to start, lighter, smaller, more stable, and performs better in wind, while being just as efficient and reliable.

The original XGK was designed to work with Sigg fuel bottles. Quite a few years ago, though, MSR introduced its own fuel bottles. Recently, Sigg has introduced a stove, the Fire-Jet, designed to work with Sigg bottles. It runs on white gas, auto gasoline, and kerosene; to use the latter you simply move a lever on the burner, by far the

easiest way of adapting a stove to a different fuel I've come across. The Fire-Jet consists of a burner enclosed in three curved pan supports (which when closed make it look like a tin can), and a flexible hose that attaches to the pump that plugs into the bottle. The fuel tube unplugs from both bottle and burner for packing. A good safety feature is a pressure valve in the pump, which means you can't over-pressurize the fuel bottle. Simmering is impossible, however—it's full blast or nothing. Even the XGK is better than this.

In the test, the Sigg was slower than other liquid-fuel stoves, though the burning performance of the latest version has been improved by 10 to 15 percent, according to Sigg. On the other hand, it weighs just 12½ ounces, making it by far the lightest stove of this type. The fuel bottles weigh 4 ounces for a 21-fluid-ounce

The Sigg Fire-Jet runs on white gas, auto gasoline, and kerosene.

capacity, and 5 ounces for a 31-fluid-ounce capacity. The quality seems good, but I did once lose the pump leather down in the depths of the pump unit and couldn't get it out until I got home. Luckily, this happened on a group trip and we had two other stoves.

Kerosene Stoves: Kerosene is *the* traditional stove fuel. It's easily obtained, reasonably cheap, and burns hot. Like gasoline, it's known under various names, some of them confusing. It pays to check carefully when abroad so that you are buying what you want to buy. In France, for example, kerosene is called *petrole,* in Germany and Scandinavia *petrolum,* in Britain *paraffin. Essence* and *benzine* always mean gasoline.

Kerosene won't ignite easily, so it is relatively safe if spilled—far safer than white gas. Conversely, it is more difficult to light, usually requiring a separate priming fuel, such as alcohol, solid-fuel tablets, or kerosene-soaked paper. The MSR WhisperLite Internationale has a wick built in to the priming cup, while the MSR XGK II has an absorbent pad at the base of the burner; both can be primed with kerosene. Kerosene tends to flare during lighting, so it should always be started outside a vestibule; once lit, it's safer than white gas and overall a better choice for cooking in a vestibule. I find it messy and hard to work with, so I use kerosene only as a last resort in a multi-fuel stove. It also stains badly and takes a long time to evaporate, leaving a strong odor. Some people swear by it, however. When I wrote in a magazine article that I disliked kerosene, I received an irate letter from a reader saying that I must be in the pay of non-kerosene stove makers and clearly had never used a kerosene stove and didn't know what I was talking about. Others who feel as strongly will no doubt continue to use kerosene. I, and I suspect many others, won't.

Recently, though, I've done two very different trips where I used kerosene simply because that's what was available. The first was the 86-day summer Scandinavian mountains solo walk, the second a ski expedition to Greenland with a party of 10. These trips haven't changed my overall views on kerosene, but I have learned that *refined kerosene* (heater or lamp fuel) is much cleaner than crude versions, like diesel, which can result—as they did when severe storms forced us to cook under cover in Greenland— in smoky fumes that can blacken the inside of a vestibule and lead to a major cleaning job.

The 96 Mini Camper and 00L Camper stoves from Optimus are the classic kerosene stoves. They've been around for decades. They are essentially the same stove in different sizes, the 96 having a ½-pint tank and the 00L a 1-pint tank. Both stoves must be assembled before use, then pumped and primed with another fuel before they can be lit—a time-consuming process. Flaring is likely during lighting, so you shouldn't light them under a tent fly sheet. The flame is controlled by opening a valve and releasing some of the pressure, a crude method. These stoves have noisy roarer burners and are relatively heavy to carry—21 ounces for the 96, 39 ounces for the 00L.

The flame is powerful, and both stoves have small wind screens to protect the burners, but their efficiency can still be enhanced in breezy conditions with a separate full wind screen. I used the 00L when I led Outward Bound treks in Scotland because these were the school's stoves—some of them dated back 40 years, which shows how durable they are. However, after one trip I reverted to my own butane-cartridge stove.

Optimus makes a much more modern, portable kerosene stove, the 85 Loke Expedition. This looks like the Trapper alcohol model; it comes complete with two pans, lid, and wind screen. Although it weighs 3 pounds 2 ounces, it would not need an additional wind screen and looks like a highly efficient unit for group use.

Butane and Butane/Propane Cartridge Stoves: Light, clean, simple-to-use cartridge stoves are the choice of many backpackers, especially those who don't undertake marathon treks or head deep into the winter wilderness. The fuel of choice is liquid petroleum gas under pressure in a sealed cartridge. Pure butane, the most common version not so long ago, has generally been replaced by butane/propane mixes or by isobutane, at least for backpacking. This is because the low pressure in the cartridges—necessary because their walls are thin to keep the weight down—doesn't allow the butane to vaporize properly in temperatures much below 40°F (4°C) at sea level, making it a poor performer in cold weather. As the cartridge empties and the pressure drops, the burning rate falls until there isn't enough heat to bring water to a boil. Cartridges can be warmed with the hands or stored inside clothing or sleeping bags to keep them warm, but I find this inconvenient.

Reports of Himalayan mountaineers successfully using butane-cartridge stoves in bitterly cold temperatures seem to contradict the fuel's bad cold-weather reputation, but there is a possible explanation: The thinner air of high altitudes means reduced air pressure outside the canister, which, in turn, means less obstruction to the gas leaving the cartridge. At 10,000 feet, butane stoves will work down to 14°F (−10°C).

Butane/propane cartridges, however, work better below freezing at all altitudes because propane vaporizes at a much lower temperature than butane. Camping Gaz says that its 80/20 mix butane/propane cartridges will work down to +19°F (−7°C). There is a problem, however,

which prevents me from using this fuel in really cold weather—butane and propane don't chemically bond very well; the more volatile propane burns off first, hence the fast boiling times with *new* cartridges. Once the cartridge is more than two-thirds empty, the gas left is mostly butane, so the performance falls. In bitter cold you have to warm the cartridge with your hands to get much power at all when cartridges are nearly empty.

Propane, however, is so volatile that it requires very thick-walled steel containers if used on its own—the lightest of these weigh several pounds. Lightweight butane/propane canister mixtures are usually 85/15 or 80/20 mixes. I find a standard 6- to 9-fluid-ounce cartridge lasts three or four days.

Isobutane is an alternative to butane/propane, but reports suggest it isn't as efficient in the cold. REI, for one, recommends that isobutane cartridges be kept above 30°F (−1°C); MSR, which markets isobutane cartridges, says they work down to 12°F (−11°C). I haven't used isobutane in temperatures below 32°F (0°C), but down to that I've found it burns hot and consistently for the life of a cartridge. On a 12-day fall trip in the Grand Canyon I used 3½ 6-ounce isobutane cartridges, fewer than I'd expected. The 2202 series cartridges from Primus, available in 6½, 8, and 16 ounces, contain 70 percent butane, 20 percent propane, and 10 percent isobutane, which Primus says "holds the low temperature performance for longer" than butane/propane alone. (Stove design also plays a part in very cold weather performance; stoves with a preheat tube that runs through the flame will work better.)

The availability of butane cartridges has improved greatly since the first edition of this book was published. Cartridges from MSR, Peak 1, Camping Gaz, and others are easier to find. I'd still check on availability in out-of-the-way places, however.

All cartridge stoves have ported burners, though these aren't as quiet as they used to be, because the latest stoves are far more powerful than in the past. The heat output is still usually easily adjusted, however, making them excellent for simmering, but the flame must be protected from wind. Most stoves come with small wind screens fitted around the burner. If you always cook in a tent vestibule, these may be protection enough, but for outside cooking you need a separate wind screen.

Cartridge stoves are best for solo or duo use because the cartridges cool as they release fuel; running a stove over a long period of time—often necessary for group cooking—leads to a much more rapid drop in performance than running it in short bursts. This also makes these stoves less efficient for melting snow than ones that run on other fuels.

There are two types of cartridge: those with a self-sealing valve that allows you to remove the cartridge at any time, and those in which the cartridge must be left on the stove until empty. Stoves using the latter are typified by the Camping Gaz Bleuet C206, probably the most popular lightweight stove in the world. Coleman makes a similar model. The weight is around 10 ounces. Both consist of a burner/pan support unit that clamps onto a 7-fluid-ounce butane cartridge; a spike at the end of the fuel column pierces the cartridge. The result is a tall, unstable structure that is even more unstable when used with large pans; an optional stabilizing base helps. Although the pan supports fold away for packing, the fixed cartridge makes it inconvenient to carry. Once three-season models at best, these stoves can be used year-round with butane/propane cartridges. They're not the most powerful stoves, but they are durable—I know of Bleuets more

than 15 years old that are still in regular use. However, the advantages of resealable-cartridge stoves are so great that I wouldn't recommend a non-resealable-cartridge stove for backpacking. Camping Gaz has accepted this: All its latest models take resealable cartridges.

The stoves most suited to backpacking can accommodate a variety of self-sealing cartridges, and thus can be broken down for easier packing. An added advantage, especially if you're trying to boil water in very cold weather, is that it's possible to change cartridges before the one in use is empty. There are more than 25 makes of cartridges worldwide, all with the same size thread and valve, including ones from Coleman Peak 1, MSR, Primus, and Olicamp. Camping Gaz uses a different thread for its CV270 and 470 cartridges, but it has the best distribution system. (Not so

The Primus Mini Stove—ultra-lightweight at 5.5 ounces.

The Coleman Peak 1 Micro, with added wind screen and pad to prevent scorching of vegetation.

long ago, Camping Gaz made three different, non-compatible, self-sealing cartridges, which made it difficult to find the one you wanted. Now, there is just one.)

Cartridge sizes range from 3½ to 17½ fluid ounces, and the cartridges come in a number of shapes. Low-profile ones, like the Coleman Peak 1 250, Primus 2207, and Camping Gaz CV270, are the most stable. Tall, thin cartridges are best used with stabilizing bases or with small stoves and pans.

Stoves attach to self-sealing cartridges two ways. The most basic models simply screw into the top of the cartridge. More complex, but usually more efficient, are stoves that have a flexible tube running from the burner to the cartridge. In these units, the burner can be safely encircled with a wind screen, something you shouldn't do with screw-in burners because the cartridge may overheat and explode. Screw-in cartridge stoves are generally lighter than hose-connected ones, making them good for solo use, especially on ultra-lightweight trips. They don't usually have pre-heat tubes, however, and so are even less suited to cold-weather use.

The lightest stove of all falls into this category: Primus' Titanium Stove, which weighs a fraction less than 3 ounces. (It's one of those products you can't afford if you have to ask the price, however. I haven't got one!) Reasonably priced and still ultralight are the Coleman Peak 1 Micro and the Primus Mini stoves, which weigh 5½ ounces each. These tiny stoves perform amazingly well, with fast boil times and good simmer control. The packed bulk is minimal, of course. The only real difference between the two is that the burner head on the Primus Mini is quite wide, so the heat isn't as concentrated as that of the Peak 1 Micro, and therefore is less likely to burn food. Both of them are excellent for solo use. Also designed for solo use is the screw-in Globetrotter, from Camping Gaz, which fits the CV270 cartridge. It comes complete with two half-quart pans and weighs 12½ ounces. The burner is small and neat, but I think I'd find the pans too small.

Other screw-in cartridge stoves, available from Camping Gaz, Primus, and Peak 1, are slightly bigger and heavier—7 ounces and up— and therefore more suited for use with larger

The Coleman Peak 1 Alpine hose-connected cartridge stove.

pans. However, they don't have the stability of hose-connected stoves, so I'd choose one of those for cooking for two or more.

While most screw-in stoves are quite simple, the latest Camping Gaz screw-in model, the Trek 270, is probably the most technically complex stove there is. It's totally unlike any other model—it's flameless. Essentially a ceramic hob cooker for the backpacker, it works by catalytic combustion and has a vitroceramic glass cooking surface rather than the usual burner head. The process also reduces pollutants. The stove was introduced too recently to allow me to test it, but Camping Gaz claims the heat output is the same as with its conventional cartridge stoves. The advantage, obviously, is that the Trek 270

The Primus Spider hose-connected cartridge stove with piezo igniter.

isn't affected by wind, because there are no flames and the pan is in direct contact with the heat source. It also can't flare or blow out. If it works well, this could be a major development in stove design.

Hanging stoves, which can be suspended from branches or other supports, are designed for mountaineers bivouacking in tight places. They also screw into cartridges. Examples are the Bibler Hanging Stove, which weighs 29 ounces complete with 2-quart pot and combined wind screen/heat reflector, and the Markill Stormy Hanging, which weighs 18 ounces. You could use one of these in a tent in winter and avoid cooling the cartridges by placing them on snow, but overall I don't think they are of great value to backpackers.

Hose-connected stoves are more stable and usually have larger pan supports than screw-in models, making them more suited for large pots. The Camping Gaz 13-ounce Tristar has a gas regulator to ensure maximum performance in cold weather, plus wide pan supports that fold flat for carrying. The Tristar gave one of the best performances in my tests. Hose-connected stoves that run off the same cartridges are available from MSR, Coleman Peak 1, Primus, Markill, and Olicamp. MSR's only cartridge stove, the RapidFire, looks like a Whisper-Lite and comes with the same foil wind screen and reflector, which make it one of the few cartridge stoves that work well in windy weather without an additional wind screen. It also has a wide burner head that spreads the flame well for use with large pans. The total weight is 12½ ounces. Coleman's Peak 1 Alpine, which I've used more than any other cartridge stove (so I can vouch for its durability), weighs 13½ ounces and has an anti-flare system—I've tested this and it works. Swedish company Primus, which introduced the first mass-produced cartridge stoves in the 1950s and whose partner Sievert made the first liquid petroleum gas stove back in 1938, makes a similar low-profile stove called

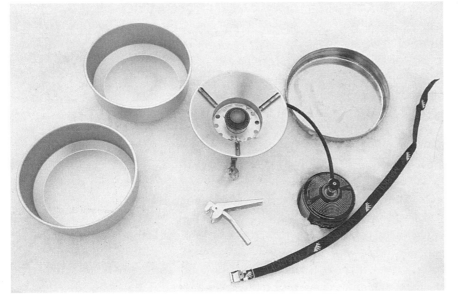

The Markill Storm-Cooker with alloy cookset.

A Trangia stove fitted with a hose-connected burner head.

the Spider, also weighing 13 ounces. (On this stove, the pre-heat tube is cleverly created by running the fuel line through one of the hollow pan supports.) The Spider also has a piezo igniter automatic ignition, which makes lighting it ridiculously easy—though I wouldn't leave the matches at home because the igniter doesn't work after you've spilled soup on it. The boil time is the fastest, barely, of any cartridge stove I've used. The power is evident by the noise too—this isn't a quiet stove!

Markill's Storm-Cooker has a unique built-in wind screen that doubles as a pan support. At 11 ounces it's lighter than average for this design. There isn't a pre-heat tube, but the wind screen acts as a heat reflector. The wide, shallow shape means that only pans with diameters of 6 inches or more can be used, and it's awkward to pack

unless it will fit inside your pans. This is a good setup for twosomes, though heavy and bulky for one.

Trangia alcohol-stove owners who want a more controllable fuel can buy burners with fuel tubes made by Primus and Camping Gaz that will fit either the standard resealable cartridge or the Camping Gaz ones. The fuel tube fits through a cutout in the Trangia wind screen. I've tried the standard one and it works well. The weight and bulk are quite high compared with a cartridge stove and foil wind screen. The wind resistance is excellent, of course.

There is one big disadvantage to cartridge stoves: empty cartridges. Too many lie glinting in the sunlight at the bottom of once-pristine mountain lakes or jut out, half-buried, from piles of rocks in wildernesses the world over.

I have no solution to this problem. Perhaps mountain stores and cartridge makers could offer a deposit system with a refund for the return of empties. Ultimately, users must be responsible enough to carry out their trash and dispose of it properly. It would also be good if the manufacturers could work out a way to recycle these cartridges.

Dungburners: There is one type of stove I haven't yet mentioned—those that burn natural materials that can be found around a forest campsite, such as twigs, pine cones, bark, charcoal, and dried dung. The last item has given these stoves the generic name *dungburners.*

All models use a tiny, battery-operated electric blower to fan the flames of a small fire lit in the well of the stove. The stoves consist of a base, mounted by a blower. Above the blower is a circular, stainless steel combustion chamber with air channels inside an aluminum shell. One C battery is said to power the fan for at least eight hours.

One version is ZZ Corp's Sierra, which weighs 15 ounces; another is Markill's Wilderness, at 18 ounces. Accessories for the Sierra include a 1-quart aluminum pot and lid, a grill, and a lightweight fire starter called Zip Fire, which comes in small blocks and is said to light even when soaked.

Such stoves may seem an interesting curiosity, but reports suggest that they work well and that the weight saved in fuel is worthwhile. So, they might be worth considering for trips in dry, wooded country. I've never used one, but I'm thinking about it.

Safety and Maintenance

All stoves are dangerous and should be used carefully. The most important safety point: Never take a stove for granted.

Before you light a stove, always check that attachments to fuel tanks or cartridges are secure, tank caps and fuel bottle tops are tight, and controls are turned off. Carefully study and practice the instructions that come with all stoves, especially kerosene and gasoline models, before heading off. When you're cold, wet, and tired, and it's half-dark and you desperately need a hot meal, it's important that you can safely operate your stove almost automatically.

A stove should be refilled with care, after you've made sure that there are no naked lights,

---

Stoves: My Choices

In order to test them for magazines (and for this book) I've acquired most of the stoves described here, so I sometimes have problems deciding which to take on a trip. For short ventures in mild conditions where weight isn't important, any one will do. Longer walks and stormy weather make me choose equipment more carefully, however.

My overall favorite stove is the Whisper-Lite Internationale, which I've used on two summer-long walks and many shorter trips, including cold-weather ones. It's light, reliable, powerful, maintainable in the field, and easy to use. If it would simmer well it would be nearly perfect. If I had only one stove, it would be the Internationale.

For trips outside North America I prefer the MSR XGK, simply because it will run on more fuels than any other stove.

The ease of use and low weight of cartridge stoves means I now use the Coleman Peak 1 Micro or Primus Mini stoves on solo trips where I don't expect temperatures to fall below freezing very often and where I know I can get the fuel. If I'm traveling with a companion, I take the Coleman Peak 1 Alpine, Primus Spider, or Camping Gaz Tristar. I wouldn't use a cartridge stove on a long hike in a remote area, however, because they aren't repairable in the field.

Cooking in a tent vestibule requires care—be sure no flammable materials are near the stove.

such as burning candles, other lit stoves, or campfires nearby. This applies whether you are changing a cartridge or pouring fuel into a white-gas stove tank. Refuel *outside* your tent or shelter to prevent spilling fuel inside.

An overheated cartridge or fuel tank is a potential hazard, though not for the tube-connected gasoline and cartridge stoves, or alcohol stoves. When the burner is directly above or alongside the fuel tank, make sure there is enough air flow around the tank or cartridge to keep it cool. It should never become too hot to touch. I've already mentioned that wind screens shouldn't fully surround such stoves. Don't use stones to stabilize them either, and if you use large pans that overhang the burner, periodically check to see if too much heat is being reflected off the pans back onto the fuel supply.

Stoves are most dangerous during lighting, when they can flare badly. For this reason, never have your head over a stove when you light it. Also, do not light a stove that is close to any

flammable material—particularly your tent. The best way to avoid trouble is to light a stove with open air above it whenever possible, even if this means sticking it out into the rain for lighting and then bringing it back into the vestibule when it's burning properly. If you do light a stove in the vestibule, the door should be open so that you can quickly push out the stove if anything goes wrong (but be careful where you push it if there are other tents around). I was once walking across a crowded campground on a cold, blustery winter day when I saw a bright yellow flash inside a nearby tent. A second later, a blazing gasoline stove came hurtling through the tent fly sheet—leaving behind a neat hole—and landed near my feet. If another tent had been close by, the results could have been disastrous.

A real threat when using a stove inside a tent is *carbon monoxide poisoning,* which can be fatal. All stoves consume oxygen and give off this odorless, colorless gas. In an enclosed space, they can use up all the oxygen, replacing it with carbon

An Optimus Svea 123 cooks away in a tent vestibule at a high camp in the Sierra on the Pacific Crest Trail.

monoxide. Ventilation is always required when a stove is in use. In a tent vestibule air can usually enter under the edge of the fly sheet, but this can be blocked by snow piling up round the edges of the tent or a wet fly sheet freezing to the ground. In those cases, having a two-way outer door zipper is useful, as the top few inches can be left open to ensure ventilation.

I don't like to use stoves in the inner tent under any circumstances, partly because of the possibility of carbon monoxide poisoning, but mainly because of the danger of fire. However, in tents without vestibules, severe weather could force you to use a stove inside the tent.

Most stoves need little maintenance. Except for those with built-in self-cleaning needles, the jets of any stove may need cleaning with the thin stove-prickers (weighing a fraction of a gram) that come with most stoves. I always carry one, and on long trips two. I use them only when the stove's performance seems to be falling off, since too much cleaning can widen the jet and lessen the burn rate. If you lose, break, or forget your jet pricker, as I did once on a winter trip, and your soup boils over and blocks the jet, a bristle from a toothbrush makes a good substitute, an idea suggested by two walkers in a mountain shelter I went to in desperate search of anything that would restore my stove to working order.

Rubber seals on tank caps and cartridge attachment points should be checked periodically and replaced if worn. I carry spares on long trips. In the case of tank caps, this usually means carrying a complete cap. On the Pacific Crest Trail I was glad I did so — the original one on my Svea 123 started to leak after four months of constant use.

Fuel Containers and Tank-Filling Devices

Liquid fuels don't usually come in containers suitable for carrying in the pack; they're either

Near Disaster

The nearest I have ever come to a serious stove accident was when I was cooking in the vestibule of a tent pitched on snow. A severe blizzard had trapped us at the same site for four nights; during the last night the wind had battered the tents so much that we'd hardly slept at all. To keep out blown snow, I lit the white-gas stove in the vestibule with the door zipped shut. The burner caught but the flame was sluggish. "Pump it some more," suggested my companion. Without thinking, I did so. There was a sudden bright surge of flame, then the whole unit was ablaze as liquid fuel shot out of the jet. Two suddenly energized bodies dived for the door zipper and yanked it open. I threw the stove out and plunged my singed hands into the snow. Later I discovered that my eyebrows and face were also slightly burned.

In retrospect, we were lucky. One moment's carelessness could have left us without our tent and gear or, worse, badly burned or even dead. My guess is that lack of air was the cause. I should have opened the door and tried to revive the stove outside. As it was, the fly-sheet zipper had partially melted and wouldn't close, so in subsequent storms we had to cook in the inner tent, which we did with great care, standing the stove on a pan lid to prevent the groundsheet from melting.

On two other occasions I've been present when a stove has caught fire, once outside and once inside a mountain hut. Each time, it was a white-gas stove. As most white-gas stove manufacturers state, these are best used outdoors, not in tents or huts. The safest stoves are alcohol-fueled ones, followed by cartridge models, which is what I use for regular tent cooking.

too large or too fragile, or leak once opened. However, Coleman Fuel and MSR White Gas are available in metal and plastic quart containers, respectively. I've carried both at times. The MSR bottle is my first choice as a fuel container; it weighs just 2¾ ounces, less than any metal container. Its flat shape is also convenient for packing.

Plastic fuel bottles are fine for alcohol, and some, such as those from Nalgene and Trangia, are suitable for white gas and kerosene, but metal bottles are generally more trustworthy for holding volatile fuels. Fuel bottles must be robust and need a well-sealed, leakproof cap. I've used the cylindrical Sigg bottles for years for all fuels. They're available in pint and quart sizes. These extremely tough aluminum bottles have leakproof screw caps with rubber gaskets, and double as fuel tanks for the Sigg Fire-Jet and Optimus Explorer stoves. MSR makes similar bottles in nearly the same sizes, but slightly heavier, which MSR says are stronger and safer. I always use an MSR bottle with my WhisperLite Internationale. On trips of a week or less, I carry just a 1-pint MSR bottle, adding a 1-pint Sigg bottle for trips where more than a week's fuel has to be carried or snow has to be melted, and the 1-quart plastic MSR container on long treks. With the Trangia, a full pint bottle sees me through three or four days, a quart one through a week.

It's almost impossible to fill small fuel tanks directly from standard fuel bottles without spilling. However, various ingenious devices help. I have a Sigg pouring cap and spout, bought many years ago for filling my Svea 123 tank. This is a standard cap with a small plastic spout inserted in one side and a tiny hole drilled in the other. By placing a finger over the hole the flow from the spout can be controlled. It's inconvenient to use—you have to remove the normal cap, screw in the pouring one, fill the stove, then change the caps again. To avoid losing either cap, I have linked them with a piece of shock cord. REI's Super Pour Spout and Olicamp's Ultimate Pour Spout/Cap, which are two versions of the same design, look better than the Sigg cap because

A fuel bottle with pouring spout and filter funnel.

each completely replaces the standard top of a fuel bottle. Turning the spout one way opens it for pouring; turning it the other way seals it. (I would recommend finding out how easily these caps open inadvertently before relying on one.) Trangia's polythene fuel bottle has a cap with a built-in safety valve, so fuel can be poured without removing it. The Trangia cap is also available separately for use with Sigg and MSR bottles.

For filling fuel bottles from larger containers, I use a small plastic funnel with a built-in filter, bought at a hardware store. I usually carry it on long treks when I may have to refill with white gas, which isn't as clean as the Coleman Fuel I normally use. For example, on the Yukon walk I often could buy only Goldex Camper Fuel, which quickly blocked the jet of my stove unless it was filtered.

Wind Screens and Accessories

All stoves need a wind screen to function efficiently. MSR stoves come with foil wind screens, while solid alloy ones are integral parts of Tran-

gia, Sigg, and Trapper alcohol stoves, the Markill Storm-Cooker, and all the natural fuel burners. No other stoves come with adequate wind screens as components. The MSR foil wind screen is ideal for low-profile, tube-connected cartridge stoves and screw-in cartridge stoves used with low-profile cartridges. The wind screen adds only 1¾ ounces to the weight.

For taller stoves with fuel tanks and cartridges that must not be fully shielded from air flow, larger, heavier wind screens are necessary. They can be made by stiffening sheets of foil-backed nylon or canvas with wire rods (knitting needles are apparently good for this) that project below the material and can be used to anchor it in the ground. When I used the Svea 123 regularly, my wind screen was a folding Coghlan one made up of five sheets of aluminum with tent-stake-like anchor rods at either end. This screen is efficient, durable, and also works well with screw-in cartridge stoves, but it adds 8 ounces to the pack. This gives the 123 a total weight of 26 ounces, versus the Internationale's 14 ounces, which is

The MSR XPD Heat Exchanger and cookset.

why I prefer the latter. A similar wind screen is the eight-section Olicamp folding aluminum shield, which weighs 9½ ounces. Traveling Light makes an interesting aluminum wind screen/ heat exchanger called the Tutu that comes in two sizes. The Standard (4.1 ounces) is for burners like the Svea that sit above the fuel tank; the Short (2.6 ounces) is for low-profile hose-connected stoves, like the WhisperLite. The Tutu is designed to direct flames up the side of the pot as well as to block wind. Whatever wind screen you use should extend well above the burner to be effective.

To make starting the Svea and Hunter stoves easier, especially in cold weather, Optimus offers a Mini Pump that replaces the fuel cap. I've never used one because it can't be fitted to the 123 when the wind screen/pot support is in place. Reports suggest that these pumps can over-pressurize the tank and perhaps blow the safety valve, so they must be used with care.

Kerosene stoves also need help priming, and there are various pastes for the purpose. Optimus Burning Paste in 1¾-ounce tubes is one example. Alternatives are broken up solid-fuel tablets, tiny amounts of alcohol, and, as a last resort, kerosene-soaked paper.

A recent innovation is the MSR XPD Cook Set with Heat Exchanger. This consists of two stainless steel pots (1½- and 2-quart capacities) with frying pan/lid, pot grab, plus a corrugated aluminum collar for the stove, which is meant to reduce boiling time by directing more heat up the sides of the pan. According to MSR, the Heat Exchanger increases the stove's efficiency by 25 percent. As the weight of the exchanger is just 7 ounces, it could save weight overall on long trips. On short ones, the main advantage would be faster boiling times. The pan set weighs 26 ounces—too heavy for solo use, but fine for duos. I would save weight by leaving the larger pan behind and substituting a stainless steel mug. The Heat Exchanger folds up to fit inside the pans for carrying. Although designed for MSR stoves, the Exchanger can be used with other brands. It won't work with pans less than 6 inches in diameter though, which cuts out many small solo units. I've used the heat exchanger when traveling with a companion and with groups of 10 and found it does speed up boiling times and save fuel, though I haven't quantified how much. I'd certainly always use it with groups of four or more and with two or three people on trips of four days or more.

Stoves with poor flame control, like the WhisperLite, can burn food that needs simmering for any length of time unless you stir constantly and lift the pot above the burner every so often. An answer to this is Traveling Light's Scorch Buster heat dispersion plate, a ribbed stainless steel disk that weighs 2.8 ounces and is, in fact, the same as the diffuser plate of the Outback Oven described below. It works well and is worth carrying if you tend to burn meals.

Also part of the Outback Oven but available separately is the Pot Parka, a heat-resistant hood (the small version weighs 2.9 ounces; the large, 4.3 ounces). By conducting heat up the sides of the pot it makes for more even heating and speeds up cooking times, saving fuel in the process.

Stove Lighters and Fire Starters: I usually carry several boxes of strike-anywhere matches, each sealed in a small plastic bag. One box is in my food bag, one in the stove bag, and one in the plastic bag with the toilet paper. I may carry an extra box in a food bag on long trips. The combined weight is only a fraction of an ounce. Waterproof metal or plastic match safes that provide extra protection are available and weigh about an ounce. I don't like book matches—the striking strip wears out quickly and half the matches never seem to work.

The likelihood of several boxes kept in different places in the pack all becoming soaked is remote, but it could happen if, for example, you fell in a river, so carrying some form of emergency backup fire starter is a good idea. In my repair and oddities bag I always keep a canister of waterproof, windproof Lifeboat matches. The waterproof plastic canister contains 25 large matches, has strikers top and bottom, and weighs ¾ ounce. They work, but beware of the hot embers after one has gone out. Less efficient alternatives are water-resistant matches available under the Greenlite and Coghlan's labels. These standard-size matches come 30 or 40 to a box and are less expensive than the Lifeboats.

An alternative to matches is a cigarette lighter, and I often carry a cheap, ¾-ounce, disposable butane lighter instead of one of the boxes of matches. Just the spark from a lighter will ignite white gas and butane, though not kerosene or alcohol (at least not easily), and if the lighter gets wet, it's easily dried; a sodden box of matches is useless. Refillable lighters like the classic Zippo (2 ounces) would be an alternative.

I've not tried the more esoteric fire lighters. Flint-and-magnesium strikers (1.3 ounces) work by scraping flakes from a magnesium block and igniting them with sparks caused by drawing a knife across a flint. The Permanent Match (½ ounce) has a brass "match" that lights a gasoline-soaked wick when struck. Carrying one might be a good idea on long, remote, wooded-country trips. Survival manuals praise other methods of fire-lighting that use natural materials, but these all strike me as unworkable in the cold and wet—the conditions under which you might need a fire most.

Transporting Stoves and Fuel: Checking in at Los Angeles International Airport a few years ago, I was asked if I was carrying a stove. When I said yes, the attendant demanded to see it. "You can't take these on the flight," she said, examining my WhisperLite and empty fuel bottle. I argued (I was very reluctant to abandon my stove), and she eventually agreed to accept the items as long as there was no smell of gasoline, something I achieved by washing out both items with huge quantities of soap in a restroom.

That's the only time I've been asked about stoves, even though I fly regularly, but others have apparently had stoves confiscated. (I usually carry my pack inside a duffel bag, so maybe I don't look enough like a backpacker to attract attention.)

The official position, according to Federal Aviation Administration regulations, is that properly purged—that is, well-aired and empty—stoves and fuel bottles are acceptable, as they clearly aren't dangerous. However, many airlines have much stricter rules of their own, and some won't carry any used stoves or fuel bottles except as freight.

If you're planning to fly with your backpacking equipment, I'd check the regulations of the airline before purchasing a ticket. The American Hiking Society (AHS) publishes a useful fact sheet on this that includes policies of different airlines, which they divide into pro-hiker, moderate hiker, and anti-hiker groups (see Appendix 3 to contact the AHS). The last usually requires used stoves and empty fuel containers to be booked as air freight or "Express Air," which is so expensive and such a hassle that you might as well buy a stove at your destination.

Fuel is obviously a hazard. Airlines will only carry it, if at all (AHS could find no airline prepared to carry it), in accordance with airline regulations and if it is accompanied by the correct shipping papers. It's much easier to buy fuel at your destination, as I've always done.

UTENSILS

Cooking habits determine what kitchen gear you carry. One advantage of minimal cooking is that it requires minimal tools. My current basic kit consists of a 0.9-quart titanium pot with lid, a 1-pint stainless steel cup, a small knife, and two spoons—total weight 11 ounces. This serves my needs both on weekends and on long summer trips.

Pans

Pots and pans for camping are hardly the most exciting items of gear, and most people give them little thought. I used the same aluminum pans for nearly a decade before switching to stainless steel ones in the late 1980s. Since then, new developments have caused me to change my pots twice more.

Aluminum, the standard backpacking cookware material for decades, is lightweight, heats evenly without hot spots, and conducts heat quickly, making for fast boiling times. However, it pits, scratches, and dents easily, which makes it hard to clean and can taint some foods with a slight metallic flavor. There is concern in some quarters about the adverse effects of ingesting aluminum.

Recently, stainless steel has become more popular for pans—it's easy to clean, non-corroding, scratch-proof, tough, long-lasting, and doesn't taint food. Unfortunately, it's significantly heavier than aluminum and also conducts heat more

A selection of cookware. From the left: MSR Alpine stainless steel pans and lid, Trangia 4-quart aluminum pot with lid, Trangia pint kettle, and Sigg Inoxal aluminum/stainless steel pans with lids.

slowly, leading to longer boiling times. Even so, many people, including myself, prefer it.

Two new materials combine the best qualities of aluminum and stainless steel. The first is a laminate of aluminum and stainless steel, with the latter as the inner surface, available from Trangia under the name Duossal, and from Sigg as Inoxal. I've used the latter and been very impressed. Sigg Inoxal Cookware is made from a light aluminum alloy with 0.2 mm layer of chrome nickel steel as a lining. Inoxal is lighter than stainless steel, though not as light as aluminum. An aluminum 1½-quart pan (without lid) tipped the scales at 4½ ounces, the stainless steel at 8½, the Inoxal pan at 7.

I always like to cut even the slightest bit of weight when I can, so I was interested to see if Inoxal pans worked better than stainless steel. I took a 1-quart Inoxal pan on a two-week trip. The first time I used it the water boiled so quickly I wasn't ready for it; during the first few days of use the pan kept boiling over and putting out the stove. I was so used to my standard stainless steel pan that I knew how long soups and meals took to come to the boil without timing them. Clearly, the Inoxal pan was more efficient.

I eventually did a comparison test using aluminum, stainless steel, and Inoxal 1½-quart pans. I wasn't too surprised when the water took longer to boil in the stainless steel pan than in the Inoxal, though a third longer was more than I'd expected. The real surprise was that water also boiled faster in the Inoxal than in the aluminum pan—one-sixth faster, in fact. I did the test again to double-check. The results were almost identical.

How much this performance is due to the Inoxal material and how much the blackened exterior (the other pans were shiny silver), I don't know. But it confirmed what my field use suggested: Inoxal pans boil water faster. This helps conserve stove fuel, and on long trips would make a difference to the amount of fuel you had to carry. The difference would be more marked when boiling larger quantities.

There are three Inoxal pans of 1-quart, 1½-quart, and 2½-quart capacities (weighing 9, 11, and 14½ ounces, respectively), each with a lid that can double as a plate, plus a 7-ounce frying pan and a 2½-ounce pot grab, called a clamp by Sigg. The clamp has a lock on it, so it can be left attached to a pan. The pans are well made and have rounded edges that make them easy to clean. My only minor complaint is that the lids aren't easy to remove unless they are put on upside down. Being deep, they then sink into your food if the pan is full.

Because Inoxal is lighter and has faster boiling times yet retains all the advantages of stainless steel, it's a better choice. The price is quite high, especially for the whole set, though few people are likely to need that. The quality and performance is such that it will never need replacing.

Titanium is lighter than Inoxal, and the latest pans are made of this material. The first ones, from Evernew, came out while I was writing this edition. The cost is about double that for stainless steel cookware. I have a 0.9-quart pan that weighs 5 ounces with lid and attached fold-out handles. I took it on a 12-day walk in the Grand Canyon and found it excellent. It doesn't pit, scratch, or taint flavor, and it cleans easily. Given the weight, it's now my pot choice for solo use.

Evernew also makes excellent stainless steel cooksets, but its smallest set—1- and ¾-quart pans, frying pan/lid, and plastic cup—weighs 21 ounces, which is three times the weight of an equivalent-size aluminum set. MSR's stainless steel Alpine Cook Set, the same as the one that comes with the Heat Exchanger, with 1½- and 2-quart pans, plus lid and pot grab, weighs 26 ounces, and makes a fine set for two people. The lightest stainless steel pans I've found are from Olicamp; I have a 1-quart copper-bottomed pan taken from a larger set that, with its lid, weighs 7½ ounces. It was my choice solo pan until Inoxal and titanium came along. Other stainless steel cooksets are available from Markill and Peak 1.

Aluminum cooksets are by far the least expensive and lightest. A quart pan weighs around 4 ounces, while the 5-quart Trangia pan I use when cooking for groups weighs only 18½ ounces. Open Country is a leading brand. Some

The author's solo cookset: 0.9-quart titanium pot, 1-pint stainless steel cup, and two Lexan plastic spoons.

aluminum pans come with non-stick coatings that overcome one of the disadvantages of aluminum. These are fine as long as you are prepared to treat them carefully and always use plastic or wooden utensils. I prefer pots I can mistreat.

Whatever they're made from, pans should be simple. Fairly shallow ones with rounded edges are best, because food is less likely to burn in these and they are easy to clean. Attached handles should be avoided on aluminum pans because they become very hot, but fold-out handles on stainless steel and titanium pans stay reasonably cool. I'd rather not have attached handles at all, but the only titanium pan I have seen has one, so at present there's no choice.

How big a pan you need depends on how many you're cooking for. I find a quart-size is easily large enough for solo cooking. For two I add a 2-quart one; when I've cooked for 10 I've found a 5-quart pot just big enough for cooking pasta or rice, with a 2-quart one adequate for sauce.

Lids are important—using one makes water boil faster. Many are designed to double as frying pans, but people who fry foods tell me that lids don't work very well this way. Lids are often heavy—the one for my quart titanium pan weighs 1½ ounces; the one for the quart Inoxal pan, 3½ ounces—so on ultra-lightweight trips I substitute a piece of heavy-duty foil (custard tins are good) that weighs just 0.3 ounce.

Ovens and Baking Devices

When I first heard about ovens for backpackers I was highly cynical, suspecting that they would be heavy and difficult to use. I couldn't imagine baking anything on a small stove in the wild. However, my assumptions started to waver with reports that Traveling Light's Outback Oven really did work well, so I decided I had to try it. I wasn't disappointed.

If you're the sort of backpacker who hates dehydrated food and dreams of pizzas, fresh bread, or apple pie, you can have them all with one of these ovens and without too much hassle.

The Outback Oven comes in two versions: the Plus Ten, which weighs 24 ounces and includes a Teflon-coated baking pan, and the Ultralight, which weighs 7 ounces. The first is fine for large groups, but most backpackers will be interested in the Ultralight. It consists of a foil reflector collar that fits under the burner of your stove and directs heat up, a stainless steel riser bar and diffuser plate to spread the heat evenly and prevent scorching, a fiberglass convection dome that fits over your pan and concentrates the heat, and a simple thermometer. All the components can be packed inside a small pan.

To use the oven you need a stove with a controllable flame—cartridge ones are ideal—plus pan supports to which the heat reflector can be fitted and which support the riser bar/diffuser

The Outback Oven Ultralight. Top: Reflector collar and convection dome; bottom: diffuser plate and thermometer.

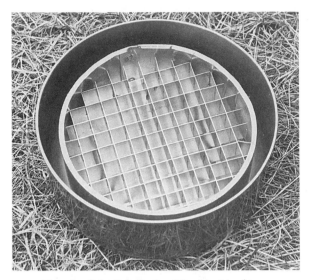

The ultralight BakePacker fitted inside a pan.

it can't produce baked goods with crisp crusts, unlike the Outback Oven, and you need a supply of plastic bags. However, it's light and easy to use.

Having eaten freshly baked food on the trail, I can't go back to living on dehydrated meals all the time. As mentioned earlier, I wouldn't carry them on a long solo trip due to the extra weight.

plate unit. Most stoves fit these criteria, but check that the oven will fit your stove before buying one. A wind screen is essential unless the wind is calm. The oven is designed to be used with pans from 6 to 8 inches in diameter and 3 to 5 inches high, which includes most 1½- and 2-quart pans, but rules out smaller ones.

Simpler and lighter than the Outback Oven is the BakePacker, described as a "cook-pot accessory," available in a standard version weighing 9 ounces, and an ultralight one weighing 4 ounces. I've tried the latter, which is designed for pots of 6 to 7 inches in diameter. The Bake-Packer consists of an aluminum grid that sits in the bottom of the pan and conducts heat up through its honeycomb. Enough water to cover the grid is put into the pot, then the food to be baked is placed on top in a plastic freezer or oven roasting bag, and spread out. The bag can then be loosely closed and the lid put on the pot. Once the water is boiling, medium heat is enough to steam-bake the mix in the bag. Because the BakePacker cooks with steam,

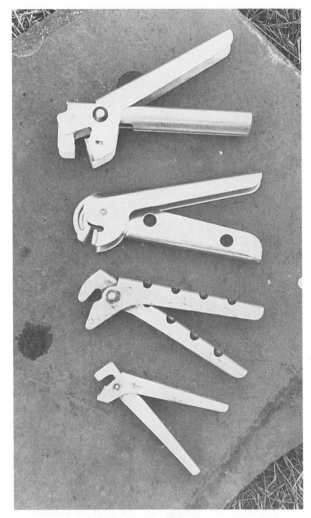

A selection of pot grabs. The smallest is fine for solo use; the larger ones are needed for big pans.

I do take them out on solo weekends and on trips with companions.

Pot Grabs

Far superior to fixed handles are simple, two-piece pot grabs that clamp firmly onto the edge of a pan when the handles are pressed together. I've used my 1-ounce Trangia pot grab on almost every trip for nearly 20 years. Sigg and MSR also make excellent pot grabs suitable for use with the biggest, heaviest pans. Not all pot grabs are of this quality, though; some thin aluminum ones quickly twist out of shape. Now that I usually use the titanium pot with its fold-out handles and a lid with a knob on solo trips, I carry a pot grab only when I intend to cook over an open fire, when the handles get hot.

Plates

I usually don't bother with plates or bowls because I eat out of the pan, but this is only practical for the solo walker. Shallow plastic utensils that look suitable spill easily and don't hold much. Stainless steel plates also are available, though these are heavier—around 4 to 6 ounces for 28- to 32-ounce capacity ones. A good alternative is a deep plastic kitchen mixing bowl. These are cheap and weigh only a few ounces. A handle can be made by melting a hole near the rim and threading it with a piece of thick cord. (This idea comes courtesy of Todd Seniff, who produced such a bowl on a six-week Canadian Rockies ski tour.) Some people eat out of their mugs, but if you do, you obviously can't

Stainless steel mugs, a Lexan plastic spoon, and plastic bowls.

Cooking with a Trangia alcohol stove at a cool-weather bivouac.

have a drink at the same time. A light wooden bowl also performs well; it insulates, is relatively tough and durable, and is organic. The weight is higher than that of plastic, however.

Mugs

These are essential and may be made of plastic or metal. The first are light and cheap, but not very durable, and if used constantly they develop uncleanable scratches, cracks, and splits in just a few months. They also retain tastes—last night's tomato soup will flavor the morning's cup of coffee no matter how well you wash the mug. A typical 0.42-quart plastic mug weighs ¾ ounce. Lexan mugs might be better, since Lexan is unbreakable and supposedly doesn't retain tastes; a 10-ounce Lexan cup from REI weighs 3 ounces.

To drink out of aluminum or enamel mugs you need asbestos lips. This means that, except for cold drinks, the one that comes with the Svea 123 stove and doubles as a burner cover is useless. The alternative is stainless steel: the lip remains cool, doesn't taint flavors, doesn't scratch, and is long-lasting. I have a pint mug, REI's Cascade Cup, which I bought many years ago. It can also be used as a small pan because it has a wide base. It weighs 4 ounces and has a clip-off handle that folds away under the cup. There are conventional stainless steel mugs available; the one I have weighs 4 ounces and holds a pint. It can just about be used as a pan on stoves with closely spaced pot supports, such as the Svea 123 and the Peak 1 Alpine, but it's not the right shape for this. If keeping drinks hot for long periods is important, then double-walled stainless steel mugs are available in 10- and 12-fluid-ounce sizes. They're heavy—the smaller one weighs 7 ounces.

Eating Implements

Lexan plastic works well for cutlery, but it discolors and can be broken, despite claims to the contrary. A soup spoon and teaspoon together weigh 0.5 ounce. Other plastic spoons break under the weight of a baked bean; forget them. Metal cut-

In the snow, comfortable outdoor kitchens can be built. This one is in the High Sierra.

lery weighs more but lasts longer; when my current Lexan spoons break, I'll go back to raiding the home cutlery drawer. Special clip-together camping sets seem unnecessarily fussy. Forks aren't needed, but a knife is an obvious accessory. Types are discussed in the next chapter.

Washing Dishes

Stainless steel and titanium clean much more easily than aluminum. Generally, a wipe-around with a damp cloth is enough, although for hygienic reasons you should sterilize pans and utensils thoroughly at least every couple of days. I do this with boiling water.

I don't carry detergent or dish-washing liquid—it's unnecessary and a pollutant, even if biodegradable. Nor do I wash dishes directly in a stream or tip waste food into one. Dirty dishwater should always be poured onto a bare patch of ground or into thick vegetation. To make dish washing easier, pour cold water into a pan once it's empty to stop food residues from cementing themselves to the inside. Some foods are worse than others—oatmeal is particularly bad. Hard-to-clean pans can be scoured with gravel or even snow to remove debris, a tip worth remembering if you forget your dishcloth.

Packing

I generally pack my stove, pans, and utensils together in a small stuff sack. I don't pack the stove inside the pans, as this tends to dirty them, although manufacturers tout this packing "convenience" as an advantage of many small stoves. I usually carry fuel bottles in outside pockets in case of leaks, or stand them upright at the bottom of the main compartment, which is where I keep fuel cartridges, too. The stove and pans also end up there, since I rarely use them during the day. If you cook at lunchtime, you will need to pack them somewhere accessible.

SITING THE KITCHEN

I like to site my kitchen next to my sleeping bag, which means either in the tent vestibule or, if I'm sleeping out, next to the groundsheet. That way I can have breakfast in bed—a good way to face a cold or wet morning, and nice any time. The stove needs to be placed on bare earth or on short, sparse vegetation, so that the heat doesn't cause any damage. If the plant growth is long and luxurious, I try to find a flat rock on which to place the stove, to avoid singeing the vegetation. You must, of course, return the rock to its proper place when you have finished. I set up the stove, then sort out the food I need for the evening. When all the kitchen items are arranged near the stove and I know where everything is, I start cooking.

This pattern requires modification in two very different circumstances. The first is anywhere bears are a potential menace. In this case, it is advisable to site the kitchen at least 100 yards downwind of where you sleep, because the smell of food might attract a bear during the night. I look for a sheltered spot with a good view, and perhaps a log or tree stump to sit on and another to use as a table. Clean utensils can be left in place overnight. Dirty ones should be hung with the food.

The other special case is camping on snow. Often, the cold makes eating from within the sleeping bag essential. The challenge is to prevent the stove from melting down through the snow; some form of insulation is needed. I often use a small square of closed-cell foam, cut from the corner of an old mat, which now has deep grooves in it where it has partially melted from the hot metal of stove bases and legs. (For some time I've meant to glue a covering of aluminum foil over it to prevent this happening.) Other insulating items could be pressed into service— I've balanced my Svea 123 on a thick natural history guide, and on the blade of a metal snow shovel. With two or more campers, you can dig out a kitchen instead of cooking in your sleeping bags.

CHAPTER EIGHT

Comfort and Safety
in Camp and on the Trail

It is one of the blessings of wilderness life that it
shows us how few things we need in order to be
perfectly happy.

—*Camping and Woodcraft,* Horace Kephart

To make any walk safe and enjoyable, numerous
small items are needed. Some are essential, some
never are necessary, though they may enhance
your stay in the wilderness. I am always surprised
at the number of odds and ends in my pack, yet
not one of them is superfluous.

LIGHT

No one goes backpacking in Alaska, Northern
Canada, Greenland, Iceland, or Lapland during
mid-winter because there is little daylight—
none at all if you're north of the Arctic Circle.
In mid-summer, however, the far north is light
24 hours a day—no artificial light is needed at
"night." Most places backpackers frequent are
farther south, though, and some form of light is
needed regardless of the time of year. How much
you need depends on where you are and when.
At Lake Louise in Banff National Park in the
Canadian Rockies, there are over 16½ hours of
daylight in mid-June, but only eight hours in
mid-December; in Yosemite you'll have 14¾
hours in June but more than 9½ in December.

You'll need one light for walking and one for

camp. A walking light will do for camp use, but
not vice versa.

Headlamps and Flashlights

These lights are for walking and setting up camp
in the dark—which you'll probably have to do
at some point, regardless of your intentions.
Flashlights had a reputation for being unreliable.
My field notes from the 1970s and early 1980s
confirm this; in 1985, two flashlights failed during my Continental Divide walk, and I finished
that trek with a large, heavy model. In the 1980s,
however, tough, long-lasting flashlights and
headlamps swept the market. Many of the newer
designs don't have on/off switches (that failed so
regularly on the older models)—you twist the
lamp housing to switch them on. Others, usually
larger ones, have recessed switches that aren't
easily damaged or accidentally turned on. Two
names dominate hand-held flashlights suitable
for backpacking: Tekna and MagLite.

A typical Tekna product is the Gear 2AA, which
has a waterproof, ABS plastic body, adjustable
focus, and runs for four hours on two alkaline
AA batteries at 70°F (21°C); it weighs 3 ounces,
including the batteries. The water-resistant Mini-
MagLite AA uses the same batteries and runs for
an hour more, but it weighs 5 ounces because
of its aluminum body. It also has an adjustable
beam, and can be turned into a small upright
lantern by using the headpiece as a stand. Other

245

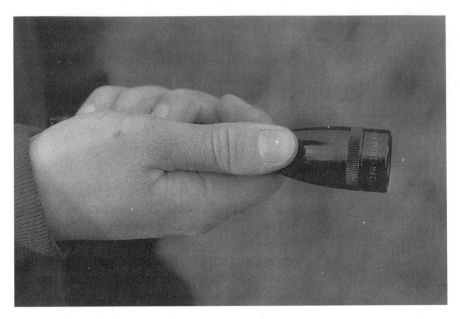

Small flashlights are adequate for three-season backpacking.

reputable names include Durabeam, PeliLite, Eveready, and Princeton Tec.

Hand-held lights are cheaper and lighter than headlamps, and buyers have a much wider choice, but I don't use them anymore—many years ago I discovered that a headlamp is far more useful because it leaves both hands free. I'd previously pitched tents and cooked while gagging on a flashlight held in my mouth, stopping every few minutes to recover. Walking is also easier with a headlamp. Because they were first developed for Alpine mountaineering, many of the best headlamps come from mountaineering equipment manufacturers. In early models, wires trailed from the lamp to battery packs, and constantly caught on things. Then came headlamps with the battery case on the headband, which made the unit uncomfortable. A few of these are still around.

There are various webbing headbands that can adapt a small flashlight into a headlamp. I haven't used these but have heard good reports.

Since the early 1980s, I've used Petzl Headlamps, French products now widely recognized as the best. They are very comfortable and reliable. The Petzl Zoom Headlamp has a battery pack that fits on the back of the head; the lamp unit pivots up and down, so it is easy to direct the beam. A twist of the lamp housing turns the light on or off and adjusts the beam from spot to flood. A spare bulb can be stored behind the lamp unit. Without batteries, the Petzl Zoom weighs 6 ounces. The standard battery is a flat Duracell MN 1203 alkaline 4.5-volt (5½ ounces), which can be hard to find in North America. However, there is an adapter that accepts three AA cells and weighs 2½ ounces with batteries. Petzl claims that at 70°F (21°C) the 4.5-volt battery provides light for 17 hours; the AA pack for eight hours. I've used a Petzl with the 4.5-volt battery for all-night winter walks without the light fading, and find that one will last for several weeks of normal use. This is with the standard bulb, which gives a 100-foot beam. If you use

Headlamps are useful for night hiking and setting up camp in the dark. This is the Petzl Zoom.

the more-powerful, long-lasting halogen bulb, which gives a 325-foot beam, the flat battery lasts 6½ hours; the three AAs 2¾ hours (at 70°F [21°C]). I've always found the standard bulbs adequate.

At 11½ ounces (with battery), the Zoom Headlamp is heavy to carry in summer, when a light isn't needed often or for very long. Petzl markets a Micro headlamp, which weighs just 5 ounces with two AA batteries. Battery life is five hours. The battery unit is mounted on the forehead, but it's so light that it's not uncomfortable. I use the Micro from May through October, the Zoom from November through April, though on long-distance hikes I generally take the Zoom for its longer battery life.

For very cold conditions, Petzl makes an Arctic Zoom Lamp, which features a battery pouch that you hang around your neck and keep next to your body. This unit takes only the halogen bulb, but will last 6½ hours with the 4.5-volt bat-tery at −40°F (−40°C)—twice as long as the Zoom version.

There are other headlamps available, including several from REI, but none I've seen look as comfortable as the Petzls. When I'm not using my light in camp, I keep it to one side of the head of my sleeping bag so that I can find it at night without too much trouble.

Whatever flashlight or headlamp you use, it's wise to carry spare batteries and bulbs. Standard tungsten bulbs are fine for camp use and don't use up batteries quickly. With lights that use only a few AA or AAA batteries, the beam is quite weak, however, and not good for walking in the dark. Halogen, krypton, and xenon bulbs are much more powerful, but use up batteries much more quickly. Alkaline batteries are standard, but alternatives are long-life lithium and rechargeable nickel-cadmium. Lithium batteries are expensive, but they last much longer than alkaline ones in cold weather; they also maintain a steadier beam until their power is completely drained. Don't bother with carbon-zinc batteries unless they are the only ones available in a remote area—they are too short-lived to be suitable for backpacking. If you use rechargeable batteries, you can't recharge them during a long trek without carrying a charger. Solar chargers are available—one from Basic Designs for AA batteries weighs 4 ounces.

CANDLES

Batteries are heavy, expensive, and polluting, so I try to minimize their use. Besides, a diffuse light is more useful in camp than a directed beam. I use candles—the short stubby ones that weigh up to 7 ounces when new and burn for 10 to 30 hours, depending on their size—because they're self-supporting. If I am sleeping out, I put the candle near the head of my sleeping bag (I make sure if it falls or is knocked over it won't land on anything flammable—I never bring a candle into the inner tent or stand it on a groundsheet). On cold, dark winter nights, I am always amazed at how much warmth and friendliness a single candle flame can give off, especially if the stove windshield is placed behind it as a reflector and to keep off breezes. Used this way, a lit candle is fairly safe, as long as you *don't leave it unattended.* After melting holes in two fly-sheet doors, I also make sure the fly sheet above the candle isn't too close.

Candle and Oil Lanterns

Candle lanterns protect the flame from wind and can be hung up so the light covers a wider area. When they work properly they are excel-

A candle lantern with candle and oil-burning insert.

A candle lantern.

lent, but problems do arise. The most common design utilizes a glass cylinder to protect the flame, and a metal or plastic cylinder into which the candle fits; the glass slides to protect it when packed. They weigh about 4½ ounces. In theory, a candle, which weighs 1.8 ounces when new, can last eight to nine hours, but in practice I've found that most candles start to sputter and overflow before they're two-thirds used, leaving the inside of the lantern covered with wax that has to be scraped off. Part of the reason for this seems to be that most wicks don't run straight down the middle of the candles, but curve off the side halfway down. After using my lantern on and off for five years, I doubt I'll use it with candles again.

I have a plastic insert for my candle lantern, however, that burns lamp oil via a wick, which is more efficient and lighter than a candle. Called the Candoil, it will work with any grade lamp oil, even kerosene, though it's very smoky with the latter. The weight of the lantern with the Candoil insert is 3½ ounces. It holds about 1.7 ounces of lamp oil and burns 10 to 12 hours.

White-Gas, Kerosene, and Cartridge Lanterns

A few experiences with fragile and heavy butane lanterns many years ago made me lose interest in them. Now, much tougher, lighter models are available, though I'm not convinced solo backpackers need to bother with them, except perhaps in winter, when a bright light can make a 16-hour night a little easier to get through. I used to think the hiss these lanterns emit would drive me crazy, but having used one of the lightest models, I've found that I can get used to it.

These lanterns have glass globes that surround and disperse the light from a glowing, lace-like *mantle,* which in turn surrounds a jet. Both the globe and the mantle are highly breakable; the lantern must be protected if it is carried in the pack.

Two of these lanterns are light enough for serious consideration. The Coleman Peak 1 Micro Lantern weighs only 7 ounces, and has protective lightweight steel bars around the globe. The output is a bright 75 to 80 watts. It runs off resealable butane/propane cartridges. I've used it on a number of winter trips and found the light welcome. Similar is Camping Gaz's Bivouac Lantern, which weighs 6 ounces and runs off CV270 cartridges. The only other lantern that approaches these for weight is the 10-ounce Primus 3230, which also runs off resealable cartridges. White-gas and kerosene lanterns are heavier; at 30 ounces, the Peak 1 Lantern is one of the lightest.

Lightsticks

Lightsticks are thin plastic tubes that when bent break an internal glass capsule, allowing two non-toxic (so they say) chemicals to mix and produce a pale greenish light. They seem no more than a curiosity to me (at least for backpacking). I've never carried one.

HEALTH AND BODY CARE
First Aid

You should be able to repair yourself in the event of most injuries or accidents—at least long enough to survive until help arrives or you can get to a road or hut. Taking a Red Cross, YMCA, or similar first aid course is a good idea. Alternatively, many outdoor schools offer courses in wilderness first aid. There are many books on the subject, too. *Medicine for Mountaineering,* edited by James A. Wilkerson (The Mountaineers) is comprehensive, while Fred T. Darvill's *Mountaineering Medicine* (Wilderness Press) is small and light enough to carry in your first aid kit. Be forewarned: A close study of these texts may convince you that you are lucky to have survived the dangers of wilderness travel, and that you'd better not go back again! (The antidote to this is a glance through the statistics of accidents that occur in the home and on the road—driving *to* the wilderness is likely to be far more hazardous than anything you do *in* it.)

First aid basics consist of knowledge and a few medical supplies. Outdoor stores carry a full line of prepackaged first aid kits—some are very good, some poor. Outdoor Research, Adventure Medical, and REI offer good ones. But the problem with even the best ones is that they usually contain items I don't feel are necessary, while items I think are essential are absent. I put together the kit I want from the shelves of the local drugstore, which is less expensive, too.

Every book on wilderness medicine features a different list of what a first aid kit should contain. I used to carry a fairly comprehensive kit (weighing a pound) on every trip, but, in keeping with cutting weight wherever possible, I now take it only into remote areas where help could be many days away and I might have to get myself out.

The kit I now carry on most trips weighs 4 to 5 ounces. It usually contains:

First aid information leaflet
6-inch-wide elastic bandage for knee and ankle sprains
2-inch-by-3-inch sheet of 2nd Skin, or 4 Compeed sections for blisters
Roll of 1-inch micropore tape for holding 2nd Skin in place
5-inch-by-5-inch wound bandage
2-inch-by-2-inch non-adhesive absorbent dressing for burns
3 antiseptic wipes for cleaning wounds and blisters
12 assorted plasters for cuts
10 foil-wrapped painkillers—ibuprofen or aspirin

I keep the kit in a small, zippered nylon case with a large white cross and the words "First Aid" written on it. Having your first aid kit clearly identified is important in case someone else has to rummage through your pack to search for it. (There are no scissors in the kit because I have these on my knife.)

For a larger kit I add the following:

6-inch-by-4-inch sterile ambulance dressing for major bleeding
2 sterile lint dressings for severe bleeding
7-inch elastic net to hold a dressing on a head wound
Extra antiseptic wipes
A second sheet of 2nd Skin
Triangular bandage for arm fracture/shoulder dislocation
4 safety pins
4-inch-by-4-inch sterile non-adhesive dressing for burns
10 extra painkillers

On long walks in remote country I also carry prescription antibiotics in case of illness or infection, though some physicians would not recommend this. If you need personal medication, it will have to be added to the kit, as well, of course. Such medicines don't last forever, though—be aware of expiration dates.

Groups need to carry larger, more comprehensive kits. The one I take when I'm leading ski tours weighs 24 ounces, though the weight can be shared. A plastic food storage container prevents a large first aid kit from being crushed. Nylon pouches are lighter, however, and are suitable for the smaller kits.

Tooth Care

If your teeth, like mine, are more metal than enamel, you should have a checkup immediately before a long trip and carry an emergency temporary dental kit on your trip. Tooth care kits contain mirror, multi-purpose tools, spatula, mixing tray, dental cement, catalyst, and instructions. They weigh around 1 ounce.

Wash Kit

There are two schools of thought regarding washing on the trail. One says "little or never." The other, in the words of Hugh Westacott in *The Walker's Handbook,* says, "before retiring for the night, and whatever the weather, the backpacker should strip off and thoroughly sponge the body from head to foot." (The very thought makes me shudder, which tells you which approach I endorse.)

It's surprising how long you can go without washing; I managed 23 days in the High Sierra during the Pacific Crest Trail walk. When every drop of water you use has to be produced laboriously by melting snow, washing becomes unimportant. On the other hand, personal hygiene suggests a minimum degree of cleanliness. In

A solo wash kit with sunscreen, one-use flannel/towel for "dry" washing, toothpaste and brush, soap.

particular, hands should be washed after going to the toilet; I usually manage to rinse my face most days as well, however cold. When it's cool, I save more thorough washings for when I get home or, on long trips, for a shower in a motel or campground. In hot weather I wash more often, if only to stay cool. Waterbags hung from a tree make good showers—if you leave the bag in the sun for a few hours beforehand, the water will be surprisingly warm.

I never used to carry soap, because even the biodegradable versions shouldn't be allowed to enter wilderness waters. However, proper hand washing is essential in a group to avoid passing stomach bugs, and the latest research suggests that solo hikers should do so, as well, to avoid the risk of getting giardiasis. There are several phosphate-free, biodegradable soaps available, including Coghlan's Sportsman's Soap, which comes in small squeeze tubes weighing an ounce; and Campsuds, which comes in 2- and 4-fluid-ounce plastic bottles. I try to use as little soap as possible, and I dispose of the wash water at least

200 feet from any lake or stream. There is now a No-Rinse Shampoo or Body Bath available in 2- and 8-ounce bottles. As the name suggests, no rinsing is necessary. I haven't tried these products yet, but I intend to.

Deodorants, cleansers, and other cosmetics have no place in the wilderness—leave them at home. However, antiseptic wipes are useful for hand and face washing when water is scarce, as long as you carry them out after use. I always carry them on winter trips. I don't carry a cotton washcloth or towel, either; both are heavy and slow to dry. A bandanna does for the former; a piece of clothing for the latter. Pile jackets make particularly good towels, and I use one after a shower at a campground. If you don't fancy using clothing to dry yourself, there are small, light pack towels available. In hot, dry areas I have recently carried the pre-moistened 12-inch-by-12-inch Shower 'n' Towel sheets—with these you can have a refreshing and cleansing "wash" without water. They weigh an ounce each.

My usual wash kit consists of a toothbrush,

a small tube of toothpaste, a couple of Shower 'n' Towel sheets, soap or antiseptic wipes, and a comb. The kit weighs 2 ounces in its Ziploc bag. Like soap, toothpaste should be deposited a long way from water. Biodegradable toothpastes are available. I carry a comb so that I can attempt to look presentable when I go into a town. Women, and men with beards, don't need to think about shaving gear, nor do those who cease their normal shaving habits while in the wilderness. (Men who do want to shave may be interested in the tiny, battery-powered travel shavers, such as Braun's Minishaver, which runs on two AA batteries.)

Biting Insects

If you are unprepared, swarms of mosquitoes or no-see-ums literally can drive you crazy in certain areas during the summer. I've yet to meet anyone immune to them, though sensitivity varies. Camping in breezy places, away from wet areas, is one way to minimize insect problems, though it's often not possible. Insects may be less of a problem when you're walking, but the moment you stop they'll appear in swarms.

Insect repellent and clothing are your main defenses. You can cover up with tightly woven, light-colored clothing (dark colors apparently attract some insects), and fasten wrist and ankle cuffs tightly. A head net (cotton mesh, 1 ounce) over a brimmed hat, and smaller nets on your hands help, too. These nets are the only defense I've found against black flies, which seem immune to repellents. Clothing made from no-see-um netting is available, but I've never used any.

Walking in long clothing in the heat is oppressive, and you won't want to keep your head and hands covered in netting all the time, so repellent is essential. The most effective one is diethylmethyltoluamide (DEET), the active ingredient in most insect repellents. Well-known brands include Muskol, Cutters, Ben's 100, Jungle Juice, Repel, and Apica. Small bottles weigh about an ounce. Creams are the easiest to apply, but liquids go farther. DEET repels most biting insects, including ticks.

Unfortunately, DEET is not very good for you—it is absorbed through the skin into the bloodstream and is toxic. Some people react badly to it almost immediately. *It shouldn't be used at all by children or for long periods by adults.* I never use 100 percent DEET. If I do use it at all it's in a 15 to 35 percent dilution, which is just as effective as the 100 percent concentration. A way to keep DEET off your skin is to apply it to clothing. I've found that repellent on the rim of a hat is good for keeping insects off my face. DEET will react with plastics, so keep it well away from pocketknife handles, cameras, and the like.

Non-DEET alternatives include Spectrum Repellent—a mix of cinnamon, clove, eucalyptus, lemon, thyme, and sandalwood in a coconut- and vegetable-oil base; and oil of citronella, a traditional insect repellent that's making a reappearance in the light of the warnings about DEET. Natrapel is one brand. Other remedies include massive doses of vitamin B, or eating lots of garlic. I cannot vouch for these; however, I know one person who crushes garlic and smears the juice on his skin, which, he says, keeps Scottish no-see-ums at bay.

My experience with various non-DEET repellents is that they don't last as long as DEET-based ones, and some hardly work at all. I shall persevere, however, because I really don't like the idea of putting a chemical on my skin that melts plastics.

In an enclosed space such as a tent vestibule, or perhaps under a tarp if it's calm, burning a mosquito coil may do the job. On a walk through the Yukon, I used to light a coil at rest stops and found that even in the open it kept mosquitoes away. Citronella candles are also available, but these are much heavier than coils. Insects are at their worst before dark, during long, light summer evenings. Twelve mosquito coils, each lasting eight to 10 hours, with holder, weigh 7 ounces.

When I must contend with no-see-ums or mosquitoes, I pitch the tent as fast as possible, fill my waterbag, climb in the tent, zip the door shut, light a mosquito coil, and stay there until dawn. No-see-ums will enter by the thousands under a fly sheet if no coil is burning, so I set up a coil last thing at night, and then sleep with the insect-netting inner door shut. By dawn, the inner door is often black with hungry no-see-ums, and the vestibule is swarming with them. I unzip a corner of the netting, reach a hand out, strike a match, and light the coil. Then I retreat and close the netting again. Within five minutes most of the insects will be dead, and I can open the inner door and have breakfast in peace. I keep the coil burning until I leave the tent. The tent often becomes hot and stuffy, and it stinks of burnt coil, but it's better than being bitten or having to eat breakfast while running around in circles, which I've seen others do. Even if you douse yourself with repellent, the no-see-ums will make your skin and scalp itch maddeningly by crawling over any exposed flesh and in your hair, even though they won't bite.

Ticks usually are no more than an irritant, but they can transmit Rocky Mountain spotted fever (found mainly in the East, despite the name) and Lyme disease. Luckily, both can be cured with timely treatment. Symptoms of the Rocky Mountain spotted fever, which include the sudden onset of fever, chills, headache, and muscle ache, general fatigue, and a loss of appetite, begin to appear two to 14 days after a bite. A rash will develop within two to five days, beginning first on wrists, hands, ankles, and feet. If untreated, the disease lasts for a couple of weeks and is fatal in 20 to 30 percent of cases, depending on one's age.

Lyme disease also appears a few days to a few weeks after a bite, and usually involves a circular red rash, though not always. It isn't fatal, but if not treated can recur and lead to bizarre symptoms and severe, crippling arthritis years later.

A more common, though less-serious tick-borne illness is Colorado tick fever, which appears four to six days after the tick bite. Symptoms are fever, headache, chills, and aching. Your eyes may feel extra sensitive to light. The illness lasts, on and off, for about a week. There is no specific cure, but most victims recover completely.

A sensible precaution is to check for ticks when you are in areas where they occur (local knowledge is useful here), and when you are walking in tick season, usually late spring and early summer. Ticks crawling on your body can be detached and crushed. *Don't twist or burn embedded ticks,* because the mouth parts will remain in the wound and could cause infection. At night, body searches usually locate most unattached ticks. (Searches work better when two people "groom" each other.) REI offers a Tick Kit consisting of a magnifier, curved tweezers, antiseptic swabs, and instructions; it weighs 2 ounces.

Bee and wasp stings can be very painful. There are various remedies. Sting Eze is a liquid antihistamine available in a 2-ounce bottle; antihistamines also come in tablet form. (Use antihistamines, however, only when there are signs of an allergic reaction, such as hives, wheezing, or facial swelling.) REI offers a Sting-X-Tractor Kit containing a suction venom extractor. I've no idea if it works. People who have adverse reactions to stings should carry medication.

Sunscreen

Protecting your skin against sunburn is *a necessity*—sunburned shoulders are agony under a pack, and a peeling nose also can be very painful. In the long run, over-exposure increases the risk of skin cancer. To minimize burning, sunscreen should be used on exposed skin whenever you are in sunlight. (Don't forget your feet if you're wearing sports sandals without socks.)

All sunscreens have a sun protection factor (SPF) number; the higher the SPF, the more protection. SPFs of 15 and above are recommended for high altitudes, where ultraviolet light (the part of the spectrum that burns) is stronger. Ultraviolet light increases in intensity 4 percent for every 1,000 feet of altitude, according to some reports. I burn easily, so I apply an SPF 10 or 12 sunscreen several times a day. A 3½-ounce tube lasts me about a week during consistently sunny weather. Snow reflects sunlight, so all exposed skin, including under your chin and around your nostrils, needs a sunscreen when you are out in snow, especially above 6,000 feet. Brimmed and peaked hats help shade the face and cut the need for sunscreen. The best sunscreens are creamy rather than greasy, and don't wash off in sweat—at least not quickly.

If you get sunburned, there are various creams and lotions that help reduce the suffering, but it's best to avoid the cause in the first place. I don't carry any sunburn treatment.

Lip Balm

Lips can suffer from the drying effects of the wind as well as sunburn, and they can crack badly in very cold conditions, so a tube of lip balm is well worth its weight. Lip balms are sold at drugstores, and even food markets.

They weigh only a few ounces, yet can save days of pain.

Sunglasses

Most of the time I don't wear sunglasses, except during snow travel, when sunglasses are *essential* to prevent *corneal burning,* a very painful condition known as *snow blindness.* This can occur even when the sun isn't bright, as I learned on a day of thin mist in the Norwegian mountains. Because visibility was so poor and wearing sunglasses made it worse, I didn't wear them, but skied all day straining to see ahead. Although I didn't suffer complete snow blindness, my eyes became sore and itchy; by evening I was seeing double, and my eyes were in pain except when closed. Luckily, it was the last day of my trip; otherwise, I would have had to rest for at least a couple of days to allow my eyes to recover. It's my guess that sunlight filtered through the fine mist and reflected off the snow.

The main requirement of sunglasses is that they cut out ultraviolet light, which most specialty ones do. Glass lenses are scratch resistant; polycarbonate lenses weigh less. Names of quality glasses include Bollé, Vuarnet, Ray-Ban, Cébé, Julbo, and Oakley. For snow use, the glacier-type glasses with side shields are good—necessary at high altitudes—but prone to fogging. I have two pairs of Bollé glacier glasses, one with gray lenses for bright light, and one with amber lenses for hazy conditions. They each weigh 1.9 ounces with cases. I always carry two pairs on trips in snow because losing or breaking a pair could be serious. I also have a very light (1 ounce) pair of simple sunglasses that I carry in summer if I might encounter snow, pale sand, or rock. I rarely wear them, however.

People who wear prescription glasses all the time tell me fogging can be a real aggravation, especially when one works up a sweat. They say anti-fogging products, such as Speedo's, work fine. I expect they work on sunglasses as well.

Keeping glasses on, especially when skiing, also can be a problem. The answer is to have a loop that goes around your head or neck. Glacier glasses often come with these, but various straps that slip over earpieces are available. These include Croakies, Chums, and I-Ties; I've used Croakies, and they work well.

In severe blizzard conditions, some people prefer goggles rather than glasses. I used to carry a pair of good-quality Alpine ski goggles (32 ounces) with an amber double lens, which improves visibility in haze. The foam mesh vents above and below the lens reduce fogging, though the goggles suffer this more than glacier glasses. A wide, elasticized, adjustable headband plus thick soft foam around the rim make them comfortable to wear. If necessary, goggles can be worn over a hat or hood, and pushed down around the neck when not needed, which is less risky than pushing them up on the forehead and having them fall off. Beware of cheap goggles; Bollé, Jones, Cébé, Smith, and Scott have good reputations.

Sanitation

All too often, every rock within a few hundred yards of a popular campsite sprouts ragged pink and white toilet paper from around its edges. Aside from turning beautiful places into sordid outdoor privies, this creates a health hazard—feces pollute. The problem stems from the sheer number of people outdoors, but unthinking toilet siting and waste disposal contribute to it. As a result, many land-management agencies provide outhouses and deep toilet pits at popular destinations—usually, but not always, backcountry campgrounds. Mount Whitney, the

highest peak in the lower 48 states, has one on its summit.

Outhouses are obtrusive and detract from the "feeling" of wilderness. Careful sanitation techniques can ensure that no more need to be built. Good methods prevent water contamination, speed decomposition, and shield waste from contact with humans and animals. Anyone concerned with minimizing impact on the wilderness should read *Soft Paths,* by Bruce Hampton and David Cole (Stackpole Books), from which my comments are derived.

There is no best method for sanitary waste disposal, but there are a number of options—the one you adopt depends on the area. You can prevent water contamination by always defecating at least 200 yards from any water. Heading uphill is usually a good way to achieve this. The best way to achieve rapid decomposition is to leave waste on the surface, where the sun and air soon break it down. (The once-prevalent practice of burying feces a few inches below the surface to hasten decomposition has been shown to be wrong—buried feces can last a very long time.)

The current recommendation is to practice surface deposition in little-used areas, well away from anywhere likely to be visited by other people, and to smear feces around with a rock or stick to maximize exposure to the sun and air. In popular areas, small, individual "catholes" should be dug about 4 inches deep (this is the level at which microorganisms that break up organic waste are most numerous). After you've finished, feces should be broken up with a stick and mixed with the soil. The hole should be filled and camouflaged. A small plastic trowel is useful for this; I carry one that weighs 1½ ounces in a pack pocket. These can and do break, however, so if weight isn't a problem a small stainless steel folding shovel is a better choice. These weigh around 6 ounces. Large groups should not dig big latrines unless there are limited cathole sites or the group is staying at a site for a long period. The idea is to *disperse* rather than concentrate waste.

There remains the problem of toilet paper. I use a standard white roll with the cardboard tube removed—3½ ounces when full. (Avoid colored paper because the dyes pollute water.) Although toilet paper seems fragile, it is amazingly resilient, lasting far longer than feces, and it shouldn't be left to decorate the wilderness. You have two options. You can burn it (I keep a box of matches in the same plastic bag as my toilet paper for this purpose). This is not an option when there is any fire risk. If you have a campfire, bring your paper bag and burn it there. If you can't burn it, then—unpleasant though it may seem—you should pack it out in a sealed plastic bag. In some areas where campfires are banned, such as Grand Canyon National Park, this is required. In fact, as long as it's kept sealed, the paper doesn't smell. The paper should be disposed of in a toilet; the plastic bag in a garbage can. Women also should pack out used tampons unless these can be burned, which requires a very hot fire. If tampons are buried, animals will dig them up. More specific advice for women, plus a lot of good general advice on backcountry toilet practices, can be found in Kathleen Meyer's humorous book, *How to Shit in the Woods* (Ten Speed Press).

For those prepared to try them, natural alternatives to toilet paper include sand, grass, large leaves, and even snow. The last, I can assure you, is less unpleasant than it sounds.

Finally, a note on urination. I wouldn't presume to advise women on this topic, but refer them to Meyer's book. For men, this is usually simple, but not when you wake in the middle of a cold, stormy night and are faced with crawling out of your sleeping bag, donning clothes, and venturing out into the wet and wind. The answer is to kneel in the tent and urinate into a wide-mouthed plastic bottle. With practice, you can do this in a very short time while half-awake. (I've been told there are devices designed to allow women to do this, as well.) I use a cheap, plastic, pint bottle (2 ounces) with a green screw top, which clearly distinguishes it from my water bottle. I carry it mainly in winter and spring. A pee-bottle could also be useful in summer, when biting insects are around, since otherwise you would have to get dressed before leaving the tent. (Not to do so is to invite disaster—when I was leading a course in the Scottish Highlands, one of the students left the tent one night clad in just a T-shirt, despite warnings. He was out less than a minute, but in the morning he emerged totally covered with midge bites from the waist down.)

EQUIPMENT MAINTENANCE AND REPAIR

It's an unusual trip when something doesn't need repairing, or at least tinkering, so I always carry a small repair kit in a stuff sack. Although the contents vary from trip to trip, the weight hovers around 4 ounces. Repair kits for specific items such as the stove and the Therm-a-Rest travel in this bag, as do backup items such as Lifeboat Matches.

The most-used item in the kit is the waterproof, adhesive-backed, ripstop nylon tape, which patches everything from clothing to fly sheets. Four strips of tape come stapled onto a card. The lot measures 9 by 3 inches and weighs about an ounce. I use Coghlan's, but many companies make similar products. When applying a patch, round off the edges so it won't peel off, and patch both sides of the hole if possible. Large holes and tears should be reinforced with stitching around the edges, or with a bigger patch. Stitch holes should be coated with glue to stop fraying or to prevent down from escaping from down-filled items. I carry either a small tube of seam seal or some sort of epoxy for this purpose, or I use the tube that comes with the Therm-a-Rest repair kit.

An alternative to sticky ripstop tape is duct tape, the mainstay of many repair kits—some even recommend it for blisters. I carry strips of duct tape and have used it to hold together cracked pack frames, split ski tips, broken tent poles, and other items. On clothing, sleeping bags, and tent fabrics, however, I find sticky nylon tape better because it is more flexible and stays on longer. It also looks better.

I carry non-adhesive pieces of nylon in case a major repair is more than the tape can handle. Since repair swatches often come with tents and packs, I've built up a collection from which I usually take two or three sheets of different weights, including a non-coated one for inner tent repair; the biggest swatch measures 12 by 18 inches. They have a combined weight of 1 ounce.

My sewing kit used to consist of needles and thread in an old film canister, along with a few spare replacement buttons. A few years ago I discovered the Black Diamond Expedition sewing kit, which contains a sewing awl, two heavy-duty sewing machine needles, two buttons, two safety pins, a cotter pin (for rethreading drawcords), two ordinary sewing needles and several weights of strong thread, all packed with instructions into a neat leather pouch. The total weight is only 1½ ounces, yet with this kit you can repair everything from packs to pants. Unfortunately, it's no longer made, but you may still find it in an outdoor store.

Also in the repair bag goes a selection of rubber bands. These have many obvious uses, and some not so obvious. A length of shock cord tied in a loop makes an extra-strong rubber band. Any detachable pack straps not in use also end up in the repair bag—perhaps "oddities bag" would be a better name.

For details of how to repair all sorts of outdoor gear see Annie Getchell's excellent book, *The Essential Outdoor Gear Manual* (Ragged Mountain Press).

Nylon Cord

The final item in the repair bag—nylon cord—deserves a section of its own because it's the most important; in fact, it's essential. The type I use is *parachute cord,* which comes in 50-foot lengths with a breaking strength of 350 pounds at a per-hank weight of 4 ounces. I always carry one length on short walks, two on long walks and in bear country. I've used it for ridgelines and guylines for a tarp, extra tent guyline, for bear-bagging food, spare boot laces, clothesline, a strap for attaching items to pack (wet socks, crampons, ice ax), a swami belt for use with a carabiner and rope for river crossings, lashing

---

Wolves

The river is a half mile or so away. I set off toward it to collect water as dusk falls. In the middle of an expansive meadow I suddenly sense that I am watched. Looking toward the forest, I freeze with a mixture of awe, excitement, and fear. A few hundred yards away, on the fringe of the timber, a pack of wolves is watching me. I count six, some of them pale gray, others almost black. After a few seconds they begin to move off slowly in single file, one of them always stationary, watching. When that one falls to the rear, another stops and the pack continues. Eventually they disappear. I do not know how long I have been holding my breath.

for a temporary repair to broken pack frame, lowering a pack down or pulling it up short steep cliffs or slopes (with the cord fed around my back, a tree, or a rock—not hand-over-hand), underfoot gaiter cords, and hat chin strap. The ends of cut nylon cord must be fused with heat, or they'll fray.

KNIFE

Some sort of knife is necessary outdoors. You don't need a large, heavy sheath or a "survival" knife for most purposes; Swiss Army knives have become the standard backpacking tools, and rightly so, but this success has fostered inferior imitations. The only genuine brands are Wenger and Victorinox. They aren't just knives—they are small tool kits.

The more complex ones are too heavy and bulky to be comfortably carried in a trouser pocket. For years I used the Victorinox Spartan, which weighs 2½ ounces and has two blades, a can opener/screwdriver, a bottle opener/screwdriver, a corkscrew, and a reamer. However, following Ray Jardine's example, I switched to the tiny Victorinox Classic, which weighs 0.7 ounce and has a small blade, a file/screwdriver, scissors, tweezers, and toothpick. I've been amazed to discover that it will do everything I want from a knife. The scissors replace the ones I used to carry in my first aid kit, and are adequate for cutting fingernails as well as cord.

I have sometimes carried a 7½-inch, folding French Opinel knife with wooden handle and carbon steel, locking single blade. It weighs just 1¾ ounces, and the blade holds an edge better than the stainless steel Swiss Army ones, though it does eventually discolor.

Swiss Army knives are now available with locking blades, but the blades are larger, so the knife weighs more. The basic Adventurer with knife blade, can opener/screwdriver, bottle opener/screwdriver, Phillips screwdriver, and reamer plus tweezers and toothpick weighs 4½ ounces, which is more than the combined weight of the Spartan and the Opinel. There are other small knives and folding tool kits around. Gerber, Tekna, and Leatherman are some of the quality ones, but there are so many Swiss Army models that every backpacker should be able to find one to suit his or her needs.

Keeping your knife blades sharp is important. I don't carry a sharpener, however, because the best place to do this is at home.

IN CASE OF EMERGENCY

You need to consider how to deal with possible emergencies on every trip, and certain ventures, particularly to remote country, snowbound mountains, and where rivers or steep, rocky terrain may have to be crossed require specialty items. Prepackaged, compact survival kits are available, but these always seem to contain some items I don't want and duplicate others I carry anyway. Whenever I walk away from camp, I always take a whistle, compass, map, headlamp, water bottle, first aid kit, knife, matches, and a few snacks with me in my fanny pack. On longer side trips, perhaps lasting all day, I take along the pack itself, with spare clothing, bivy bag, and more food.

Signaling

If you are injured or become seriously ill in the wilderness, you need to be able to alert other people and rescuers to your whereabouts. Displaying a bright item of clothing or gear is one way to do this. At night, your headlamp or flashlight can be used for sending signals. Six regular flashes, a pause, then six more flashes is the international distress signal. Noise can bring help, too, and I always carry a plastic whistle in a pocket or my fanny pack for this purpose. (My current one is a Storm Whistle, from the All-Weather Whistle Company of St. Louis, which is said to be one of the loudest available, reaching almost 95 decibels—and is audible under water. It weighs 0.8 ounce. I've never used it to signal distress, but it has come in handy for warning bears of my presence.) Again, six blasts, pause, six blasts should be used when calling for help.

In most remote areas, most initial searches are made by aircraft, so you need to be seen from above and from afar. A fire, especially with wet vegetation added, should create enough smoke to attract attention. Ideally, three fires should be lit in the form of a triangle, an internationally recognized distress signal. Flares are quicker and simpler to use, and there are various packs available. I've never carried flares, but they would have been a reassurance at times during the Canadian Rockies and Yukon walks, and I intend to take some on my next remote wilderness walk. Carrying several small flares seems to make more sense than one big one; packs of six to eight waterproof mini flares with a projector pen for one-handed operation weigh only 8 ounces or so. The flares reach a height of around 250 feet and last six seconds. Larger flares last longer, but unless you carry several of them, you have only one chance to draw attention to your plight.

The alternative to flares is a strobe light, which I'd always thought of as big and heavy until I discovered the waterproof Medik C.I. emergency strobe, which sends out a light flash every second that is visible for 3 miles. It weighs only 8 ounces, including the D battery that powers it, and is another likely addition to my pack for my next walk in remote country.

Mirrors can be used for signaling, though obviously only in sunlight. However, any shiny object, such as aluminum foil (stove wind screens), a polished pan base, a watch face, a camera lens, or even a knife blade could be used instead. Smoke and flares are likely to be more effective, though.

If you are in open terrain and have no other signal devices, spreading light- and bright-colored clothing and gear out on the ground could help rescuers locate you. I always carry at least one yellow or orange item for this purpose.

Cellular Phones

Although unusual, cellular phones are starting to appear in the wilderness. Many backpackers feel that phones have no place in the backcountry, but the likelihood is that more and more hikers will carry them as service becomes more accessible. Though their usefulness in an emergency is undeniable, there already have been problems with people calling for help for what can only be regarded as frivolous reasons—such as feeling thirsty. It also seems that some people think the phones are a substitute for wilderness skills—if you get lost, you can just pick up the phone. This is irresponsible. Relying on a phone is unwise: they can break, batteries can fade, not all areas are covered, and they may not work deep in canyons even in areas of good reception.

Rescue Procedures

If you are alone and suffer an immobilizing injury, all you can do is make yourself as comfortable as possible, send out signals, and hope someone will respond. In popular areas and on trails, attracting attention shouldn't be too difficult, but in less-frequented places and when traveling cross-country you may be totally dependent on those who have details of your route to report you missing when you don't check in as arranged.

If you are in a group, someone can be sent for help if the group can't manage together. It is important that whoever goes has all the necessary information: the location of the injured person(s), relevant compass bearings, details of local features that may help rescuers find the place, the nature of the terrain, the time of the accident, a description of the injuries, and the size and experience of the group. This should be written down so that important details aren't forgotten or distorted. Once out of the wilderness, the messenger should contact the local law enforcement official, park or forest service office, or other organization that can arrange a rescue.

In North America, there are volunteer mountain rescue teams made up of locals who come out to help people, often at great personal risk. (If you need their services, make a generous donation to the organization afterward; they are not government funded.) Other areas, such as the Alps and the Pyrenees, use professional rescue teams and charge high fees. If you are going to such an area, take out *mountain rescue insurance*. For more on mountain rescue, see Chapter 17 of *Mountaineering: The Freedom of the Hills*.

Rope

Roped climbing is for mountaineers. However, there are situations when a backpacker needs a short length of rope when crossing deep, fast-flowing rivers or scrambling steep, rocky slopes. Full-weight climbing rope isn't necessary; I've found ¼-inch line with a breaking test of 2,200 to 3,400 pounds perfectly adequate. A 60- to 65-foot length (the shortest that's much use) weighs 20 to 26 ounces.

Ropes need proper care. They should be stored out of direct sunlight and away from chemicals. A car seat or trunk is not a good place to keep ropes. Even with minimum use and careful storage, ropes deteriorate and should be replaced every four or five years.

Snow Shovel

In deep snow, a shovel is both an emergency tool and a functional item. The emergency uses range from digging a shelter to digging out avalanche victims. More mundane uses are for leveling out tent platforms, digging out buried tents, clearing snow from doorways, digging through snow to running water, collecting snow for water, serving as a stove platform, and many other purposes. I find a snow shovel essential in snowbound terrain. They come with either plastic or metal blades, but most plastic blades won't cut through hard-packed snow or ice. There are many models available, usually with folding blades and weights from 20 to 25 ounces. Shovel blades that attach to ice axes are lighter, but they only work if you carry an ax, which I don't always do.

Fishing Tackle

I once carried a length of fishing line and a few hooks and weights on a deep wilderness trip, in case I ran out of food. I duly ran short of food, and on several nights put out a line with baited hooks. On each successive morning I pulled it in empty. Experienced anglers probably would have more success, and if you're one, I'm sure it's worthwhile to take some lightweight fishing tackle, depending on where you're headed.

Navigation

Route finding as a skill is discussed in the next chapter, and it therefore makes sense to leave any detailed discussion of equipment until then. Here I will mention the effect navigation may have on your load. On any trip a compass and a map, weighing between 1 and 4 ounces, will be the minimum gear you'll need. On most trips, more than one map will be needed, and you also may have to carry a trail guide. On trips of a fortnight and longer, I usually end up with 25 to 35 ounces of maps and guides. In remote, trailless country, you might want a GPS receiver, which adds another 8 to 16 ounces. The next chapter contains details of these.

OFFICE

I carry writing materials and paper on trips, so I need to keep them somewhere, both for protection and convenience. There are many different pouches available; most are made of nylon, contain several compartments, and are designed to be fastened to pack hipbelts or shoulder straps. Weights range from a few ounces to a pound and more. I currently use a very simple pouch with just two compartments and a Velcro-closed flap that weighs 2 ounces.

Writing Paper and Notebooks

On trips of more than a week, I send postcards to family and friends, buying them at supply points. I often carry a few between post boxes, writing in camp at night. Many other backpackers do likewise. On long trips, I also carry airmail paper and envelopes. My correspondence materials never weigh more than 3½ ounces.

Keeping a journal on a walk is perhaps the best way of ensuring you will remember what it was like. I've kept one for each of my walks, long before I began writing for anyone other than myself, and I can spend hours reliving a trip I'd almost forgotten by reading them. In order to record as much as possible, I try to write in my journal every day, often making a few notes over breakfast and more during the evening. This is

Chair kits can make camping luxurious, but they do add unnecessary weight.

difficult enough to do on solo trips; when I'm with companions, I'm lucky if I write in it every other day.

There are many lightweight notebooks around, many with tear-out pages, but I prefer something more durable. Since the 1970s, I've used weather-resistant oilskin notebooks, with easily identifiable black covers. In my notebook I also keep my route plan, addresses of people at home and people I meet along the way, lists of how far I go each day and where I camp, reminders of bus and train times, and any other information I may need or collect along the way. Looking at my Canadian Rockies journal, I see I kept records of my resting pulse rate (which ranged between 44 and 56), and how much fuel my stove used (10 to 14 days per quart). I also made shopping lists and, toward the end, a calendar on which I crossed off the days. (There was an ulterior motive for this—buses at the finish ran only three times a week.) Such trivia may not seem worth recording, but for me they bring back the reality of a trip very strongly.

I always carry at least two pens with waterproof ink in case my notebook gets wet. They weigh a mere 1 ounce.

Documents and Papers

The number of documents you need to carry on a trip can amount to quite a collection, though they never weigh more than an ounce. On trips close to home, you may need none. On any trip abroad, you'll need your passport and insurance documents, and you'll probably end up carrying your airline or other tickets as well. It's useful to carry some form of identification in case of emergency; I usually take my driver's license. While walking I keep my papers sealed in a plastic bag in the recesses of my "office." Trail permits, if required, also go in a plastic bag, but they often get carried in a pocket or my fanny pack

so they're ready when I'm asked for them, as I have been in both Yosemite and Grand Canyon National Parks in recent years.

Wallet and Money

Small wallets weigh so little that I carry mine with me, after removing the extra clutter it somehow generates. In the wilderness, money serves no purpose, and on short trips, when I am never far from home, I carry no more than I need for the return journey. On long trips money is essential for food, but also perhaps for accommodation, the laundromat, and postage. I try not to carry loose coins, which are relatively heavy, except for phone change. Notes in small denominations are the best form of cash to carry, since in remote places there may be no way to change large bills. I also carry a credit card, because these are more widely accepted than traveler's checks, which I no longer bother with.

Watch

I'm often tempted to leave my watch at home, but unfortunately a watch has its uses, even in the wilderness. It's helpful to know how many daylight hours are left when you must decide whether to stop at a good campsite or push on. When the sun's visible, you can estimate time fairly accurately, but on dull, overcast days it's almost impossible. A watch with a built-in calendar also helps keep track of the days, something I find confusing on long trips. Checking your watch when you stop for a break may also help get you moving again, especially when you realize that the intended "couple of minutes" has somehow become a half hour. If your watch has an alarm, you can set it to wake you up for morning starts. These days I carry a wrist altimeter, the Avocet Vertech, that also tells the time and date and has an alarm (though the makers stress that it isn't a watch).

The Avocet Vertech altimeter.

BINOCULARS

Few walkers carry binoculars, which surprises me. They're practical for scouting the trail or the country ahead, and for checking out whether that dark lump under the tree you're approaching is a mossy stump or a bear. I use mine regularly, and they've often prevented me from

taking a route that would have led to a dead end or an obstacle. In Glacier National Park, for example, I took a lower route after seeing that the main trail was banked with steep, soft snow where it cut around the side of a high cliff. The avalanche danger was high then, and the snow looked difficult to cross safely, so we stayed in the forest. Without the binoculars, we would have had to double back after following the trail to the snowbank. I also often use binoculars to survey a river valley for possible fords.

Aside from functional uses, binoculars open up the world of birds and wildlife to the walker. Whether it's otters playing in a lake, a grizzly rooting through a meadow, or an eagle soaring overhead, binoculars allow you to watch wild creatures from a safe distance (both for you and for them).

The last decade has witnessed the development of a wealth of ultra-lightweight mini binoculars, most of which are ideal for backpacking. Mine are an 8-power Sirius with a 21 mm objective — at 5½ ounces the lightest I could find. They're so small I carry them in a pocket or my fanny pack. Such glasses aren't as good as full-spectrum ones, and the light-gathering power is likewise compromised. However, they are so light that I am never tempted to leave them at home. There are many good mini binoculars; the heaviest weigh 12 ounces.

PHOTOGRAPHY

Taking photographs is probably the most popular non-essential backpacking activity. People like to have a visual record of their trips. But those who simply point the camera and shoot every pretty scene regardless of the light or viewpoint may reduce it to a quick postcard view. Those who take time and care to study the details of a place in order to make the best picture, the one that most reflects how they see it, may share my feeling that this process helps them achieve a deeper appreciation of the wilderness.

Anyone wanting to pursue the subject of wilderness photography further will probably learn a lot from Galen Rowell's marvelous *Mountain Light: In Search of the Dynamic Landscape* (Sierra Club Books), and from *Outdoor Photographer* magazine.

Photography is about seeing, not equipment. No amount of expensive gear will make someone a good photographer. That said, the more ambitious you become, the more gear you end up carrying. On the Canadian Rockies, Yukon, and Scandinavian mountain walks, I carried 9 pounds of cameras and accessories, which seems an enormous amount to the non-photographer. I have, however, become something of a professional over the years, and I go on most walks knowing that I have to come back with a set of pictures. Most people could take less camera equipment than I do just by leaving behind the second camera I take as a backup in case my main one breaks.

Cameras

There are two choices for packable cameras: A small, lightweight compact ("point and shoot"), or a single lens reflex (SLR) with interchangeable lenses. Compacts now come with a variety of lens choices, and are usually fully automatic, including auto focus. Weights run from 5 or 6 ounces to 1½ pounds, heavier than some SLRs. For someone who has no interest in photography but would like to take pictures, the most basic compact is ideal.

However, even the best compacts cannot match an SLR for versatility. There are two reasons for this. The main one is that SLRs take interchangeable lenses, so focal lengths are limited only by what you can carry. Secondly, with an SLR you look directly through the lens, which helps with composition.

My main camera for more than a decade has been an SLR. On long walks, I carry a second body as a backup; on shorter trips, I take a compact.

There is a wide choice of SLRs, most of them of high quality. Choosing one is really a question of which features, price, and weight suit you. Top names are Canon, Nikon, Pentax, Minolta, Olympus, Yashica, and, if you have enough money, Leica.

One big problem with most cameras today is that they're totally dependent on batteries to operate the auto-focus, auto-exposure, motor-wind, and self-timer mechanisms. As with other battery-dependent accessories such as lights, always carry spares.

Lenses

There is no point in having an SLR unless you also have a selection of lenses. I carry a 24 mm wide angle, and 28 to 70 mm and 75 to 150 mm zooms. The first (weighing 8 ounces) is for wide-angle landscapes, the 28 to 70 zoom is my most useful lens, good for landscapes, portraits, and detail. The big zoom is for distant detail, portraits, and animal shots. I'd like a longer lens, but they generally weigh too much. I use zooms because they are lighter than the three or four fixed-focal-length lenses they replace, and they aid composition—wilderness pictures are often taken from positions you can't change, like the edge of cliffs and the sides of mountains.

Filters

These are the most overused items in photography, and I carry very few of them. I want the light and colors in my pictures to look natural. For protection and to cut out ultraviolet light,

I keep a skylight filter fitted to every lens. I also use a polarizer to cut glare and to darken blue skies. If the sky is bright and the land dark, I use a graduated neutral-density filter in a filter holder, and I sometimes use an orange filter with black-and-white film to bring out clouds. Each filter weighs about ¾ ounce with case.

Film

I nearly always take color transparency (slide) film because this works best for publications and slide shows. The ISO number of the film, its *speed,* is important. For fine detail and the best colors, 100 speed film is the fastest I use; Kodachrome, Ektachrome, Agfachrome, and Fujichrome are the main brands. I mostly use film with prepaid mailers so that I can send it home to be developed during a long walk—the results are waiting for me when I get back.

Individual rolls of film don't weigh much, but a half-dozen 36-exposure rolls with canisters weigh around 7 ounces. I average a roll a day.

Supports

In low light and with slow film (ISO 25 and 50), you need something to steady the camera. (As a rough guide for hand-held shooting, the shutter speed should approximate or be faster than the focal length of the lens. For example, a 28 mm lens shouldn't be hand held at slower than ⅟₃₀ second; a 200 mm lens no slower than ⅟₂₅₀.) A camera support can be as simple as propping your arms on a rock, bracing yourself against a tree, or even laying down.

There are alternatives to using natural supports: monopods, mini-tripods and clamps, and full-size tripods. I use them all. My Tracks walking staff has a screw hidden under the handle to which a ball-and-socket tripod head can be mounted, making it a monopod. I use this for wildlife photography when I don't have time to remove my pack and set up the tripod. There are many small tabletop tripods and clamps around, but the lightest I've seen is the REI Ultrapod (2 ounces), an ingenious little device that can be used as a tripod, and by using a Velcro strap, as a clamp. I sometimes use it on ski trips, strapping it to a pole. It's too light for long lenses, but works well with wide-angle ones.

I use a tripod most of the time, both for self-portraits and for low-light photography. The problem is finding a lightweight one that doesn't develop the shakes after minimal use. After destroying several cheap but lightweight models I finally settled on a 27½ ounce Gitzo 001 Loisir.

Protection and Carrying

You can protect your camera by carrying it in your pack, but you won't take many pictures that

Extra lenses can be carried in padded cases.

Padded camera bags protect against shocks and keep out rain, snow, and dust.

way. I like to carry a camera slung across my body so that I can access it quickly. But it's vulnerable there, so I generally keep it in a foam-padded, waterproof case. There are many such cases available from Tamrac, Lowe, Photoflex, and others. Weights of padded cases range from 3 ounces for compact cameras or wide-angle lenses, to 12 ounces for ones for SLRs with telephoto lenses. For carrying my cases and cameras around my neck and shoulders I use the broad, comfortable, stretch neoprene rubber straps (2½ ounces) from Op-Tech. Filters and film rolls travel in a small stuff sack that goes in the fanny pack or the top pocket of the pack.

Cleaning

I carry lens-cleaning cloths for removing marks from lenses, and a blower brush for puffing out the inside. But the dangers of damaging equipment in field conditions makes me keep cleaning and tinkering to an absolute minimum.

Recording

You may think that you'll remember the details of every photo you shoot, but you won't—unless you take very few pictures or have a phenomenal memory. You need some method of recording each roll of film or photo as it's shot. I keep a tiny notebook (½ ounce) and pen in a plastic bag in my fanny pack, and note down when and where I start and finish each roll, plus any particular details I want to remember about the pictures. To relate the film to the notes, I photograph this page on the last few frames.

ENTERTAINMENT

Reading Matter

Because I'm a book addict, I always carry at least one paperback on every walk. Too often I end up with several. There are three books that might find their way into your pack: trail guides, natural history guides about the country you're passing through, and ones for entertainment. On my 124-day Canadian Rockies walk, I read 36 books, an average of one every 3½ days—24 were fiction and 12 were nonfiction. This doesn't include an area guide that I carried all the way, parts of which I read several times, and a trail guide I carried on the first half of the walk.

Natural history guides are a problem because you usually need several if you want to identify trees, flowers, mammals, and birds in a given region. In a group, each member can carry a different volume, but the solo walker has to be selective. I usually carry the smallest bird and tree guides I can find, sometimes adding a flower guide if the weight can be kept down. I always look for a guide that covers everything, but sadly these are few. The best I've found is Ben Gadd's *Handbook of the Canadian Rockies,* which is a complete natural history field guide and also covers geology, history, weather, and much more. I wish other areas had such a comprehensive single-volume guide.

A map of the night sky that you can rotate to show the stars in position for each month is well worth carrying, if you're interested in such things. It weighs less than ¼ ounce and takes up no space. I don't use mine often, but when I do, I'm very glad I remembered to bring it.

Radios and Cassette Players

Tiny radios weighing in the 3- to 7-ounce range could be worth carrying if you grow bored with reading or need to rest your eyes. Himalayan mountaineers now regularly take portable stereos for use on the climb as well as in camp. I used to carry a radio now and then (on the pretext that it was for weather forecasts), but I rarely used it because, even in the tent, it cut me off

from the world I'd come to experience. Proponents of radios point out that books do the same, but to my mind they do not have the same effect. My opinion, however, should not prevent you from carrying a radio or portable tape player if you find it enjoyable. But please use headphones, because sounds carry in the quietness of the wilderness and not everyone shares your taste in music or noise. I remember coming off a high Pyrenean peak, my eyes set on a necklace of mountain tarns far below with green sward, ideal for camping—only to be greeted, while still a half mile away, by the tinkling sounds of music coming from the only tent I could see in the whole basin. Once down there, I found the sound permeated the whole area, so I pushed on, down into the next valley bottom to camp, much later than I'd wanted to, but in quiet.

Cards and Games

There are various games that groups can take along for entertainment, and, of course, you can make up your own, but a deck of cards is the most obvious lightweight entertainment to carry. You can buy miniature decks, though a standard one weighs just 3½ ounces. I've never carried cards, but a companion did on the ski crossing of the Columbia icefield in the Canadian Rockies, and we played many games during the four days we spent stormbound in the tents. Cards could be carried on solo trips for playing solitaire, though I can't imagine wanting to do so. A hill-walking book I read many years ago did recommend carrying a deck in case you became lost. Don't panic if this happens, the author recommended, just sit down and start playing solitaire, because some damn fool is then bound to pop up behind you and tell you which card to play next!

Thermometer

Few people carry these, but I'm fascinated by the temperature data I've collected over the years. My immediate finding, reinforced whenever I camp with others, is that it's never as cold as people think. Also, I've noted that you really do feel warmer when the temperature drops a few degrees below freezing and the humidity falls than when it's a few degrees above. On the Canadian Rockies walk, I recorded no temperatures below freezing during July and August and only three nights when they occurred in September; yet, by the middle of October, it was freezing hard every night. During the four days we spent stormbound on the Columbia icefield, the temperature in the tent ranged, astonishingly, from 28°F (−2°C) to 75°F (24°C), depending on whether we were cooking and whether the doors were open. Having such data gives me a reference for the temperatures to expect when I revisit an area, which helps with planning.

To entertain myself with such detail, I currently carry a metal-clad Minimum-Register mercury thermometer with an aluminum case, which weighs 1 ounce. There are also tiny mercury thermometers, with windchill charts on the reverse, attached to split rings for hanging off jacket and pack zippers. These come under a variety of labels, and their weight is negligible. They provide only a rough idea of temperature. My altimeter, the Avocet Vertech, has a thermometer on it, but it isn't accurate once the temperature drops much below freezing, and it can't tell you the maximum or minimum temperature.

CHAPTER NINE

On the Move: Skills and Hazards

Pushing on through rain and mud and sludgy snow, crossing many brown, boulder-choked torrents, wading, jumping, and wallowing in snow up to my shoulders was mountaineering of the most trying kind.

—*Travels in Alaska,* John Muir

Walking is very easy. Walking in the wilderness with a pack isn't quite so simple: You have to find your way, perhaps in dense mist or thick forest; cope with terrain, which may mean negotiating steep cliffs, loose scree, and snow; and you must deal with hazards ranging from extremes of weather to wild animals. Most wilderness walking, however, is relatively straightforward as long as you are reasonably fit, have a few basic skills, and know a little about weather and terrain.

FINDING THE WAY
Maps

Knowing how to read a map is a key wilderness skill, yet there are many walkers who can barely do so. I have one regular backpacking companion who has little understanding of maps and is quite happy to allow me to plan and lead. The only solo backpacking he's ever done was on a coastal footpath, where route finding consisted of keeping the sea to the same side. There are also some inland areas where trails are so well posted and trail guides so accurate that a map isn't needed. Even in such areas, though, you may turn blithely down an unmarked or unmaintained trail—not thinking about where you are until you realize that it's been too long since you've seen a trail marker. Without a map you are lost.

With a map, you plan walks, follow your route on the ground, locate water sources and possible campsites. But maps also can open an inspiring world—I can spend hours poring over a map, tracing possible routes, wondering how to connect a mountain tarn with a narrow notch, whether it's possible to follow a mountain ridge or if it will turn out to be a rocky edge that forces me to another route. A few months before writing this, I planned to link two regions in the Pyrenees, with no trails visible on the maps, via a high mountain pass. I was delighted when, despite a day of thick mist and rain, my route turned out to be possible—the untracked slopes of steep scree and small crags on the far side of the pass were navigable, with care, on foot.

Every map has a key. Using this to interpret the symbols, you can build a picture of what the terrain will be like. There are two types of maps: *planimetric* and *topographic.* The first represents features on the ground; the second the topography, or shape of the ground itself. Topographic maps use *contour lines,* which join together

Cross-country travel in steep, rocky terrain is slow and requires good route-finding skills.

less height than the contour interval won't show on the map). Some maps mark cliffs, others don't; check the key to see if you may encounter cliffs not shown on the map.

The patterns contour lines form represent the three-dimensional shapes of features. Once you can interpret them, you can tell what the hills, valleys, and ridges of an area are like, and plan accordingly.

The *scale* tells you how much ground is represented by a given distance on the map. The standard scale for USGS topo maps outside of Alaska is 1:24,000. These are known as *7.5-minute maps,* because of the area of latitude and longitude they cover. On a 1:24,000 map, 1 inch equals 24,000 inches on the ground, which works to roughly 2½ inches per mile. In Alaska, 1:62,500 maps—about 1 inch to the mile—are the norm. These *15-minute maps* are still available for some other areas, but are being replaced by 1:24,000 ones—a pity, since the scale is adequate for backpacking and each sheet covers a larger area. USGS topo maps, sometimes known as *quads* (from quadrangle), are the standard in the United States.

For most of the world, metric scales are standard, with 1:25,000 and 1:50,000 the most useful

points of equal elevation starting from sea level. Contour lines occur at given intervals, usually from 15 to 500 feet. Standard United States Geologic Survey (USGS) 1:24,000 maps have a contour interval of 40 feet. Metric intervals are starting to appear on maps. The latest Bureau of Land Management topo maps use a 50-meter (160 feet) interval. On most maps, every fifth contour line is thicker and has the elevation indicated, though you may have to trace it for some distance to locate this marker. The closer together the contour lines, the steeper the slope. If they're touching, expect a cliff (though cliffs of

---

A Mountain Storm

The wind whipping along the rocky ridge drives sheets of rain into my face. Clouds swirl all around, ripped apart at times to reveal sharp pinnacles soaring above me or the dark outline of a lake far below in the valley. I scramble along the narrow crest, exhilarated by the storm's fury and reveling in the rough rock under my hands. I am at the heart of the world. There is no sense of time; it is a shock when I come to the top of the talus slope that leads safely down into the valley. I hesitate to leave the storm, but the thought of dry clothes and warmth of camp spurs me into the long descent.

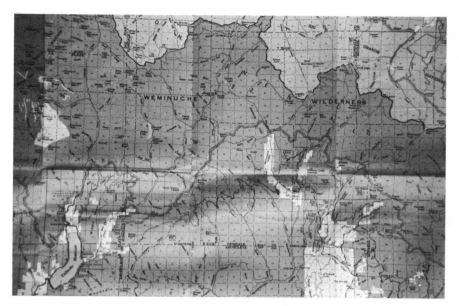

A Forest Service planimetric map.

for walkers. Smaller-scale maps covering larger areas, such as 1:100,000 and 1:250,000, are helpful for planning. Although the greater detail of large-scale maps is best for walking, it is possible to use smaller-scale ones in the wilderness. In remote areas they may be all that's available. I've used 1:250,000 maps in Greenland and even 1:600,000 in the northern Canadian Rockies.

Most Forest Service maps are planimetric, but there are some topographic ones covering designated wilderness areas, such as the 1:63,360 ones covering the Ansel Adams and John Muir Wildernesses in the Sierra. The Bureau of Land Management also makes an increasing number of metric topo maps at different scales, such as 1:100,000, with contour intervals of 50 meters.

Several companies produce maps for wilderness use that are more up to date and have more trail information than USGS topo maps (see Appendix 3). Those from Trails Illustrated are excellent. Printed on a paper-like recyclable plastic called Polyart, they are tearproof and waterproof. The maps are also attractively designed, clear, and easy to read. The scale varies from

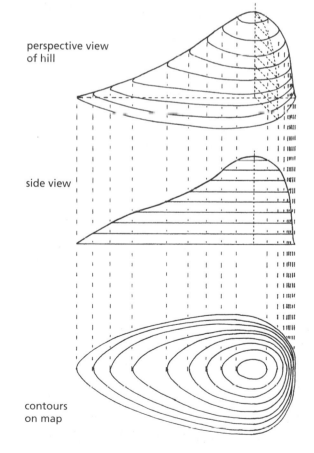

perspective view of hill

side view

contours on map

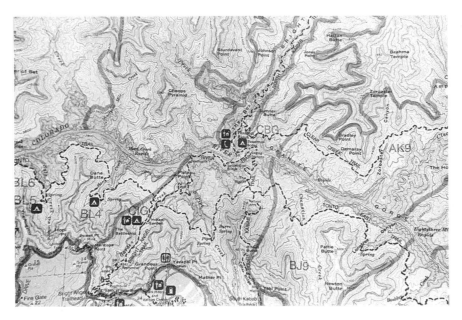

This section of a Trails Illustrated topo map shows specific information for hikers.

map to map. Unfortunately, they cover only certain areas, though new maps are being issued all the time—more than 60 maps, covering national parks, monuments, and seashores, currently are available, plus extensive coverage of Colorado and Utah. Each map is based on USGS data, but this is customized for outdoor recreation and updated every year or two to keep the maps accurate. Trails Illustrated maps are topographic, but they also contain information needed for planning trips, such as the location of trailheads, ranger stations, campsites, plus the precise route of trails, advice on bearbagging, giardia, park and wilderness area regulations, and outlines of topics like wildlife, history, geology, and archaeology. Wilderness Press offers 1:62,500 topo maps covering much of the High Sierra. These also are printed on plastic and show trails and other information for backpackers. Earthwalk Press maps are worth looking out for, too; I found the 1:48,000 one covering part of the Grand Canyon very good.

For planning, the state atlases and gazetteers published by DeLorme are useful. The maps are topographic (mostly 1:250,000 or 1:300,000, though national parks may be shown at 1:70,000). There is also a great deal of other information. I've used the Arizona and Utah atlases for planning a 1,000-mile walk in the Southwest canyons. I haven't done the walk yet, but the planning has been fun! DeLorme atlases don't yet cover all states.

Many topographic maps have a grid superimposed on them; each line in the grid may be numbered. If it is, you can record the grid reference for precise location. Also, counting the number of squares that a route crosses is a quick way to estimate the distance.

To work out distances on maps without grids (such as those covering the Alps, the Pyrenees, Iceland, and some of the United States), a map measurer is useful. This is a calibrated wheel that you set to the scale of the map, then run along your route. You can then read the distance off

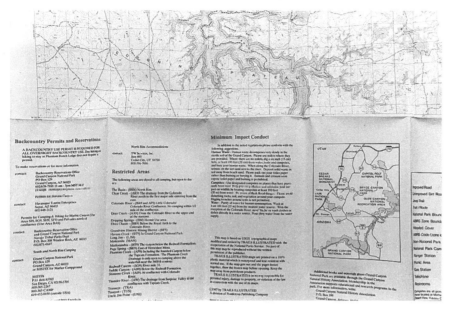

Trails Illustrated maps contain information on wilderness permits.

a scale on the device. They weigh only a fraction of an ounce, but I've never carried one. You could draw a grid on a map, but I've never done this, either. A piece of string laid along the route and measured is another way of determining distance.

While large-scale topographic maps are the best for accurate navigation, other maps offer information useful to the walker. Land-management agencies, such as the National Park Service, often issue their own maps showing trails and wilderness facilities. These maps are more up to date than the topographic ones for the same area. Forest Service and Bureau of Land Management planimetric maps (usually ½ inch to the mile) often show roads and trails that don't appear on topo maps. These planimetric maps don't have contour lines, so they don't tell you how much ascent and descent there is over a particular distance. (The 1:600,000 map I used in the northern Canadian Rockies was planimetric; I worked out when I would be going uphill

and downhill by studying the drainage patterns of streams, but I had no way of knowing whether I was headed for a 300- or a 3,000-foot climb.) Some planimetric maps are shaded to show where the higher ground lies, but this only gives a rough idea of what to expect.

Maps normally have the date of publication listed with the key, along with any revisions. Remote areas are rarely remapped, and you may find some maps are decades old. Obviously, the older the map, the less accurate the information may be, especially with regard to man-made features like roads. The maps I used in the northern Yukon in 1990 didn't indicate the Dempster Highway, built in the 1960s and '70s. I added it myself from highway maps, which are updated regularly. Features can disappear as well, of course, and trails on maps may be hard or impossible to follow if they haven't been maintained. Current guidebooks and ranger stations are worth consulting if you don't want to risk a nasty surprise.

I am a firm believer in doing virtually all navigating with only a map. As long as you can see features around you and relate them to the map, you know where you are. The easiest way to do this is by setting, or orienting, the map, which involves turning the map until the features you can see are in their correct positions relative to where you are. If you walk with the map set, it is easier to relate visible features to it.

Many people automatically use a compass for navigating, ignoring what they can actually see around them, yet even at night you can navigate solely with a map. I once completed a night-navigation exercise on a mountain leadership training course and was the only person to travel the route without relying on a compass. It was a clear night, and the distinctive peaks above the valley were easily identifiable on the map, while the location of streams showed me where I was on the valley floor. The others in the group navigated as though we were in total darkness, relying on compass bearings and pace counting. If you always rely on such methods, you cut yourself off from the world around you, substituting figures and measurements for a close understanding of the nature of the terrain. I don't like my walking to be reduced to mathematical calculations.

When following a trail, an occasional map check is enough to let you see how far along you are. When going cross-country, however, study the map carefully, both beforehand and while on the move. Apart from working out a rough route, note features such as rivers, cliffs, lakes, and, in particular, contour lines. Be prepared not to always find what you expect, though. The lack of contour lines around a lake may mean you'll find a nice, flat, dry area for a camp when you arrive, or it may mean acres of marsh (as happened to me a few times in the Canadian Rockies). Close-grouped contour lines at the head of

a valley may mean an impassable cliff or a steep but climbable grass slope. You have to accept that sometimes you'll have to turn back and find another route, that sometimes it will take you twice as long and you'll have to walk twice as far as planned to reach your destination. No map will tell you everything. Flexibility in adapting your plans to the terrain is important.

Always keep your map handy, even if the route seems easy or you are on a clear trail. A garment pocket or a fanny pack is the obvious storage place. Unless the maps are waterproof plastic, it's essential to protect them from weather. Unfortunately, most map cases are bulky, awkward to fold, and hard to fit into a pocket or fanny pack. Those from Ortlieb (a fraction over 2 ounces) are quite flexible; they're what I now use. Plastic bags work well, but they don't last very long. You can cover maps with special clear plastic film, and some hikers use waterproofing sprays, such as Texnik, which I'm told are effective. I don't bother with waterproofing maps. Although some of mine look disreputable, I've never had one disintegrate on me.

Maps can be bought at outdoor stores, bookstores, agency offices, and direct from the publishers. There may still be problems finding out which maps you need, especially for trips to remote areas. For advance planning, the USGS offers free small-scale maps and catalogs for every state, listing every topo map; the Canada Map Office does the same. The Bureau of Land Management and the Forest Service can send you lists of maps for their different regions as well. Local guidebooks and tourist offices can provide information on which maps you need for a particular area. For the United States, *The Map Catalog*, edited by Joel Makower (Vintage Books), tells you what maps are available and where to order them. Those who wander widely may be interested in *World Mapping Today*, by R.B. Parry and C.R. Perkins (Butterworth), which describes maps available for each country.

The Compass

Although I prefer to navigate with just a map, I always carry a compass. For trail travel, I hardly need it, except perhaps when at an unsigned junction in thick mist or dense forest. For cross-country walking, though, a compass may prove essential, especially when visibility is poor.

The standard compass for backpacking is the *orienteering* type, with a liquid-damped needle and transparent plastic base plate. Silva is the best-known brand; Suunto, Recta, and Brunton are others. I now use the smallest, lightest model available—the Silva 7NL—which weighs 0.8 ounce. This is just 0.2 ounce lighter than the Silva Type 3 I used to use. But that's still a 20 percent weight saving. For backpacking, models with sighting mirrors and other refinements are unnecessary.

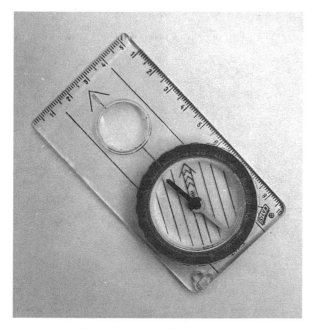

A basic orienteering compass.

The heart of the compass is the magnetic needle, which is housed in a rotatable, fluid-filled, transparent, circular mount marked with north, south, east, and west, plus degrees. The base of the dial is marked with an orienting arrow, fixed toward north on the dial, and a series of parallel lines. The rest of the compass consists of the base plate, with a large direction-of-travel arrow, and a set of scales for measuring distances on a map. Some base plates, like that on the Silva Type 3, also have a small magnifying glass built in to help read map detail.

A compass helps you walk toward your destination, even if you can't see it, with no reference to the surrounding terrain. Without a compass, you would veer away from the correct line. The direction you walk is called a *bearing.* Bearings are given as degrees, or the angle between north and your direction, reading clockwise. To set a bearing, you use the compass base plate as a protractor. Point the direction-of-travel arrow toward your destination, then turn the compass housing until the red end of the magnetic needle aligns with the orienting arrow. As long as you keep these two arrows pointing to the north and follow the direction-of-travel arrow, you will reach your destination, even if it is hidden.

However, you can rarely take a bearing on something several hours away and walk straight to it (although it's possible in desert and wide-open tundra). It's better to locate a visible, stationary feature that lies along your line of travel, such as a boulder or a tree, and walk to that—a *checkpoint.* You may have to leave your bearing to circumvent an obstruction, such as a bog or a cliff, but that's okay as long as you keep the chosen feature in your sights. Once you reach a checkpoint, you can check your bearing and find another object to head for. In poor visibility, a solo walker may have to walk on his bearing by holding the compass and literally following the

Taking a map bearing between the trail east of East Fork and Sadler Lake.

arrow. Two or more walkers can send one person ahead to the limit of visibility. (The scout stops so the other walker can check the position with the compass, and direct the scout to move left or right until he or she is in line with the bearing. Then everyone else joins the scout and the process is repeated. It's a slow but very accurate method of navigation, particularly useful in whiteout conditions. I've used it many times when skiing.)

If you know where you are but not which way you need to go to reach your destination, then you need to take a bearing off the map. To do this, place an edge of the base plate on the spot where you are, then line up the edge with your destination. Rotate the compass housing until the orienting arrow is aligned with north on the map. Remove the compass from the map and turn it, without rotating the housing, until the magnetic needle and orienting arrow are aligned. The direction-of-travel arrow now points in the direction you want to go. The number on the compass housing at this point is your bearing.

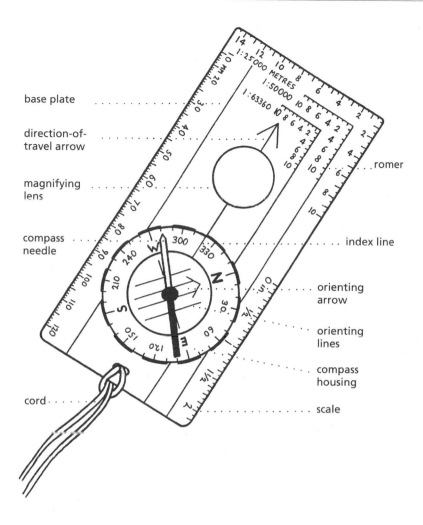

base plate

direction-of-travel arrow

magnifying lens

compass needle

cord

romer

index line

orienting arrow

orienting lines

compass housing

scale

1:25 000
1:50000
1:63360
METRES

The main features of an orienteering compass, including a magnifying lens. The compass housing is a rotating ring, also known as the azimuth.

This process is straightforward, but you must account for *magnetic variation.* Most topographic maps have three arrows somewhere in the margin showing three norths. Grid north can be ignored; the other two are very important. One is magnetic north, the direction in which the compass needle points. The other is true north. The top of the map is always true north, so if your map has no grid marked on it, the margins can be used. Because compasses point to magnetic north and maps are aligned to true north, the difference between them should

be taken into account when using the two in conjunction. This angle is measured in degrees and minutes (60 minutes equal 1 degree) and is called the magnetic variation or *declination.*

As magnetic north lies in the far north of Canada, true north can be either east or west of magnetic north. In parts of Michigan, Indiana, Ohio, Kentucky, Tennessee, and North and South Carolina, however, magnetic north and true north coincide. In areas of North America east of those states, true north is west of magnetic north, but in areas west of them, true north

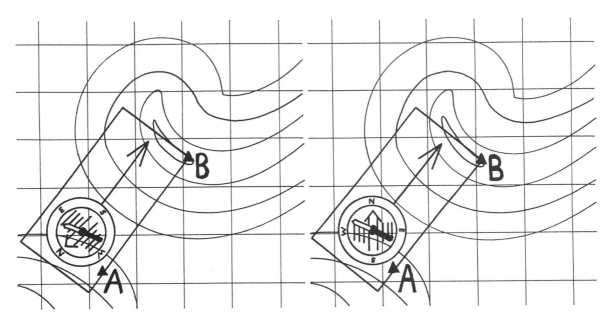

Align the compass with your objective on the map . . .

. . . then rotate the housing to line up the orienting arrow with the north-south grid lines.

Taking a compass bearing from a map.

is east of magnetic north. The actual difference between true and magnetic north is often marked on maps.

Just to confuse matters further, magnetic north moves in a predictable pattern. The declination on an old map will not reflect the current position of magnetic north, but many maps list the rate of change so you can work out the current figure. (For example, The Trails Illustrated 1:37,700 Zion National Park map notes the approximate 1995 magnetic variation was 14°00′ east, and the approximate annual change is 3.0 west.) If your map isn't new and doesn't show the rate of change, you may be able to find it in a trail guide. You also can calculate the magnetic variation yourself by taking a bearing from one known feature to another, recording the bearing (without taking any declination into account), and then taking the same bearing from the map.

The difference between the two is the current declination. If you stick a piece of tape on the compass as a declination mark, you won't have to recompute it every time you use the compass. You will have to remember to move it if you visit different areas, though. Some compasses come with adjustable declination marks.

In the eastern United States, because magnetic north lies west of true north, when you take a bearing from the map you add the declination figure. However, if your bearing is taken from the ground and transferred to the map (not something you're likely to do often), you subtract the declination. A mnemonic for remembering this is "empty sea, add water"—MTC (map to compass), add. Of course, in western states, the opposite applies; you subtract declination when taking a bearing from the map, and add it when taking one from the ground.

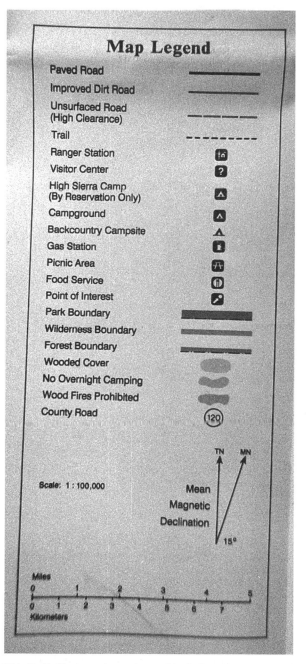

Map Legend

Paved Road	
Improved Dirt Road	
Unsurfaced Road (High Clearance)	
Trail	
Ranger Station	
Visitor Center	
High Sierra Camp (By Reservation Only)	
Campground	
Backcountry Campsite	
Gas Station	
Picnic Area	
Food Service	
Point of Interest	
Park Boundary	
Wilderness Boundary	
Forest Boundary	
Wooded Cover	
No Overnight Camping	
Wood Fires Prohibited	
County Road	120

Scale: 1 : 100,000

TN   MN

Mean
Magnetic
Declination

15°

Miles
0   1   2   3   4   5

0   1   2   3   4   5   6   7
Kilometers

This Trails Illustrated map legend includes the magnetic declination.

There's always an element of error in any compass work. If your bearing is 5° off, then you'll be 335 feet off the correct line of travel after walking 0.6 mile, 650 feet after 1.2 miles, and more than half a mile after 6.2 miles. This makes it difficult to find a precise spot that lies some distance from your starting point, unless you can take a bearing on some intermediate feature. One of the few compass techniques I use, other than straightforward bearings, is *aiming off*, which is especially handy in poor visibility. If your destination lies on or near an easy-to-find line such as a stream, you can make a deliberate error and aim to hit a line on one side or the other of your destination. When you reach the line, you know which way to turn to reach your destination. I used aiming off on a large scale in the Canadian Rockies. I knew that hundreds of miles somewhere to the northwest was the little town of Tumbler Ridge, which I wanted to reach, and that a road ran roughly east-west to the town. By heading north rather than northwest, I knew I'd hit the road east of Tumbler Ridge, which, after several days' walking I did—and found myself 46 miles away. But I knew where the town was, and, more importantly, where I was.

The compass has other, more complex uses, instructions for which you should consult a good orienteering book. Don't rely on your compass blindly, though. There are areas high in iron ore where a compass won't work. The Cuillin Hills on the Isle of Skye in Scotland is one such area; at spots on the main ridge, the compass needle can turn in a full circle in the space of just a few yards, something Outward Bound students found unnerving when I demonstrated it for them while we were enshrouded in a thick mist.

Keep your compass where you can reach it easily; otherwise, you might be tempted to forgo checking it when you are unsure of your direc-

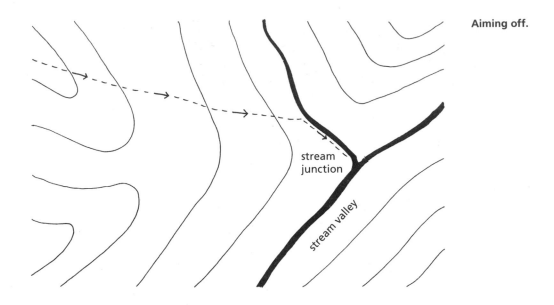

Aiming off.

stream
junction

stream valley

tion. The result, as I have learned, can mean retracing your steps a considerable distance. Like most people, I have a loop of cord attached to my compass (most come with small holes in the base plate for this purpose), though I don't often hang it around my neck. I may tie the loop to a zipper pull on a pocket or my fanny pack so that I don't lose the compass and can refer to it quickly whenever I want to.

GPS Receivers

The use of electronic gadgets in the wilderness has become controversial in the last few years due to the increasing use (misuse, some would say) of cellular phones and satellite navigation devices. Whatever you think about the place of electronics in the wilds, one thing is clear: This new technology will not go away. Indeed, its use will increase as more devices designed for wilderness use are developed. It is, I think, futile to debate whether the wilds are an appropriate place for such technology. The point is to look at electronic devices exactly as we would any other

new gear, to consider what purpose they serve and just how useful they are. After all, they are only tools, like packs or stoves.

I've tried a number of satellite navigation devices, and have reached some tentative conclusions. This is an area of rapid development, so even more than with other gear, before buying a unit I'd recommend getting up-to-date, expert advice.

GPS stands for *Global Positioning System.* It's a government-operated system that consists of 28 satellites 12,000 miles up, four of which are used for backup. Each satellite orbits the Earth twice a day and sends out a continuous signal, giving its position and the time. By locking onto a minimum of three satellites, a GPS receiver on the ground can *triangulate* its position. You won't get your position as accurately as you could, however, because the Department of Defense, which owns and runs the satellites, introduces what it calls Selective Availability so that GPS isn't too accurate (presumably for defense purposes). Silva says that this "gives an

A global positioning satellite (GPS) receiver.

accuracy within 100 meters 95 percent of the time," which is fine for general navigation across open moors, but not accurate enough for getting off the summit of a mountain in a blizzard. However, from early 1996, receivers will be available that bypass selective availability to give an accuracy of a few feet. Even then, though, an accurate fix may not be obtainable if the satellites aren't in the right alignment. Also, line of sight is required between the receiver and the satellites; it can be impossible to get a fix through dense forest or below steep cliffs.

For all these reasons, GPS should not be considered a substitute for a map and compass (and the skills required to use them), but rather as a backup. On a few occasions, I've been unable to confirm my position with GPS because the receiver wouldn't give a reading; each time I was very glad I'd been checking my progress on the map.

Once a receiver has a fix, it will show the position on its screen. This can be in latitude or longitude, or UTM (universal transverse Mercator), the grid used on USGS topo maps. To translate this reading onto the map you must be able to plot grid references accurately. All receivers can be set to give positions for the maps of different countries. These are known as *map datums*. Not all maps have enough information on them to use with a GPS receiver, but this is changing. Trails Illustrated, for example, has latitude and longitude on all maps, and grids on some. They also show selected GPS waypoints on an increasing number of maps.

Using a GPS Receiver: Anyone familiar with computers should have no problem with GPS. If you find programming a video recorder difficult, however, be warned that GPS receivers are more complex. Studying the manuals carefully (which takes several hours) and practicing with the receiver at home are essential if you are to fully utilize it in the field.

GPS receivers have multiple functions. In addition to indicating your position, they tell you the approximate altitude, and can be programmed to guide you to a specific destination via a series of legs—they can store from dozens to hundreds of locations, called *waypoints*—or take you back to your starting point. They can tell you how far you have to go to reach your goal, which direction to go, the speed at which you are traveling, how long it will take you to get there, and the estimated time of arrival. If you stray from the route they'll warn you of that, too.

To utilize all these functions requires power, and that means batteries. Most receivers run off four to six AA batteries, and though figures for battery life given in manuals are quite impressive (20 hours and more) these are usually for temperatures of around 70°F (21°C). In colder temperatures (I've used receivers at 0°F [−18°C]), battery life is much shorter, even when the receiver is kept warm inside your clothes and you use lithium batteries.

The most common use of GPS is to guide you toward a destination. To do this you first enter the grid references of the destination and waypoints into the receiver's memory, and then follow the direction indicators on the screen to each point, or transfer the bearings given to your compass. Of course, the receiver can direct you only in straight lines, though most will indicate how far off your line of travel you are.

Using GPS like this means walking with the receiver in your hand and consulting it regularly. I tried this on a cross-country walk in view-less forest, and it worked well. However, I don't go for walks in order to stare at a screen; I do enough of that when I'm writing. There are times and places—when I was unsure of my

whereabouts for nearly a week in the Canadian Rockies, for example, or in a whiteout in winter anywhere—when I could see the usefulness of following a pre-set course. However, for most walking it's unnecessary and a waste of batteries. I think GPS is better used as a means of checking your position when it's important you know *exactly* where you are. I've used it for this in trackless, snow-covered terrain in poor visibility, and felt reassured when the receiver confirmed I was where I thought I was. For this, a simple, tiny, lightweight receiver would be adequate. Unfortunately, one isn't available at present, complexity apparently being the aim of receiver designers, as it is in other areas of electronics.

The GPS receivers I've tried perform well once the necessary procedures and the technical jargon of the instructions have been mastered. The exception is altitude. Receivers regularly gave wildly inaccurate heights, often 300 feet or more off. This is due, again, to Selective Availability, which allows for an accuracy only within about 500 feet. This is useless for navigational purposes. If you want to use elevation for navigating, then one of the new electronic altimeters, such as the Avocet Vertech, or one made by Casio, are far more accurate than GPS.

Current GPS units are expensive and relatively heavy, but lighter, less-expensive models are likely to appear soon. Current manufacturers include Magellan, Silva, Trimble, Panasonic, and Garmin.

Altimeters

Until recently, altimeters were used mainly by Alpine and Himalayan mountaineers, for whom they are essential navigational aids. For backpackers, a map and compass have always been adequate. Initially, I was dubious about the usefulness of altimeters for backpacking (and I still don't think they are essential), but after using one for a few years, I can see that they can make navigation easier, especially for cross-country travel.

On an ascent, knowing the height and the time means you can monitor progress and work out how long it will take to reach the top. If you know the height at which you need to leave a ridge or start an ascent from a wooded valley, an altimeter will tell you when you reach that point. (During a long traverse on steep, difficult terrain during a ski tour in the High Sierra, I could see from the map that the only safe descent to the valley was through a tiny notch that led into a wide, shallow gully. By using the altimeter I was able to ski through trees in growing darkness directly into the notch. It would have been much harder to find by map and compass alone.)

Altimeters are barometers—they work by translating changes in air pressure into vertical height. To maintain accuracy, they must be reset at known heights. (The barometer function is also useful as a forecasting aid, especially on long trips. There is nothing so heartening as seeing that the pressure is rising after several days of bad weather. Unfortunately, the converse also is true.) Temperature changes can cause inaccurate altimeter readings. Some altimeters are tempera-

GPS: My Choice

The Garmin GPS 40 is the best receiver I've used. It is lighter and smaller than most other receivers, weighing 9½ ounces with four AA batteries, and can easily be held in the palm of one hand and operated with the thumb. The batteries are said to last 10 hours in Normal Mode, and 20 hours in Battery Saver Mode; the latter is adequate for most functions. There is also a battery-life indicator, which is very useful. You can't accidentally turn the unit on either—the on/off switch is small and requires firm pressure.

The GPS 40 instruction manual is easy to understand, even if you're not familiar with computer technology. A short video is also provided. (It shows a walker using the GPS 40 on a cross-country route; it's a good introduction to satellite navigation, as well as a guide to this particular receiver.) The device has a Simulator Mode, which lets you practice all the functions without having to access satellites.

The receiver itself is as user-friendly as the manual and video—I found it far easier to use than the other receivers I've tested. The controls are well placed, the screen is bright and clear, and all the functions are easily accessed. It also gives more useful information than other receivers, including a representation of the sky above, with the positions of the satellites at the time. Each satellite is numbered and an indicator shows which ones the receiver can pick up and how strong the signal is. Once sufficient signals have been acquired, your position is given. Once you start walking, the receiver also tells you the direction you're heading and how fast you're going. The altitude is given, with an accuracy indication—plus or minus 100 feet, for example. The receiver will hold 250 waypoints and 20 reversible routes. One display "page" is a moving map, with an adjustable scale, which actually traces your route onto the screen. The most useful information is displayed on the navigation page, which has a moving track on the screen with an arrow that always points to your destination. If you go astray the track moves, showing you how much and in what direction you are off route. The page also tells you how fast you are moving, how fast you are approaching your destination, the estimated time to your destination, plus the compass bearing and the bearing you are walking.

In featureless terrain, the GPS 40 is easy to use and quicker than a compass. It changed my opinion about GPS receivers. I still wouldn't carry it on walks on clear, well-signed trails, but in remote, trackless areas and snow-covered terrain, it could prove very helpful.

ture compensated, but the least-expensive ones usually aren't. The best way to minimize inaccuracies is to avoid temperature variations by keeping the altimeter at the same temperature as the outside air. For quick reference, wrist altimeters can be worn on the outside of your jacket cuff.

The altimeter I use is the temperature-compensated Avocet Vertech, which provides more data and is much easier to use than other watch-style altimeters. I wear it on my wrist, though the temperature reading isn't accurate if it's worn this way, of course. My only complaint is that the battery (said to last two years, though mine have given up in less time than that) can be changed only by the manufacturers, which means sending the device back to California. Other altimeters come from Casio and Thommen.

Navigating by Natural Phenomena

There are many ways to navigate without a map or compass, but I habitually use only two—the sun and the wind, and then only as backups. Knowing where they should be in relation to my route means I am quick to notice if their position has shifted. If I've veered off my intended line of travel—easy to do in rolling grassland or continuous forest—I stop and check my location. I also check that the wind hasn't shifted, and what the time is so that I know where the sun should be.

Learning More

There are many helpful books for those who want to learn more about navigational techniques. The classic is *Be Expert with Map & Compass* by Bjorn Kjellstrom (Charles Scribner); a good modern one is David Seidman's *The Essential Wilderness Navigator* (Ragged Mountain Press). To learn more than these books can teach, you'll need to take a course at an outdoor center or join an orienteering club.

Waymarks and Signposts

Paint splashes, piles of stones (cairns, or ducks), blazes on trees, posts, and other devices mark trails and routes throughout the world. (In Norway, wilderness ski routes are marked out with lines of birch sticks.) These waymarks, combined with signposts at trail junctions, make finding most routes easy, but I have mixed feelings about them—part of me dislikes them intensely as unnecessary intrusions into the wilderness; another part of me follows them gladly when they loom up on a misty day. But waymarking of

Stone cairns, or ducks—such as these granite slabs in Yosemite—are used to mark trails in open areas.

Blazes on trees are often used to mark trails.

routes doesn't mean you can do without map and compass or the skills to use them.

Useful though it is, I would not like to see waymarking increase. I'd rather find my own way through the wilderness, and I don't build cairns or cut blazes, let alone paint rocks. In fact, I often knock down cairns that have appeared where there were none before, knowing that if they are left, a trail will soon follow. The painting of waymarks in hitherto unspoiled terrain is an act of vandalism. On a week-long trek in the Western Highlands of Scotland, I was horrified to discover a series of large red paint splashes daubed on boulders all the way down a 3,300-foot mountain spur that is narrow enough for the way to be clear. There wasn't even a trail on this ridge before. Now it has been defiled with paint that leaps out of the subtle colors of heather, mist, and lichen-covered rock. May the culprit wander forever lost in a howling Highland wind, never able to locate a single spot of paint!

Guidebooks

There are two kinds of wilderness guidebooks: area guides and trail guides. The first give a general overview, providing information on possible routes, weather, seasons, hazards, natural history, and so on. Often lavishly illustrated, they are usually far too heavy to carry in the pack. I find such books interesting when I return from an area and want to find out about some of the places I've visited and things I've seen. They're also nice to daydream over.

Trail guides are designed as adjuncts to maps. Indeed, some of them include the topographic maps you need for a specific location. If you want to follow a trail precisely, they are very useful, though your sense of discovery on a trail is diminished when you already know in advance about everything you'll see along the way. Some cover only specific trails; others are miniature area guides, with route suggestions and general information. Most popular destinations or routes have a trail guide, and many have several. Since trail guides frequently contain up-to-date information not found on maps, I often carry one, especially if I'm visiting an area for the first time.

On Being "Lost"

What constitutes being lost is a moot point. Some people feel lost if they don't know to the yard exactly where they are, even if they know which side of which mountain they're on, or which valley they're in. It's possible to "lose" a trail you're following, but that doesn't mean you are lost.

I think it's very hard to become totally lost when traveling on foot; I've never managed it. I was "unsure of my whereabouts" during the week I spent in thick forest in the foothills of the Canadian Rockies, but I knew my general position, and I knew which direction to walk to get to where I wanted to go. Although I couldn't pinpoint my position on a map (indeed, I couldn't locate myself to within 25 miles in any direction, and I've never been able to retrace my route on a map), I wasn't lost, because I didn't allow myself to think I was. Being lost is a state of mind.

The state of mind to avoid is panic. Terrified hikers have been known to abandon their packs in order to run in search of a place they recognize, only to die of hypothermia or from a fall. As long as you have your pack, you have food and shelter and can survive, so you needn't worry. I've spent many nights out when I didn't know precisely where I was. But, I had the equipment to survive comfortably, so it didn't matter. A camp in the wilderness is a camp in the wilder-

---

Sort of Lost

On the Pacific Crest Trail, two of us mislaid the trail in the northern Sierra Nevada after taking a "shortcut" that took us off the map. The evening this happened we "camped above a river we think may lead to Blue Lake" (journal entry, June 22, 1982), the lake being the next feature we expected to recognize. My rather confused journal entry for June 23 describes what happened next: "Took three hours before we were back on the trail and even then we weren't sure where. We must have been farther north and east than we thought. The hill we thought was The Nipple wasn't and when we'd finally given up trying to reach it we found ourselves traversing the real Nipple just after I'd been talking about Alice in *Through the Looking Glass* only reaching the hilltop by walking away from it."

We didn't know we were back on the Pacific Crest Trail until we found a trail marker telling us so. Once we knew exactly where on the trail we were, all the other features fell into place and the terrain we'd been crossing suddenly made sense. That's when we realized we couldn't reach the peak we were seeking because we were already on it!

---

ness, whether it's at a well-used, well-posted site, or on the banks of a river you can't identify.

The first thing to do if you suspect you are off course is to *stop* and *think*. Where might you have gone wrong? Check the map. Then, if you think you can, try to retrace your steps to a point you recognize or can identify. If you don't think you can do that, use the map to figure out how to get from where you are (you always know the area you are in, even if it's a huge area) to where you want to be. It may be easiest to head directly for a major destination, such as a road or town, as I did in the foothills of the Canadian Rockies, rather than try to find trails or smaller features.

Good backpacking skills open up wilderness from the deserts to the high mountains. This is the Grand Canyon.

Often it's a matter of heading in the right direction, knowing that eventually you'll reach somewhere you want to be.

I have to say that I don't mind not knowing exactly where I am—sometimes I enjoy it. There is a sense of freedom in not being able to predict what lies over the next ridge, where the next lake is, and where the next valley leads. I enjoy the release of wandering through what is, from my perspective, uncharted territory. I never intend to lose myself, I just view it as an opportunity, rather than a problem, when it happens.

COPING WITH TERRAIN
On and Off Trail

As long as you stick to good, regularly used trails, you should have no problems with terrain, except for the occasional badly eroded section. Don't assume that because a trail is marked boldly on a map it will be clear and well maintained. Sometimes the trail won't be visible at all; other times it may start off clearly, then fade

away, becoming harder to follow the deeper into the wilderness you go. Trail guides and ranger stations are the best places to find out about specific trail conditions, but even their information can be inaccurate.

Many people never leave well-marked trails, feeling that cross-country travel is simply too difficult and too slow. They are missing a great deal. Going cross-country differs from trail walking and requires a different approach. The joys of off-trail travel lie in the contact it gives you with the country you pass through. The 15- to 20-inch dirt strip that constitutes a trail holds the raw, untouched wilderness a little at bay. Once you step off it, the difficulties you will encounter should be accepted as belonging to that experience. You can't expect to cover the same distance you would on a trail or to arrive at a campsite before dark. Uncertainty is one of the joys of off-trail travel, part of the escape from straight lines and the prison of the known.

Learning about the nature of the country you're in is very important. Once you've spent a little time in an area—maybe no more than a few hours—you should be able to start interpreting the terrain and modifying your plans accordingly. In the northern Canadian Rockies, I learned that black spruce forest meant muskeg swamps so difficult to cross that it was worth any length detour to avoid them; if the map showed a narrow valley, I knew it would be swampy, so I would climb the hillside and contour above the swamps; if it showed a wide valley, I would head for the creek because there probably would be shingle banks I could walk on by the forest edge. It's useful to be able to survey the land ahead from a hillside or ridge where possible—for which binoculars are well worth their weight—and I often plan the next day's route from a hilltop.

Compared with walking on trails, cross-country travel is real exploration, of both the world around and yourself. To appreciate it fully you need to be open to whatever may happen. Distances and time matter far less once the trail network has been shrugged off. What matters is being there.

The Steep and the Rough

Steep slopes can be unnerving, especially on descents. If you're not comfortable going straight down and there is no trail, take a switchback route across the slopes. Look for small, flatter areas where you can rest and work out the next leg of the descent. A careful survey of the slope before you start down is always a good idea. Work out a route between small cliffs and drop-offs.

Slopes of stones and boulders, known as *talus,* occur on mountainsides the world over, usually between timberline and the cliffs above. Trails across them are usually cleared and flattened, though you may still find the going tricky. Balance is the key to crossing rough terrain—a staff is a great help. Cross large boulder fields slowly and carefully, test each step, and try not to slip. Unstable boulders, which may move as you put your weight on them, easily can tip you over. The key to good balance is to keep your weight over your feet, which means not leaning back when descending and not leaning into the slope when traversing.

When descending a talus slope, take short steps and keep your weight over your feet.

You may go crazy trying not to slip on the smallest stones, known as *scree,* though, so you just have to let your feet slide. Some people like to run down scree—a fast way to descend—but the practice damages scree slopes so quickly that it should no longer be practiced—too much scree-running turns slopes into slippery, dangerous ribbons of dirt embedded with rocks. Be very careful if you can't see the bottom of a scree slope—it may end at the edge of a cliff. Because climbing, descending, or crossing a scree slope without dislodging stones is impossible, a party should move at an angle or in an arrowhead formation so that no one is directly under anyone else. Because other parties may be crossing below you, if a stone does start rolling, you should shout a warning—*below!* or *rock!* are the standard calls. If you hear this call, *do not look up,* even though you will be tempted to.

Traversing steep, trail-less slopes is tiring and puts great strain on the feet, ankles, and hips. It is preferable to climb to a ridge or flat terrace, or to descend to a valley, rather than to traverse slope for any distance. You may think that traversing around minor summits and bumps on mountain-ridge walks requires less effort than going up or down, but in my experience it won't. (Still, I'm frequently drawn to traversing. Heed my words, not my practice!)

In general, treat steep slopes with caution. If you feel unhappy with the angle or the ground under your feet, retreat and find a safer way. Backpacking isn't rock climbing, though it's surprising what you can get up and down with a heavy pack if you have a good head for heights and a little skill. *Don't climb what you can't descend* unless you can see your way is clear beyond the obstacle. And remember that you can use your cord for pulling up or lowering your pack if necessary.

However, it's unwise to drop packs down a slope, as they may go farther than you intend. Bad route finding once left two of us at the top of a steep, loose and broken limestone cliff in Glacier National Park in Montana; foolishly, we decided to descend rather than turn back, and it

Even in summer, patches of old snow may have to be crossed—this one is in the High Sierra in August.

Good wilderness skills are needed to travel in snow-covered mountains. The Sierra Nevada in spring.

took us several hours of heart-stopping scrambling to reach the base. At one point, my companion decided he could safely lower his pack to the next ledge, even though he would have to let go before it reached it—the pack bounced off that ledge and a few more before being halted by a tree 200 or so feet below. Amazingly, nothing broke—not even the skis strapped to the pack. If we'd lost the pack or the contents had been destroyed, we would have had serious problems.

Snow

Much of what was said about traversing rock slopes applies to crossing snow. However, you may come upon small, but steep and icy snowfields in summer when you aren't carrying ice ax or crampons. Having a staff makes it easier to balance across snow on small holds kicked with the edge of your boots. Without the staff, take great care and, if possible, look for a way around a snow slope, even if it involves descending or climbing.

Bushwhacking

Bushwhacking is the apt word for thrashing through thick brush and scrambling over fallen trees while thorny bushes tear at your clothes and pack. It's the hardest form of "walking" I know, and it's to be avoided whenever possible—though sometimes you have no choice.

Bushwhacking takes a long time and a lot of energy, with very little distance to show for it; a half mile per hour can be good progress. Climbing high above dense vegetation or wading up rivers are both preferable to prolonged bushwhacking. But if you like to strike out across country, bushwhacking eventually will be essential.

Bushwhacking can be necessary even during ski tours. On one occasion in the Allgau Alps, four of us descended from a high pass into a valley. The snow wasn't deep enough to cover fully the dense willow scrub that spread over the lower slopes, and rose a yard or two high. Luckily, the scrub didn't spread very far, but skiing

Be sure to stay on the switchback—taking shortcuts, particularly on steep slopes, causes erosion.

through it was a desperate struggle, since the springy branches constantly knocked us over and caught at our poles and bindings.

Unmaintained trails can quickly become overgrown, too. I made the mistake of wearing shorts while descending one in the Grand Canyon; the upper part of the trail ran through dense thickets of thorny bushes and small trees, and my legs were soon bloody. It was quite a relief to reach the desert farther down, where the cacti and yuccas were at least widely spaced.

MINIMIZING IMPACT

A trail is a scar on the landscape, albeit a minor one. But where there is a trail, you should use it—not wander away from it. Cross-country travel is for areas where there are no trails. You shouldn't parallel a trail in order to experience off-trail walking. Most damage is caused when walkers walk along the edges or just off a trail, widening it and destroying the vegetation along-side. Always stick to the trail, even if it means walking in mud.

On steep slopes, in particular, switchbacks should always be used in their entirety. Too many hillsides have been badly damaged by people short-cutting switchbacks, creating new, steeper routes that quickly become water channels. In meadows and Alpine terrain, where it's easy to walk anywhere, multiple trails often appear where people have walked several abreast. In such terrain, you should follow the main trail, if you can figure out which it is, and walk single file. When snow blocks part of a trail, try to follow the line of where the trail would be; don't create a new trail by walking around the edge of a snow patch unless you need to do so for safety.

When you walk cross-country, your aim must be to leave no sign of your passing—that means no marking with blazes, cairns, or subtle signs like broken twigs. It also means avoiding fragile surfaces where possible, walking around damp meadows, and not descending onto soft ground.

Rock, snow, and non-vegetated surfaces suffer the least damage; gravel banks of rivers and streams are regularly washed clean by floods and snowmelt, so walking on them causes no harm.

It would take a skilled tracker to follow a good solo walker's cross-country route. Groups of four or more have a more difficult time leaving no sign of their passage. The answer is to keep groups small and to spread out, taking care not to step in each other's boot prints. As few as four sets of boots can leave the beginnings of a trail that others may follow in fragile meadows and tundra. Where these new trails have started to appear, walk well away from them so that you don't help in their creation. The aim should be to use obvious trails but not make new ones or expand signs of faint ones.

In many areas, land-management agencies maintain and repair trails, often using controversial methods. However, wide, eroded scars made by thousands of boots (and sometimes horses) hardly create a feeling of wilderness, either. Unfortunately, some popular trails may be saved only by employing drastic regulations. Walkers can assist by following trail-management instructions, staying off closed sections, and accepting artificial surfaces as necessary in places.

Generally, when walking cross-country you should always consider what your impact on the terrain will be, and always pick the route that will cause least damage.

WILDERNESS HAZARDS
Weather

The cause of most outdoor hazards is the weather. Wind, rain, snow, thunderstorms, freezing temperatures, heat waves, and thaws all introduce difficulties or dangers. Coping with weather is the reason backpackers need tents, sleeping bags, and other specialty equipment.

Learning about weather is useful, but don't think that you can forecast as well as expert meteorologists—even they do not fully understand weather.

For any given trip, knowing what weather generally to expect is important, and should be part of your trip planning. Area guides, local information offices, and ranger stations are the places to get specific details of regional weather patterns. For a specific day, check radio, television, and newspaper forecasts if you can; park and forest service ranger stations often post daily weather forecasts. If you don't see one, inquire. If you monitor forecasts for an area you visit regularly, you will soon be able to develop an annual weather overview.

Even the most detailed, recent forecast can be wrong. Regional patterns can mean rain in one valley, sun in another just over the hill. Mountains are particularly notorious for creating their own weather. Weather has less impact on travel over low-level and below-timberline routes—if it rains, you don rain gear; if it's windy, you keep an eye out for falling trees.

High up, however, a strong wind can make walking impossible, and rain may turn to snow. On any mountain walk you should be prepared to descend early or take a lower route if the weather worsens. Struggling on into the teeth of a blizzard when you don't have to is foolish and risky. It even may be necessary to sit out bad weather for a day or more. I've done so on a few occasions and have been surprised at how fast the time passes.

A useful book on this subject is *Weathering the Wilderness,* by William F. Reifsnyder (Sierra Club Books). It describes the weather you can expect in the Sierra, Cascades, Rockies, Appalachians, Olympics, and the Great Lakes Basin at different times of year, and includes tables covering temperatures, rainfall, hours of sunshine, and more.

Altitude

As you go higher, atmospheric pressure lessens, making it harder for your body to extract oxygen from the air. This may result in *acute mountain sickness* (AMS), typified by headaches, fatigue, loss of appetite, dizziness, and a generally awful feeling. AMS rarely occurs at altitudes below 8,000 feet, so many backpackers never need worry about it. But if you do ascend high enough and experience AMS, the only immediate remedy is to descend; the effects usually pass in a few days.

To minimize the chances of AMS, acclimatize slowly by gaining altitude gradually. If you're starting out from a high point, you will aid acclimatization by spending a night there before set-ting off. It's also important to drink plenty of fluids—dehydration is reckoned to worsen altitude sickness. Most backpackers won't get higher than the 14,000 feet of the Sierra or Rockies; spending three or four days hiking at 6,000 to 8,000 feet should minimize altitude effects, but it's not always easy to do this. The altitude at which you sleep is important too; apparently, if you sleep below 8,000 feet you can ascend to 14,000 feet without much likelihood of altitude sickness.

The only time I've suffered from mountain sickness was when I took a cable car up to 10,600 feet on the Aiguille du Midi in the French Alps. The moment I stepped out of the cable car I felt dizzy and a little sick, and had a bad headache. However, we'd gone up in order to ski down, so I was soon feeling fine again.

Much more serious than AMS are *high-altitude cerebral* and *high-altitude pulmonary edema* (fluid buildup on the brain or lungs), which can be fatal. Cerebral edema rarely occurs

In snow-covered mountains, avalanches are a real danger.

In some areas of the far north, glaciers may be an impediment to travel.

below 12,000 feet; pulmonary rarely below 10,000 feet. Lack of coordination and chest noises are among the symptoms, but you may not be able to differentiate between AMS and edema. Your only course is to descend—quickly.

Medicine for Mountaineering, edited by James A. Wilkerson (The Mountaineers), has a detailed discussion of high-altitude illness that is worth studying by those planning treks in high mountains.

Avalanches

Avalanches are a threat to every snow traveler who ventures into mountainous terrain, more so for the skier than the walker. In spring, great blocks of snow and gouged terrain stripped of trees mark avalanche paths and show the power of these snow slides. Avalanches can be predicted to some extent, and many mountain areas, especially ones with ski resorts, post avalanche warnings. These should be heeded. Anyone heading into snow-covered mountains should study one

of the many books on the subject. *Avalanche Safety for Skiers & Climbers,* by Tony Daffern (Rocky Mountain Books/Alpenbooks), is one of the best for home study, while *The ABC of Avalanche Safety,* by Ed LaChappelle (The Mountaineers), is light enough at 2 ounces to carry in the pack.

Lightning

Lightning is both spectacular and frightening. Thunderstorms can come in so fast that reaching shelter before they break may be impossible (although I have learned that I can run very fast with a heavy pack when scared enough). In thunderstorms, avoid summits, ridge crests, tall trees, small stands of trees, shallow caves, lake shores, and open meadows. Places to run to include deep forests, the bases of high cliffs, depressions in flat areas, and mountain huts (these are grounded with metal lightning cables). Remember that, statistically, being hit by lightning is very unlikely, though this may fail to comfort you when you're out in the open and the flashes seem to be bouncing all around.

During a storm, there is danger from *ground currents* radiating from a lightning strike; the closer to the strike you are, the greater the current. Wet surfaces, whether hard or soft, can provide pathways for the current, which may also jump across short gaps rather than go through the ground. If part of your body bridges such a gap, some of the current will probably pass through it. Your heart, and therefore your torso, are the parts of your body you most need to protect from electric shocks, so it might be advisable to crouch on all fours rather than sit on insulating material, so that any ground current passes through your limbs only. I'd also keep away from damp patches of ground and wet gullies and rock cracks.

Metal can burn you after a nearby strike—if you are caught in a storm, move away from pack frames and tent poles. The most frightening storm I've encountered woke me in the middle of the night at a high and exposed camp in the Scottish Highlands; all I could do was huddle on my foam pad and wait for it to pass, while lightning flashed all around.

If someone in a group is hit by lightning and knocked unconscious, he (or she) should be given immediate mouth-to-mouth resuscitation if breathing or the heart has stopped.

Hypothermia

Hypothermia occurs when the body loses heat faster than it produces it. It can be a killer. The causes are wet and cold, abetted by hunger, fatigue, alcohol, and low morale. The initial symptoms are shivering, lethargy, and irritability, which develop into lack of coordination, collapse, coma, and death, sometimes very quickly.

Because wind whips away heat, especially from wet clothing, hypothermia can occur in temperatures well above freezing. Indeed, it is often in summer that unwary dayhikers get caught, venturing high into the mountains on a day that starts sunny but becomes cold and rainy. Too many people die or have to be rescued because they weren't equipped to deal with stormy weather.

If you start to notice any of the symptoms of hypothermia in yourself or any of your party, take immediate action. The best remedy is to stop, set up camp, get into dry clothes and a sleeping bag, start up the stove, and have plenty of hot drinks and hot food. Pushing on is foolish unless you've first donned extra clothes and had something to eat. After you're clothed and fed, exercise will help warm you up, since it creates heat. Even then you should stop and camp as soon as possible.

The best solution to hypothermia is to prevent it happening. If you are properly equipped, stay warm and dry, and keep well fed and rested, you should be in no danger.

Frostbite

When body tissue freezes, that's frostbite. It can be avoided by covering and by keeping warm. Minor frostbite is most likely to occur on the extremities—the nose, ears, fingertips, and toes. If any of these feels numb and looks colorless, it may be frostbitten. Rewarming can be done with extra clothing, by putting a warm hand over the affected area or, in the case of fingers or toes, holding them in someone's armpit, groin, or stomach. I've only come across mild frostbite once, to a companion's nose on a windy mountain top in February with a temperature around 0°F (−18C); she pulled a woolen balaclava over it and within a half hour color had returned. Deep frostbite is a serious condition, and can be properly treated only in a secure shelter with a reliable source of heat. *Frostbitten areas shouldn't be rubbed, as this can damage the frozen tissue.*

Heat Exhaustion

Most walkers are afraid of the cold, but heat can be dangerous, too. The opposite of hypothermia, heat exhaustion is caused by the body being unable to cool itself sufficiently. Typical symptoms are muscle cramps, nausea, and vomiting. Because the body uses respiration for cooling, the main cause of heat exhaustion is dehydration and electrolyte depletion—if you are severely dehydrated, you cannot sweat.

The main way to prevent heat exhaustion is to drink plenty of water, *more than you think you need* on hot days. If you still start showing symptoms, then stop and rest somewhere shady—exercise produces heat. If you feel dizzy or weak, you should lie down out of direct sunlight and drink water copiously. In very hot weather, travel in the early morning and the late afternoon, and take a mid-day siesta in the shade to minimize the chance of heat exhaustion. A sun hat also helps.

Fording Rivers and Streams

In many areas, major hazards are presented by unbridged rivers and streams. Water is more powerful than many people think, and hikers are drowned every year fording what may look like relatively placid streams. If you don't think you can cross safely, don't try.

If no logs or boulders present a crossing, wading a stream or river may be the only option. Whether you prospect upstream or downstream for a potential ford depends on the terrain. If you can view the river from a high point, you may be able to see a suitable ford. Otherwise, check the map for wide areas where the river may be braided and flowing more slowly. Several shallow channels are easier to cross than one deep one, and wide sections are usually shallower and slower than narrow ones. (Check the map for bridges, too—many years ago, after tor-rential rain had turned even the smallest streams into raging torrents, two companions and I walked many extra miles upstream and camped far from where we'd intended because we didn't notice on the map that there was a bridge not far downstream of where we were.)

On a week-long trip during the height of the spring snowmelt in Iceland, my route was almost totally determined by which rivers I could cross and which I couldn't (which was most of them). During my walk along the northern Canadian Rockies, I spent many hours searching for safe fords across the many big rivers there.

In the end, only experience can tell you whether it's possible to cross. If you decide fording is feasible, study your crossing point carefully before plunging in. In particular, check that the far side isn't deeper or the bank undercut. Then cross carefully and slowly with your pack hip-belt undone so that you can jettison it if you are washed away. (If you get swamped, try to hang on to the pack by a shoulder strap—it will give extra buoyancy and you'll need it and its contents later.) You should cross at an angle facing upstream so that the current won't cause your knees to buckle. Feel ahead with your leading foot, but don't commit your weight to it until the riverbed beneath it feels secure. Your staff, ice ax, or a stout stick is essential in rough water. If the water is fast-flowing and starts to boil up much above your knees, *turn back*—the water could easily knock you over, and being swept down a boulder-littered stream is not good for your health, nor fun.

If I'm wearing sandals, fords are no problem as far as wet feet are concerned. For shallow crossings, I don't even break my stride. If I'm wearing shoes or boots and carrying sandals, I change into the latter unless my footwear is already wet. If there are lots of fords, I keep the sandals on, even in cold weather, so I have dry

Rivers in flood season may be impossible to ford safely—it is better to retreat than take risks.

shoes for campwear. If I can see that the river bottom is flat and sandy or gravely rather than rocky, I sometimes cross wearing just a pair of dirty socks.

Mountain water is very cold, and you will often reach the far side feeling shivery. I find that the best way to warm up is by gulping down some carbohydrates, like a few granola bars, then

Some creeks can be crossed by balancing on rocks and using a staff for added support.

Fording a creek with ski pole as a third leg. Such fords should be made with your pack hipbelt undone.

hiking hard and fast. Unless the weather is hot, the best clothes for fording are shorts and a warm top. Long pants can drag in the water and when sodden aren't very warm.

Groups can use various techniques to make fords safer. Three people can cross in a stable tripod formation, or a group can line up along a pole held at chest level. In the past, I've used a rope to belay forders, but the current thinking is that roped crossings are dangerous—the chance of someone slipping and being trapped under water by the rope is too great.

An easy creek ford with an ice ax used as a third leg. If you carry your boots in your hand like this, make sure you don't drop them!

I have never swum across a river—the water in the areas I frequent is generally too cold, too fast, and too boulder-strewn for this to be practical. Bigger, warmer, slower rivers can be swum, however. For a detailed look at how to do it, see Colin Fletcher's *The Complete Walker* (Knopf).

If you can't find a safe crossing, you have one final option before you turn back—wait. In areas where mountain streams are rain-fed, they recede quickly once the rain stops; a raging torrent can turn into a docile trickle in a matter of hours. (Conversely, placid streams can swell just as quickly, so you should camp *after* you've crossed a river, or you may wake to a nasty shock. Glacier- and snow-fed rivers are at their lowest at dawn. If you camp on the near side, you may be able to cross in the morning.) Meltwater streams are the worst to ford because you can't see the bottom through the swirling silt.

Poisonous Plants

There are a few poisonous plants that can harm you by external contact. One is the *stinging nettle*, which has a sharp but transitory sting. Although painful, it's nothing to worry about unless you dive naked into a clump. At low elevations, the nastier *poison oak, poison ivy,* and *poison sumac* may be found. These closely related shrubs can cause severe allergic reactions, resulting in rashes and blisters in many people. If you brush against this stuff, you should immediately wash the affected area well with water, if you have any, since the oil that causes the problems is inactivated by water. It's also tenacious and long-lived, so also wash any clothing or equipment that has come into contact with the plants. If you still start to itch after washing the affected area, calamine lotion and cool saltwater compresses can help. Some cortisone creams can help with red and itchy rashes where no blisters have yet developed, as well as later when the rash has healed and is scaly, yet still itchy.

A final plant to watch out for is *devil's club,* whose stems are covered with poisonous spines that cause inflammation on contact. It's found in montane forests in the Cascades and British Columbia. I came across large stands of this head-high, large-leafed shrub mixed in with equally tall stinging nettles in the Canadian Rockies, just south of the Peace River. I normally

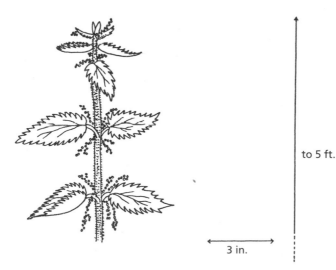

Stinging nettle (*Urtica dioica*).

to 5 ft.

3 in.

Poison ivy (Rhus radicans).

6 in.

try to avoid any unnecessary damage to plants, but on this occasion, I used my staff to beat my way through the overhanging foliage.

Many agencies, park offices, and guidebooks provide identification information; they're worth studying and carrying. You may also find warning notices at trailheads. If you rely on plants for food you need to be very sure you know what you're eating, especially fungi. There are numerous guides available.

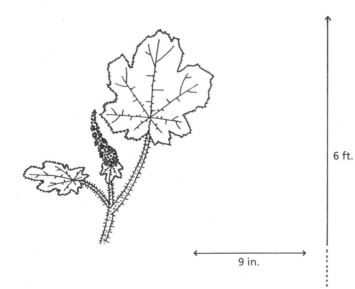

Devil's club (Oplapanax horridum).

6 ft.

9 in.

DEALING WITH ANIMALS

Encountering animals in the wilderness, even potentially hazardous ones, is not in itself a cause for alarm, though some walkers act as if it is. Observing wildlife at close quarters is one of the joys and privileges of wilderness wandering, something to be wished for and remembered long afterward.

You are the intruder in the animals' world, so do not approach closely or disturb them, for their sake and your safety. When you do come across animals unexpectedly and at close quarters, move away slowly and quietly, and cause as little disturbance as possible. With most animals, you only need fear attack if you startle a mother with young, and even then, as long as you back off quickly, the chances are that nothing will happen.

Some animals pose more of a threat and need special attention, however. (Insects, of course, are also animals, and the ones most likely to be a threat—to your sanity if not your physical health. The items and techniques needed for keeping them at bay were discussed in Chapter 8.)

Snakes

The serpent is probably more feared than any other animal, yet most species are harmless, and the chances of being bitten by one are remote. In the major North American wilderness areas there are four species of poisonous snakes—the *coral snake, rattlesnake, copperhead,* and *water moccasin* (also called a *cottonmouth*). Not all areas have them. They are rarely found above timberline or in Alaska and Maine. Their venom is unlikely to seriously harm fit, healthy persons. In tropical areas in Asia, Africa, and Australia, however, more poisonous—even deadly—species exist, and anyone intending to walk there should obtain relevant advice.

Snakebites rarely occur above the ankle, so wearing boots and thick socks in snake country minimizes the chances of being bitten. Snakes will do everything possible to stay out of your way; the vibrations of your boots are usually enough to send them slithering off before you even see them. However, it's wise to be cautious around bushes and rock piles in snake country—there may be a snake sheltering there. Do not pad around at night in a snake-country campsite barefooted or in sandals or light shoes without checking the ground first.

Rattlesnakes seem to strike more fear into people than other snakes do, though I don't understand why. By rattling, at least they warn you of their presence so that you can avoid them.

In some areas, walking at night can present difficulties. On the Pacific Crest Trail walk, I traveled through the Mojave Desert with three other hikers. Battered by the heat of the day, we decided to take advantage of a full moon and hike at night. However, we quickly found that rattlesnakes, which abound in the Mojave, come out at night, and we couldn't distinguish them from sticks and other debris. Several times we stopped and cast around anxiously with our flashlights for the source of a loud rattle. Once, we found a snake, a tiny sidewinder, between someone's feet. We didn't hike at night again.

On that trip, I carried in my shorts pocket a Coghlan's Snake Bite Kit (2 ounces) containing suction cups, antiseptic ampule and swab, scalpel blade, lymph constrictor, and instructions. The current advice, though, is *not to use such kits,* because an untrained person could easily cause more harm than the bite itself. Instead, the recommendation is to wash the bite with soap and water, then bandage it and keep the limb hanging down to minimize the chance of venom entering the bloodstream. The victim should stay still and rest while someone goes for assistance.

If you're on your own, you may have to sit out two days of feeling unbelievably awful unless you're close enough to habitation or a road to walk to aid quickly.

If you're interested in knowing more, there is a detailed and interesting discourse on snakes and the legends surrounding them in Colin Fletcher's *The Complete Walker.* For those who want to know more about snakebite treatment, I recommend *Medicine for Mountaineering,* edited by James A. Wilkerson.

Bears

In many mountain and wilderness areas, black and grizzly bears roam, powerful and independent. Knowing that they are out there gives an edge to one's walking; you know you're in real wilderness if bears are around. In many areas though, bears no longer roam. Grizzlies, in particular, have been exterminated in most of the lower states; there are now just tiny numbers in small parts of Montana, Idaho, and Wyoming (mainly in Glacier and Yellowstone National Parks). They are only found in any numbers in Alaska and in western Canada (the Yukon, Northwest Territories, British Columbia, and western Alberta). I like knowing they're there, lords of the forests and mountains, as they have been for millennia.

The chances of seeing a bear, let alone being attacked or injured by one, are remote. In Glacier National Park in Montana, one of the last strongholds of the grizzly and a place many hikers avoid because of the bears, there were nine deaths between 1913 and 1994 due to bear attacks, but 48 deaths from drownings, 27 from heart attacks, 25 from vehicle accidents and 21 from falls while hiking. In 8,000 miles of walking in bear country, most of it alone, I've seen only 10 black bears and three grizzlies, and none has threatened me—most have run away.

However, you should minimize the chances of encountering a bear. Stephen Herrero's *Bear Attacks: Their Causes and Avoidance* (Nick Lyons Books), is recommended reading for anyone venturing into bear country. I'd also suggest reading Doug Peacock's *Grizzly Years* (Henry Holt), an excellent personal account of two decades of living among and studying grizzlies.

When you're on the move, you want bears to know you're there so they'll give you a wide berth. Most of the time, their acute senses of smell and hearing will alert them to your presence long before you're aware of them. However, a wind blowing in your face, a noisy stream, or thick brush can all mask your signals. In these circumstances, make a noise to let any bears know you're around. Many people wear small bells on their packs for this purpose, but these aren't really loud enough. It's better to shout and sing, clap your hands or blow your safety whistle. Don't forget to use your eyes—in the Canadian Rockies I once came across another hiker sitting on a log eating his lunch, all the while calling out to warn bears he was there. I walked toward him for several minutes without his seeing me, and finally startled him by calling out a greeting when I was a few steps away.

In open terrain and on trails, scan ahead for bears. A pair of binoculars helps greatly with this. Binoculars will help you determine if a tree stump ahead is actually a grizzly sitting by the trail. Look for evidence of bears, too—paw prints and scat (dung) are obvious signs, but also look for scratch marks on trees and mounds of freshly dug earth in Alpine meadows, where grizzlies have been digging for rodents.

If you see a bear before it sees you, detour quietly and quickly away from it. Be particularly wary of female grizzlies with cubs—70 percent of known attacks are by mothers defending young. If the bear is aware of you, move away from it, perhaps waving your arms or talking to help it identify what you are. Don't stare at it or act aggressively; you don't want to be seen as a threat. The only grizzly I've met at fairly close quarters moved slowly away from me once I'd made a noise and let it know I was there. The nearest it came was about 50 yards.

In wooded country, look for a tree to climb as you move away, in case the bear comes after you. Black bears can climb trees but may not follow you up one, and grizzlies supposedly can't climb—although they can reach amazingly high. (One bear-country saying is that the way to tell the difference between black and grizzly bears is to climb a tree—the first will climb up after you, the second will knock down the tree.) If the bear keeps coming and you do climb a tree, you need to get at least 30 feet up to be safe.

Very occasionally, a grizzly will charge. Advice is mixed regarding what to do if one does. It's only worth trying to climb if a tree is very close—*you can't outrun a bear.* Dropping an object, such as a camera or item of clothing, may distract it and allow you to escape. Don't drop your pack—if the bear eats your food, it may learn to regard future walkers as food sources. Your pack will also help protect your body if the bear actually attacks. If dropping something doesn't work, your choices are trying to frighten the bear by yelling, banging objects together (metal on metal may be effective), hitting it while standing your ground or backing away slowly, acting non-threateningly by talking quietly to the bear (the option Herrero says he would choose), dropping to the ground and playing dead, and running away (which isn't advised, because the bear may chase you).

You could also use a spray repellent called Counter Assault. This is a strong version of cayenne pepper-based anti-dog sprays that has been shown to repel bears both in the field and in controlled tests. In one case, a grizzly that had already knocked a man down and was biting him ran off when sprayed in the face with Counter Assault. The makers stress that it isn't a substitute for knowing about bear behavior and taking the usual precautions, but, the advertising says, "it's better than no protection at all." It's non-toxic (the bears aren't harmed) and available in 8-ounce canisters. There's also a holster for carrying it on your belt. I'll probably carry a canister the next time I head into grizzly territory.

Bear-country ranger stations and information offices have up-to-date reports on areas that bears are using and whether any have caused trouble. Trails and backcountry campsites may be closed if necessary. For your own safety and that of the bears, obey any regulations that are in force.

HUNTERS

In many areas, the late summer and autumn sees wildernesses fill up with hunters carrying high-powered rifles and looking for something to shoot. Make sure it isn't you—wear something bright, like an orange hat or jacket. In some areas, officials recommend wearing two or more pieces of blaze orange. Hunting season is not the time to be wearing camouflage in the wilderness.

BACKPACKING WITH CHILDREN

I can give no personal advice on this. Three books on the subject that are well regarded include *Starting Small in the Wilderness: The Sierra Club Outdoors Guide for Families,* by Marlyn Doan (Sierra Club Books); *Backpacking with Babies and Small Children,* by Goldie Silverman (Wilderness Press); and *Take 'Em Along: Sharing the Wilderness with Your Children,* by Barbara J. Euser (Cordillera Press).

CHAPTER TEN

Adventure Travel: Backpacking Abroad

North America is arguably the best place for backpacking in the world: It's got a good trail network and vast areas of protected wilderness. Ironically, the excellence of the trails and the numerous published trail guides available can lessen the adventure.

Trekking abroad can be different. There are few places in the world where hiking isn't possible, though it may be very different from what you're used to at home. In Europe, there is a huge network of well-maintained trails; mountain lodges that provide beds, meals, and heating are found in many areas, including the Alps, the Pyrenees, and the Scandinavian mountains, making long-distance walks with very light loads possible. To explore the more remote areas, "primitive" camping is still necessary, of course (and preferred by many, including myself, at least in good weather).

European hikers carry their own gear, but in many countries porters or pack animals are used, as in that ultimate hiking destination, the Hima-

Inside a self-service hut in Norway.

layas. Treks there usually involve porters—one or two for small groups, up to 40 for large, organized trips. Tea houses are found on the most popular routes, such as the Annapurna Circuit or the Everest Base Camp Trek, but in most areas all your supplies have to be carried in. The same system is used in Africa for ascents of mountains like Kilimanjaro.

Other foreign hiking opportunities range from the rain forests of Costa Rica and other Central and South American countries, to the deserts of Australia or Israel.

Not all these areas are "wilderness" by the American definition; in the Alps, the valleys are cultivated (in fact, *Alp* means mountain meadow); in the Himalayas, the hiking trails literally are highways for the local people, used for trading and travel. Some areas *are* untouched and remote: Most of Greenland is a mass of uninhabitable ice, as is Antarctica.

Long-distance trails exist in many countries. You can walk from the Atlantic Ocean to the Mediterranean Sea along the spine of the Pyrenees on the 500-mile Pyrenean High Level Route, or cross the Arctic Circle on Sweden's 280-mile *Kungsleden* (The King's Way). Other well-known trails are New Zealand's Milford Track in the Fiordland Mountains, the Tour of Mont Blanc in the French Alps, England's 270-mile Pennine Way, the High Level Route in Corsica, the Concordia Trek in the Karakorum, the Ascent of Kilimanjaro in Tanzania, and the Circuit of Annapurna and the Everest Base Camp Trek in Nepal.

Two books with general introductions to these and other international hikes are *Classic Walks of the World,* edited by Walt Unsworth (Oxford Illustrated Press/Interbook, 1985), and *Trekking: Great Walks of the World,* edited by John Cleare (Unwin Hyman, 1988). Where long trails don't exist, it's usually easy to link shorter trails to make through-routes or circuits, just as you would at home.

The problems of hiking in some of these areas

On the Pointe du Dard, Vanoise Glacier, in the French Alps.

mainly concern information and organization. Only the most experienced travelers can set out for unknown foreign destinations on short notice and with minimal planning—and even then chances are something important will be overlooked.

Foreign adventure travel is often considered to be expensive, but this is only true if you want to visit a place like Antarctica. Indeed, many places can be visited for less than it would cost to hike in some areas of North America. If you live on the East Coast, a visit to Costa Rica or even

Nepal may be less expensive than an airline flight to the Southwest—and certainly less than one to Alaska. A main reason for this is that although the airfares may be higher, the ground costs are much, much less.

INFORMATION AND PLANNING

It's not difficult to learn about what to expect at most hiking destinations. At an outdoor store, book shop, or library you should find guidebooks to most countries and areas. Many, of course, are designed for auto travelers and those intent on being "tourists" rather than trekkers. Lonely Planet, Rough Guides, Bradt Publications, Sierra Club Books, and The Mountaineers publish books covering areas suitable for hiking outside North America. Most of these publications include general information about the countries, along with details of towns and popular destinations. Some have details of specific hikes, as well. Trekking guides are available for many areas such as Nepal and other Himalayan countries. John Hatt's *The Tropical Traveler* (Penguin Books), covers everything a first-time traveler could want to know in an entertaining and informative way. It's focus is the tropics, but the general information is just as useful for trips to other areas.

Travel guides can never be completely up to date, however, and they may not include the information you require. Tourist boards can be helpful, as can national park and other land-management agencies, especially for European countries, Australia, and New Zealand. Much information is now available on the Internet, so those with access can find data quickly.

Many trekking guides contain maps; some, such as those for many European long-distance paths, may even contain topographic maps. However, for most trips you'll want separate

Hiking in the Austrian Alps.

maps. These can be ordered at home or (usually) bought at your destination. I prefer to buy maps before the trip so I can use them for planning. Map quality varies enormously from country to country; some are barely more than sketches. I used basic 1:250,000 maps on a trek in the remote Dolpo region of Nepal. We crossed three 17,000-foot passes on that trip, none of which was named or had a height assigned on the map. Adapting to the scale was difficult, and the lack of detail made walking interesting in places — cliffs and gullies not on the map appeared in front of us. Most foreign maps and trekking guides use metric measurements, so you should become familiar with measuring in meters and kilometers in advance of a trip. (There are 3.28 feet in a meter; a kilometer is 0.6 mile.)

Once you have general information and an idea of where you want to walk, you can get to the specifics. Making lists may seem tedious, but I find them the only way to ensure I don't forget anything. One is a gear list, tailored to the area and weather conditions expected; a separate list covers items needed for travel but which won't be taken backpacking, such as extra toiletries and clothes. Perhaps the most important list is for the essentials — passport, airline tickets, foreign currency, and addresses of hotels, contacts, and embassy. (I leave a copy of this list at home, along with an itinerary, in case people need to contact me.) This last list should be kept in a secure place while you travel; I use a small nylon pouch that can be hung around my neck or over my shoulder (under my clothes) for all documents, including passport and tickets. When hiking, I keep it in an internal pack pocket.

A typical information list contains two sub-lists: information common to every trip, and that specific to a trip. John Hatt describes a good way to organize this in *The Tropical Traveler*. The list below is adapted from his.

Permanent Trip List

Passport Number with date and place of issue.
Credit card numbers and bank telephone number.
Home doctor's name and telephone number.
Camera equipment and serial numbers.
Camera insurance policy number and insurance company phone number.

Specific Trip List

Embassy address and telephone number.
Travel insurance number and telephone number for claims.
Medical emergency telephone number.
Air ticket booking reference number.
Ticket serial number and date of issue.
Dates and times of flights.
Air ticket booking agent, telephone number, and booking number.
Phone card numbers.
Telephone code from home.
Telephone code to home.
Traveler's check numbers.
Contact address.

ORGANIZED TRIPS

One way to avoid having to do all the trip organization yourself is to go with an adventure travel company. These trips vary from "catered" ones — your gear is carried by porters or animals, all the cooking, and even tent-pitching, is done for you — to ones where you carry everything and do most of the work yourself. (The ski tours I lead in Scandinavia fall into the latter category.)

Organized trips can be fun, and a good way to experience a new country. You do need to be comfortable traveling and hiking with a group, and with a specific itinerary, however. Most companies give you all the details, such as how many people will be on the trip, how far you'll walk each day, how many days will be spent walking and how many traveling in motorized transport (some trips can involve more motor travel than walking), how difficult the walking will be, what to bring, and the type of weather to expect.

IMMUNIZATIONS AND HEALTH

Foreign travel, especially to the Third World, often raises health concerns. The first thing to do is to discuss the trip with your doctor to find out what immunizations you'll need. Do this well in advance of the trip—some shots may be necessary weeks before you go. You also need to know what other medication it would be advisable to carry, such as malaria pills. I always take a broad selection of antibiotics, plus a strong prescription painkiller.

Water can be a problem in the Third World, or indeed in any remote area—some foreign waterborne diseases make giardia look like a slight cold. The biggest danger is from viruses—*unless they have a chemical disinfectant built in, filters do not remove viruses.* Iodine is the standard water treatment; I used the Polar Pure Iodine Crystal Kit when I went trekking in Nepal for two weeks, and had no problems, though I did come down with a nasty stomach ailment in Katmandu (which I blamed on brushing my teeth with unpurified tap water in my hotel). I found being careful in the city much more difficult than in the wilderness.

FOOD AND SUPPLIES

Eating different foods is one of the joys of adventure travel. Finding quick-cooking ones suitable for backpacking can be difficult, though,

so I usually carry some dehydrated meals. This applies even in Europe; I've resupplied with some very odd selections from tiny village stores in the Pyrenees, and ended up carrying loaves of bread and tins of beans at times because I couldn't find dried items.

Fuel supplies can be even more of a problem. White gas is almost impossible to find outside North America. If this is all your stove runs on, you'll need gasoline (which could cause clogging). Far better is a stove that will run on kerosene, a common fuel in the Third World. (It's usually not very clean, though, so bring a filter funnel.) The MSR XGK II is the best stove for international travel because it will run on any type of petroleum, clean or dirty, and is easily maintained in the field. In Europe, butane/propane cartridges are common, and alcohol can be found in many countries, especially Norway and Sweden. By the way, knowing the local name for your fuel is important: In France kerosene is called *petrol,* but in Britain *petrol* means gasoline.

If you plan to take photographs, take all the film you expect to need with you when visiting Third World countries; spare batteries should be carried, too. In Europe, film is readily available but more expensive than in North America. On long trips, bringing a second camera is a good idea because making repairs or finding spare parts is likely to be impossible in most places. I know people who carry three cameras—the third usually is a small compact, carried "just in case."

INSURANCE

Comprehensive travel and medical insurance is essential. For backpacking, it's important to check that hiking and camping are covered in your policy—many general travel policies don't cover such activities. Gear and cameras need insurance, too. Carry a list of camera gear serial numbers, both in case of a claim and in case a customs inspector asks you where you bought your gear. If you can't show where you purchased it, you could face hefty import charges.

DIFFERENT CULTURES

Meeting people from different cultures can be one of the great pleasures of adventure travel. But it is important to learn something about their culture in advance so you can avoid behaving offensively or disrespectfully. Good guidebooks have details for specific countries. Knowing just a few phrases of the local language can help with communication; phrase books can be useful, but most are geared to general tourism and don't have the words needed for backpacking. Trekking guides are usually better. Stephen Bezruchka's *Trekking in Nepal* (The Mountaineers) has an excellent appendix on Nepali for trekkers.

When employing local people as porters, you have a responsibility if problems arise. You're on a vacation, but they are working. In the fall of 1995, a huge snowstorm swept areas of the Himalayas in Nepal, killing many people—locals and trekkers—and causing serious problems for trekking groups. Some of the stories that came out of this disaster are very disturbing, including tales of trekkers abandoning porters to die in the snow while they took helicopter flights back to Katmandu, or refusing to allow locals the use of tents and other equipment. Some of those involved were trekking companies. I would suggest quizzing any company you're thinking of traveling with about how they treat their porters and what provisions are made for them in emergencies. (On the other hand, in Nepal, some trekkers went out of their way to assist porters and local people, and some companies treated porters and clients exactly the same, which is as it should be. I don't want to imply that all trekkers behave badly.)

INTERNAL TRAVEL

Internal travel can be exciting. I've been petrified in a taxi on narrow winding mountain roads in the Spanish Pyrenees, bumped in a car on a pot-holed highway in Nepal, chugged down an iceberg-dotted fjord in a fishing boat in Greenland, and helicoptered just above glacier-filled valleys in the same country.

The most exhilarating, overwhelming, and downright terrifying journey I've ever made was in a small passenger plane in Nepal, from Nepalgunj in the lowlands to Juphal, high in the Himalayas. The little plane, packed to bursting with people and baggage, flew into a narrow mountain valley with dense conifer forests on each side, the treetops so close it seemed you could pluck the cones from them through the windows. Our altitude was 17,000 feet, high enough to clear most mountain ranges, but here the peaks soared to 26,000 feet and more on each side, towering masses of rock and ice. I checked my watch, which indicated we should be landing in a few minutes. I looked down: Below, a winding river slid through the dense forest; clearings or flat land were nowhere to be seen. Through the cockpit window I could see a spur of the mountainside cutting across the valley—we were flying straight at the top of it. Surely the pilot would climb, I thought. But no, on we went toward what seemed an inevitable crash. Finally, we cleared the rocky edge of the spur, the wheels touched down and we bumped to a halt on the sloping field that constituted Juphal airport. These are known as STOL airstrips—Short Take Off and Landing.

In other places, internal travel can be the

310 THE BACKPACKER'S HANDBOOK

opposite, a time to relax in comfort. I especially love the train journey through Norway and Sweden to the Arctic, the big, well-appointed trains drifting north through increasingly wild, snowy northern landscapes. At night, there are comfortable beds to sleep in, while for breakfast coffee and donuts are served in the restaurant car.

Whether by car, coach, train, boat, or plane, internal travel can take time. Rather than view it as a means to reach the mountains or trailhead, it's better to treat it as part of the adventure, as part of experiencing what a new country has to offer.

A FINAL WORD

When I finished the first edition of this book, I was surprised—I didn't know I had so much to say. Well, this time I've said even more. I hope you still find my thoughts interesting and useful, and I'd like to know what you think.

Last time, I finished as spring was coming to the hills, the first flowers were appearing, and every dawn brought new birdsongs. These words are written in December, just four days before the shortest day, and snow lies on the mountainsides. However, the familiar feelings of wanting to see what's over the next hill, to head into the sanctuary of the wilderness, are still there. Before the month ends I'll be out on my skis, exploring the snow-quieted forest.

As before, I will see you out there—in spirit, at least.

—Chris Townsend

Equipment Checklist

This is a list of every item you might take on a backpacking trip. No one would ever carry everything listed below; I select items from this master list to create smaller, specific lists of what I need for each particular trip.

Packs

Backpack
Fanny pack
Daypack

Footwear and Walking Aids

Boots/trail shoes
Running shoes
Sandals
Insoles
Wax
Socks
Liner socks
Pile socks
Insulated booties
Gaiters
Staff/trekking poles
Ice ax
Crampons
Snowshoes

Skis
Ski poles
Ski boots
Climbing skins
Ski wax

Shelter

Tent with poles and stakes
Tarp
Bivouac bag
Groundsheet
Sleeping bag
Sleeping bag liner
Insulating mat

Kitchen

Stove
Fuel
Fuel bottles
Pouring spout
Windshield
Pan(s)
Mug
Plate/bowl
Spoon(s)
Pot grab
Baking accessory (such as an Outback Oven or BakePacker)
Pot scrub

Water container (large)
Vacuum flask
Water bottle(s)
Insulating water bottle cover
Water purification tablets
Water filter
Matches/lighter
Plastic bags
Bear bag and cord
Bear-resistant containers
Food

Clothing

Inner layer

T-shirt
Shirt
Long underwear
Underpants

Warmwear

Shirt, synthetic
Shirt, wool
Shirt, cotton
Wool sweater
Pile/fleece top
Insulated top
Vapor-barrier suit

Shell

Windproof jacket
Wind shirt

Rain jacket
Rain pants

Legwear

Shorts
Walking trousers
Fleece/pile trousers
Knickers
Bib overalls

Headwear

Sun hat
Bob hat
Thick balaclava
Thin balaclava
Neck gaiter
Pile-lined cap
Bandanna

Hands

Liner gloves
Thick wool/pile mittens
Overmitts
Insulated gloves

Miscellaneous: Essential

Flashlight/headlamp and
   spare bulb and battery
Candles
Candle lantern
Oil lantern
Pressure lantern
First aid kit

Compass
Whistle
Map
Map case
Altimeter
Pedometer
Map measurer
Guidebook
GPS receiver
Repair kit:
   Ripstop nylon patches
   Duct tape
   Needles and thread
   Tube of glue
   Stove maintenance
      kit/pricker
   Rubber bands
Waterproof matches
Wash kit
Dark glasses
Goggles
Sunscreen
Lip balm
Insect repellent
Mosquito coils
Head net
Bear-repellent spray
Flares
Strobe flasher
Emergency fishing tackle
Cord

Knife
Notebook, pen, and docu-
   ments
Watch
Toilet trowel
Toilet paper
Rope
Plastic bags

Miscellaneous: Optional

Binoculars
Photography equipment:
   Cameras
   Lenses
   Flash
   Spare batteries
   Tripod
   Mini tripod/clamp
   Filters
   Cable release
   Lens tissue
   Film
   Padded camera cases
Books
Cards
Games
Radio
Portable tape player (Walk-
   man)
Thermometer

Suggested Reading

This is a list of books that I have found inspirational, helpful, or at least interesting. It is by no means comprehensive, and some of them may be out of print. Check your library or used-book store. Many are not backpacking books as such, but all of them are about, or have relevance to, wilderness travel. Many are referred to in the text.

Techniques and Equipment

Axcell, Claudia, Diana Cooke and Vikki Kinmont. *Simple Foods for the Pack: The Sierra Club Guide to Delicious Natural Foods for the Trail.* Rev. ed. San Francisco: Sierra Club Books, 1986.

Berger, Karen. *A Trailside Guide: Hiking/Backpacking.* New York: W.W. Norton, 1995.

Daffern, Tony. *Avalanche Safety for Skiers & Climbers.* 2d rev. ed. Seattle: Cloudcap, 1992.

Darvill, Fred T. *Mountaineering Medicine: A Wilderness Medical Guide.* 13th ed. Berkeley: Wilderness Press, 1992.

Doan, Marlyn. *Starting Small in the Wilderness: The Sierra Club Outdoors Guide for Families.* San Francisco: Sierra Club Books, 1979.

Fleming, June. *The Well-Fed Backpacker.* New York: Random House, 1986.

Fletcher, Colin. *The Complete Walker III.* 3rd ed. New York: Knopf, 1984.

Frazine, Richard. *The Barefoot Hiker.* Berkeley: Ten Speed Press, 1993.

Getchell, Annie. *The Essential Outdoor Gear Manual: Equipment Care & Repair for Outdoorspeople.* Camden, ME: Ragged Mountain Press, 1995.

Gillette, Ned, and John Dostal. *Cross-Country Skiing.* 3rd ed. Seattle: The Mountaineers, 1988.

Graydon, Don, ed. *Mountaineering: The Freedom of the Hills.* 5th ed. Seattle: The Mountaineers, 1992.

Greenspan, Rick, and Hal Kahn. *The Camper's Companion: The Pack-Along Guide for Better Outdoor Trips.* 2d ed. San Francisco: Foghorn Press, 1991.

Hampton, Bruce, and David Cole. *Soft Paths: How to Enjoy the Wilderness Without Harming It.* Mechanicsburg, PA: Stackpole, 1988.

Hart, John. *Walking Softly in the Wilderness: The Sierra Club Guide to Backpacking.* Rev. ed. San Francisco: Sierra Club Books, 1984.

Hatt, John. *The Tropical Traveler: The Essential Guide to Travel in Hot Countries.* 2d ed. New York: Penguin Books, 1993.

Herrero, Stephen. *Bear Attacks: Their Causes and Avoidance.* New York: Lyons & Burford, 1988.

Ilg, Steve. *The Outdoor Athlete: Total Training for Outdoor Performance.* Boulder, CO: Cordillera Press, 1987.

Jardine, Ray. *The Pacific Crest Trail Hiker's Handbook: Innovative Techniques and Trail Tested Instruction for the Long Distance Hiker.* 2d ed. LaPine, OR: AdventureLore Press, 1996.

Kesselheim, Alan. *The Lightweight Gourmet: Drying and Cooking Food for the Outdoor Life.* Camden, ME: Ragged Mountain Press, 1994.

Kjellstrom, Bjorn. *Be Expert with Map & Compass: The Complete Orienteering Handbook.* New York: Macmillan, 1994.

LaChapelle, E.R. *The ABC of Avalanche Safety.* 2d ed. Seattle: The Mountaineers, 1985.

Manning, Harvey. *Backpacking, One Step At A Time.* New York: Random House, 1986.

Meyer, Kathleen. *How to Shit in the Woods: An Environmentally Sound Approach to a Lost Art.* 2d ed. Berkeley: Ten Speed Press, 1994.

Miller, Dorcas S. *Good Food for Camp & Trail: All-Natural Recipes for Delicious Meals Outdoors.* Boulder, CO: Pruett Publishing Company, 1993.

Parker, Paul. *Free-Heel Skiing: Telemark and Parallel Techniques For All Conditions.* 2d ed. Seattle: The Mountaineers, 1995.

Parry, R.B., and C.R. Perkins. *World Mapping Today.* Newton, MA: Butterworth-Heinemann, 1987.

Prater, Gene. *Snowshoeing.* 3rd ed. Seattle: The Mountaineers, 1988.

Prater, Yvonne, and Ruth Dyer Mendenhall. *Gorp, Glop & Glue Stew: Favorite Foods from 165 Outdoor Experts.* Seattle: The Mountaineers, 1981.

Randall, Glenn. *Modern Backpacker's Handbook.* New York: Lyons & Burford, 1993.

Reifsnyder, William E. *Weathering the Wilderness: The Sierra Club Guide to Practical Meteorology.* San Francisco: Sierra Club Books, 1980.

Ross, Cindy, and Todd Gladfelter. *A Hiker's Companion: Twelve Thousand Miles of Trail-Tested Wisdom.* Seattle: The Mountaineers, 1993.

Rowell, Galen. *Galen Rowell's Vision: The Art of Adventure Photography.* San Francisco: Sierra Club Books, 1993.

————. *Mountain Light: In Search of the Dynamic Landscape.* San Francisco: Sierra Club Books, 1986.

Schad, Jerry, and David S. Moser. *Wilderness Basics: The Complete Handbook for Hikers & Backpackers.* 2d ed. Seattle: The Mountaineers, 1993.

Seidman, David. *The Essential Wilderness Navigator: How to Find Your Way in the Great Outdoors.* Camden, ME: Ragged Mountain Press, 1995.

Silverman, Goldie. *Backpacking with Babies & Small Children.* Berkeley: Wilderness Press, 1986.

Spangenberg, Jean S. *The BakePacker's Companion: An Outdoor Cookbook.* 2d ed. Sylva, NC: Sylva Herald Publishing, 1996.

Townsend, Chris. *Wilderness Skiing & Winter Camping.* Camden, ME: Ragged Mountain Press, 1993.

Waterman, Laura, and Guy Waterman. *Backwoods Ethics: Environmental Issues for Hikers & Campers.* 2d ed. Woodstock, VT: Countryman, 1993.

Wilkerson, James A., ed. *Medicine for Mountaineering & Other Wilderness Activities.* 4th ed. Seattle: The Mountaineers, 1994.

Backpacking Stories and Tales of Adventure

Abbey, Edward. *Desert Solitaire: A Season in the Wilderness.* Tucson: University of Arizona Press, 1988.

Essays and anger about the deserts of the Southwest. All his other books are highly recommended, too.

Adkins, Jan, ed. *The Ragged Mountain Press Portable Wilderness Anthology.* Camden, ME: Ragged Mountain Press, 1993.

A packable selection from Thoreau to Edward Abbey.

Annerino, John. *Running Wild: Through the Grand Canyon on the Ancient Path.* Tucson, AZ: Harbinger House, 1992.
> Stories of multi-day solo runs through the deserts of the Southwest.

Berger, Karen, and Dan Smith. *Where the Waters Divide: A Walk Across America Along the Continental Divide.* New York: Crown, 1993.
> Story of a CDT through-hike.

Brown, Hamish. *Hamish's Mountain Walk: The First Traverse of all the Scottish Munros in One Journey.* London: Gollancz, 1978.
> The best backpacking book about Scotland.

Fletcher, Colin. *The Man Who Walked Through Time.* New York: Random House, 1989.
> First trek through the whole of the Grand Canyon.

———. *The Secret Worlds of Colin Fletcher.* New York: Knopf, 1989.
> Backpacking stories and philosophy.

———. *The Thousand-Mile Summer.* New York: Random House, 1989.
> Walking the length of California.

Hillaby, John: *Journey Through Europe.* Chicago: Academy Chicago Publishers, 1982.
> Hiking Europe north-to-south.

———. *Journey Through Love.* Boston: Houghton Mifflin, 1977.
> Includes account of an Appalachian Trail hike.

———. *Walk Through Britain.* Boston: Houghton Mifflin. No date.
> Hiking Britain from end to end.

Kephart, Horace. *Camping & Woodcraft: A Handbook for Vacation Campers and for Travelers in the Wilderness.* Knoxville: University of Tennessee Press, 1988.
> A classic on how it used to be done.

Lopez, Barry. *Arctic Dreams: Imagination and Desire in a Northern Landscape.* New York: Macmillan, 1986. Will inspire you to visit the Far North.

Matthiesen, Peter. *The Snow Leopard.* New York: Viking, 1987.
> A story of a trek in Nepal interwoven with personal philosophy.

Mikkelsen, Ejnar: *Two Against the Ice.* London, Rupert Hart Davis. No date.
> Sled journeys and survival in Greenland early this century.

Muir, John. *The Eight Wilderness Discovery Books.* Seattle, The Mountaineers, 1992.
> Classics from the pioneer of wilderness preservation.

Newby, Eric. *A Short Walk in the Hindu Kush.* New York: Viking Penguin, 1987.
> Hilarious story of a mountaineering misadventure.

Peacock, Doug. *Grizzly Years: Encounters with the Wilderness.* New York: Holt and Co., 1990.
> Two decades of wilderness bear-watching.

Powell, J.W. *The Exploration of the Colorado River and its Canyons.* New York: Dover, 1961.
> A classic.

Rawicz, Salvomir. *The Long Walk.* New York: Lyons & Burford, 1988.
> An amazing journey by escapees from a Siberian labor camp through the Gobi desert and the Himalayas.

Rice, Larry M. *Gathering Paradise: Alaska Wilderness Journeys.* Golden, CO: Fulcrum, 1990.
> Wilderness backpacking and canoe-touring tales.

Ross, Cindy. *Journey on the Crest: Walking 2,600 Miles from Mexico to Canada.* Seattle: The Mountaineers, 1987.
> Story of one woman's Pacific Crest Trail through hike.

Rowell, Galen. *High and Wild: Essays on Wilderness*

Adventure. 2d ed. San Francisco: Lexicos, 1983.
Compelling tales of treks, climbs, and ski tours.

————. *In the Throne Room of the Mountain Gods.*
2d ed. San Francisco: Sierra Club Books, 1986.
One of the best Himalayan mountaineering expedition accounts.

Shipton, Eric. *The Six Mountain-Travel Books.* Seattle:
The Mountaineers, 1985.
Classic tales.

Simpson, Joe. *Touching the Void: The Harrowing First-Person Account of One Man's Miraculous Survival.*
New York: Harper Collins, 1990.
Intense, almost unbelievable tale of survival after a mountain accident.

Steger, Will, and Paul Schurke. *North to the Pole.* New
York: Random House, 1987.
Story of successful unsupported dog-sled journey to the North Pole with much interesting detail on camping techniques at −40°F (−40°C).

Thayer, Helen. *Polar Dream: The Heroic Saga of the
First Solo Journey by a Woman and Her Dog to the Pole.* New York: Simon & Schuster, 1993.
Story of solo trip to magnetic North Pole.

Tilman, H.W. *The Eight Sailing/Mountain Exploration
Books.* Seattle, The Mountaineers, 1987.
Classic tales.

————. *The Seven Mountain-Travel Books.* Seattle:
The Mountaineers, 1983.
More classic tales.

Townsend, Chris. *The Great Backpacking Adventure.*
Somerset, England: Oxford Illustrated Press, 1988.
Includes accounts of Pacific Crest Trail and Continental Divide walks.

————. *High Summer: Backpacking the Canadian
Rockies.* Seattle: Cloudcap, 1989.
First continuous walk along the whole range.

————. *Walking the Yukon: A Solo Trek Through the
Land of Beyond.* Camden, ME: Ragged Mountain Press, 1993.
Story of my 1,000-mile, south-to-north walk through Canada's Yukon Territory.

Vickery, Jim Dale. *Wilderness Visionaries.* Rev. ed.
Minocqua, WI: NorthWord, 1994.
Short biographies of Thoreau, Muir, Service, Marshall, Calvin Rutstrum, and Sigurd F. Olson, with an emphasis on their wilderness travels.

Waterman, Laura, and Guy Waterman. *Forest & Crag:
A History of Hiking, Trail Blazing, and Adventure in the Northeast Mountains.* Boston, MA: The Appalachian Mountain Club, 1989.
Fascinating and encyclopedic.

Selected General and Regional Guidebooks

There are a vast number of guidebooks available, covering every wild area. Good trail guides include *100 Hikes,* from The Mountaineers (the Pacific Northwest); *Fifty Hikes,* from Countryman Press (the East); the Sierra Nevada guides from Wilderness Press; the Sierra Club's Totebooks, which cover areas from the Smoky Mountains to the Grand Canyon; and the Hiker's Guides, from Falcon Press, which cover a selection of states and wild areas.

The big three long-distance trails all have detailed guidebooks. Those on the Appalachian Trail are published by the Appalachian Trail Conference, those on the Continental Divide Trail by the Continental Divide Trail Society, and the two-volume Pacific Crest Trail guides from the Wilderness Press, which also publishes a guide to the John Muir Trail.

There are also a couple of very useful annual guides to the AT: Dan "Wingfoot" Bruce's *The Thru-Hiker's Handbook: A Guide for End-to-End Hikes of the Appalachian Trail* (published by the Center for Appalachian Trail Studies), and Joe and Monica Cook's *Appalachian Trail Companion* (published by the Appalachian Trail Long Distance Hikers Association).

Good regional guides are published by the Sierra Club in its adventuring series, which covers Arizona to Alaska, plus several overseas destinations. Bradt

Publications publishes a series of invaluable trekking guides to remote places, from South America to Spitsbergen, while Lonely Planet does an excellent travel guide series of use to backpackers.

The following is a selection of guides I've found particularly good, and readable enough for armchair browsing. I've included two of mine that are intended for the latter purpose.

Annerino, John. *Hiking the Grand Canyon.* Rev. ed. San Francisco, Sierra Club Books, 1993.

Bezruchka, Stephen. *Trekking in Nepal: A Traveler's Guide.* 6th ed. Seattle: The Mountaineers, 1991.

Gadd, Ben. *The Handbook of the Canadian Rockies.* 2d ed. Jasper, Alberta: Corax, 1995.

Hodgson, Michael. *America's Secret Recreation Areas: Your Travel Guide to the Forgotten Wild Lands of the Bureau of Land Management.* San Francisco: Foghorn Press, 1993.

Kelsey, Michael R. *Canyon Hiking Guide to the Colorado Plateau.* 2d ed. Provo, UT: Kelsey, 1991.

Patton, Brian, and Bart Robinson. *The Canadian Rockies Trail Guide.* 6th ed. Banff, Alberta: Summerthought, 1994.

Satterfield, Archie. *Chilkoot Pass. The Most Famous Trail in the North.* 6th ed. Seattle: Alaska Northwest, 1988.

Schatter, Jeffrey P. *Yosemite National Park.* 3rd ed. Berkeley: Wilderness Press, 1992.

Schmidt, Jeremy. *Adventuring in the Rockies: The Sierra Club Travel Guide to the Rocky Mountain Regions of Canada and the U.S.A.* Rev. ed. San Francisco: Sierra Club Books, 1993.

Simmerman, Nancy Lange. *Alaska's Parklands: The Complete Guide.* Seattle: The Mountaineers, 1983.

Spangler, Sharon. *On Foot in the Grand Canyon.* 2d ed. Boulder, CO: Pruett, 1989.

Steck, George. *Grand Canyon Loop Hikes I,* and *Grand Canyon Loop Hikes II.* Evergreen, CO: Chockstone Press, 1989 and 1993.

Swift, Hugh. *Trekking in Nepal, West Tibet & Bhutan.* San Francisco: Sierra Club Books, 1989.

Townsend, Chris. *Adventure Treks: Western North America.* Seattle: Cloudcap, 1990.

———. *Long Distance Walks in the Pyrenees.* Swindon, England: The Crowood Press, 1992.

Wayburn, Peggy. *Adventuring in Alaska: The Ultimate Travel Guide to the Great Land.* Rev. ed. San Francisco: Sierra Club Books, 1994.

Useful Addresses

Walking and Backpacking Clubs

These are associations that organize backpacking and walking ventures, and campaign on behalf of walkers. They publish journals, newsletters, and hold regular meetings, which members can use to swap information about equipment, techniques, and places to visit; some organize trail maintenance programs. I've listed only national organizations there are many local and regional ones.

The American Hiking Society
1701 18th Street NW
Washington, DC 20009

Appalachian Long Distance Hikers
    Association
30 Donovan Court
Merrimack, NH 03054

Appalachian Trail Conference
Box 807
Harpers Ferry, WV 25425

Continental Divide Trail Society
3704 N. Charles St.
Baltimore, MD 21218-2305

The Pacific Crest Trail Association
1350 Castle Rock Road
Walnut Creek, CA 94598

The Sierra Club
730 Polk Street
San Francisco, CA 94109

Conservation Groups

These environmental organizations emphasize wilderness preservation.

The Sierra Club
730 Polk Street
San Francisco, CA 94109

The Wilderness Society
900 17th St. NW
Washington, DC 20006-2501

Magazines

Backpacker
Rodale Press
33 E. Minor Street
Emmaus, PA 18098

Explore Magazine
Suite 420
301-14th St. NW
Calgary, Alberta T2N 2A1

Outdoor Photographer
12121 Wilshire Boulevard
Suite 1220
West Los Angeles, CA 90025-1123

Outside
400 Market Street
Santa Fe, NM 87501

Mail-Order Catalogs

These companies offer a full selection of gear, including brand items.

Campmor
810 Route 17 North
Paramus, NJ 07653-0999

L.L. Bean
Freeport, ME 04033-0001

REI
P.O. Box 1938
Sumner, WA 98390-0800

Bootmakers

Peter Limmer & Sons Inc.
P.O. Box 88
Route 16A
Intervale, NH 03845

Specialty Backpacking Food Suppliers

Adventure Foods
Route 2, Box 276
Whittier, NC 28789

AlpineAire Foods
13321 Grass Valley Ave.
Grass Valley, CA 95945-9046

Backpacker's Pantry
6350 Gunpark Drive
Boulder, CO 80301

Harvest Foodworks
RR1
Toledo
Ontario, Canada, K0E 1Y0

Indiana Camp Supply
P.O. Box 2166
Loveland, CO 80539

Trail Foods
124555 Branford Street, #6
Arleta, CA 91331

Traveling Light
4000 1st Ave. S.
Seattle, WA 98134
510-526-8401

Uncle John's Foods
500 Hathaway
Fairplay, CO 80440

Maps

Canada Map Office
Department of Energy, Mines, and
    Resources
615 Booth Street
Ottawa, Ontario K1A 0E9

Department of the Interior
National Park Service
Office of Public Inquiries
1849 C St. NW
Room 1013
Washington, D.C. 20013

Earthwalk Press
2239 Union Street
Eureka, CA 95501

Trails Illustrated
P.O. Box 4357
Evergreen, CO 80437-4357

U.S. Forest Service
Public Affairs Office
P.O. Box 96090
Washington, D.C. 20090-6090

U.S. Geological Survey
Branch of Information Services
Box 25286
Denver, CO 80225

Wilderness Press
2440 Bancroft Way
Berkeley, CA 94704

Equipment Suppliers

This is a fairly comprehensive list of backpacking equipment suppliers. I haven't included ski companies unless they make other products, and I've only mentioned companies whose products aren't available in North America if they're mentioned in the text. Where a company handles several brands I've listed the latter separately, so some addresses appear more than once. Companies move, get taken over, and go out of business, of course, so this list is only a guide.

Acorn Products Co., Inc.
PO Box 7780
Lewiston, ME 04243
Fleece socks

Adidas
541 N.E. 20th St., Suite 207
Portland, OR 97232
Footwear

A.D. One
1500 Fashion Island Boulevard
San Mateo, CA 94404
Footwear

Alico Sport
RR3, Box 9D
Newport City, VT 05855
Footwear

Alpina Sports Corp.
P.O. Box 23
Hanover, NH 03755
Footwear

Alpine Design
500 Coffman St., Suite 201
Longmont, CO 80501
Clothing

Arc'Teryx
170 Harbour Avenue
North Vancouver
BC, Canada V7J 2E6
Packs

American Recreation Products
1224 Fern Ridge Parkway
St. Louis, MO 63141-4451
Kelty packs, tents, sleeping bags

Appalachian Mountain Supply
731 Highland Avenue NE
Atlanta, GA 30312-1425
Self-inflating sleeping pads

Avid Outdoor
1120 W. 149th Street
Olathe, KS 66061
Tents

BakePacker
Strike 2 Industries, Inc.
508 E. Augusta Ave.
Spokane, WA 99207-2418
Baking accessory

Basic Designs
335-A O'Hair Court
Santa Rosa, CA 95407
*Self-inflating sleeping pads, water
    filters*

Bergsport International
P.O. Box 1519
Nederland, CO 80466
Markill stoves, cooksets

Bibler Tents
5441-D Western Avenue
Boulder, CO 80301
Tents, bivy bags, hanging stove

Black Diamond Equipment, Ltd.
2084 E. 3900 South
Salt Lake City, UT 84124
*Megamid tent, waterproof stuff
    sacks, gaiters, gloves, backcountry
    skis, mountaineering and Nordic
    ski boots, ski poles*

Blue Magic Products, Inc.
4445 E. Fremont
Stockton, CA 95215
*Tectron boot and clothing proofings,
    cleansers*

Boreal USA
P.O. Box 7116
Capistrano Beach, CA 92624
Footwear

Camp 7
3701 W. Carriage Drive
Santa Ana, CA 92704
Packs, sleeping bags, clothing

Camp Trails
1326 Willow Road
Sturtevant, WI 53177
Packs

Caribou Mountaineering
400 Commerce Rd.
Alice, TX 78332
Packs, sleeping bags

Cascade Designs Inc.
4000 First Avenue S.
Seattle, WA 98134
*Therm-a-Rest and Ridge-Rest sleep-
    ing pads, sleeping bags, Tracks
    staffs*

Century Tool
P.O. Box 188
Cherry Valley, IL 61016
Primus stoves and lanterns

Chuck Roast Equipment, Inc.
29 Odell Hill Road
P.O. Box 2080
Conway, NH 03818
Fleece clothing

Climb High
1861 Shelburne Road
Shelburne, VT 05482
*Full range of outdoor equipment and
    supplies*

The Coleman Company/Peak 1
P.O. Box 2931
Wichita, KS 67201
Stoves, packs, sleeping bags

Columbia Sportswear
6600 N. Baltimore
Portland, OR 97203
Clothing

Crazy Creek Products
1401 S. Broadway
Red Lodge, MT 59068
Chairs and sleeping pads

Critter Mountain Wear
108 W. Tomachi Ave.
Gunnison, CO 81230
Clothing

Dana Design
333 Simmental Way
Bozeman, MT 59715
Packs

Danner Shoe Manufacturing Co.
12722 N.E. Airport Way
Portland, OR 97230
Footwear

Deckers Corp.
1140 Mark Avenue
Carpinteria, CA 93013-2998
Teva sandals

Design Salt
P.O. Box 1220
Redway, CA 95560
Cotton and silk sleeping bag liners

Devold
5151 Edina Industrial Boulevard
Suite 200
Edina, MN 55439
Wool underwear, sweaters, and socks

Diamond Brand Canvas Products
P.O. Box 249
Naples, NC 28760
Packs, tents

Dolomite
1 Sellec Street
Norwalk, CT 06855
Footwear

Duofold
Valley Square Mall
Tamaqua, PA 18252
Underwear and fleece clothing

DuPont/SealSkinz
1002 Industrial Road
Old Hickory, TN 37138
Oversocks

Eagle Creek, Inc.
1740 La Costa Meadows Drive
San Marcos, CA 92069
Travel packs, duffel bags, and accessory pouches

Eastern Mountain Sports
One Vose Farm Road
Peterborough, NH 03458
EMS is a chain of shops with much own-brand gear, including packs, tents, sleeping bags, and clothing

EC-camp
P.O. Box 27208
San Diego, CA 92198
Ferrino packs, tents, sleeping bags

Ecotrek
P.O. Box 9638
Amherst, MA 01060
Packs and clothing made from recycled materials

Edko Alpine Designs
P.O. Box 17005
Boulder, CO 80308
Packs, limited edition sleeping bag

Envirogear Ltd.
127 Elm Street
Cortland, NY 13045
Down-filled inflatable cocoon sleeping bags with optional canopies

Expedition Trails/MZH, Inc.
80 E. State Rt. 4
Paramus, NJ 07652
Sleeping bags

Fabiano Shoe Co.
850 Summer Street
S. Boston, MA 02127-1576
Scarpa footwear

Feathered Friends
1415 10th Ave.
Seattle, WA 98122
Sleeping bags, down, fleece, and waterproof/breathable clothing

Five.Ten Co.
P.O. Box 1185
Redlands, CA 92373
Footwear

Foam Design, Inc.
444 Transport Ct.
Lexington, KY 40511-2502
Sleeping pads

Fox River
P.O. Box 298
Osage, IA 50461
Socks

Frelonic Corp.
63 Grove Street
Salem, MA 01970
Sleeping pads

Gander Mountain
P.O. Box 128
Wilmot, WI 53192
Packs, tents, sleeping bags

Garcia Machine
14097 Avenue 272
Visalia, CA 93292
Bear-resistant containers

Garmin International
1200 E. 151st St.
Olathe, KS 66602
GPS systems

Garmont
1 Second Street
Peabody, MA 01960
Packs, boots

Garuda Mountaineering
333 Simmental Way
Bozeman, MT 59715
Tents

Gates Mills, Inc.
P.O. Box 547
Johnstown, NY 12095
Ov'r'sox

General Ecology, Inc.
151 Sheree Boulevard
Exton, PA 19341
Water filters

Georgia Boot, Inc.
P.O. Box 10
Franklin, TN 37068-0010
Footwear

Gerry Sportswear
1051 First Avenue S.
Seattle, WA 98134
Down and waterproof/breathable clothing

Gold-Eck of Austria
6313 Seaview Avenue NW
Seattle, WA 98107
Sleeping bags

Granite Gear
P.O. Box 278
Two Harbors, MN 55616
Packs, mitts, gaiters, hats

Gregory Mountain
    Products/Bianchi
100 Calle Cortez
Temecula, CA 92590
Packs

Helly-Hansen
17275 N.E. 67th Court
Redmond, WA 98073
Clothing

High Country Outdoor Products
19767 S.E. Sunnyside Road
Boring, OR 97009
Sleeping pads

Hilleberg
Box 144
S-840 43 Hackas
Sweden
Tents

Hind, Inc.
P.O. Box 12609
San Luis Obispo, CA 93406
Clothing

Hi-Tec Sports USA, Inc.
4801 Stoddard Road
Modesto, CA 95356
Footwear

Integral Designs
P.O. Box 40023, Highfield P.O.
Calgary, AB, Canada T2G 5G5
*Tents, bivy shelters, sleeping bags,
   clothing*

Jandd Mountaineering
P.O. Box 4819
Santa Barbara, CA 93140
Packs

JanSport
10411 Airport Road SW
Everett, WA 98204
Packs, clothing

Jinwoong, Inc.
569 Charcot Avenue
San Jose, CA 95131
Quest packs, tents

Johnson Worldwide Associates
1326 Willow Road
Sturtevant, WI 53177
*Eureka! tents, packs; Silva com-
   passes, headlamps; Jack Wolfskin packs, tents, sleeping bags,
   clothing*

Karrimor International Ltd.
Petre Road, Clayton-le-Moors
Accrington, Lancashire
BB5 5JZ, England
Packs, clothing

Kenyon Consumer Products
141 Fairgrounds Road
W. Kingston, RI 02892
Underwear and fleece clothing

K-Swiss Corp.
20664 Bahama Street
Chatsworth, CA 91311
Footwear

Lake of the Woods
P.O. Box 79
Prentice, WI 54556
Footwear

La Sportiva USA
3235 Prairie Avenue
Boulder, CO 80304
Footwear

Legend Footwear
14450 Chambers Road
Tustin, CA 92680
Footwear

Leki-Sport USA
60 Earhart Drive
Williamsville, NY 14221
Hiking poles

Liberty Mountain Sports
9325 S.W. Barber Street
Wilsonville, OR 97070
Scorpion Stoves

Life-Link International
P.O. Box 2913
Jackson, WY 83001
*Backcountry ski accessories including
   shovels, avalanche beepers, poles,
   and packs*

Liquipak
154 Pirates Cove
Vallejo, CA 94591
Water containers

Longworth Industries/PolarMax
480 E. Main St.
Candor, NC 27229-9095
Underwear

Lowe Alpine Systems
P.O. Box 1449
Broomfield, CO 80038
Packs, clothing

Madden Mountaineering
2400 Central Avenue
Boulder, CO 80301
Packs

Magellan Systems Corporation
960 Overland Court
San Dimas, CA 91773
GPS systems

MAG Instrument, Inc.
1635 S. Sacramento Avenue
Ontario, CA 91761
MagLite flashlights

Manzella Productions
5684 Main Street
Buffalo, NY 14231
Gloves, oversocks

Marker USA
1070 West 2300 South
Salt Lake City, UT 84119
Clothing

Marmot
2321 Circadian Way
Santa Rosa, CA 95407
Sleeping bags, clothing

McHale & Co.
29 Dravus Street
Seattle WA 98109
Packs

Medalist Apparel, Inc.
4201 Pottsville Pike
Reading, PA 19605
Base-layer clothing

Merrell Boots
P.O. Box 4249
Burlington, VT 05406
Footwear

Metolius Mountain Products
63189 Nels Anderson Rd.
Bend, OR 97701
Sleeping pads

Modan Pack Systems/Explore Out-
    door Systems
395 Bigelow Hollow Road
Eastford, CT 06242
Packs

MontBell American
940 41st Avenue
Santa Cruz, CA 95062
Packs, sleeping bags, clothing

Moonstone Mountaineering
5350 Ericson Way
Arcata, CA 95521
Sleeping bags, clothing

Moss Tents
P.O. Box 577
Camden, ME 04843
Tents and tarps

Mountain Equipment, Inc.
4776 E. Jensen Avenue
Fresno, CA 93725
Packs

Mountain Hardwear
950 Gilman Street
Berkeley, CA 94710
Tents, sleeping bags, clothing

Mountain Safety Research
4225 Second Avenue S.
Seattle, WA 98134
*Trangia stoves, cooksets, water
    filters, waterbags*

Mountainsmith, Inc.
18301 W. Colfax Ave.
Building P
Golden, CO 80401
Packs, sledges

Mountain Tools
140 Calle del Oaks
Del Ray Oaks, CA 93940-5711
Packs

Natural Balance
503 S. Main St.
Fairfield, IA 52556-3611
Packs

New Balance Athletic Shoe, Inc.
61 N. Beacon Street
Boston, MA 02134
Footwear

Nike, Inc.
One S.W. Bowerman Drive
Beaverton, OR 97005
Footwear, clothing

Nikwax
P.O. Box 1572
Everett, WA 98206
*Waterproofing and cleansing prod-
    ucts for footwear and clothing*

Noall Tents
59530 Devils Ladder #26 GV
Mountain Center, CA 92561
Tents

Nordica USA
139 Harvest Lane
Williston, VT 05495
Asolo footwear

North By Northeast
PO Box 398
Lincoln, RI 02865
Fleece clothing and accessories

Northern Lights
P.O. Box 3413
Mammoth Lakes, CA 93546
Candle lanterns

The North Face
2013 Farallon Dr.
San Leandro, CA 94577
Tents, sleeping bags, packs, clothing

Not Just Johns
219 Grant St., Unit A
Newport Beach, CA 92663
Long johns and union suits

One Sport, Inc.
1003 Sixth Avenue S.
Seattle, WA 98134
Footwear

The Original Bug Shirt Co.
908 Niagara Falls Boulevard
North Tonawanda, NY 14120
Insect-proof clothing

Osprey Packs
P.O. Box 539
Dolores, CO 81323
Packs

Outbound
Box 56148
Hayward, CA 94544
*Sigg stoves, cooksets, and bottles.
    Packs, tents, sleeping bags, sleep-
    ing pads, clothing, water filters,
    headlamps, candle lantern*

Outdoor Research
1000 First Avenue S.
Seattle, WA 98134
*Bivy bags, clothing, hats, gloves,
    gaiters, accessories*

Outdoor Sportswear
1419 Elliott Avenue West
Seattle, WA 98119
Clothing

Overland Equipment, Inc.
2145 Park Avenue, Suite 4
Chico, CA 95928
Packs

Patagonia, Inc.
P.O. Box 32050
Reno, NV 89533-2050
Clothing

Phoenix
Karrimor International Ltd.
Petre Road, Clayton-le-Moors
Accrington, Lancashire
BB5 5JZ, England
Tents

PMI/Petzl Distribution
P.O. Box 803
Lafayette, GA 30728
Headlamps

Premier International (USA) Ltd.
901 N. Stuart Street
Suite 804
Arlington, VA 22203
Packs

Raichle Molitor USA, Inc.
Geneva Road
Brewster, NY 10509
Footwear

Rainfair
3600 S. Memorial Drive
Racine, WI 53403
Coated nylon rainwear

Recovery Engineering
2229 Edgewood Avenue S.
Minneapolis, MN 55426
PUR Water filters

Red Wing Shoe Company
314 Main Street
Red Wing, MN 55066
Vasque footwear

Reebok Outdoor
100 Technology Center Drive,
 Annex 2
Stoughton, MA 02072
Footwear, clothing

Relags USA, Inc.
1705 14th Street
Boulder, CO 80302
Water filters

Ridge Outdoor
205 Suburban Road #6
San Luis Obispo, CA 93401
Footwear

Rockport Co.
220 Donald Lynch Boulevard
Marlboro, MA 01752
Footwear

Rocky Shoes & Boots, Inc.
39 E. Canal Street
Nelsonville, OH 45764
Footwear, oversocks

Royal Robbins
1314 Coldwell Avenue
Modesto, CA 95350
Clothing

Rugged Footwear Co.
4701 N. Federal Highway
Lighthouse Point, FL 33064
Footwear

Salomon North America
400 E. Main Street
Georgetown, MA 01833
Footwear

Sequel Outdoor Clothing
P.O. Box 409
Durango, CO 81302
Clothing

Serratus/Pelion Mountain Products, Ltd.
3103 Thunderbird Crescent
Burnaby, BC, Canada V5A 3G1
Packs

Sierra Designs
1255 Powell Street
Emeryville, CA 94608
Tents, sleeping bags, clothing

Slumberjack
1224 Fern Ridge Parkway
St. Louis, MO 63147
*Sleeping bags, self-inflating sleeping
 pads*

SmartWool/Duke Designs, Inc.
P.O. Box 771143
Steamboat Springs, CO 80477
Socks

Solstice
60 NW Davis
Portland, OR 97209
Clothing

SportHill
1690 S. Bertelsen Road
Eugene, OR 97402
Clothing

Stephensons-Warmlite
22 Hook Road
Gilford, NH 03246
*Tents, sleeping bags, down-filled
 sleeping pads, clothing, vapor
 barriers*

Sun Dog, Inc.
6700 S. Glacier Street
Seattle, WA 98188
Packs, camera bags

Sun Precautions
2815 Wetmore Ave.
Everett, WA 98201
Sun-protection clothing

Suunto USA
2151 Las Palmas Drive
Carlsbad, CA 92009
Compasses, Camping Gaz stoves,
    Optimus stoves

SweetWater, Inc.
2505 Trade Center Ave.
Suite D
Longmont, CO 80503
Water filters

Tecnica USA
19 Technology Drive
West Lebanon, NH 03784
Footwear

Tekna/Rayovac
630 Forward Drive
Madison, WI 53711
Flashlights

Terramar Sports Worldwide, Ltd.
10 Midland Avenue
Port Chester, NY 10573
Silk base layers

Teton, Inc.
P.O. Box 12601
Tucson, AZ 85732
Pants and shorts

Thorlo
2210 Newton Drive
Statesville, NC 28677
Socks

Timberland Co.
200 Domain Drive
Stratham, NH 03885-2575
Footwear, clothing

Timberline Filters, Inc.
P.O. Box 20356
Boulder, CO 80308
Water filters

Tough Traveler
1012 State Street
Schenectady, NY 12307
Children's packs and sleeping bags

Trail Designs
350 Fifth Avenue
Suite 5515
New York, NY 10118
Clothing

Traveling Light
4000 1st Ave. S.
Seattle, WA 98134
Outback Oven

Trek Sport
114 17th Place
Kirkland, WA 98033-4906
Packs

Trigon Design Works
306 Westlake Avenue N. #313
Seattle, WA 98109
Packs

Trondak, Inc.
11710 Airport Road, Suite 300
Everett, WA 98204
Proofing and cleaning agents
    (Aquaseal) for footwear, clothing,
    tents, and maps

Ultimate Direction
1488 N. Salem Road
Rexburg, ID 83440
Small and medium packs with built-
    in water holders with feed tubes

vauDe Sports, Inc.
P.O. Box 3413
Mammoth Lakes, CA 93546
Packs, tents, sleeping bags, clothing

Voilé Equipment
2636 South 2700 West
Salt Lake City, UT 84119
Nordic ski bindings, snow shovels

Vortex
1414 South 700 West
Salt Lake City, UT 84104-1604
Packs

Walrus
P.O. Box 3875
Seattle, WA 98124
Tents

Western Mountaineering
840 Town and Country Village
San Jose, CA 95128
Sleeping bags

Wiggy's, Inc.
P.O. Box 2124
Grand Junction, CO 81502
Sleeping bags, sleeping pads, packs,
    tents, clothing

Wigwam Mills, Inc.
3402 Crocker Avenue
Sheboygan, WI 53081
Socks

Wild Country, Ltd.
230 E. Conway Road
Center Conway, NH 03813
Tents, gaiters

Wilderness Experience
333 Simmental Way
Bozeman, MT 59715
Packs

Wild Things, Inc.
P.O. Box 400
North Conway, NH 03860
Packs, climbing equipment

Wisconsin Pharmacal Co., Inc.
P.O. Box 198
Jackson, WI 53037
Potable Aqua iodine tablets

Wolverine Worldwide, Inc.
9341 Courtland Drive
Rockford, MI 49351-9778
Coleman Footwear

Woolrich
1 Mill Street
Woolrich, PA 17779
Clothing

WTC Industries/Ecomaster
14405 21st Avenue N.
Minneapolis, MN 55447
PentaPure water filters

Wyoming Woolens
3103 Big Trails Drive, Box 3127
Jackson Hole, WY 83001
Clothing

Zanika
P.O. Box 11943
Minneapolis, MN 55411
Women's clothing

ZZ Corp.
10806 Kaylor Ave.
Los Alamitos, CA 90720
Stoves

Metric Conversions

Length

1 mile = 5,280 feet = 1,609 kilometers
1 yard = 3 feet = 0.9114 meter
1 foot = 12 inches = 30.48 centimeters
1 inch = 2.54 centimeters = 25.4 millimeters
½ inch = 12.7 millimeters
¼ inch = 6.35 millimeters

Weight

1 ounce = 28.35 grams
1 pound = 16 ounces = 453.6 grams
2.2 pounds = 1 kilogram

Capacity

(U.S. liquid measure)
1 gill = 4 ounces = 1 cup = 0.1 liter
1 pint = 4 gills = 0.5 liter
1 quart = 2 pints = 0.9 liter
1 gallon = 4 quarts = 3.8 liters

Capacity

(British imperial liquid and dry measure)
1 gill = 5 ounces = 142 cubic centimeters
        = 0.142 liter
1 pint = 4 gills = 568 cubic centimeters = 0.568 liter
1 quart = 2 pints = 4.5 liters
1 gallon = 4 quarts = 4.5 liters

Temperature

0° centigrade (Celsius) (C) = 32° Fahrenheit (F)
100°C = 212°F
To convert Fahrenheit to centigrade, deduct 32, multiply by 5, and divide by 9.
To convert centigrade to Fahrenheit, multiply by 9, divide by 5, and add 32.

Index